4907

SCOPE ENGLISH

Writing and Language Skills

LEVEL FOUR

CONSULTANTS

Venita Bridger
Secondary Language Arts Supervisor
Springfield Public Schools
Springfield, Missouri

Diane E. Bushner
Director, Chapter 1
Cambridge Public Schools
Cambridge, Massachusetts

Dr. Ray Crisp
Co-ordinator, English Language Arts Education
Wichita Public Schools
Wichita, Kansas

Adrian W. McClaren
Supervisor of English
Memphis City Schools
Memphis, Tennessee

Margaret A. Reed
Resource Teacher for Secondary English
Minneapolis Public Schools
Minneapolis, Minnesota

SCOPE ENGLISH

ENGLISH

Writing and Language Skills

LEVEL FOUR

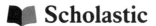 Scholastic

STAFF

Publisher: Eleanor Angeles
Project Editor: Marjorie L. Burns
Level Four Editors: Savannah Waring Walker, Lauren Weidenman, John
    Simmons
Level Four Writers: Jan Freeman, Alan Hines, Carol Klitzner, Julia Piggin,
    Stella Sands
Art Director: Marijka Kostiw

DESIGN AND PRODUCTION

Taurins Design Associates

CREDITS

ILLUSTRATION

Graphic Chart and Map Company: 322
Taurins Design Associates: 290, 292, 294, 295, 296, 313, 323, 324, 325

COVER

After the Storm, 1960. Climbers in the snow at 11,500 feet on the
    Durrenhorn, Switzerland.
Museum of Science, Boston

PHOTO RESEARCH

Linda Sykes, Chris Wohler

Photo credits appear on page 672.

ISBN 0-590-34675-X

12 11 10 9 8 7 6 5 4 3 2 1   3   7 8 9/8 0/1/9

CONTENTS

LEVEL FOUR

UNIT 3: WRITING PARAGRAPHS

UNIT 4: WRITING A JOURNAL

UNIT 5: WRITING A DESCRIPTION

UNIT 6: **WRITING INSTRUCTIONS**

UNIT 7: **WRITING COMPARISONS**

UNIT 8: **WRITING A BUSINESS LETTER**

UNIT 9: **WRITING TO PERSUADE**

UNIT 10: **WRITING A REVIEW**

UNIT 11: **WRITING AN AUTOBIOGRAPHICAL NARRATIVE**

UNIT 12: IMPROVING YOUR WRITING STYLE

UNIT 13: PREPARING A RADIO TALK

COMMUNICATOR'S

HANDBOOK

UNIT 17: LIBRARY AND RESEARCH SKILLS

UNIT 18: STUDY SKILLS

UNIT 19: **THE PARTS OF SPEECH**

UNIT 20: **UNDERSTANDING SENTENCES**

UNIT 21: **COMPLEMENTS**

UNIT 30: SPELLING

UNIT 31: SENTENCE PATTERNS

UNIT 32: DIAGRAMING SENTENCES

I
WRITING

Thinking and Writing

The cellist Baquet playing chamber music in the Alps, 1957
Robert Doisneau, Photo Researchers, Inc., New York

Thinking and Writing

When you are asked to write a composition on any topic at all, how do you react? Which of these two things do you do?

☐ You quickly decide on a topic and begin to write. It's easy because you've already done quite a bit of thinking about this topic.

☐ You sit and stare at your paper, racking your brains for an idea. "What's the matter with me?" you say to yourself. "My mind is a blank!"

If your usual reaction is more like the second than the first, here's some good news. Your mind is *not* a blank; it is filled with ideas that you can write about. If it often seems blank, that's only because you haven't had enough practice in tapping its resources.

In this unit, you will learn several techniques for finding and using the ideas you have stored in your mind. By the time you finish doing all the exercises, your reaction to a writing assignment will probably be like the first one mentioned above. You will quickly decide on a topic and begin to write.

Finding Ideas

Your ideas are stored in the form of memories, beliefs, feelings, and pieces of information, and all of them can serve as raw material for writing. Of course, it's one thing to know that the ideas are "in there somewhere," and quite another to be able to get them out when you need them. If retrieving your ideas is ever a problem for you, here are four techniques that you might like to try.

☐ free writing

☐ brainstorming

☐ writing daily in a notebook or diary

☐ keeping a scrapbook

Free Writing

In free writing, you write about anything at all for a pre-set amount of time. The only rule is this: you must not stop writing for the entire time period. If you can't think of anything to write about, you can write a letter or a word or a sentence or anything at all until you come up with an idea.

When you free write, you are writing for yourself alone. No one else will evaluate your work or even see it. Therefore, you shouldn't force yourself to stick to one topic or try to make the ideas fit together logically. Instead, you should just let your mind wander from thought to thought as it will.

Exercise One   For five minutes, practice free writing. When the time is up, look over your work. Does it reveal what is or has been on your mind?

Following is the beginning of a free writing exercise that Vera wrote. Yours will be longer, as you will be writing for five minutes.

busy rushing all day live-long day hurrying feet talking voices yelling voices honking traffic blaring horns screaming alarms rocketing trains lunch dinner tea six o'clock seven o'clock eight o'clock all of a sudden quiet quiet peace

Brainstorming

Brainstorming is another useful technique for writers. It is similar to free writing but more focused. Instead of changing topics as different ideas occur to you, when you brainstorm you stay on the topic you started with. Brainstorming can help you explore more specific aspects of a topic you have already decided on.

You can brainstorm by yourself, or work with one or two others, jotting down notes on what each person says. But whichever way you choose to brainstorm, remember to stick to one general topic.

Exercise Two   For five minutes, brainstorm with a classmate or classmates on a topic of your choice. When time is up, think about the many different ideas that were presented about the topic. Would they be useful in a writing assignment?

Kenny and Wayne decided to brainstorm about music. They were both interested in music, but wanted a more specific idea of what they might discuss if they wrote about it. Following is their conversation.

Kenny: Have you heard the Treadmills' latest album? They're unbelievable.

Wayne: Unbelievably bad, you mean. Their music is so monotonous. I can't listen to it for more than two minutes. The kind of thing I like has more of a tune and some interesting words.

Kenny: Oh, you mean like the Doorjambs? They put me to sleep. You can't dance to a nonexistent beat.

Wayne: So for you music is only something to dance to? What about great tunes? What about great lyrics? Don't they ever inspire you?

Kenny: Just sitting and listening is a waste of time for me. It's obvious that we don't look for the same things in music.

Wayne: Yeah, I guess you're right. Sitting and listening is a lot more fun than you make it out to be, you know.

The brainstorming session made both Kenny and Wayne give more thought to the qualities they most admired in music. Writing a paper on the topic now seemed like an easier task.

Writing Daily in a Notebook or Diary

"Practice makes perfect" is a saying you have probably heard many times. Although it is doubtful that anyone can achieve absolute perfection, it is true that you can become better at almost anything you do—if you practice. Athletes, musicians, scientists—almost anyone who is striving for excellence—practice as often and as diligently as possible. These people know that the time they spend practicing is time well spent.

As a writer you, too, can strive for perfection, by practicing writing as you have the time. If possible, set aside a certain amount of time each day to record your ideas and feelings. After a while, you will probably find that your ideas flow more easily, that you can come up with the right words more readily, that your sentences have become more varied in length and structure, and that your spelling, grammar, and punctuation have improved.

Exercise Three   Write the name and date of each day for the next week on separate notebook pages. Set aside some time each day to write in your notebook. Write about anything at all that interests you.

Keeping a Scrapbook

By keeping a scrapbook and filling it with articles, pictures, bits of conversation, jokes, drawings, or anything else of this nature that captures your imagination, you will be creating a ready source of possible writing topics. Whenever you are looking for something to write about, you can browse through your scrapbook.

Exercise Four   Each day for a week, try to find at least one interesting article or picture from a newspaper or magazine. If possible, cut out the article or picture and paste it in a notebook.

If you find you have enjoyed collecting this kind of information, hold on to the notebook and add to its pages as you find interesting items.

Organizing Ideas

You have just been learning about ways to come up with ideas for a composition. The writer's work doesn't stop there, though. Once you have collected the ideas for a writing assignment, you have to organize them.

Composition writing, unlike free writing or diary writing, is done for an audience, so your ideas should be presented as logically as possible. It helps to be well aware of the purpose of your composition before you even begin writing. And once you do begin, you will probably get your best results if you have spent a little advance time grouping your ideas in an outline. That way, you will know where to start, how to proceed, and what to say in conclusion.

Classification

Imagine going into a large department store to look for a sweater to buy. In front of you are dozens of racks. You look through one. On it are babies' clothes, men's slacks, kitchen towels, and women's sleepwear. On the second rack, you find men's shirts, women's raincoats, and children's bathing suits. You hope that the entire store is not organized in this haphazard fashion, because if it is, it will take you hours to find a sweater. However, as you continue looking through the racks, your worst fear becomes reality: there is no rhyme or reason to the way things are arranged in this store.

If items were arranged this carelessly in libraries, doctors' offices, record stores, supermarkets, department stores—in practically any place that houses a number of different kinds of items—even the simplest tasks would become nearly impossible. A doctor would have a hard time locating an important instrument during surgery. A student would find it difficult or impossible to locate a specific book to study for a test. Shoppers would spend hours trying to locate something that should have taken them only minutes to find.

Luckily, most things that you need to use or understand are organized according to special systems of classification. Items in department stores, for instance, may be grouped according to age or size of the buyer: babies' items, children's items, teenagers' items, adults' items, and so on. These items may be further divided into items for females and items for males.

When you classify items, you divide them into groups, or classes. Movies, for example, are classified according to certain ratings: G, PG, and so on. However, you and your friends may classify movies in other ways. For example, you could group them according to type: science fiction, mystery, comedy, documentary, and so on.

There are usually several ways of classifying a group of items. But it is important to remember that items are only classified according to characteristics that matter. For example, you would not classify movies according to the height of the leading actor or the birthplace of the casting director. Those facts are not important in any broad discussion of movies.

Exercise Five   Write a short answer to each of the following questions.

1. Suppose you've been asked to organize items that belong in kitchen cupboards and drawers. Into what categories would you place all the different items you might find in a kitchen?

    You could begin, for example, by grouping together all canned and dry goods.

2. Suppose you have decided to write a book on all the different means of transportation. What characteristics would you use to categorize them?

    One characteristic might be "used today." You could put all the methods of transportation that people use today into one category.

Exercise Six   Complete one or more of the following activities.

1. Suppose a new bakery has just come to your town. The owner has asked you to help arrange the display shelves. It's up to you to decide what items to put where. What principle or principles will you use to classify the items?

2. Imagine that the country's largest furniture store is about to open in a shopping mall near your home. You have been hired to divide the store into departments. Make a list of the departments you would set up.

3. Make a list of at least ten sports, and think of different ways in which to classify them.

Classifying Ideas for a Composition

Ideas for writing assignments, like items in department stores, libraries, supermarkets, and so on, are easier to handle if they are first classified. When you classify ideas for a composition, you put together those ideas that share an important characteristic.

Suppose you have decided upon a topic for a composition and have written down about twenty ideas that you feel will help serve your purpose in writing. Your next job is to decide how to group your ideas.

One tenth-grade student, Mary, decided to write a composition about the red dirt road on which she lived. Here are some of her notes:

beautiful—lots of trees

in summer, dozens of different flowers and trees in bloom

very dusty

in winter, can be used to cross-country ski and sleigh ride

It's a bridle path.

only three dirt roads left in our town

Many ride bikes there, though it's hard.

sometimes like a washboard it's so bumpy

The town may pave it.

There's the water supply for the town below the area.

The way the road is treated affects the water supply.

Street is not maintained well.

Plow never comes in winter.

People throw garbage on side of road.

Many deer, foxes, raccoons, and other animals live and roam near the dirt road.

wildflowers blooming practically all year on the side of the road

many joggers on the road

When Mary looked over her list of ideas, she first thought that she would write a composition describing the dirt road. She would divide her ideas into two groups: the road in winter and the road in the summer. She then realized that some of the ideas didn't fit into either of those categories. If she didn't think of another way to organize her composition, she would be forced to leave those ideas out, even though she wanted to include them.

She looked again at her notes, and decided to write about the advantages and the disadvantages of dirt roads. But then it occurred to her that these categories, too, would force her to leave out some of her ideas.

She looked yet again at her notes and realized that one fact about the dirt road interested her the most: The town was going to vote on whether or not to pave the road. She didn't want it to be paved. On the other hand, she thought it should be kept in better condition.

Once she knew what interested her the most, she saw that she could group her ideas as follows:

Describe dirt road.

reasons why the road should not be paved

details on how to take better care of the road

By dividing her notes into these three groupings, Mary felt she could write an interesting essay.

Exercise Seven   Following is a list of ideas for a paper on leisure time. See how many different ways you can think of to group the ideas. For example, some of the leisure activities take place indoors and some outdoors. What other categories can you think of?

You do not have to include all the ideas in your groups. Leave out any ideas that do not fit into the categories you come up with.

aerobics

painting, sculpting, drawing

growing flowers, weeding gardens, planting trees, cutting lawns

singing

playing board games

collecting items, such as stamps, records, or baseball cards

learning another language

cooking

practicing a musical instrument

reading in the library

researching information about the stars and planets

lifting weights

going to the movies or a show

writing a short story, poem, or novel

playing tennis, volleyball, baseball, hockey

learning a new skill, such as using a computer or fixing a car

teaching others to swim

thinking

sleeping

General and Specific

Sometimes you make general statements:

Everyone in my family is an excellent mechanic.

Winding country roads are dangerous.

Both of these statements apply to all members of a class: every person in your family; all country roads. Statements of opinion that apply to all members of a class are sometimes considered "sweeping generalizations." A sweeping generalization does not allow for the possibility that one or more members of the group it refers to may be exceptions. For example, there may be one member of your family who is only a fair mechanic, and there are probably some winding country roads that are not dangerous at all.

If you do make a general statement, it's helpful to follow it with one or more examples to help support your point of view:

> Everyone in my family is an excellent mechanic. Yesterday, my mother fixed her car by changing the pistons herself, and my brother put new sparkplugs in his car.

> Winding country roads are dangerous. There have been four accidents in two weeks on Old Country Road, on the part that twists and turns for half a mile.

These examples help make the meaning of the statements clearer, but they do not prove that the original statements are true. Examples show only that certain members of a class behave according to the general statement.

It is usually best to avoid making statements about all members of a class, as there are bound to be some exceptions.

Exercise Eight   For each of the following general statements, write one or more examples that help clarify its meaning.

1. There are many pleasant ways to spend a rainy day.
2. Sporting events are thrilling to watch.
3. Students work hard.
4. Both men and women have interesting hairstyles.
5. Sweet desserts are bad for your health.
6. There are many opportunities to help others in our community.
7. Foreign travel is exhausting but rewarding.
8. Italian food has too much garlic in it.
9. Parades provide a grand spectacle.
10. Our town has changed a lot during the past five years.

Using Specific Words

Sometimes when you speak or write you use general words instead of specific ones. For example, you may say, "I worked yesterday." The verb *worked* is a general word. By using a more specific verb, you could make your meaning clearer.

I babysat yesterday.

I studied yesterday.

I lifeguarded yesterday.

A specific word applies to fewer members of a class than a general word, but it also gives more information than a general word. Here's another example.

> I bought an outfit.

Instead of using the general noun *outfit*, you could be more specific:

> I bought a pair of pants and a sweater.
> I bought a dress and tights.
> I bought a business suit.

Exercise Nine   Following are five general nouns and verbs. For each one, write as many specific synonyms as you can.

EXAMPLE: flower

daisy, rose, petunia, tulip, gardenia, hyacinth, dahlia, violet, lilac, pansy, begonia

1. tree
2. went
3. spoke
4. clothing
5. fruit

Facts and Opinions

As you saw earlier in this unit, writers sometimes make general statements that seem to be facts:

> Winding country roads are dangerous.

This statement is not a fact; it is an opinion. A statement of fact can be proved or disproved. A statement of opinion cannot. It presents a person's point of view and is open to disagreement. An opinion may be based on careful observation or on personal experience, but it cannot be definitively proved either true or false.

If, when you write, you want others to be convinced of your point of view, try to present facts. They are more persuasive than personal opinions.

Exercise Ten   On your paper, write whether each of the following statements presents a fact or an opinion.

1. Watching television is a waste of time.
2. Cigarette smoking should be banned from all public places.
3. Dogs should be kept on leashes.
4. Thyme, rosemary, and sage are herbs.
5. The capital of France is Paris.
6. No state should allow drivers to exceed 55 miles per hour.
7. Jogging is fun.
8. If you read too much, your eyesight will suffer.
9. A mongoose is a meat-eating mammal.
10. John F. Kennedy was assassinated in 1963.

Exercise Eleven   For each of the following topics, write one fact and one opinion.

EXAMPLE: Kentucky

Fact: The capital of Kentucky is Frankfort.

Opinion: Kentucky is the most beautiful state in the United States.

1. Alaska
2. Presidents
3. television
4. books
5. South America

Cause and Effect

Were you the kind of child who is continually asking "why"? If you were, you are probably the kind of young adult who still asks the same question. Of course, you no longer begin every question with the all-purpose word *why*. Instead you may say, "What factor or combination of factors caused this problem?" Or you may say, "If I do thus-and-so, what will happen as a result?" Nor do you always expect a simple, direct answer, as you did when you were a child. In fact, you know that sometimes there is no answer at all.

Still you keep on asking, because cause-and-effect relationships are extremely important in every aspect of life. The better you understand what causes certain things to happen, the better you can control what happens to you. Naturally, there are some events that no human being can prevent, no matter how well their causes are known. But there are many that might be controlled if people understood them better. For example, if doctors knew exactly what causes cancer, they might be able to find ways to prevent or cure it.

As a writer, you often need to explain the cause-and-effect relationships that underlie your ideas. This is especially important if your readers have enquiring minds. You should keep your readers constantly in mind when you are stating important facts or offering an opinion. Do you hear these imaginary readers asking, "Why?" If you do, try to explain the cause of the condition or problem you are discussing. Or, do you hear your readers saying, "I don't agree that event B always results from event A"? If you do, try to give some evidence that A leads to B.

Exercise Twelve   Number your paper from 1 to 5. Read each of the five items that follow. If an item states or hints at an answer to the question *Why?* write *Yes* after its number. Then write the answer in a few words. If the item does not offer any answer to the question *Why?* write *No* after its number.

EXAMPLE: No fish live downstream of the point where that factory dumps chemicals into the river.
Yes. Water pollution has killed the fish.

1. The little girl asked why Rover didn't talk to her, and her mother answered, "Dogs don't talk."
2. You left the milk out of the refrigerator, and now it's sour.
3. Sue did poorly on the Spanish test; in fact, she couldn't translate any of the passages.
4. A gallon of water usually weighs eight pounds, but, after a rain, a gallon of water from the Colorado River weighs almost nine pounds.
5. If you exercise regularly, you will feel better.

The Writing Process

Left: "José," from The Lower West Side Revisited series, around 1985 (Buffalo, New York)
Right: "José," from The Lower West Side Revisited series, around 1972 (Buffalo, New York)
Copyright Milton Rogovin, Courtesy Daniel Wolf, Inc., New York City

The Writing Process

There is really no such thing as a born writer. Even the best professional writer has to put in long years perfecting his or her craft. Should this discourage you? Not at all. In fact, it should encourage you. It means that you, too, can learn to write. Writing is a skill, like performing gymnastics or playing the piano. You can develop it through practice.

Or, here's another way to think about writing: It is a step-by-step process, like building something. You gather tools and materials. You make a plan, and then you shape the parts and put them together. Finally, you smooth away any rough edges and add the finishing touches.

Four Steps to Good Writing

There are four steps that can help both beginning and advanced writers to get their ideas down on paper, and then to improve and refine their work.

- ☐ **Step One: Set Your Goal.** The first step has three parts. First you choose a suitable topic. Next, you decide on the purpose of your writing. Then you identify the person or persons who will read your work.

- ☐ **Step Two: Make a Plan.** The second step has two parts. First you gather ideas for your topic, writing them down in your notes. Then you organize these ideas.

- ☐ **Step Three: Write the First Draft.** The third step is to get your thoughts down in sentences and paragraphs. Your first draft is like a rough sketch. It doesn't have to be polished or free of mistakes.

- ☐ **Step Four: Revise.** To revise is to "look again." In this step you reread your first draft to see how you can improve it. You may want to reorganize or reword certain parts to make them clearer. Then you proofread your revised draft and correct any mistakes in grammar, spelling, and punctuation that you find.

In this book, you will practice many kinds of writing. But for each kind you do, you will follow the same four steps to good writing—set your goal, make a plan, write the first draft, and revise.

Warming Up

It's easier to begin writing if you prepare yourself first. You need to warm up, just as a baseball player needs to warm up before a game. The following exercises will help you get ready to begin writing.

Exercise One   Take out some paper and a pencil or pen and find a pleasant place to sit. Look around you. Make a list of some of the things that you see. Then listen to the sounds around you. Make a list of the sounds you hear.

Exercise Two   Free writing is a good way to get yourself started. You may have already tried free writing if you studied the first unit in this book. Begin by writing down the first thing that comes to your mind. Then continue to write anything at all for five minutes, without stopping. Don't worry about making sense or being correct. Just relax and write. When five minutes is up, read over what you've written. Is there an idea on your paper that interests you? If so, write it at the top of a new sheet. Use it as the starting point for another round of free writing.

Setting a goal in writing, as in anything, involves making certain decisions. Naturally, you have to decide what you want to accomplish before you can work toward accomplishing it. You will make a decision in each of the three parts of this step.

A. Choose a Topic.

B. Define Your Purpose.

C. Identify Your Audience.

A. Choose a Topic

The first and most important thing you have to decide is what you are going to write about.

Suppose your teacher asks you to write about a topic of your own choice. How do you begin to choose? One way to begin is to think about interesting things that you've done or seen or read about. You could choose a topic you know well or one that you would like to know more about. The main thing to consider is whether the topic interests you.

Sometimes your teacher will assign a specific topic, and you won't have a choice. For example, your teacher might ask you to write about the surprise ending of the O. Henry story "The Green Door" (*Scope English Anthology*, Level Four).

Or, your teacher may assign a topic that is very general. Then it is up to you to decide which aspect of the topic you wish to focus on. Again, it's best to choose an aspect that interests you. For example, if you were asked to write about something having to do with transportation, you could choose to write about airplanes, trains, cars, bicycles, or any other means of transportation. Each of these topics is still too general for a short composition, however, so you would have to narrow down your choice even further. Suppose you chose bicycles as your topic. A narrower topic might be professional bicycle racing, or how to maintain a bicycle in good working order.

Exercise Three   Make two lists of broad, general topics that you might like to write about. For the first list, choose three or more topics that you know well. For the second list, choose three or more topics that you would like to know more about.

Following are two lists to help you get started. If the ideas you see interest you, choose a couple of them to include in your own lists.

Things I know well	Things I would like to know more about
cooking	music
movies	camping
sports	art

Limit Your Topic

When your teacher gives you a writing assignment, he or she usually tells you how long the composition should be. The length of the composition determines the breadth of your topic. The shorter the composition is, the narrower the topic should be.

Suppose the teacher who assigned the paper on transportation asked you to write one page on the topic. You have decided to limit your topic to bicycle maintenance. But one page is short, and the topic of bicycle maintenance is still broad enough to fill a book. You need to choose one aspect of the topic that can be covered in one page. Think about the specific problems you have had with your bicycle. Maybe you have had to fix a flat tire or install new brakes. You could cover either of these narrower topics adequately in one page.

Exercise Four   Look at the topics you listed for Exercise Three. Choose one that you would like to write one or two pages about. Decide whether the topic you've chosen is narrow enough to be covered in that length. If it isn't, make your topic more specific. Keep limiting your topic until you arrive at something that can be treated in one or two pages.

Holly chose sports as her topic. She narrowed it down several times before she arrived at a topic she could use for her paper.

Sports
Competitive sports
Team sports
The importance of team spirit

B. Define Your Purpose

You speak and write for many different reasons. You might want to tell an amusing story or describe a beautiful scene. Or perhaps you want to express an opinion or explain how something works. Whatever your purpose is, defining it will help you decide what to include in your composition and how to present it. For example, suppose that your teacher asks you to explain how to make something, and you write about making chocolate cake. You would not discuss the history of chocolate cake or describe in detail the best chocolate cake you ever ate. You would simply explain the procedure, step by step.

Stating your purpose before you start to write will help you decide what to say and how to say it.

Exercise Five   Look at the topic you came up with for Exercise Four. Ask yourself this question: *What do I want my reader to know, think, feel, or do after reading my writing?* Then in one sentence state the purpose of your writing.

Holly decided to write her paper about the importance of team spirit. She had recently joined an after-school softball team, and she felt the players' lack of team spirit was hurting them. Writing about this, she thought, might possibly benefit the team. Here are her topic and statement of purpose.

Topic: The importance of team spirit

Purpose: To find ways to improve the spirit on my softball team, the After-School Ramblers

Keeping your statement of purpose in mind as you write will help you to keep your composition focused.

C. Identify Your Audience

Who will your readers be? The answer to this question affects the tone and the content of your writing. For example, if you were writing a story intended for children, you would have to write about something that children would understand and find interesting. You would use an informal tone and a simple vocabulary. If you were writing a history term paper for your teacher, however, you would include complex words and ideas, and use a formal tone.

Once you have a clear idea of your audience, you can make the necessary decisions at each step of the writing process. You can decide what information is too basic or too difficult. You can decide what may be simply stated and what needs more explanation. And when it's time to revise your first draft, you can read your composition from your reader's point of view.

Exercise Six   Under your statement of purpose, write down who your readers will be. Consider their interests, opinions, age, and knowledge of the subject you are writing about.

Holly planned to submit her composition to the school paper. Her audience would be the whole student body, but she was hoping that her teammates, especially, would read the article. She knew that she would have to present the problem tactfully, so as not to offend them.

A. Gather Ideas

The method you use for gathering your ideas will depend on the type of paper you are writing. For example, to gather information for a research paper or a report, you would consult an encyclopedia or other reference materials. If you were writing an essay on a short story, you would read and reread the story to get ideas.

The two ways of gathering ideas that you will learn in this unit are observing your subject and brainstorming. These are useful methods of generating ideas for descriptive essays, firsthand news accounts, and narratives.

Observing

You can often gather ideas for a composition by simply looking around you. Even the most ordinary object can become interesting if you look at it closely. And the more carefully you observe something, the more vivid your description of it will be. For example, if you wanted to describe a pair of jeans, you might get out your favorite pair and take a good look at them. As you look, you begin to see details that make your jeans unique: grass stains from that time you stole third base, your lucky rabbit's foot attached to the belt loop, and the faded spots from the time you accidentally washed your jeans with bleach. Your jeans suddenly seem to have a story in them worth writing about.

Brainstorming

Brainstorming is a good way to generate ideas for your topic. Start by writing down your topic. Then relax and let your mind wander, jotting down whatever ideas come to you. As you brainstorm, you'll find that each idea automatically triggers a new idea.

When you have collected enough ideas, measure each idea against the statement of purpose for your composition. Discard any ideas that will not help you accomplish this purpose.

Making Notes

You can make notes on paper or on index cards. If you use paper, it's a good idea to write on only one side of each sheet. This way you can see what you've written on each piece without having to flip it over.

If you prefer to write your notes on index cards, it's a good idea to write only one idea on each card. Then you can try out different ways of organizing your ideas by arranging and rearranging the index cards.

Exercise Seven   Review the statement of purpose that you wrote in Exercise Five. Then jot down ten or more ideas for your topic. Your notes do not have to be complete sentences.

B. Organize Ideas

As you look at your list of ideas, you may notice that some of the ideas are closely related to each other. These can be grouped together under their own heading. The main idea of this new group is a *subtopic* (a division of the overall topic) of your paper.

Here is Holly's list of ideas. As you read it, think about which ideas you would group into subtopics.

Topic: The importance of team spirit

Purpose: To find ways to improve the spirit on my softball team

> People don't come to practices and games, or they come late.
>
> lack of equipment
>
> lack of a catcher with a good throwing arm
>
> People should come to practices and games.
>
> People should try not to be late.
>
> Someone should be in charge of equipment.
>
> Teammates should talk to each other during game.
>
> congratulate other team after game
>
> raise money for new uniforms
>
> hold a team picnic

Holly divided her ideas into two main groups. She saw that the first three ideas on her list described the problems that her team had during practices and games. So she put those three ideas under the heading *What Practices and Games Are Like*. Holly saw that the other ideas all suggested ways of solving the team's problems. So she grouped those ideas into a subtopic titled *How We Might Change Things*.

Holly's next step was to arrange her ideas in a rough outline. As she did this, she added some ideas for an introduction and a conclusion. Here is her outline:

I. Introduction

    a. joined the After-School Ramblers

    b. discovered there was no team spirit

II. What Practices and Games Are Like

    a. People don't come to practices and games, or they come late.

    b. lack of equipment

    c. lack of a catcher with a strong throwing arm

III. How We Might Change Things

    a. People should come to practices and games.

    b. People should try not to be late.

    c. Someone should be in charge of equipment.

    d. Teammates should talk to each other during game.

    e. congratulate other team after game

    f. raise money for new uniforms

    g. hold a team picnic

IV. Conclusion

    a. better team = more fun

POINTS TO REMEMBER

▷   Group related ideas into subtopics.

▷   Decide on the order of your subtopics.

▷   Feel free to add or cross out ideas as you make your outline.

Exercise Eight   Look over your notes and group your ideas into subtopics, giving each subtopic its own heading. Write a rough outline.

When you write your first draft, you should have one goal in mind: getting your ideas down on paper in sentences and paragraphs. The first draft does not have to be perfect. In fact, you will probably end up changing it quite a bit before you are satisfied with it. So don't worry about making mistakes in grammar or punctuation, or writing awkward sentences. You will have plenty of time to correct these mistakes later.

Just relax and write. If you get blocked at a particular point, just skip over the idea that's troubling you and keep writing. You can come back to it later when you revise.

Exercise Nine   Write the first draft of your composition. It should be one to two pages long. Use your rough outline and statement of purpose as guides as you write.

Here is the first draft of Holly's paper on team spirit.

When I first joined the after-school ramblers softball team, I was hoping to find a realy enthusiastic group. But was I ever disappointed! There wasn't no team spirit whatsoever. Hardy anybody seemed to care whether we won or lost, or whether we even played at all.

On the day of the first game things weren't much better. You might have expected people to shape up then, but it didn't seem to make any difference. We didn't have enough people to feild our own team, so we had to steal some extra players. After the second inning, enough team mates arrived and we had our own team. And guess what? You'll probably never guess in a hundred years. We won. We actually won that silly old ballgame. The final score was 13-10. But league rules being what they are, we had to forfeit the game. That certainly didn't improve our team spirit. Also, on my first day at practice half the team wasn't there until it was half over. And as if that wasn't bad enough, no one had remembered to bring a bat and a ball.

I think there are many things we could do to improve the team spirit on the After-School Ramblers. Everyone should attend practices & games and be on time. A committee should be chosen to be in charge of bringing the softballs/bats. During games we should talk to each

other. And after the game no matter who has won we should congratulate the other team. If someone misses a ball at bat or in the field, offer
encouragement. I think we should hold a car wash in order to buy new
jerseys and caps. It may seem silly, but I think new uniforms would give
us a sense of pride and to try harder. And a team picnic would really
help to boost morale.

Doing all these things, I believe, will not only increase our team
spirit, it will also increase our fun. And that, after all, is why we joined
the After-School Ramblers in the first place.

Compare Holly's first draft with her outline. Which ideas in the outline
did she leave out of the draft? Which ideas in the first draft were not in
the outline?

As you write your first draft, you will change certain things in your
outline. You will see that some things work and some things don't, and
you will probably add some ideas that you had not thought of before.

Allow as much time as you can between finishing your first draft and picking it up again to revise it. This will make it easier for you to approach your writing with a fresh, critical eye.

Try reading your paper as though someone else had written it. As you do so, check it for problems in content, organization, and style. The revision checklist that follows can help you identify these problems in your paper.

Revision Checklist

Content

1. Does your draft include the important ideas in your outline?
2. Do the majority of the ideas relate to your statement of purpose?
3. Have you supplied enough facts and details to support your main point?

Organization

1. Does your draft follow the order of your outline? If you departed from your outline, did you have a good reason for doing so?
2. Is the order of your ideas effective?

Style

1. Is the way you've stated things appropriate for your topic, purpose, and readers?
2. Is each word specific and correct?
3. Is each sentence clear and concise?

Exercise Ten　　Revise your first draft. As you revise, try reading your work aloud. Your ear will tell you whether you have created the overall impression you want. Use the revision checklist as a guide.

Holly put her paper away for a couple of days before she revised it. Notice the changes that she made.

When I first joined the after-school ramblers softball team, I was hoping to find a really enthusiastic group. But was I ever disappointed! There wasn't no team spirit whatsoever. Hardly anybody seemed to care whether we won or lost, or whether we even played at all.

On the day of the first game, things weren't much better. You might have expected people to shape up then, but it didn't seem to make any difference. We didn't have enough people to field our own team, so we had to ~~steal~~ borrow some extra players (of the other team's). After the second inning, (You could still tell who our players were by our shabby uniforms.) enough team mates arrived and we had our own team. And guess what? ~~You'll probably never guess in a hundred years.~~ We won! ~~We actually won that silly old ballgame.~~ The final score was 13-10. But, because of league rules ~~being what they are~~, we had to forfeit the game. That certainly didn't improve our team spirit! ~~Also,~~ on my first day at practice, ~~half~~ most of the team ~~wasn't there~~ didn't arrive until it was half over. And as if that ~~wasn't~~ were bad enough, no one had remembered to bring a bat and a ball.

I think there are many things we could do to improve the team spirit ~~on~~ of the After-School Ramblers. First of all, Everyone should attend practices

and   (make an effort to)
~~&~~ games and be on time. A committee should be in
                              equipment
charge of bringing the ~~softballs/bats~~. During games we should talk to

each other. And after the game, no matter who has won, we should

congratulate the other team. If someone misses a ball at bat or in the
     (we should)   (also)
field, offer encouragement. I think we should hold a car wash in order
              eys   #
to buy new ~~jersies~~ and caps. It may seem silly, but I think new
(maybe, if we had any money left over, we could have)
uniforms would give us a sense of pride and to try harder. And a
          (That)   (inspire us)
team picnic would really help to boost morale.
                              would   improve
     Doing all these things, I believe, ~~will~~ not only ~~increase~~ our team
        would
spirit, it ~~will~~ also increase our fun. And that, after all, is why we

joined the After-School Ramblers in the first place.

Proofread

After you have revised your work, you should proofread it for mistakes
in spelling, grammar, and punctuation. This step is often overlooked,
but it is important. Careless errors can distract your readers, and make
your composition less effective. You should also check your work for
proper word choice and sentence structure. If you're not sure how to
use or spell a word, consult a dictionary. If you have any questions
about grammar or punctuation, ask your teacher or consult a textbook.

Exercise Eleven   Proofread your work carefully. Now you are ready
to make a final copy. Use a word processor, a typewriter, or a pen to
make it letter-perfect. Although this is the last part of the last step, it is
very important to do the neatest job you can. Your paper deserves the
best.

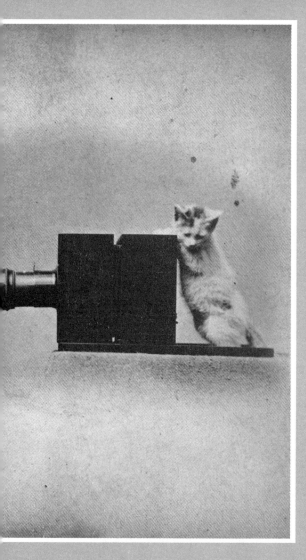

Writing Paragraphs

"Photographic Students," 1871
This is a stereograph, which is a set of two almost identical images mounted side by side on a card. When viewed through a device called a stereoscope, the image appears to be three-dimensional.
Culver Pictures, Inc.

Writing Paragraphs

Imagine that you are a movie director shooting a Western. You've reached the point in the story where some ranchers come into conflict with a tribe of Indians. Three leaders from each side meet to see if they can settle their differences without fighting. How will you film this meeting?

You decide to shoot it in three scenes. For the first scene, you position the camera so that it looks down on the actors from a distance. You get a broad view of the plateau, with forested hills and a snow-capped mountain in the background. In the midst of this spectacular scenery, the men and their quarrel seem quite small.

Your second shot shows the two groups of leaders, on horseback, lined up facing each other. The camera is close enough now so the movie audience will be able to identify the six men.

Your third shot shows the chief of the Indians close up. He is about to tell the cattlemen that this land belongs to his people.

Now suppose you are asked to put this part of the story into writing. Where before you used pictures, you must use words and sentences to tell what happens. However, you can organize the written version the same way you did the filmed version, by arranging your statements in three scenes. At the beginning of each scene, instead of moving the camera to a new position, you will start a new paragraph.

As you know, a paragraph is a group of sentences that work together to express one main idea. Usually, one of the sentences in the paragraph states the idea in general terms. The other sentences give details or examples, or they explain the main idea.

The standard way to show that you are starting a new paragraph is to write the first word a few spaces (usually five) in from the left-hand margin. This is called *indenting*. In some books—the one you're reading now, for example—not every paragraph is indented. (The artist who designed this book has found other ways to show you where each new paragraph starts.) When you write, however, you should indent all your paragraphs. The indentations will make it easier for the reader to follow your train of thought.

53

P O I N T S   T O   R E M E M B E R

▷ A paragraph is a group of sentences that relate to one main idea or topic.

▷ A paragraph indentation is a signal to your reader that you are going to present a new thought.

In the following paragraph, all the sentences discuss the same topic.

In the emperor penguin family, it's Father who hatches the children. Each mating season, as soon as her one egg is laid, the female goes out to sea to dine on fish and krill. The male holds the egg on the top of his feet and covers it with the soft, warm roll of fat that he has on his lower belly. Sixty-four days later he is still standing there, a shadow of his former self. He has lost from one third to one half of his body weight. At last his mate returns with food for the newly hatched chick, and Father takes off for a well-earned vacation.

The first sentence in this paragraph states the main idea: The male emperor penguin hatches the chicks. The other sentences tell what he goes through to hatch them. When all the sentences in a paragraph work together in this way, the paragraph is said to have *unity*.

As you read the following paragraph, look for two sentences that do not relate to the main idea.

Boomeranging, a sport that is very popular in Australia, is catching on in the United States. Many Americans are finding out how much fun it is to throw a boomerang and watch it come sailing back. The English distance record for throwing a boomerang is over 180 yards. According to Benjamin Ruhe, the author of *Many Happy Returns,* the sport appeals mostly to people who are a little "offbeat." Ruhe warns that a sudden gust of wind can spoil the most perfect throw.

The main idea of this paragraph is stated in the first sentence. The two sentences that do not support the main idea are the third (*The English distance record . . .*) and the last (*Ruhe warns . . .*).

Exercise One   Find the main idea in the following paragraph. Write it on your paper. Then copy the other sentences that support the main idea. Omit any sentences that do not help make up a unified paragraph.

Popular dance styles can tell us a great deal about the social customs of a particular period. The minuet is a good example of this fact. It was popular in the eighteenth century. This was a time when meetings between unrelated men and women were usually public and formal. According to the dictionary, *minuet* comes from a word in both Latin and French meaning "small," and probably refers to the dancers' tiny steps. When dancing the minuet, partners stayed quite far apart and touched only each other's hands. You can see the minuet danced in the opera *Don Giovanni.*

Choose a Topic

In this unit you will write a paragraph on a topic of your own choosing. Select a topic that you are genuinely interested in. It may be one that you know quite a lot about, or one that you know a little about and would like to explore further. It should be something that can be covered in six to ten sentences. In other words, it must be a fairly narrow topic.

Limit Your Topic

Suppose you're interested in becoming a forest ranger some day, so you choose "forests" as the topic of your paragraph. Right away you have a problem: the topic is far too broad. You would have to write a whole book to cover it adequately. The solution is to divide "forests" into parts, and then divide each of those parts into still smaller parts. Eventually you should arrive at a topic that's small enough for a one-paragraph paper.

Here are some possible divisions of the broad subject "forests."

forest trees and plants	how forests safeguard water
how forests prevent soil erosion	national and state forests
animal life in forests	careers in forestry

As you probably noticed, each of these narrower topics is still too large to cover in only one paragraph. You need to develop a still narrower topic. Suppose you choose "forest trees and plants" from the list above. Here are some possible subdivisions of that topic.

flowering plants	types of trees
logging	forest fires
tree diseases	fungi

Although these topics are narrower, each one is still too broad to be discussed adequately in one paragraph. If you chose a topic from this list, you would need to narrow it even further. For example, you might narrow "flowering plants" down to "the trailing arbutus." You might narrow "types of trees" down to "the giant sequoia."

Exercise Two   Select four of the following broad topics. Then divide each of them into smaller and smaller parts until you get a topic that is narrow enough to be covered in a single paragraph.

EXAMPLE:

Topic: Education

Narrower Topic: Tests

Still Narrower Topic: Math tests

One-Paragraph Topic: Why I Find Math Tests Difficult

Broad Topics:

Careers

Education

Families

Fashion

Food

Movies

Sports

Travel

P O I N T S   T O   R E M E M B E R

▷ Choose a topic that you know well, or that you are interested in learning more about.

▷ Make sure your topic is narrow enough to be discussed in one paragraph.

A. Gather Ideas

You now have four narrow topics to choose from. Your next step will be to brainstorm a list of ideas that you might use in your paragraph. When you brainstorm, you relax and let ideas about your topic pop into your mind in any order. Here are the notes Gerard came up with in a brainstorming session:

One-Paragraph Topic: Why I Find Math Tests Difficult
Notes:

> never seem to study the right thing
>
> get too nervous to think straight
>
> don't really understand problems when doing daily homework
>
> stay up too late studying the night before
>
> try to cram too much information into my head at last minute so I don't seem to remember anything
>
> don't stay current with homework
>
> have always had a problem with math
>
> don't really like numbers
>
> never learned all the multiplication tables
>
> don't ask questions in class when don't understand something

Exercise Three   Select a one-paragraph topic from the work you did in Exercise Two. Brainstorm a list of ideas on this topic. (Let your mind wander freely over the topic, and write down whatever occurs to you.) You can record your thoughts in the form of complete sentences, phrases, single words, or a mixture of these forms.

While brainstorming, just relax and don't worry about the results. Your only goal is to make a list of ideas that have some connection with your topic. A few of them may sound silly to you later when you read over your list, but that's all right. At least some of the ideas on the list will be usable.

After you have finished brainstorming and listing ideas, take another look at the topic you chose. Now pretend that you are allowed to make only one statement on that topic. Of all the points you would like to make, which is the most basic? Write one complete sentence that states that point. This sentence will become the topic sentence of your paragraph.

Develop Your Paragraph

There are three main ways to develop a paragraph. You can use facts, you can use examples, or you can use an incident. The method you choose will depend upon what you are writing about and how you want your paragraph to affect your reader.

When might you choose to use facts? You would probably use them if you were writing something technical or scientific and you could look up the information you needed.

Here is an example of a paragraph developed with facts.

A well-known woodland flower in central and eastern Canada and the United States is the trailing arbutus. It is a creeping plant whose tiny blossoms are sometimes hard to find among the leaves on the forest floor. Each white or pink flower has five petals and gives off a delightful fragrance. In New England the trailing arbutus is called the mayflower, and some people claim that the Pilgrims gave it this name. Both the state of Massachusetts and the province of Nova Scotia have adopted it as their official flower.

The first sentence in the paragraph is the topic sentence. It states that the trailing arbutus is well known in certain parts of North America. The rest of the sentences in the paragraph give facts about the plant: how it grows, what its flowers look like, and so on.

The writer of the following paragraph used examples to support the main idea.

Stamp collecting is more than just arranging small printed rectangles in an album. It's witnessing the signing of our Declaration of Independence. It's hearing the "westward ho" cries from the wagon trains. It's smelling the excitement in the air as prospectors look for gold. It's observing Emily Dickinson penning one of her poems. It's waiting in the crowd outside Paris for the landing of Charles Lindbergh after his transatlantic flight. It's feeling awe as astronauts walk on the moon. It's admiring the skills of the athletes at the Olympic Games.

Stamp collecting is all these things because stamps record many of the memorable moments in our history.

This paragraph gives examples of some of the people and events that are pictured on U.S. postage stamps. The examples support the main idea of the paragraph. Notice that the main idea is expressed in two sentences, the first and the last.

Sometimes—as in the following example—a topic is best explained with the help of an incident or an event.

Have you ever noticed that *first day* rhymes with *worst day*? I know it's just a coincidence and doesn't mean anything. Still, *first* and *worst* seem to go together in my life. Take, for example, my first day in this school. I overslept, so I knew I would have to hurry to get here on time. I looked frantically for the piece of paper on which I had written the school's address, but it was nowhere to be found. However, I knew the school was a few blocks north and a few blocks east of our new house—so I walked south and west because I didn't have the directions straight yet. After a while I stopped somebody on the street and asked where the high school was. I had forgotten the name of the school, but I figured there was probably only one in this part of town. Of course there are two, and my guide kindly directed me to the nearest one, which was the wrong one. By the time I finally got to Crestview, I was forty-five minutes late. But, strangely enough, I didn't feel too bad. I told myself that since this was my first and worst day, the rest were bound to be better.

The main idea of this paragraph is that the writer always has trouble coping with a new situation. As evidence of this fact, the writer relates an incident.

Exercise Four Look at the work you did in Exercise Three. You should have a list of ideas on a topic, as well as a topic sentence that states the main point you want your paragraph to express.

Look over your list again. Cross out any ideas that do not relate to your main idea. And if in the meantime you have thought of other ideas that relate to your topic, add them to your list. Remember, you want your paragraph to have unity.

Now decide how you will develop your paragraph. You can use facts, examples, or an incident. If you find that you don't have enough of one type of detail to support your main idea fully, you might want to use a combination: facts and examples, for instance, or examples and an incident.

POINTS TO REMEMBER

▷ Make sure that every detail explains or supports your main idea.

▷ There are three types of details that you can use to support your main idea: facts, examples, or an incident.

▷ If you find that you don't have enough details to support your main idea, try changing the type of details you're using. If that doesn't work, you may want to change your main idea.

B. Organize Ideas

In this unit we will discuss two methods of organizing the information in a paragraph. You can arrange your ideas according to their logical relationships. This is called *logical order.* Or, if you are talking about an event or a procedure, you can arrange your details according to their relationship in time. This is called *chronological order.*

Logical Order

If you are developing your paragraph with facts or examples, you will probably want to use logical order. There are two main kinds of logical relationship that may exist between ideas. One is the relationship of cause and effect. For example, suppose the main idea of your paragraph is that the city should let homeless families take over and repair abandoned buildings owned by the city. To support this suggestion, you could mention the good results that you think such action would bring. You could point out, for instance, that the families would be decently housed and the city's welfare costs would be reduced.

Another type of logical relationship is the one that exists between a general statement and the details that support it. Two of the sample paragraphs in this unit—the one about the trailing arbutus and the one about one student's first day at a new school—are examples of this kind of logical relationship.

Chronological Order

When you develop a paragraph by describing an incident, you will usually use chronological (time) order. You will always use this method of organization when you are explaining a process or giving how-to instructions. The following paragraph, which outlines a process, is organized according to chronological order.

A 3-D movie tricks your eyes into seeing three dimensions (height, width, and depth) where only two exist. Here's how the trick works: The camera operator takes each shot twice, from two different viewpoints. These two viewpoints are—like your eyes—side by side and about two inches apart. The two pictures are printed on film one over the other. When you look at the screen through special polarizing glasses, your left eye sees one image and your right eye sees the other. As usual, your brain puts the two images together and presto: the scene before you comes to life. It looks so much like the real world that you feel as if you could get up from your seat and walk right into the picture.

Exercise Five   Organize the details you listed in Exercise Four. Use either logical or chronological order. Before you begin, think about which method of organization would be more suitable for your topic.

Write the First Draft

Now it's time to write the paragraph that you have been planning. You know your topic and your purpose, you have a list of ideas, and you have chosen a method of organization. You should begin by deciding what the main idea of your paragraph will be and stating it in a topic sentence.

The Topic Sentence

A sentence that expresses the main idea of a paragraph is called the *topic sentence*. When you wrote your main idea as a complete sentence in Exercise Three, you wrote a topic sentence. What does a topic sentence do? It directs the reader's attention to the main idea. It also acts as a guide for the writer, helping her or him make sure that all the sentences in the paragraph relate to the main idea.

Does a topic sentence always appear at the beginning of the paragraph? Often it does. But a topic sentence could appear anywhere in the paragraph—at the beginning, in the middle, or at the end.

Notice where the topic sentence in the following paragraph occurs.

When I entered the room, I was standing next to Sigourney Weaver and Mel Gibson. Across the room, Tom Cruise was dancing with Kelly McGillis. Whoopi Goldberg was whooping it up with Jack Nicholson. Sam Shepard, wearing a cowboy outfit, stood talking to Meryl Streep. The Three Stooges were there, too, trying to decide which way to leaf through a magazine. *I had just arrived at Shelley's "come as your favorite movie star" costume party.* I stood there in my top hat and tails, leaning on my walking stick. I looked around the room, searching for a dance partner worthy of me, the great Fred Astaire. I was just about to give up when I spied a tall, strawberry blonde in a pink chiffon gown. "Ginger," I said with a bow, "may I have this dance?"

The topic sentence—the one that explains what is going on—appears in the middle of the preceding paragraph. A topic sentence in the middle is less common than one that appears at the beginning or at the end. For that very reason, it can add interest and variety to writing.

Why would anyone want to put a topic sentence at the end of a paragraph? Doing so could make things more interesting—it could heighten the sense of drama by keeping the reader in suspense. Read the following example.

They number more than 6,000 species. Their name comes from the Latin word meaning "to creep." They are so named because creeping is their chief means of locomotion (movement). They prefer warm cli-

mates because they are *ectothermic*. This means that the temperature of their blood is the same as that of their surroundings. Although many of them live in or near water, they have lungs rather than gills. Most of them lay eggs to produce their young. And even though many people call them slimy, their skin is covered with dry scales. These creatures make up the class of animals known as *reptiles*.

P O I N T S   T O   R E M E M B E R

▷ The topic sentence expresses the main idea of a paragraph.

▷ The topic sentence can appear at the beginning, in the middle, or at the end of a paragraph. It should be placed where it is the most effective.

Exercise Six   Look at the topic sentence and the details (facts, examples, or incident) you arranged (in logical or chronological order) in Exercise Five. Experiment with your topic sentence. Read it at the beginning of your list of details, then in the middle, and then at the end. Where does it sound the best? When you have decided on the most effective placement of your topic sentence, write the first draft of your paragraph in ten to fifteen sentences.

As you write your first draft, keep the following guidelines in mind.

☐ The first sentence of your paragraph should catch the reader's attention and should be indented.

☐ The topic sentence should be placed where it is most effective.

☐ Keep your main idea in mind as you write. You want all your sentences to relate to the main idea so that your paragraph will have unity.

☐ Use facts, examples, or an incident—or a combination of these— to develop your main idea.

☐ Use either logical order or chronological order.

☐ Don't worry about minor mistakes at this stage. Concentrate on making the paragraph say what you want it to. You can correct your work later.

Now that you have written your first draft, wait a day or two if possible before looking at it again. If you can do this, you will be more objective and able to approach your paragraph as if you had never read it before. You will be better able to see what needs to be added, deleted, moved, or made clearer.

Polishing Your Topic Sentence

A topic sentence should do more than simply state a main idea. It should state the main idea in a clear and interesting manner. Now is the time to make sure your topic sentence accomplishes this.

Dana was writing a paragraph on circus clowns. Here is the first topic sentence she wrote:

Circus clowns are not all alike.

Dana reread the sentence and decided that it did not really say very much. She tried again.

Circus clowns come in all shapes and sizes.

This sentence was all right, she thought, but she had written a paragraph that she felt deserved something livelier. She wanted a topic sentence with more zip. Here is the one she finally developed:

Circus clowns come in all shapes and sizes and degrees of funniness.

Read the following groups of topic sentences. Compare the topic sentences in each group and decide which one is the best.

Jack London was a very successful author.

Jack London had more money and fame than almost anyone else during his day.

Jack London had more riches and fame than any character he could have thought up.

Sailing is my dad's favorite sport.

There is nothing my father enjoys more than going sailing.

My father's life took a new tack the first time he set sail.

The bookshelf in my room holds many books.

Last time I counted, there were forty-seven books on my bookshelf.

My library covers subjects from A to Z, though there are usually a few letters scattered under the bed or forgotten at a friend's house.

Transitional Words

As you revise your paragraph, you may want to add some *transitional words*. These words can help your paragraph flow smoothly from one idea to the next. The following list contains some of the more commonly used transitional words.

first	second	third	finally
after	now	then	sometimes
above	below	next to	opposite
because	therefore	so	consequently
but	however	even so	for example

Exercise Seven   Reread and revise the first draft of the paragraph you wrote. Try to think of ways in which the writing can be improved. Does the paragraph flow smoothly from one idea to the next? Is every word the best word you can think of?

Here are some questions to ask yourself as you revise your work.

☐ Can I state the topic sentence more clearly or make it more interesting? Is the topic sentence placed where it works best in the paragraph?

☐ Will the first sentence make the reader want to read more? Is the first sentence indented?

☐ Do all the details support the topic sentence? Will these details be clear to the reader?

☐ Are there any important details that I have left out? Do I need to add another type of detail (fact, example, incident)?

☐ Are the details in the best logical or chronological order?

☐ Do I need to use any other transitional words?

Proofread and Edit

Now it is time to go over every sentence carefully. As you proofread, look for mistakes in grammar, spelling, capitalization and punctuation. Are there any words you need to check in the dictionary? Have you capitalized all proper nouns? Are there any words capitalized that should not be? Are the final punctuation marks correct? Do you need to add or delete any commas? Is the first sentence of your paragraph indented? Is each sentence a complete sentence? Are there any sentences that do not look or sound right? If so, you might want to ask your teacher for help in correcting them.

Exercise Eight   Proofread the revised paragraph you wrote. Correct all your mistakes. If you have the time, set your work aside and then reread it. You will probably notice that you can find mistakes or things to change each time you return to your paper. (As a famous writer once said, good writing is never finished. It is merely abandoned.)

After you have made all the necessary corrections, make a clean copy of your work. Remember to write neatly. Before you hand in your paper, proofread it one more time.

Writing a Journal

*Main Street, Cazenovia, New York, 1971. Local merchants in
this town of 2,600 received the Governor's Award for their
restoration of these 19th-century buildings.
David Plowden*

Writing a Journal

One basic rule of good writing is that you should write about a topic that you know well. And there is at least one topic on which you are an expert: yourself. One of the best places to establish yourself as the main topic is in a journal.

A journal, as you probably know, is usually kept in a book or a notebook of blank pages. But why do you need to use a notebook rather than just a blank sheet of paper? Because that way you won't have to hunt around for paper when something important occurs to you, and you will always know where to look if you want to reread one of your previous journal entries.

A journal is written by and for yourself. In other words, you don't have to worry about your audience. Keeping a journal is a very good way to remember what you have seen, what you have done, and what you have learned.

Keeping a journal will improve your writing, because it will give you practice. There is simply no substitute for writing practice if you want to strengthen your skills. Also, by recording your thoughts in a journal, you will get a better idea of what things in life are most important to you. This can help you know yourself better. It can also help you find interesting topics for your other writing projects.

In this unit you will start writing in a journal on a regular basis.

POINTS TO REMEMBER

▷ Record in your journal what you have seen, what you have done, and what you have learned from your experiences.

▷ You can improve all the writing that you do by keeping a journal.

▷ A journal can also help you know yourself better and find writing topics.

Set Your Goal

It is important that you set an easy goal for yourself as you start your journal writing. Don't worry too much about whether your writing is good or not. This is not a time for you to be a perfectionist. You are simply trying to get in the habit of writing. It is better to write something every day, whether you feel inspired or not, than it is to wait until you feel inspired. So, even if it is only a few sentences, write something in your journal regularly. The more you write, the easier it will become. Journal writing may even start to be something you look forward to.

Exercise One   Make lists in your journal on each of the following topics. It's all right if you can only think of two or three items for each topic. You can always add items to your list later as you think of them.

EXAMPLE: Things That I Regret

Not knowing how to ride a bike

Not being able to play the piano

Not trying out for the tennis team

Not studying for the last math test

Things I Would Like to Accomplish

People I Would Like to Know

Places I Would Like to Visit

Things I Would Like to Be Able to Do Over Again

Whenever you don't feel capable of writing a lot in your journal, try making a list instead. Lists can often lead you to think of other important details and ideas to write about.

Journal writing can also help you find out what you think. Writing involves some physical effort, but it is basically a mental act. Even if you tried, you could not put meaningful words and sentences down on a page without thinking.

Exercise Two   Choose an evening during the past week. Write down a key word that comes to mind about the evening. It can be the name of someone you talked to, a TV or radio program you enjoyed, an emotion you felt, or anything else that you remember clearly. Let that one word trigger other thoughts. Write them down as quickly as you can, so that your mind keeps making rapid associations. Do not worry about writing correctly or neatly. Just write.

Charlotte decided that her key word would be *music.* Following is part of her journal entry.

Listening to jazz on the radio. Liked the rhythm section. I play drums so I enjoy hearing drummers. One drum solo went on for longest time. Wondered if the record was stuck. Imagined how tired I would be.

Before now you may have sat trying to write, staring at a blank page, thinking you'd never be able to fill it with writing. You can overcome that feeling by writing regularly in a journal. With practice, writing becomes more familiar and easier to do—a helpful way of sorting out your thoughts. Eventually, you may even start to feel that you don't really know your own mind until you have had the chance to write your thoughts down in your journal.

Exercise Three   Imagine that the following list of questions has been sent to you by a college you are applying to. Answer the questions in your journal. Each of your answers should be no less than three sentences long.

1. What important change has taken place in your life this year?
2. Which school course do you like best and why?
3. What statement do you make about yourself by the way you dress?
4. What are your best qualities? What are your worst qualities?
5. How do you like to spend your free time?

Following is the answer Charlotte wrote in her journal to the question *How do you like to spend your free time?*

I like to divide my free time between activities done with other people and activities done by myself. With friends and family I like to bike, dance, and cook. By myself, I like to read and take photographs.

Exercise Four   Imagine that you are writing the story of your life in your journal. Naturally, it is such a fascinating and eventful story that it takes ten chapters. Each chapter has a title. Following are the titles. For each one, write the first two sentences of the chapter.

After you have completed all your two-sentence chapter beginnings, look them over. Which one of these chapter topics especially interests you? Choose one and write a little more about it.

74

Writing in your journal can be a minor part of your life, but make it a regular one. You don't have to spend a huge chunk of time on it. Just plan to spend a few minutes a day.

Finding Your Voice

Just as your manner of speaking gives you a style all your own, the way you express yourself in writing can be distinctive and original. Since journal writing is less formal than writing for regular school assignments, you can have fun with your journal. You can use it to develop your own writing voice without having to worry about what anyone else might think.

To take an example, here is how a student named Sam wrote about a camping trip for a school assignment:

My brother and I went camping for two weeks in the Rockies. We pitched our tent next to a mountain stream. It was cold at night. We spent our days hiking and fishing. Two nights in a row, a bear tried to get our food.

Later, when Sam met a friend of his, he told the story much differently:

You wouldn't believe how loaded down my brother's car was when we went camping in the Rockies. We had a tent, sleeping bags, a stove, lots of food, and fishing gear. We set up camp next to this ice-cold stream. Would you believe the water was so clear you could see the trout just waiting to be caught? But Bill is one serious fisherman, I'll tell you. My legs would ache after a long day of fishing. Every night it was so cold that all I did was wrap up in my sleeping bag after we had eaten our day's catch. One night as I was falling asleep there was this big bear outside the tent, trying to swipe some of our leftovers. I found out that my big brother is no hero. He buried his head in his sleeping bag until the bear was gone.

Sam's spoken words have a style and rhythm that his written words do not have. His writing could be made more lively and interesting if he would only listen to his speaking voice and use the same style in his writing.

Exercise Five   Think of something that happened to you in the not-so-distant past. Maybe you had an unexpected adventure on what began as a typical Saturday afternoon. Perhaps you visited a fascinating museum or you went on a long hike or an all-day canoe trip. In your journal, write a brief description of what happened.

After you have written about it, tell your story out loud to a friend. If possible, tape-record your account. Compare the written and the spoken versions. How do they differ? How could you use some of your speaking style in your writing style? Study the differences in word choice, sentence patterns, and content.Then rewrite your story so that it more closely resembles your spoken account.

In addition to finding your own voice, you should feel free to experiment and take risks in journal writing. Write about things you have never written about before. Don't restrict yourself to only a few subjects. Expand your interests. Surprise yourself. Your journal is a place for you to grow as a person and as a writer.

Exercise Six   Daydreaming about the future can be useful. It can help you find out what you would like to happen, and what goals you want to work toward.

Read the following questions. Then imagine yourself twenty years from now, and write a journal entry answering each question.

1. Where do you live?
2. What kind of work do you do?
3. What do you do for recreation?
4. What have you accomplished that you are proud of?
5. What are your goals for the next twenty years?
6. Looking back, how do you feel about the kind of person you were in high school?

Memories of the past, thoughts about the present, or daydreams about the future may pop into your mind at any time. Try to have your journal at hand to jot down these ideas whenever they occur. Journal entries can help you understand where you've been, where you are, and where you would like to go.

Write the First Draft

Anything Goes

Anything can go into a journal. You can include drawings or descriptions. You can put in letters you've received or letters you've never sent. You can paste in pictures or other mementos. You can write about your daydreams or your real dreams. You can record your most intimate feelings and important discoveries. Your journal can be a daily account of every aspect of your life, from the most important detail to the least important. There are few things that allow you as much freedom as a journal. You may even begin to regard your journal as a good friend.

Many professional writers keep journals. They write down page after page of ideas, conversation, and observations. They often pull out this raw material to use in their later writing. You can do the same. When you are asked to write a composition or prepare a speech, you can pick up some good ideas from your journal entries.

John Updike once wrote an account of a walk in New York City. Read this selection from "Central Park" (*Scope English Anthology*, Level Four). You can almost imagine the writer as he recorded his observations in his journal.

M O D E L . . . .

On the afternoon of the first day of spring, when the gutters were still heaped high with Monday's snow but the sky itself was swept clean, we put on our galoshes and walked up the sunny side of Fifth Avenue to Central Park. There we saw:

Great black rocks emerging from the melting drifts, their craggy skins glistening like the backs of resurrected brontosaurs.

A pigeon on the half-frozen pond strutting to the edge of the ice and looking a duck in the face.

A policeman getting his shoe wet testing the ice.

Three elderly relatives trying to coax a little boy to accompany his father on a sled ride down a short but steep slope. After much balking, the boy did, and, sure enough, the sled tipped over and the father got his collar full of snow. Everybody laughed except the boy, who sniffed.

Four boys in black leather jackets throwing snowballs at each other.
(The snow was ideally soggy, and packed hard with one squeeze.)
    Seven men without hats.
    Twelve snowmen, none of them intact.
    Two men listening to the radio in a car parked outside the Zoo; Mel
Allen was broadcasting the Yanks-Cardinals game from St. Petersburg.

Exercise Seven   Go for a walk around your school, or in your neighborhood, or through your community. Then, in your journal, describe what you have seen. Try to do it as though you've just seen everything for the first time.

A writer may also take an imaginary walk. Read this paragraph from "400 Mulvaney Street" (*Scope English Anthology*, Level Four). In it, the writer Nikki Giovanni is remembering her old neighborhood in Knoxville, Tennessee.

M O D E L . . . .

And I remember Mulvaney Street where I grew up. Mulvaney Street looked like a camel's back with both humps bulging—up and down. We lived in the down part. At the top of the left hill a lady made ice balls and would mix the flavors for just a nickel. Across the street from her was the Negro center, where the guys played indoor basketball and the little kids went for stories and nap time. Down in the valley part were the tennis courts, the creek, most of the park, and the beginning of the right hill. The houses started on the side of the left hill. In the middle, people got regular flat front lawns. Then the right hill started. On it was a big apartment building that didn't have a yard at all.

. . . .

Exercise Eight   Recall a place from your past. It might be a town or a house or a neighborhood where you once lived. It could be a school or a summer camp you once attended, or a trip you once took to an interesting place. Go for an imaginary walk through this place and describe what you remember about it.

Much of the information we receive comes to us through our ears. We listen to the radio and the TV; we listen to stories from our friends; we listen to our teachers. We listen all the time, but do we *really* hear? We may get the gist of a person's conversation, but do we recall the words the person used—the turns of phrase and the colorful expressions?

It takes a good ear to capture exactly what people say. But doing so can liven up your writing. Careful listening is something you can train yourself to do. A journal is a good place to start collecting some of the conversation you hear.

You might consider carrying a small notebook in which you can jot down snatches of conversation that you hear during the day. Write on only one side of each page, so you can tear out the notes that you want to keep and tape them onto the pages of your journal.

Exercise Nine   Think of a conversation you have had or overheard in the past week. Write it in dialogue form, as if it were in a play. Make it look like the sample dialogue below, which was written by Nell. She based it on a conversation she had had.

Mr. B.: This is going to be the warmest winter we've had in years.

Me: How can you tell?

Mr. B.: Well, one sure sign is the wooly worms. *(Sees the puzzled look on my face.)* You know—caterpillars. Usually they have a yellow or orange stripe down their backs, but this year they're completely black.

Me: I don't see the connection.

Mr. B.: Neither do I, actually. But you can be sure the wooly worms do!

Daydreams are not the only dreams that are important in journal writing. Night dreams can provide a backdrop against which to view your waking hours. Many writers keep records of their dreams, to understand themselves better, and to use the details of dreams in stories and other imaginative writing.

Exercise Ten   Dreams are like movies running through your mind. They give clues to your innermost feelings. Write down in your journal a dream you have had. As you write, see if you can answer the following questions.

1. Who was in your dream, what happened, and where did it take place?
2. What did the people in your dream look like?
3. Do you remember anything that was unusual?
4. Use your five senses to add details to the dream.
5. How do you feel about what happened in the dream?
6. Do you see any connection between your dream and your waking life? If so, what is it?

Strictly speaking, there is no place for "Step Four: Revise" in a unit on journal writing. Unless you enjoy revising, you have no reason to correct or try to improve a journal entry. However, there is definitely a place for reviewing and making use of what you've written. Your journal entries can be a rich source of ideas for school writing assignments and for the letters, stories, and poems that you write on your own.

Thinking About Journals

Your mind operates on three levels of awareness. On the first level you are aware of the physical world around you. You see, hear, taste, smell, and touch objects. You observe people and events.

On the second level your awareness is turned inward. You observe your own reactions to people, objects, and events. You watch yourself thinking and feeling.

On the third level of awareness you are busy drawing conclusions. You try to figure out the meaning of things you see happening outside you and within you. For example, how would a quarrel between two of your good friends affect you? If you were extremely upset by the quarrel, what would that mean?

Since writing is a way of recording your awareness, you write on three levels, too. On the first level you describe the world around you. On the second level you tell how you feel about the world and yourself. On the third level, you try to answer the questions *why?, how?,* or *so what?*

An entry in your journal may involve all three levels of awareness. For example, suppose you are trying to decide what to write about, and you remember the joke that Kathy told this morning. You write down the facts about the setting and record the joke exactly as Kathy told it. That is the first level of awareness.

Then, perhaps, as you are writing down the joke, you remember how you felt at the time. You were just a little jealous of Kathy. She was speaking very well and was the center of attention. You record your feeling. That is the second level of awareness.

Then you draw a conclusion. You decide that you would like to learn some jokes and be able to tell them well. That is the third level of awareness.

In making this one entry in your journal, you have not only practiced your writing skills. You have also gained some insight into your own thought processes and feelings. You have even discovered something you want to change about yourself.

Exercise Eleven   Write a journal entry about yesterday. Recall something that happened that is still of interest to you. It can be an event that seemed significant at the time or a quiet moment that almost went unnoticed. Write how you felt about it. If you can draw any conclusions from the experience, write them down.

Writing a Description

*Grass in Rain, Glacier Bay National Monument, Alaska, 1948
Ansel Adams, Ansel Adams Publishing Rights Trust*

Writing a Description

You and your friends use descriptions all the time. You tell each other about people you have met, objects you have seen, and places you have visited. You describe things in order to give your listeners a mental picture, so that they can see in their minds what you have seen. Suppose, for example, that you wanted to tell your friends about a beautiful sunset. You could say, "The sunset on the bay was beautiful." They would know what you meant, but they wouldn't see it for themselves. Instead, you could say, "The sky was crimson and the clouds were tinged with gold, and all of it was reflected in the glassy water of the bay." This description would recreate the beauty of the sunset for your friends, so that they could experience it, too.

Following are two more examples of descriptions. See which one gives you a more vivid mental picture.

I had my first taste of a persimmon the other day. It looked good when I bought it, but it wasn't ripe enough, so it tasted terrible.

I was in the mood for something sweet and juicy, so I decided to try a persimmon. I looked at the display and picked out one that looked delicious. It had a shiny orange-red skin and was shaped like a perfect heart. I chomped into it, and for a second it tasted pleasantly sweet. But as I chewed it, its texture became dry and mealy. It was like having a mouthful of sawdust. As I spat out what was in my mouth, I promised myself that I would learn to tell a ripe persimmon from an unripe one!

The first description is an abstract statement. It communicates the idea but not the experience. The second description, on the other hand, provides concrete details that stimulate your imagination. In your imagination, you "experience" biting into an unripe persimmon, chewing it, and spitting it out.

Sensory Details

What makes the second description of the unripe persimmon interesting to the reader is the *sensory details* that the writer has included. *Sensory details* are details that appeal to the five senses: sight, hearing, smell, taste, and touch. Following are some examples.

sight: The icicles sparkled in the sunshine.

sound: We heard a thundering crash.

smell: This milk smells sour.

taste: Indian food is too spicy for some people.

touch: Cashmere feels soft against your skin.

▷ Create clear and vivid word pictures to help your reader "experience" what you are describing.

▷ Concrete details that appeal to one or more of the five senses make
a description come alive.

Exercise One   Following are ten abstract statements. Choose three
and, for each, list some concrete details that you could use to describe
the stated idea more vividly. Try to use details that appeal to as many
different senses as possible.

EXAMPLE: Visiting the bakery was fun.

Every time a customer came through the door, a bell jingled.

The aroma of freshly baked bread lingered in the air.

The glass case displayed brightly decorated cakes, whipped-cream
topped pies, and perfectly browned loaves of bread.

The lemon meringue pie tasted sweet and tangy.

It felt cool and smooth in my mouth.

1. We had a great time at the beach.
2. The prom was a success.
3. Flying in an airplane is very interesting.
4. I've just finished redecorating my room.
5. We had a wonderful view from the roof of the tallest building in
   town.
6. We went ice skating on the frozen pond.
7. Peter won the prize for the most imaginative costume.
8. I did all my holiday shopping in one day.
9. My sister tried out for the gymnastics (hockey, bowling, etc.) team
   and made it.
10. That ride was the scariest I've ever had.

A. Choose a Topic

For the description that you are going to write, you should choose a topic that gives you a chance to use sensory details. A good choice would be any subject that is concrete—something that can be seen, heard, smelled, tasted, or felt. For example, you would have a hard time creating a vivid picture of "loyalty" because loyalty is an abstract quality. You could, however, describe a friend who is loyal. By using sensory details that describe your friend's actions, facial expressions, and tone of voice, you could give the reader concrete evidence of your friend's loyalty.

Exercise Two   Choose three concrete topics, one in each of three categories: person, object, and place.

EXAMPLES:

my friend Hank   a special cap   an old classroom

B. Define Your Purpose

Your overall purpose is to write an effective description. But you should have an additional purpose that relates specifically to the person, object, or place you have chosen as your subject. You may be able to discover this purpose by asking yourself the following questions about your subject: "Out of all the things in the world I might describe, why did I choose this? What makes it special? What is the main impression that it makes on me? If I could make just one statement about this person, object, or place, what would I say?" Your specific purpose is to convey the answers to these questions to your reader.

Exercise Three   For each topic that you chose in Exercise Two, state the specific purpose of the description you are going to write.

EXAMPLES:

Topic: my friend Hank

Purpose: to show that he seems tough, but really isn't

A. Gather Ideas

To gather ideas for your description, simply observe your subject. Make a list of the concrete details that relate to your purpose. If you can't observe your subject directly, try to remember as much as you can about it. Then list the details that support your purpose.

Details About People

When you describe a person, your purpose is to reveal an interesting quality that the person has. To do so, you need to find concrete details that suggest that quality. For example, suppose you wanted to describe a vain person named Elmer. You could suggest the idea of vanity by describing Elmer's actions, such as his habit of constantly looking in the mirror. You could also suggest vanity by describing Elmer's expensive and fashionable clothes.

Following is a description from Hugh Garner's "A Trip for Mrs. Taylor" (*Scope English Anthology,* Level Four). The story is about a lonely elderly woman who decides to take a train ride just to relieve her boredom. In this description, she is preparing to leave. As you read it, look for concrete details that show how she feels about herself.

M O D E L . . . .

When she returned to her room, her 76-year-old face shone with the excitement of the day. She combed her thinning gray hair and did it up with pins into a bun. Going over to her old trunk in the corner, she took out two pieces of jewelry. One was a gold locket holding a faded photograph of her dead husband Bert. The other was an old-fashioned gold chain bracelet. Her hands were so thin now that it slipped easily over her wrist.

When she had made sure the jewelry was on just right, she put on her old black straw hat. She smiled at herself in the mirror, wishing that her false teeth were a little whiter.

. . . .

Garner has included several concrete details that reveal Mrs. Taylor's youthful spirit. She is looking forward eagerly to whatever adventures the day may bring. And she takes as much pride in her appearance as a young woman would. For example, she arranges her hair carefully, and she makes sure her jewelry is on "just right."

As you gather ideas for your description of a person, try to think of details that reveal the person's character.

Exercise Four   Review the purpose you defined in Exercise Three. Keep your purpose in mind as you gather details about the person you're going to describe.

EXAMPLE:

Topic: my friend Hank

Purpose: to show that he seems tough, but really isn't

   biggest person in our class

   deep voice

   scowl on his face makes him look angry

   often wears black sweatshirt, black jeans, and heavy black boots

   cracks his knuckles frequently

   rough hands, dirty fingernails

   often smells of gasoline from working at his uncle's garage

   scar on his cheek from a childhood accident

   stares at you when he talks

   hangs out with older students

   can beat everyone in school at arm wrestling

   good student and plans to go to college

   helps his mother take care of younger brothers and sisters

   cooks chili for family's annual Halloween party

Details About Objects

When you describe an object, your purpose is to help the reader see the object as you see it. You want the reader to appreciate the special qualities that make the object interesting to you. To accomplish your goal, you need to choose details that suggest these special qualities.

Following is a description of a pair of work shoes. See if you can tell what main idea about the shoes the author is trying to convey.

These shoes had weathered many hard days. Deep creases cut across the toes. The toes curled up slightly, and the tops leaned against one another as if for comfort. There were scratches and scuffs that no polish would ever be able to hide. Knots on each shoelace showed where it had snapped and been retied again and again.

The details in this description all add up to one main idea: the shoes are old and well-worn. The author's purpose was to help you, the reader, to see this fact for yourself.

Exercise Five   Gather details about the object you're going to describe. Refer to the purpose you defined in Exercise Three as you list your ideas.

EXAMPLE:

Topic: a special cap
Purpose: to show what makes the cap special
>   visor of cap is curved down at sides
>   special pocket sewn on the left side to hold whistle
>   the whistle is so loud you can hear it several blocks away
>   a pocket sewn onto the right side to hold food
>   rubber band was wound around wet visor to make it curve
>   silver whistle hangs from a cord attached to racing stripe on top
>   red-and-white racing stripe down middle of the cap

Details About Places

A place can seem friendly or hostile or peaceful or sad to the person who is looking at it. When you describe a place, you can make it seem to have any qualities you like. Just mention details that will make the reader think of those qualities.

To see how this works, think of a place that affects your mood in a certain way. For example, suppose there's a room in your home that makes you feel relaxed and contented. Try to decide what characteristics of the room make you feel the way you do. Could it be the color of the walls? The music playing on the radio? The shelves cluttered with keepsakes?

Following is a description of a ghost town. Notice that the author has chosen details that suggest a feeling of loneliness and desolation.

The town had been empty for so long that it was beyond hope. If the people had come back ten years ago, they could have saved it from the desert. Even five years ago those sagging roofs could have been propped up. Those faded signs on the grocery store, advertising long-forgotten brands of food, could have been painted over with new signs. Now it was too late. A car passing through the main street slowed down to look for signs of life. Finding none, it picked up speed, kicking up dust on the unpaved road.

Exercise Six   Refer to the purpose you defined in Exercise Three. Then gather details about the place you're going to describe. Try to include details that will help the reader understand the mood of the place and how it makes you feel.

EXAMPLE:

Topic: an old classroom

Purpose: to show how run-down and old-fashioned the classroom is

    classroom in the old wing of the school

    chipped desks with holes cut out for inkwells

    high windows that rattle in the wind

    cloakroom doors that stick when you push them

    smells musty

    warm water in the antique water fountain

Exercise Seven   Review the work you did in Exercises Two through Six. Of the three topics you worked on in those exercises (person, object, place), choose one that you would like to develop into a descriptive composition for this unit. Copy your chosen topic, purpose, and list of ideas onto a clean sheet of paper.

B. Organize Ideas

There are three basic ways to organize your ideas in a description. You can present details in spatial order, in chronological order, or in natural order.

Spatial Order

When you arrange details in spatial order, you show how the parts of the item being described relate to each other in space. You start by describing one part, usually a prominent feature. Then you describe the other parts in relation to the first part or to each other.

Following is an example of a description that is organized according to spatial order. It is taken from O. Henry's story "The Green Door" (*Scope English Anthology*, Level Four).

M O D E L . . . .

The building was five stories high. A small restaurant was in the basement. The first floor seemed to be a fur shop. The second floor was the dentist's. His name appeared in winking electric letters. The next floor had signs for dressmakers, musicians, and doctors. Still higher up, on the fourth and fifth floors, curtains were hung in the windows and milk bottles could be seen on the ledges. It seemed that people lived on these floors.

. . . .

O. Henry describes the building as it would be seen by someone standing outside in the street. He mentions the floors in order, starting with the basement and moving up to the top floor. He uses certain words, such as *in the basement, the next floor,* and *still higher up,* to draw your attention first to one floor, then to the next. These words help you see, for example, where the apartments were in relation to the business and professional offices.

Chronological Order

When you arrange details in the order in which they occurred in time, you are using chronological order. It is best to use chronological order when the item being described goes through changes in time. You might also use chronological order when the description you are writing is part of a narrative.

Following is an example of a description in which the details are presented in chronological order. It is an excerpt from *The Pearl*, by John Steinbeck (*Scope English Anthology*, Level Four).

The dawn came quickly now, a wash, a glow, a lightness, and then an explosion of fire as the sun arose out of the Gulf. Kino looked down to cover his eyes from the glare. He could hear the pat of the corncakes in the house and the rich smell of them on the cooking plate. The ants were busy on the ground, big black ones with shiny bodies, and little dusty quick ants. . . . A thin, timid dog came close and, at a soft word from Kino, curled up, arranged its tail neatly over its feet, and laid its chin delicately on the pile. It was a black dog with yellow-gold spots where its eyebrows should have been. It was a morning like other mornings and yet perfect among mornings.

. . . .

This description of Kino's morning is part of a narrative. Steinbeck uses sensory details to help you imagine that you are Kino, seeing what he sees and hearing what he hears as he starts his day.

Natural Order

When you use "natural" order, you mention details in the order in which the viewer would notice them when looking at the item for the first time. You start with the feature you would notice first (this is usually the most prominent or important), then go on to the one you would notice next, and so on. For example, if you were describing Grandpa's easy chair, you might first mention the fact that it's roomy and soft-looking, with a wide seat and a high back. Then you might say that when you sit down in it, you notice that the springs are broken and the stuffing feels lumpy.

Following is an example of a description arranged in natural order. It is also taken from *The Pearl,* by John Steinbeck.

M O D E L . . . .

A stout slow man sat in an office waiting. His face was fatherly and benign, and his eyes twinkled with friendship. . . . This morning he had placed a flower in a vase on his desk, a single scarlet hibiscus, and the vase sat beside the black velvet-lined pearl tray in front of him. He was shaved close to the blue roots of his beard, and his hands were clean and his nails polished.

. . . .

In this description, Steinbeck calls attention to the man's stoutness first, because that is the first thing one would notice about him. On taking a closer look, one might notice his benign (kindly) face and his twinkling eyes. From his cheerful face, one's gaze might travel to the flower in the vase on his desk and then to the tray next to the vase. Then the viewer might glance again at the man's face and notice signs that he shaved very carefully this morning. Finally the viewer might look at the man's hands and see that they, too, are well groomed. The details that Steinbeck mentions give you a clear picture of the man's appearance and suggest the kind of person he is. The order in which the details are presented recreates the experience of seeing this man for the first time.

Exercise Eight   Decide which method of organizing ideas is best for your topic. Arrange the details you have gathered according to this method. As you read over your list, you may want to add new ideas or delete ones that don't work.

The topic shown in the following example, "a special cap," was mentioned earlier in this unit. If you compare the rearranged list of details below with the original list on page 91, you will notice that some of the original details have been deleted and some new ones have been added.

EXAMPLE:

Topic: a special cap

Purpose: to show what makes the cap special

Method of Organization: spatial order

Details:

> red-and-white racing stripe runs down middle from front to back
>
> silver whistle hangs from cord attached to racing stripe on top
>
> special pocket sewn on left side to hold whistle
>
> pocket sewn onto right side to hold food
>
> food pocket has zipper
>
> visor of hat is curved down at sides to shade eyes better
>
> rubber band was wound around wet visor to make it curve

Write the First Draft

You have listed sensory details to describe your topic, and you have arranged them in spatial, chronological, or natural order. Now you are ready to write the first draft of your description.

When you write a first draft, concentrate on turning the details into sentences and paragraphs. Use your list as a guide, but don't be afraid to experiment. You may suddenly remember an important detail about your topic that you forgot to put on your list.

Don't worry about errors in grammar, spelling, or punctuation at this point. You will have time later to correct any mistakes you make.

Exercise Nine   Write the first draft of your description. Use the following checklist as a guide.

☐　Keep your purpose in mind as you write.

☐　Try to avoid abstract statements; instead, use concrete details.

☐　Do your words create a clear and vivid picture for your reader?

When you have completed your first draft, put it aside for a day or two if possible. A rest from thinking about your paper will help you to approach it more objectively when you revise it. It's a good idea to read your paper as though someone else had written it. This makes it easier to spot problems and mistakes.

Finding the Right Word

It is not easy to say exactly what you want to say. It takes skill to find the right words to express your ideas. As Mark Twain once stated, "The difference between the right word and the almost right word is the difference between lightning and the lightning bug."

Using Specific Words

One way to find the right words when you write is to use a reference book called a *thesaurus.* In a thesaurus, you can look up general words and find more specific words that will fit your meaning. For example, here are some of the specific words a thesaurus gives for the general word *walk*:

march, shuffle, plod, trudge, lumber, hobble, strut, tread, pace, step, hike, tramp, shamble, stagger, toddle, stride, swagger, mince, scuttle, prance, flounce, trip, skip, amble, creep, stomp, promenade

Obviously, these words don't all mean exactly the same thing. To select the one that best expresses your thought, you need to understand the different shades of meaning. Or, you need to check the exact meanings of some of the words in a dictionary.

Look at the pairs of sentences that follow. Notice that the second sentence in each pair contains a more specific noun and verb than the first sentence.

The child cried.   The mechanic fixed the car.

The **infant screamed.**   The mechanic **replaced** the **fan belt.**

Exercise Ten   Each of the following sentences has one general word in italics. Rewrite each sentence, changing the general word to a more specific word. You may use a dictionary or a thesaurus if you like.

EXAMPLE: George *looked* at his watch.

George glanced at his watch.

1. I *cleaned* the floor today.
2. My uncle brought a bouquet of *flowers*.
3. The noisy children *ran* onto the playground.
4. Judy went to the store to buy *vegetables*.
5. Michael *hates* spinach.

Exercise Eleven   Reread your first draft to see how you can improve it. Revise it, using the checklist that follows as a guide.

Revision Checklist

1. Does the description create a vivid picture for the reader?
2. Do all the details support your purpose?
3. Are the details organized in a way that makes sense?
4. Do the details appeal to the senses?
5. Are the words specific and precise?
6. If you have used a comparison, does it help to make your description clearer?

Proofread

Proofreading is an important part of this last step of the writing process. It is possible to write a wonderful description but still lose your reader's attention. This can happen if your reader is distracted by mistakes in grammar, spelling, and punctuation. So, read your revised draft again carefully.

Exercise Twelve   Proofread your revised draft. Check the spelling of unfamiliar words. If you have any questions about grammar or punctuation, ask your teacher. Then make a fresh, neat copy of your composition.

Writing
Instructions

Construction of the Panama Canal, 1913
Library of Congress

Writing Instructions

H ave you ever tried to follow instructions that were incomplete or confusing? Probably you have, at least once. Perhaps you had trouble setting up your little brother's new electric train because two important steps had been left out of the instructions. Or perhaps you were late for the party at a classmate's new house because her directions for getting there were unclear. Even if you didn't complain out loud, you probably said to yourself, "I could write better instructions than these without even trying!"

In this unit you are going to live up to those words—except, possibly, the last three, "without even trying." To master the skills you'll need for writing good instructions, you may have to do a little trying. These necessary skills include the following:

- ☐ picturing the whole activity, or process, clearly in your mind
- ☐ breaking the process down into separate steps
- ☐ presenting the steps in the proper order
- ☐ giving just the right amount of information about each step

You will learn all these skills and more as you plan and develop two kinds of instructions. In the first kind, you will tell your reader how to make or do something. For example, you might explain the steps involved in baking bread or flying a kite. In the second kind, you will give your reader directions for traveling from one place to another. For example, you might explain how to get from your school to a store.

P O I N T S   T O   R E M E M B E R

▷   Instructions describe a process, or series of steps.

▷   Instructions tell the reader how to make or do something, or how to go from one place to another.

A. Choose a Topic

When you write any kind of composition, a thorough knowledge of the topic is very helpful. But when you write instructions, a thorough knowledge of the topic is not just helpful, it's necessary. Before you can teach other people to do something, you must be able to do it yourself.

You might start your search for a topic by asking yourself this question: "What things do I know how to do?" On a clean sheet of paper, list as many things as you can think of.

Now read over your list and cross out any topic that does not refer to a process. (As you know, a process is a series of steps that must be taken in a certain order.) For example, "How to Carry on a Conversation" is not a good topic for instructions because conversing is not a process.

Next, cross out any topic that is either too complicated or too simple. For example, "How to Decorate a Room for a Party" is too complicated; it involves too many decisions and too many steps. "How to Make Balloons Stick to the Ceiling" is too simple; you could probably explain it in a sentence or two.

Finally, read over the topics remaining on your list. As you consider each topic, pretend that you are the reader. Is this an activity that you would like to learn about? If it is, mark the topic with a star or check mark.

On the next two pages, you will find two sample sets of instructions. As you will see, the writers have chosen topics that are either interesting or useful or both.

The first example is a set of "how-to" instructions. Notice that the topic is announced in the title: "How to Estimate the Height of a Tree." Notice, also, that there is a short introduction. The first sentence of the introduction announces the topic again in different words, so you will be sure to understand what the instructions are for. The second sentence tells you what preparations you must make before you can carry out the instructions. It explains that you will need one simple tool and the help of a friend.

How to Estimate the Height of a Tree

Here's an easy way to figure out approximately how tall a tree is without actually measuring it. All you need is a straight stick about a foot long and a friend whose height you know.

1. Have your friend stand against the tree.
2. Move back a distance from the tree.
3. Take the stick in one hand and hold it up vertically in front of you at arm's length.
4. Close one eye and sight past the stick to your friend.
5. Position your thumb on the stick so that the height of your friend is between your thumbnail and the top end of the stick. This distance on the stick is your unit of measurement.
6. Still sighting with one eye, raise the stick so that your thumb is where the top of the stick was before (that is, at the top of your friend's head). Keep moving the stick up in this way, to see how many units there are in the height of the tree.
7. Multiply the height of your friend times the number of units you measured from the ground to the top of the tree. This will give you the height of the tree.

In these instructions, you can see why it's sometimes useful to number the steps. The numbers help the reader see where one step ends and the next begins.

Exercise One   Choose a topic for a set of "how-to" instructions. Be sure to pick an activity that you understand well and have carried out successfully. Also, make sure that the activity is a process (series of steps) that is neither too complicated nor too simple.

EXAMPLES:

How to develop black-and-white film

How to grow a new plant from a cutting

How to make spaghetti (or some other dish)

The second sample set of instructions is a memo for a school bulletin board; it gives directions for travel. Here again, the title announces the topic, and there is a short introduction. Notice that the second sentence tells what means of transportation the directions apply to.

Picnickers: Here's How to Reach the Coleman Farm on August 9

The annual Summer School Picnic will be held on August 9, from noon to five o'clock, at the home of student Karen Coleman. The Coleman family farm is only five miles west of town, so it's easy to reach by driving, biking, or even walking.

Go west on Main Street, which becomes M-20 once you pass the village limits. After three miles you will come to the Four Corners shopping mall, at the junction of M-20 and Tustin Road. Turn right (north) on Tustin Road and go one mile to 92nd Road. There, turn left (west) and go one more mile to Karen's house.

After turning into 92nd Road, you will pass a faded red barn on the left, close to the road. A little later you will go around three sharp curves. As you come out of the third, look up the hill to your left. You will see the Coleman farm buildings with green roofs. Turn into the driveway; there's a mailbox with the name Coleman at the entrance.

Picnic tables will be set up behind the house, in the peach orchard. Mr. Coleman says we are welcome to pick our dessert right off the trees!

These directions give you all the necessary facts, plus a few extra details to reassure you as you go along. The extra details are landmarks that you can look for: the shopping mall, the faded red barn, the three curves in the road. As each landmark comes into view, you can say to yourself, "Good! I'm still on the right track."

Exercise Two   Decide what place will be the destination in the travel directions you are going to write. You should choose a place to which you have traveled at least a few times. It does not have to be far away, but the route there should be fairly complicated. (If it's very simple, it won't need any explanation.) Also, the route should be one that you can travel any time you please—you may need to check a few details.

When you've chosen a destination, write the title of your directions on a piece of paper.

EXAMPLES:

How to Go From the School to the Public Library by Bus

Directions for Walking to Dana's House From the Stadium

B. Identify Your Audience

In your writing, as in your conversations, you sometimes need to adjust your style to make it fit your audience. When you are talking, you can watch your listener's reactions. If the person seems to be puzzled by what you are saying, you can try another way of explaining it. When you are writing, however, you don't receive any instant feedback. You have to plan your adjustments beforehand.

Basically, there are two kinds of adjustments that you can make in your writing. You can adjust the *vocabulary* you use, and you can adjust the *amount of detail* you include.

Adjusting Vocabulary

The words you use in instructions or directions should be right for the age and experience of your reader. For example, suppose you were giving young children instructions for making and using a toy telescope, and you explained the first step like this:

First, take a sheet of notebook paper and make a cylinder 11 inches long and about one inch in diameter. Secure it with a rubber band.

You would probably lose some of your readers at the first hard word: *cylinder.* Others would give up after *diameter* or *secure.* But, as you know, there is almost always more than one way to express an idea. The first step in your instructions would be just as clear if you wrote it like this:

First, take a sheet of notebook paper. Hold the paper by one of the long edges, and roll it up into a tube. The hole at each end of the tube should be about the size of a quarter. Put a rubber band around the tube to keep it from unrolling.

Your young audience should be able to read all the words in this revised version. But can you see another difference between the two versions besides the difference in vocabulary? The second version is much longer. One reason is that, in the second version, there is a separate sentence for each important point. Another reason is that a difficult word with a very specific meaning (such as *diameter*, for example) has no synonyms. Often you have to use many words to express the meaning of the one you can't use.

Adjusting the Amount of Detail

Different readers require different amounts of information. Before you start writing, you should try to guess how much your reader probably knows already. Then you can decide whether or not you need to explain every step in great detail. You can also decide whether you should provide background information at the beginning of the instructions.

For example, imagine that you are writing instructions for changing the oil in a car. If you are an expert on cars, you might not realize how difficult the task appears to someone who has never tried it. You might write something like the following.

1. Use an open-end wrench on the oil filter plug.
2. Turn the plug with the wrench until the plug comes out completely, letting out a stream of oil.

But these instructions assume that the reader already knows quite a bit about tools and car engines. Now turn to page 109 and read those same steps written so that an inexperienced person could understand them.

Before you can put fresh oil in your car, you must first remove the oil plug and drain the old, dirty oil out of the engine block.

1. Find a wrench suited to removing the oil plug. The best kind is an open-end wrench. (Its end is like a circle with the top removed, or like a U. The sides of the U hold the bolt.)

2. Get an empty can or other container that can hold at least two quarts. You will use this container to catch the dirty oil as it drains, so pick something that you can throw away afterward.

3. Locate the oil plug on the bottom surface of the engine block, and firmly grip the sides of the plug with the wrench. (The oil plug is a bolt. It is sometimes hard to remove because the heat of the engine makes it stick.)

4. Turn the wrench counterclockwise. If this does not loosen the bolt, take a hammer and tap the edge of the wrench handle near its end, using a series of light blows.

5. Once the bolt is loosened, keep turning it until it is almost ready to come out. Then stop turning for a moment and put the empty can where it will catch the oil.

6. Remove the plug.

To make these instructions as easy to follow as possible, the writer explains each step in detail. He tells the reader exactly what kind of wrench to use, how large the empty container must be, and when to place the container under the plug. He even thinks of a problem that might arise—the oil plug might refuse to move—and tells the reader how to solve it.

Exercise Three   Look at the topics you chose in Exercises One and Two. For each topic, write down the name of a person to whom you would like to show your instructions. Then write brief answers to the following questions.

1. How old is the reader?
2. How much does the reader probably know about the topic?
3. What vocabulary level would be comfortable for the reader?
4. How detailed should the instructions be? How much background information does the reader need?

Make a Plan

A. Gather Ideas

Gathering ideas for a set of instructions is quite easy. The "ideas" consist mostly of the steps in the process you are going to explain.

Frank decided to write instructions for separating egg yolks from egg whites—something he had to do when he made waffles. Here is his first list of ideas. Has any important information been left out?

Take the egg out of the refrigerator.

Crack it.

Separate the shell into halves and hold one half in each hand.

Pass the yolk back and forth from one half-shell to the other, spilling the egg white into the bowl.

Continue doing this until all the white is in the bowl.

When he read over his list, Frank noticed some omissions. There was no title, so the reader wouldn't be able to tell what the instructions were for. He had forgotten to mention that the egg should be at room temperature. He had also forgotten to tell the reader to have a bowl ready. And, he decided, the second step, "crack it," was too brief to be useful. He should probably add some advice on how to crack the egg.

Here is Frank's second, improved, list of ideas.

> Title: How to Separate an Egg
>
> When you need to do this (waffles, omelette, meringue).
>
> Take egg out of refrigerator; let warm to room temperature.
>
> Take out bowl of right size for beating egg white(s).
>
> Crack egg by striking center against hard surface (edge of counter, another bowl, etc.). Don't use beating bowl—might get bits of shell into batter.
>
> Separate shell into halves; hold one half in each hand over bowl.
>
> Pass yolk back and forth from one half-shell to other, spilling egg white into bowl.
>
> Continue till all white is in bowl.

Exercise Four   Make a list of ideas for each of the two topics that you chose in Exercises One and Two. Use a separate sheet of paper for each topic. At the top of the paper, write your topic and a sentence describing your audience. (Refer to the notes you made in Exercise Three.) Try to keep the reader's needs in mind as you gather ideas.

B. Organize Ideas

As you know, a process is a series of actions or steps that are connected. Each new step develops from the one just before it. That's why, when you explain a process, you must present the steps in a certain order. You must present them in *chronological* (time) order.

One way to make sure you've put the steps in the right order is to try following your own instructions. Frank did this with his instructions for separating an egg, and found that they worked fine. He was pleased because he had listed his ideas in the right order on the first try. He could go ahead and write the first draft of his instructions.

Then Frank checked the list he had made for his second project, a set of directions for travel. This list needed further work, he decided.

Here is Frank's list; see if you can figure out what is wrong with it.

TOPIC: How to drive to the ice rink in Taylor Park

1. Turn right at intersection of Aldeah Avenue and West Broadway.
2. Go three blocks to flashing yellow light at Stewart Road.
3. Make sure you're in left-turn lane.
4. Turn left onto Stewart Road.
5. Drive one mile to park.
6. Go to parking lot B. You can see rink from there.
7. Entrance is just past Soup 'n' Sandwich restaurant, on right.

Frank realized that the confusion started with the very first step: turn right at the intersection of Aldeah Avenue and West Broadway. Which of those two streets was the reader on? And in which direction was the reader driving? Step 1 made sense only if the reader was driving north along Aldeah Avenue. Frank decided to add a line at the beginning that would answer these questions.

The next thing that Frank noticed was that step 3 was out of order. He decided it belonged before step 2. The driver must get into the left-turn lane as soon as possible after turning right on West Broadway. Step 7 was also out of order; it belonged between 5 and 6.

Here is Frank's corrected and reorganized list.

TOPIC: How to drive from Maple Grove to the ice rink in Taylor Park

1. From Maple Grove, drive north along Aldeah Avenue.
2. Turn right at intersection of Aldeah Avenue and West Broadway.
3. Get into left-turn lane as soon as possible.
4. Go three blocks to flashing yellow light at Stewart Road.
5. Turn left onto Stewart Road.
6. Drive one mile to Taylor Park.
7. Entrance is just past Soup 'n' Sandwich restaurant, on right.
8. Go to parking lot B. You can see rink from there.

Exercise Five   Look again at the two lists of steps you made in Exercise Four. Check each list twice. The first time, ask yourself whether you have left out any important steps. The second time, ask yourself whether the steps are in the right order. Make whatever changes are needed, and copy each list onto a fresh sheet of paper.

Write the First Draft

It's now time to write one of the sets of instructions that you planned in Step Two. You can use your list of steps as an outline as you write your first draft. If the list is well organized, you will probably not have to make any changes in it.

However, you may need to make some additions to your outline. For example, you might add a short introduction. In it, you could try to catch the reader's interest and convince him or her that your instructions are useful.

If the reader will need certain materials or tools to carry out your instructions, you should mention these at the beginning. You can list them in the introduction, or you can include them in the first step or two of your instructions.

You may need to add details to your explanation of certain steps. Sometimes a step is easy to jot down in a list but hard to describe. The instructions for removing an oil filter plug are an example. Step 1 in the first version (page 107) tells the reader to "use an open-end wrench." Step 1 in the second version (page 109) is much more helpful because it describes an open-end wrench in detail.

Exercise Six   Choose one of the two topics that you worked on in Exercises Three through Five. Write a set of step-by-step instructions or directions on that topic. Use the list that you completed in Exercise Five as an outline. Refer to the following guidelines as you work.

1. Write a title that tells the reader what your instructions or directions are meant to accomplish. You might start with the words "How to . . . ."

2. Start with an introduction. Here you might tell more about the purpose of the instructions, give background information, or list tools and materials that the reader will need.

3. Next, present the major steps in the process. If your reader doesn't know much about the process, you may need to explain some steps with smaller sub-steps. If there are many steps, you may wish to number them.

4. As you explain each step, ask yourself, "Is there any mistake that the reader might make at this point?" If there is one, give some extra information or advice to prevent the person from making that mistake.

5. Keep your reader's age and reading ability in mind as you write. Try to explain the steps in words that your reader will understand.

6. You may want to add a concluding statement after the last step in the process. However, it is not necessary to do so. If you prefer, you can simply end with the last step.

Jacklyn chose "parallel parking" as her topic. Her purpose was to tell the reader how to back a car into a parallel parking place. Here is her first draft.

How to Park a Car Paralel to the Curb

What is paralel parking? Paralel parking is one of the more difficult skills needed for for driveing a car. It is parking a car parallel to the curb between a car in front and a car behind in a space large enough for the driver's car. You have to back into the space. It can take a whole lot of practice to learn how to do this sucessfully.

My brother says that paralel parking was the hardest part of the test he took for a drivers licence. In fact, the first time he took the test he failed that part of it. Then a friend taught him the following surefire method and he passed it on the next try. He says this will help me when I learn to drive I hope it will help you, to.

STEP ONE Pull up alongside the car in front of your space. The rear bumper of your car should be even with the rear bumper of the other car. Leave one or two feet of space between your car and it.

STEP TWO Look to the rear over your shoulder and make sure the oncomming traffic will pass too close beside you.

STEP THREE Start to back slowly. As you back, turn your steering wheel sharply to the right. Your car will move into the parking space at 45 degrees to the curb. Keep going until your right door is even with the rear bumper.

STEP FOUR Turn your steering wheel sharply to the left. Make sure you are clearly the car in front. Keep backing slowly until your right wheel is about eight inches from the curb.

STEP FIVE Stop before you bump the car in back. Turn the steering wheel sharply to the right and forward slowly. This will bring your car parallel to the curb in the middle of the parking space.

If possible, put your rough draft away for a few days. Then read it as if you were someone else who was seeing these instructions or directions for the first time. Try following them step by step. Do they work? Or are there places where a word is confusing or some necessary detail seems to be missing? If there are such places, you will want to concentrate on them as you revise your paper.

Exercise Seven   Revise the rough draft that you wrote in Exercise Six. Here is a checklist that will help you remember what to look for.

Revision Checklist

1.   Does your title announce your topic?
2.   If an introduction is needed, have you provided one?
3.   Have you included all the necessary steps?
4.   Are the steps in the right order?
5.   Have you explained each step in sufficient detail?

Proofread and Edit

When you revise, you take care of big problems, such as gaps in information or confusing sentences. When you proofread, you take care of little problems, such as mistakes in spelling, punctuation, and grammar. Of course you're aware that little problems sometimes cause big trouble. So you know it's important to proofread your work.

One good way to proofread your paper is to read through it three times. The first time, look for mistakes in grammar. The second time, look for mistakes in spelling. The third time, check the punctuation.

Exercise Eight   Proofread the revised draft you wrote in Exercise Seven. Read through the paper three times, once for grammar, once for spelling, and once for punctuation. Correct any errors you find. If you make so many corrections that your composition looks messy, copy it on a clean sheet of paper. Proofread it once more before handing it in.

Here is Jacklyn's revision of her instructions for parking a car.

How to Park a Car Paralel to the Curb

~~What is paralel parking?~~ Paralel parking is one of the more difficult skills needed for ~~for~~ driveing a car. It is parking a car paralel in the middle of a marked space. If there are cars ~~to the curb between a car in front and a car behind in a space, large enough for the driver's car.~~ You have to back into ~~the~~ space. It can take ~~a whole lot of~~ practice to learn how to do this sucessfully.

My brother says that paralel parking was the hardest part of the test he took for a drivers licence. In fact, the first time he took the test, he failed that part of it. Then a friend taught him the following surefire method, and he passed ~~it~~ the test on the next try. He says this method will help me when I learn to drive. I hope it will help you, too.

STEP ONE: Pull up alongside the car in front of your space. The rear bumper of your car should be even with the rear bumper of the other car. Leave one or two feet of space between your car and ~~it~~ the other one.

STEP TWO: Look to the rear over your left shoulder and make sure the oncomming traffic will not pass too close beside you.

STEP THREE: Start to back slowly. As you back, turn your steering wheel sharply to the right. Your car will move into the parking space at a 45-degree angle. ~~45 degrees to the curb.~~ Keep going until your right front door is even with the rear bumper of the other car.

STEP FOUR: Turn your steering wheel sharply to the left. Make
sure you are clearing the car in front. Keep backing slowly until your
rear right wheel is about eight inches from the curb.

STEP FIVE: Stop before you bump the car in back. Turn the
steering wheel sharply to the right and move forward slowly. This will bring
your car parallel to the curb in the middle of the parking space.

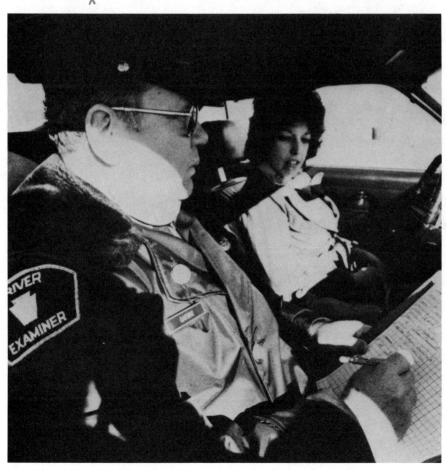

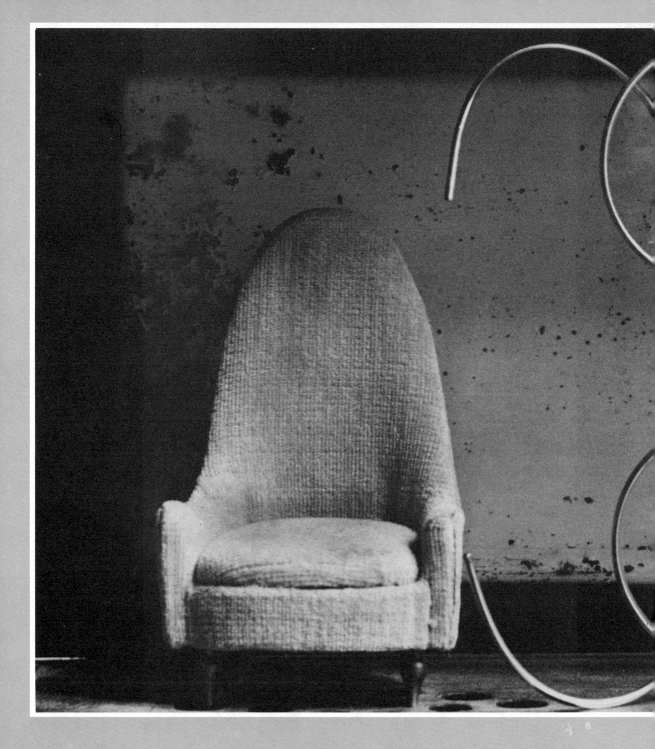

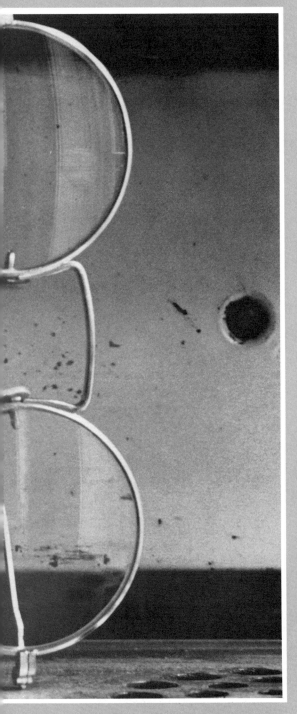

Writing Comparisons

"Alice's Mirror," 1974
One photo in a series of seven inspired by the book Alice in
Wonderland, *by Lewis Carroll*
Duane Michals, Sidney Janis Gallery, New York

Writing Comparisons

In *Alice's Adventures in Wonderland*, by Lewis Carroll, the Mad Hatter offers a riddle to Alice: "Why is a raven like a writing desk?" When Alice gives up and asks for the answer, the Mad Hatter admits, "I haven't the slightest idea." Lewis Carroll intended the Mad Hatter's riddle to have no answer. But throughout the years, readers of *Alice* have suggested answers. Here are a few of them:

1. Both a raven and a writing desk produce flat notes. (When a raven sings, it makes musical notes that are flat. A desk can be used for writing notes—short letters—which, of course, are flat.)

2. Both should be made to shut up. (A raven should be kept quiet, and a writing desk should have a lid that closes.)

3. Edgar Allan Poe wrote on both. (Poe wrote a famous poem about a raven, and he wrote on a desk.)

Can you think of any other answers to the Mad Hatter's riddle?

Finding Similarities

Finding similarities can be an amusing pastime. But it can also serve a serious purpose. Dr. Joseph R. Wilder, a surgeon and a member of the Lacrosse Hall of Fame, has a purpose in mind when he likens surgeons to athletes. Like an athlete, he says, a surgeon must have strength and endurance (it may take ten to twelve hours to perform a complicated operation). Like an athlete, a surgeon must have excellent coordination and sharp lateral (side) vision. But there is one way in which surgeons should be like athletes but aren't. Most athletes are ambidextrous—able to use both hands equally well—whereas most surgeons are one-handed. The point of Dr. Wilder's comparison is that surgeons should follow the athletes' example and train themselves to be two-handed.

Sometimes the similarities are obvious. For example, a car and an airplane are similar in several ways that are easy to see.

1. Both are vehicles that carry people and goods.
2. Both run on gasoline.
3. Both are made in factories that employ many people.
4. Both are sometimes involved in accidents.

Sometimes, however, finding the similarities between two things takes a little imagination. For example, in what ways is a duck similar to a marshmallow? You may say, "There are no similarities between a duck and a marshmallow." But think again.

1. Both can be roasted.
2. Both are sold in supermarkets.
3. Both are soft.

Finding the similarities between two things that seem very different may not be easy. But if you think carefully about the two things, you will probably be able to find some similarities.

Exercise One   Choose three of the five pairs of objects in the following list. On your paper, note three or more similarities between the objects in each pair you chose.

1. a door and an umbrella
2. a leaf and a potato chip
3. a flag and a curtain
4. a postcard and a book
5. a cup and a helmet

Finding Differences

No matter how similar two things are, there are almost always some differences between them. "What about identical twins?" you might ask. But even identical twins have different habits, different ways of walking and talking, and different kinds of facial expressions. Two things that seem identical are almost always slightly different, even though you must look closely to find their differences.

For example, take the famous "two peas in a pod." People often refer to them when they want to say that two things are exactly alike: "They're as like as two peas in a pod!" But if you examine any two peas, you'll find that they are not exactly alike. One may be slightly larger than the other. One may be a lighter green than the other. One may be round, while the other is flattened on one side.

In the following example, taken from an article called "Dolphins" (*Scope English Anthology*, Level Four), the writer Alice Herman Lehrer discusses differences between two animals that seem at first to be very much alike.

M O D E L . . . .

The dolphin is often confused, even by scientists and fishermen, with its look-alike, the porpoise. But a close look shows important differences. The dolphin's teeth are cone-like and pointed, rather than spade-shaped like the porpoise's. A dolphin's dorsal fin is curved toward the tail, while most porpoises have triangular fins. And the dolphin has a much larger brain than its porpoise relative. That is where the intelligence that so interests its other relative, humankind, is stored.

. . . .

Exercise Two   Choose three of the five pairs of objects in the following list. Look closely at specific examples of each pair of objects you chose. On your paper, list three or more differences between the objects in each pair.

1. two blossoms or leaves on the same plant   4.   two pennies
2. two oranges   5.   two belts
3. two pairs of trousers

Finding Similarities and Differences

When you look closely at the features that make two things similar and different, you are making a *comparison*. You make comparisons all the time, sometimes without knowing it. You might compare two record albums when deciding which one you want to buy. You might compare one movie with another when deciding which one you'd enjoy seeing. In choosing a way to travel across town, you might compare taking the bus to riding your bike. You would probably make these comparisons quickly.

There are other situations in which you need to *write* a comparison. In school, for example, you may be asked a question on a test that calls for a comparison: "Compare the character of Tom Sawyer with that of Huckleberry Finn," or "Compare the natural resources of Nevada with those of Michigan."

Someday you may need to write a comparison on the job. For instance, your boss may ask you to test two computers and write a comparison to help the company decide which computer to buy. A written comparison takes more time and thought than one that you make only in your mind.

P O I N T S   T O   R E M E M B E R

▷   You make a comparison by looking closely at similarities and differences between things.

▷   Finding similarities and differences between things can help you understand and analyze them.

Set Your Goal

A. Choose a Topic

Sometimes you are given a topic for a comparison. In school, for example, you may be asked to compare two books, two periods of history, or two animals or plants. At other times, however, you have the opportunity to come up with your own topic.

Exercise Three   Following are ten pairs of items that could be compared. Choose two pairs. On your paper, list as many similarities and differences as you can think of between the items in each pair. You should have at least three similarities and three differences.

1. two sports (You name the sports.)
2. two singers or musicians you like (Name them.)
3. two books you have enjoyed (Name the books.)
4. two kinds of pet (Name the kinds.)
5. two forms of transportation (Name them.)
6. two famous people from history (Name the people.)
7. two of your favorite movies (Name the movies.)
8. two hobbies (Name the hobbies.)
9. two jobs (Name the jobs.)
10. two magazines you like to read (Name them.)

Muriel decided to choose her two favorite breeds of dog, German shepherds and Yorkshire terriers. Following are some of the similarities and differences she found between them.

German shepherds and Yorkshire terriers

Similarities:

Both are very loyal to their owners.

Both are good watchdogs.

Both are very intelligent and can be trained to do many things.

Differences:

German shepherds are short-haired and Yorkshire terriers are long-haired.

Yorkshire terriers are more high-strung than German shepherds.

German shepherds offer a lot of protection as guard dogs; Yorkshire terriers are too small to protect people.

Exercise Four   Think of at least two sets of things you might like to compare in a short essay. Do not use any of the ideas from Exercise Three. On your paper, list at least five similarities and five differences between the items or activities you have chosen.

Exercise Five   Look at the two pairs of items you chose in Exercise Four. Decide which pair you know more about. You will use this one as the basis for a written comparison.

B. Define Your Purpose

There are many different purposes for making comparisons. The three following situations illustrate the most common purposes for which comparisons can be used.

☐   Mike and Lucy are outside the Twin Cinemas. They are trying to decide whether to see *It Came From Planet X* or *The Thing That Ate Des Moines*. Mike and Lucy compare what they know about each of the two movies: the stars, the stories, and what their friends have said about them.

☐   Pedro has agreed to lend his car to his friend Anthony. But Pedro's car has a standard transmission, while Anthony has only driven cars with automatic transmissions. Pedro is showing Anthony the similarities and differences between automatic and standard transmissions, so that Anthony will be able to drive Pedro's car.

☐   Coach Robbins is teaching the players on the girls' softball team two ways to slide into second base: the *hook slide* and the *bent-leg slide*. Coach Robbins compares the two slides so the players will understand why each one is used in a different base-running situation.

A comparison can be used in making decisions or judgments. This is the most common purpose for a comparison. When Mike and Lucy try to decide which movie to see, they are making a comparison for this purpose. Newspapers and magazines often contain articles that compare two or more products—two shampoos, for instance, or two compact cars—to help people decide which one to buy.

A comparison can help explain something unfamiliar by comparing it to something familiar. Pedro describes the standard transmission to Anthony by comparing it with the automatic transmission. The workings of the English Parliament could be explained to an American if they were compared to the workings of the United States Congress.

A comparison can be used to illustrate or clarify a fact or idea or to support an opinion. Coach Robbins uses a comparison of the two types of slide to help players understand certain techniques of softball. A writer who wanted to support the opinion that people of today are better informed than those of the past could compare TV news shows and news magazines of today with newspapers of previous centuries.

In some circumstances, your purpose might not be obvious to you right away. You might want to make notes on the similarities and differences between the two elements of your comparison before deciding on a purpose. Your notes may offer a suggestion.

For example, an English test might contain this question: "Compare any two characters from Stephen Crane's novel *The Red Badge of Courage*." The question allows you to select your own purpose. After choosing two characters to compare and thinking about them, you might decide that the comparison illustrates some fact or idea about Stephen Crane's novel. This purpose is the third one mentioned in the list on page 127.

Exercise Six   Look back at Exercise Five and your choice of two items or activities to compare. Then study the list of similarities and differences you made for these items. Does your list suggest a purpose?

Decide on a purpose. Could it be to help yourself make a decision or a judgment? Are you trying to learn about something unfamiliar by studying something familiar? Or is there a fact or idea about your topic that the comparison will illustrate or clarify? On a sheet of paper, write the purpose of your comparison.

C. Identify Your Audience

The Glee Club of Oakglen High School is planning a lip-syncing contest. Each contestant must pretend to be a famous singer doing a live performance of a popular song. This involves mouthing the lyrics to the song, while dancing along in a specially choreographed routine.

First prize will be tickets to a Pointer Sisters concert. A student named Neil decides he will enter the contest. He wants to take his sister Patti to see the Pointer Sisters for her birthday, and thinks he might win the tickets, as he has been practicing lip-syncing for years at home, singing along with every new hit on the radio.

The trick will be to convince the judges of the contest, the Glee Club members, that he should be allowed to compete. They require each would-be contestant to submit a written comparison of the two songs he or she would most like to perform.

Neil has begun planning his comparison of two of the likeliest songs he can come up with. In doing this, he has been trying to keep the judges in mind. They would not, of course, be his entire audience if he were actually performing, but they are the audience that counts now. After reading his comparison, they will decide whether he can compete. If they say he can, they will then decide which of the two songs he will perform.

You may not have as much at stake as Neil does, but before you begin writing a comparison, think about your audience. If you do, you'll have a clearer idea of what information to include.

For instance, if you were writing your best friend a letter comparing your family's new house to the house you used to live in, you might emphasize the great new stereo in the basement, or the amount of space you have in your new bedroom. But if you were writing on the same subject to your grandmother, you might decide to discuss the kitchen, the family room, or the guest bedroom, in which she will stay on her next visit.

Exercise Seven   Look at the items or activities you chose to compare in Exercise Five. Decide on your audience for this comparison. Are you presenting the comparison to a sports committee? Your brother? A teacher? A friend?

A. Gather Ideas

How do you begin to write a comparison? First you think about the two items or activities you want to compare. Then you jot down your ideas in two lists—one for similarities and one for differences.

Some comparisons are easier to make than others. For example, suppose you are comparing a lemon and a lime. Your list of similarities might show that both are egg-shaped and small. Three differences might be their color, taste, and price.

The lists Neil had to make for the song comparison were more complicated. He had to consider vocals, instrumental performance, the beat, and the tune, as well as the popularity of the recording artist and his own resemblance to the artist. He couldn't do a good imitation if he didn't look right for the part.

Neil's two top record choices were "The Tears of a Clown," by Smokey Robinson and the Miracles, and "Monster Mash," by Bobby "Boris" Pickett. He felt he could come up with very effective choreography for either song, and he knew the words to both by heart. But he was still hesitant about which one to choose. He began jotting down all the factors he could think of that were important to the comparison. The main ones seemed to him to be the following:

1. tune and lyrics of song
2. recording artist
3. rhythm and style of song

On a clean sheet of paper Neil made a chart, with the names of the two songs at the top and the three headings running down the side. Read the following list to see how he grouped the similarities and differences he had thought of.

	"Tears of a Clown"	"Monster Mash"
tune/lyrics:	sentimental	funny
	touching	silly
artist:	looks like me	looks different
	well known	obscure
rhythm/style:	good beat	good beat
	romantic	comic

Now Neil could look over the lists to see how the two records compared. He could see that both records had strong points.

Exercise Eight   Using the similarities and differences you listed in Exercise Four as a guide, make a list of the factors that are important in your comparison. If you are comparing two forms of transportation, for example, you might discuss cost, speed, availability, and comfort. List at least three factors on which to base your comparison.

B. Organize Ideas

Neil had made an excellent start in preparing his comparison. But he had to do more than make lists. He had to organize the lists into a well-written, clearly organized comparison.

Here are three ways of organizing a comparison.

1. In one paragraph, tell all the similarities between the two things. In another paragraph, tell all the differences.

2. In the first paragraph, describe one of the two things you want to compare. In the second paragraph describe the other.

3. Alternate between the items, discussing the points of comparison one by one.

The method you choose for your comparison will depend on the nature of your topic. If you have many factors, or points of comparison, to discuss, your reader might be confused if you constantly went back and forth between the items in the comparison. It would be better in that case to choose one of the other two methods.

On the other hand, you might be writing a fairly simple comparison, discussing a limited number of factors. If so, the alternating method is a good choice, as it will keep the reader's interest and clearly enumerate the similarities and differences.

All three methods of organization can work equally well. It's up to you to decide which method you want to use.

Exercise Nine   Following is a list of notes to be used in writing a comparison. The notes are in no particular order. Read them. Then copy them onto your paper in an order that makes sense to you, using one of the three ways of organizing a comparison.

Do not write the comparison; just group the ideas according to one of the three organizational methods described on page 131.

Notes for a comparison of two restaurants:

Beef 'n' Bun serves only hamburgers.

A meal at Beef 'n' Bun costs about three dollars.

Captain Jack's is decorated to look like the inside of a sailing ship.

Service at Captain Jack's is usually fast.

The food at Beef 'n' Bun is usually fresh.

The food at Captain Jack's is usually fresh.

A meal at Captain Jack's costs about five dollars.

Service at Beef 'n' Bun is very slow.

Beef 'n' Bun is always crowded at lunchtime.

Captain Jack's is very clean.

Beef 'n' Bun is very clean.

Beef 'n' Bun is decorated to look like a cattle ranch in Texas.

Captain Jack's serves only seafood.

Captain Jack's is always crowded at lunchtime.

Exercise Ten   Decide which method of organization you will use for your comparison. The factors, or points of comparison, that you listed in Exercise Eight might influence your choice.

Then group the similarities and differences you listed in Exercise Four, along with any others you may have thought of, according to the method you have chosen.

Since he had only three main points of comparison, Neil felt he could afford to use the alternating method of organization for his essay. With his list of details about the two records, he was ready to write the first draft. He did not worry about writing "perfectly" this first time. Getting his ideas down in an organized fashion was the important thing. He knew he would have time to polish his draft later.

"The Tears of a Clown and "Monster Mash" both have a good, danceable beat and would both be great for this contest, but there the similarities end. The style of "Tears" is romantic, while "monster Mash is more commic than anything else. The tune and lirics of the two songs are also vastly different. "Tears" is sentimental and touching; while "Mash" is funny to the point of sillyness.

The artists who sing the two songs aren't anything alike, either, and only one of them, Smokey Robinson, looks enough like me that I could imitate him. But that wouldn't pose a problem for my performing of the other song. I would dress up as Frankenstein if I were doing the "Monster Mash."

I like both songs, and feel their different moods relate to two different sides of my personality. Also, I feel able to act out either one.

133

P O I N T S   T O   R E M E M B E R

▷ Choose the organizational method that best serves your purpose.

▷ The method you choose, along with the points of comparison you have outlined, will guide you as you write.

▷ A first draft provides a chance to explore your topic. Do not spend time worrying about word choice or grammatical problems.

Exercise Eleven Write a first draft of your comparison, using the method of organization you chose in Exercise Ten.

Revise

Once you have written a first draft, you can look it over with an eye to polishing it. Look for vague words and replace them with clearer ones. Try to find ways to make your statements more specific.

Following is the revised version of Neil's comparison. Notice the improvements that he made. He corrected errors. He added a few details. His main change, however, came in the last paragraph. He decided he didn't like the tone of the paragraph in the first draft, and wanted to conclude on a more down-to-earth note.

"The Tears of a Clown" and "Monster Mash" both have a good, danceable beat and would both be great for this contest, but there the similarites end. The style of "Tears" is romantic, while "monster Mash" is more commic than anything else. The tune and lirics of the two songs are also vastly different. "Tears" is sentimental and touching, while "Mash" is funny to the point of sillyness.

The artists who sing the two songs aren't anything alike, either, and To begin with, one is well known and the other isn't. Also, only one of them, Smokey Robinson, looks enough like me that I could imitate him. But that wouldn't pose a problem for me in performing of the other song. I would dress up as Frankenstein if I was doing the "Monster Mash."

I like both songs, and feel that either one would be their different moods relate to two very exciting to perform. different sides of my personality. Also, I feel able to act out either one.

Exercise Twelve   Write a revised draft of your comparison, adding details wherever you feel they are needed. You may want to have a classmate read your first draft and tell you what points could be made more clear. Use the following checklist as you revise.

1. Does the comparison include both similarities and differences?
2. Is the comparison organized clearly according to one of the methods discussed on pages 131-132?
3. Does the comparison include details that make the similarities and differences clear?

Proofread and Edit

This final part of the writing process should not be taken lightly. It would be a shame if a composition filled with good ideas was marred by careless mistakes. So be sure to reread your work thoroughly, looking for mistakes in grammar, spelling, and punctuation.

Exercise Thirteen   Go over your paper carefully, checking for errors in punctuation, grammar, and spelling. After you've made the necessary corrections, type or rewrite your work on a clean sheet of paper.

Writing a Business Letter

Oil wells in Oilton, West Virginia, in the 1870's
Culver Pictures, Inc.

Writing a Business Letter

People in business aren't the only ones who write business letters. Business letters are formal letters written for many purposes by many people.

You could write a business letter to order something—for example, a pair of sneakers from a sporting goods store. Or you might write a business letter to request information—perhaps a list of camping sites from the parks department. You could write a business letter to thank a museum director for conducting a tour for your class. You could write a business letter to complain to the traffic department about all the potholes in your street. You could write a business letter to the editor of a community newspaper, expressing your opinion on the construction of a teen center. Finally, you could write a business letter to apply for a position somewhere—say, a place at college, or a job you read about in the want ads.

In this unit you will write the last-mentioned type of business letter: a letter of application. The skill of writing letters of application will be useful to you often in the future, as you apply for jobs or for admission to school or college. And, of course, once you've mastered the letter of application, you'll be able to handle most other kinds of business letters, too.

P O I N T S   T O   R E M E M B E R

▷ A business letter is a formal letter that can be used for many purposes: to order something, to request information, to thank someone, to complain, to express an opinion, to apply for a position.

▷ A letter of application is appropriate when you are applying for a job or for admission to a school or college.

▷ A letter of application uses the standard business letter format.

A. Choose a Topic

What would you like to apply for? Perhaps you're interested in a part-time job after school or a full-time job next summer. Maybe you would like to apply for a special class that meets at night or on weekends.

Exercise One   Read the following advertisements for jobs and school courses. Choose one to write a letter of application for. If none of them interest you, look in a newspaper and choose a real want ad for a job, or find a school catalog and choose a class.

1. Wanted: Part-time assistant for a small community zoo. Must get along with others, enjoy working outdoors, and be calm under stress. (The monkeys sometimes get loose.) Some experience with animals helpful. Hours flexible. Write: Mr. Philip Brock, 3212 Pines Plaza, Pfafftown, NC 27040.

2. Wanted: Young man or woman to work in small office weekends. Typing skills helpful. Will train in duties, including use of computer. Opportunity for some travel and meeting celebrities. Need steady, reliable person who doesn't require constant supervision. Write: Lori Ray, LaSalle Talent Agency, 14 Covena Street, Mystic, CT 06355.

3. A Wonderful Place to Spend the Day is now hiring student help for after school or next summer. This marvelous combination restaurant/bookstore/sporting goods shop/gym/pool needs waiters, waitresses, chefs, clerks, storytellers, salespeople, demonstrators, recreation assistants, lifeguards, guides for hiking, camping, white-water rafting, etc. If you're the right person, we'll train you for the job. Good starting salary and chance for advancement. Write: Regina Maxwell, Department of Recruitment, A Wonderful Place to Spend the Day, 444 Seaside Boulevard, Santa Barbara, CA 93102.

4. Why not use your spare time to improve yourself? Hundreds of courses to choose from. Whatever subject you're interested in, we've got a course in it. Courses at night, weekends, and summer, or by correspondence. Apply to Director of Admissions, The School of Self-Improvement, 3150 Century Blvd., Des Moines, IA 50316.

5. Make up a want ad for a job of your choice or make up a school and a course to further your education.

B. Identify Your Audience

Usually, when you write a letter of application, you are writing to a person you have never met. Sometimes you will know the person's name. If you don't, however, it is acceptable to write "Dear Sir or Madam," or to use the person's title (for example, "Dear Director of Admissions"). If you are fortunate, you will know both the person's name and her or his business title. Use both if you know them (for instance, "Dear Mayor Jones").

Exercise Two   Decide whom you will write your business letter to. Do you know the person's name? Do you know his or her business title? What is the name of the business or school, and where is it located? It is important to know the exact street address, the city, the state, and the ZIP code; you will use them for the inside address of your business letter, as well as on the envelope.

Make a Plan

A. Gather Ideas

There is some standard information that you will need or want to include in your letter of application. Some of it is information about yourself that you should supply no matter what position you're seeking.

1. your address (street, town, state, and ZIP code), your telephone number, and the date
2. the name of the person you are writing to, the person's title, the company or school, and its address (street, town, state, and ZIP code)
3. the job or course you are applying for, how you heard about it, and why you are interested
4. biographical information about yourself (age, level in school, experience, interests, and schooling that might help qualify you)

Exercise Three   Write down the basic information you will need in your letter of application. Supply what is asked in the list above, as well as any other information you feel is important.

Your Special Qualifications

As you saw in the examples in Exercise One, job advertisements often list the qualifications that are wanted in applicants. The list may include specific skills or knowledge. It may also include personality traits that are needed to do the job well.

If qualifications are stated in a job advertisement, you need to be able to show that you have them. Suppose, for example, that one of the requirements for the job you want is typing skills. If you have studied typing in school, tell what course you have taken and what your typing speed is in words per minute. Or suppose you want a job as a camp counselor and the work requires a knowledge of the woods. You might tell about the many times you have hiked and camped in the woods, or the camping merit badge you earned in scouting.

Sometimes job advertisements do not list specific qualifications. In those cases it is up to you to decide what abilities would be most important for the job. For example, suppose you are applying for a job as a lifeguard. You know that a knowledge of lifesaving techniques is the first requirement. However, you should also mention other abilities or character traits of yours that might be important. These might include a sense of responsibility and the ability to act fast in a crisis.

Exercise Four   Look at the advertisement you chose in Exercise One and the information you collected in Exercise Three. Write a list of the special abilities and helpful traits that you will be bringing to the job or course of study you're applying for. Mention experiences that show you have the abilities you describe.

Following are the qualifications Mollie listed for the job of assistant playground supervisor for seven- to nine-year-old children.

> I have had regular baby-sitting jobs for three years.
>
> I know a lot of games to teach children.
>
> I sing and play the guitar.
>
> I have had a course in first aid in school.
>
> I know a lot about crafts from scouting and camp.

References

Your letter of application should also include the names, addresses, and telephone numbers of two or three people not related to you who know your work and character and would be willing to vouch for you. Be sure to ask the people you choose as references whether they are willing to recommend you. Once they have agreed to do so, they should, of course, be prepared to hear from your prospective employers, either by phone or by mail.

You might ask some of these people to be your references:

1. Teachers who have seen you try hard and do good work.
2. Coaches or faculty advisors who know that you do your share on a team and do not give up easily.
3. Scout or religious leaders who know that you try to help others.
4. Friends of the family who have known you for years.
5. Former employers who can say that you have good work habits.

Exercise Five   Make a list of three people who might act as your references. List people who could talk about your abilities, personal traits, and work or study habits. After each name, write one or more sentences explaining why that person might be a good reference.

Darren decided that Mr. Allen Brady of the City Parks Department might be willing to recommend him. Following is what he wrote about Mr. Brady.

> Mr. Brady is in charge of the summer lifeguard program for city pools. He knows that I'm responsible and always on time. He was there once when I helped a tired swimmer out of the pool.

B. Organize Ideas

Now that you have located all the details you will need to present in your letter of application, it is time for you to organize the information. Since a letter of application is a business letter, you will need to follow the format for a business letter.

Following is a letter of application written by a student named Jesse. It shows the standard format you should follow.

1506 Maple Avenue
Takoma Park, Maryland 20012
February 27, 19XX

Ms. Sandra Eichner
Director of Operations
Camp Elwood
R.D. 1, Box 156
Bear Claw, Minnesota 55601

Dear Ms. Eichner:

I would like to apply for one of the cabin counselor jobs at Camp Elwood for this coming summer. I read about your camp and your need for counselors in the *Camp News Digest*.

I am fifteen years old and a sophomore at Hickory High School in Takoma Park. I am a member of the cross-country track team, the school band, and the school service organization.

I think I would be a good cabin counselor because I especially enjoy working with younger people. I have cared for a younger brother and sister at home and have been a baby-sitter for the last three years throughout our neighborhood. I also have a lot of experience camping. I have gone camping many times with The Outdoor Club, family, and friends. In addition, being a cabin counselor would fit in with my long-range goals. These are to study psychology in college and become a school counselor.

The following people have agreed to give me references:

Ms. Francine Billows
School Counselor
Hickory High School
330 Taylor Avenue
Takoma Park, MD 20012
(301) 555-7042

Mr. William Loomis
Staff Member
The Outdoor Club
51 East 97th Street
Silver Spring, MD 20910
(301) 555-8951

I look forward to hearing from you. My address is in the upper right-hand corner. My home phone number is (301) 555-9224.

Sincerely yours,

Jesse Mentken

Notice that Jesse's paragraphs are single-spaced. They are separated from each other by a line of blank space, and are not indented.

Jesse's letter is divided into six parts: the heading, the inside address, the greeting or salutation, the body of the letter, the complimentary close, and the signature.

The Heading

The heading of a letter is written in the top right-hand corner of the page. It includes the *return address* (street, town, state, and ZIP code), which tells the person receiving the letter where to reach you. The heading also includes the *date* on which you wrote the letter.

You may use the Postal Service abbreviations for the states (for example, MN for Minnesota). But nothing else should be abbreviated in the heading, unless it is a commonly accepted abbreviation, such as St. Paul. All street names should be written out (North York Street, not N. York St.), but you may use suffixes after numbered avenues and streets (42nd Street). Write out the months in the heading (February, not Feb.), and do not put suffixes after the day in the date (October 12, 1990, not October 12th, 1990).

The Inside Address

Write the inside address two lines below the heading, but on the left-hand side of the paper. The inside address consists of the *name* and *business title* of the person to whom you are writing, the name of the *company* or *school*, the *street address*, the *city*, the *state*, and the *ZIP code*. If you don't know the name or the title of the person you are writing to, it is acceptable to write only the company's name and address.

The Greeting or Salutation

Skip two lines after the inside address and write the greeting on the left-hand side of the paper. The greeting or salutation will begin with *Dear*, then follow with the name and a colon (*Dear Ms. Eichner:*). If you do not know the name, use *Sir or Madam* (*Dear Sir or Madam:*).

The Body

Skip two lines after the greeting and then start the body of the letter. The body of a business letter is the part that contains the message. It is what your letter is about. Indicate each new paragraph by skipping a line.

The Complimentary Close

Skip two lines after the body of the business letter to write the complimentary close—the word or words you use before signing your name. Capitalize the first letter of the first word in the close, and follow the close with a comma. Here are some examples of complimentary closes:

Formal	Less Formal
Sincerely yours,	Sincerely,
Respectfully yours,	Respectfully,
Cordially yours,	Cordially,
Yours truly,	Truly,
Very truly yours,	

The left margin of the complimentary close should be even with the left margin of the heading.

The Signature

About four lines below the complimentary close, print or type your name. This is necessary because so many signatures are difficult to read. Above this write your signature. The signature of a business letter consists of the *handwritten name* and the *typed or printed name.*

Exercise Six   Doing this exercise will help you organize the information you have collected for your letter. Down the side of a clean sheet of paper, write the names of the different parts of the business letter (Heading, Inside Address, Salutation or Greeting, Body, Complimentary Close, Signature). Then, next to each part, write the information from your notes that belongs in it.

When writing a business letter, try to put yourself in the place of the person receiving it. Doing so will help you maintain a polite tone, no matter what business you are transacting.

It is also important to state the facts and support them with specific details. Jesse, for instance, stated that he enjoyed working with younger people and then supported his claim with proof: the jobs he'd had that involved taking care of children.

A business letter should be friendly but not chummy. For example, if Jesse had been writing a personal letter instead of a letter of application, he might have mentioned that one of his major reasons for wanting the job was to get out of his hometown for the summer. But he maintained a detached and businesslike tone, which was more appropriate in this case.

Remember also that it is better not to make outright demands in a business letter. Write *I look forward to hearing from you soon* rather than *You'd better write back right away.*

Exercise Seven   Now write the first draft of your letter of application for the job or course of study you chose in Exercise One. As you go through each of the six parts of the business letter, use the information you organized in Exercise Six. Following are some guidelines.

1. Put yourself in the place of the reader.
2. Be complete. Give all the necessary information.
3. Be accurate. Double-check your information, including facts, figures, dates, and addresses.
4. Be friendly but not too familiar.
5. Make sure your letter follows the correct form for a business letter.
6. Be brief and to the point.

A business letter, like other kinds of writing, will turn out better if you regard the first draft as a trial run. If you're not worrying about possible mistakes, you are free to think about the most important part of your letter: its content.

To revise means to "re-see." In this step, you will have a chance to make sure your letter of application says exactly what you want it to say. Read it closely to make sure you have included all the necessary facts and information about yourself. If you have forgotten to include a special qualification you have for the job, add it now.

Exercise Eight   Use the following checklist to revise and refine the first draft of your letter of application.

1. Did you use the correct form for a business letter?

2. Is the information in the heading, the inside address, the salutation, and the body of the letter accurate? Is it complete? Has all unnecessary information been eliminated? Have you double-checked all your facts? Are the names, addresses, and telephone numbers of your references correct?

3. Read your letter of application as you imagine your reader will. Is the tone of the letter appropriate for the situation? Did you choose the best complimentary close?

Proofread Your Letter

Once you are satisfied with the format, content, and tone of your letter of application, turn your attention to its spelling, punctuation, and grammar.

Exercise Nine   Read through your application letter three times. The first time look for mistakes in grammar. The second time be on the lookout for mistakes in punctuation. Pay attention to the spelling the third time through.

The Final Draft

When you write a letter to someone, especially a business letter, try to write as neatly and correctly as possible. It is a matter of courtesy to your reader. It is also a way of making sure that your reader will understand what you are saying.

Use unlined paper when writing a business letter, and type the letter if possible. If you do not have a typewriter or word processor, write your letter in blue or black ink. If your script is not easy to read, print neatly. Keeping the lines straight on unlined paper is sometimes difficult, so place a sheet of lined paper underneath your letter as you write. The lines should show through to guide you.

Exercise Ten   Make a final, neat copy of the letter of application—a copy that you could actually send. Your letter will determine your reader's first impression of you. You want to make sure the impression is a good one.

The Envelope

As good as your letter might be, it will not be complete until you prepare an envelope in which to send it. The address to which you are sending the letter should be placed near the center of the envelope. It should be identical to the inside address in the letter. Your return address should contain your name, street address, city, state, and ZIP code. It should be placed in the upper left-hand corner of the envelope.

Exercise Eleven   Address the envelope, using the inside address from the letter. Do not forget to include your return address in the upper left-hand corner.

Writing to Persuade

*Visitors to Tower Grove Park, in St. Louis, Missouri, 1900
The giant lily pads on which they are standing are protected
by blankets and weight-distributing frames. The lilies were
grown from Amazon River seeds. Being photographed while
perched on one of these pads was a popular pastime.
Photo probably by Charles C. Holt, Collection of Dick Lewen*

Writing to Persuade

Megan is trying to persuade her brother Ethan to help her with the dishes, but she is not succeeding. Can you tell what's wrong with her approach?

Megan: Hey, Jughead, get over here and help me with these dishes, or I'll tell Mom about that glass you broke!

Ethan: You can tell her whatever you want to. I'm not doing any dishes.

Megan: Why not? You're just loafing around.

Ethan: I see no reason why I should help you.

Megan: I knew I couldn't count on you, you lazy bum!

Megan fails to persuade her brother because she is unpleasant and rude. She seems to think that insults and threats will make him do what she wants. But they have just the opposite effect on Ethan, as they do on most people.

What Megan doesn't know is that persuasion is a gentle art. The root of the word "persuade," *suade*, comes from a word in Indo-European (an ancient, "dead" language) that meant *sweet* or *pleasant*. When you try to persuade someone, you present your ideas in a polite, kindly manner. You try to make it pleasant for the person to see things your way.

Following is an example of how Megan might persuade Ethan to help her.

Megan: I hate to disturb you when you're busy, but I could certainly use your help with these dishes.

Ethan: What do you want me to do?

Megan: If you dried and put away the ones in the drainer, I'd really appreciate it. Then I would have some extra time to help you learn your lines for the play.

Ethan: Okay.

Megan: Thanks, Ethan. I knew I could count on you!

In this approach Megan shows consideration for Ethan. She asks him the favor in a calm and pleasant way and tells him exactly what she would like him to do. She also points out how his cooperation will benefit him (she'll help him with his homework).

P O I N T S   T O   R E M E M B E R

▷ Be polite and show consideration for your audience.

▷ Recognize the needs and desires of your audience.

▷ Express your wishes calmly, reasonably, and precisely.

In this unit, you will try to persuade someone through the written word. You will write a letter explaining your point of view on a matter that is important both to you and to your reader. To present your beliefs effectively, you must plan, step by step, how you are going to influence your reader.

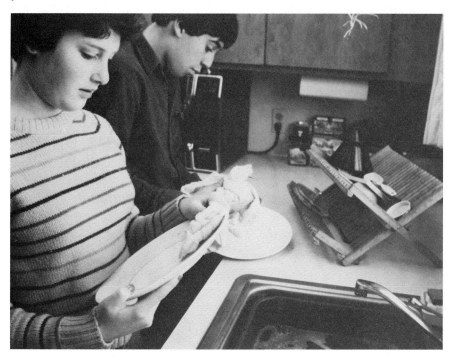

In your letter you will try to guide your reader toward your point of view. But before you can change someone's mind or move a person to action, you must know exactly what your goal is. What do you want to convince your reader of? What effect do you want your letter to have?

A. Choose a Topic

The topic you choose should be one that matters to you. If you care about the issue, you'll try hard to be as persuasive as possible. It also helps if you have a strong opinion about the issue. It's easier to present your case effectively when your point of view is clear in your mind.

Your topic should also be one that you know well. If you know what you are talking about, your reader will pay attention to what you have to say.

Try to choose a topic that people do not automatically agree on. Your ideas should meet with some resistance, so that you have a reason to be persuasive. There is no point in trying to convince someone of something he or she already believes.

Finally, make sure that your letter of persuasion is aimed at a realistic goal. If your goal is unrealistic, then no matter how effective your letter is, you will not be able to persuade your reader. For example, suppose you tried to persuade the governor of your state that all colleges and vocational schools should be free. Students should not have to pay tuition, and they should get their books and other supplies free, too. The governor would probably answer, "It's a wonderful idea, but it can't be done. The state does not have enough money. Even if we did have the money, the voters might not want to spend it as you suggest." In other words, your goal is unrealistic.

Exercise One   Think of three possible topics you might like to discuss in a letter of persuasion. The following questions may help you think of a topic.

1. Try to recall an argument you had with another person recently. What did you disagree about? Perhaps your side of the argument would make a good topic.

2. What problem are you concerned about? What is your "pet peeve"? Can you suggest a solution? You might write a letter of persuasion about it.

3. What changes would you like to see made in your town, school, or neighborhood? You might write a letter of persuasion asking for one of these changes.

4. What favor would you like to have someone do for you? You might write a letter of persuasion asking for this favor.

B. Define Your Purpose

You had a general purpose in mind when you chose your topic. Now it's time for you to decide on a specific purpose. For example, suppose you have decided to write about the safety hazards that bicycle riders face in your town. Your general purpose is to convince your reader that something should be done to make bicycling safer. Your specific purpose will be to persuade the reader to take the specific actions that you recommend.

Following is another example.

Topic: Improving school lunches

Specific Purpose: To persuade the reader that a salad bar should be added to the lunch menu in the school cafeteria

Exercise Two   List the three topics you chose in Exercise One. For each topic, write a sentence stating your specific purpose.

EXAMPLE:

Topic: Sharing household chores fairly

Specific Purpose: To persuade brother and sister to help set up weekly chore schedule and actually do chores assigned to them

A student named Walter chose "need for more extracurricular activities" as one of his topics for Exercise One. His specific purpose was to persuade school officials to let students start a bowling team.

C. Identify Your Audience

After you've chosen a topic and defined a specific purpose, you need to identify your audience. Ask yourself: "Whose opinion do I want to change?" If your topic involves community action, ask: "Who has the power or the authority to do what needs to be done?" This is the person to whom you will address your letter.

Once you determine whom you should write to, it's important to think about what kind of person your reader is. What are his or her interests, concerns, and attitudes? How much does this person know about the subject? How does this person feel about the subject? The answers to these questions will help you decide what information to include in your letter.

Walter decided to write his letter to the principal of his school, Ms. Diana Carter. He thought about what kind of person Ms. Carter was, what she valued, and what she worried about. He decided to make a list of facts about Ms. Carter. Here it is:

Topic: Need for more extracurricular activities

Specific Purpose: To persuade school officials to let students start bowling team

Audience: Ms. Carter, the school principal

Facts About Audience: She puts academic achievement first.

She is concerned about not having enough money to hire more teachers.

She likes to see students take part in extracurricular activities.

She thinks sports should be for everybody, not just talented athletes.

She encourages parents to take an active part in school affairs.

She would like to see more school spirit.

She likes to see girls as well as boys compete in after-school sports.

Exercise Three   For each of the three topics you listed in Exercise One, name the person who will read your letter. Then write as many statements as you can about each person's attitudes and concerns.

Look over the notes you have made for your three topics, and choose the topic you would most like to develop into a persuasive letter for this unit.

Make a Plan

A. Gather Ideas

You have chosen a topic for your letter of persuasion and have decided on your purpose and audience. Your next step is to gather ideas to support your point of view. Think about the reasons why you feel your proposal is a good one. Your reasons can be based on facts, feelings, experience, or a combination of these. If you feel you need to know more about your subject, you may want to do some research.

Arguments that support your point of view are called *pros,* from the Latin word meaning "for." Following is a list of pros that Walter gathered to show Ms. Carter why a bowling team would be a good idea.

Pros

1. Other schools in the district have bowling teams.
2. Bowling is fun, and it's good exercise.
3. Both boys and girls can be on a bowling team.
4. Students who don't take part in other sports might try out for a bowling team.

Before you can change your reader's mind, you need to understand his or her point of view. You have already listed facts about your reader. Now try to guess how he or she will react to your ideas. Make a list of the objections you expect your reader to raise. These arguments against your point of view are called *cons.* The word *con* is short for the Latin *contra,* meaning "against."

After you have listed the possible objections, prepare a reply to each. You will try to convince your reader that his or her objections are not valid. Presenting both the pros and the cons of the argument can be a very persuasive technique. It shows the reader that you considered both points of view thoroughly before you formed your opinion.

Walter studied his list of facts about Ms. Carter. He thought of four objections that she would probably have to his proposal for a school bowling team. Following is his list of cons.

Cons

1. There is no money in the school budget for a new extracurricular activity.

2. The school bus could not take us to the bowling alleys to compete with other teams.

3. We do not have a staff member who could coach a bowling team.

4. There are not enough interested students to form a team and keep it going.

Walter studied his list of cons and thought of a reply to each one.

Replies

1. The school would not have to spend money on this project. A local business has offered to sponsor the team. The sponsor would provide shoes and gloves. Also, the owner of a nearby bowling alley will let us practice free of charge if we go there when the lanes are not busy.

2. The place where we will practice is within walking distance of the school. As for getting to meets with other teams, we can go by car. Some of the students' parents will set up a car pool.

3. The sister of one of our students is an expert bowler. She has offered to coach the team without pay.

4. We have put a notice about the bowling team on the bulletin board of every homeroom. The notice invites students to sign their names if they would like to join the team. So far we have twenty-six signatures, enough for several teams.

Exercise Four   List the pros and cons for your point of view. Reread the list of facts about your audience that you wrote in Exercise Three. These will help you think of possible objections (cons). Then write a reply to each objection.

B. Organize Ideas

Now that you have gathered all your information, your task is to organize it in an outline. Your letter will have three parts: an *introduction*, a *body*, and a *conclusion*. You can organize your notes under these three headings in your outline.

The purpose of your introduction is to present your proposal and explain what you want from your reader. You did this in Exercise Two, when you wrote your statement of purpose. You can begin your outline by writing your statement of purpose under the heading "Introduction."

Under the heading "Body," your outline will have two subheadings: "Pros" and "Cons." Under "Pros," list reasons that support your proposal. It is a good idea to give your most important reason first. That way you may be able to win your reader's agreement early in the letter.

Under "Cons," list the objections you think your reader may have. Follow each objection with the reply you wrote in Exercise Four.

For the "Conclusion" section of your outline, restate your proposal and briefly sum up the points in its favor.

Following is Walter's outline.

I. Introduction

I would like to start a bowling team at my school. I believe it would benefit the school and would not be expensive.

II. Body

A. Pros

1. Bowling is fun, and it's good exercise.

2. Both boys and girls can be on a bowling team.

3. Students who don't take part in other sports might try out for a bowling team.

4. Other schools in the district have bowling teams.

B. Cons

1. There is no money in the school budget for a new extra-curricular activity.

Reply: A local business has offered to sponsor the team. Also, the owner of a nearby bowling alley will let us practice free of charge.

2. The school bus could not take us to the bowling alleys to compete with other teams.

Reply: Some of the students' parents will set up a car pool to take the team to meets.

3. We do not have a staff member who could coach a bowling team.

Reply: The sister of one of our students is an expert bowler. She has offered to coach the team without pay.

4. Many of the people who say they are interested will not actually join, or will join but will drop out later.

Reply: So far we have twenty-six people interested, enough for several teams.

III. Conclusion

I believe a bowling team would be a good thing for the school.

Exercise Five Write an outline for your letter of persuasion, using the notes you have made for your topic so far. Use Walter's outline on this page as a model.

Write the First Draft

When you write a first draft, you translate your notes into sentences and paragraphs. Your goal is to get down all your ideas without worrying about grammar, spelling, punctuation, or handwriting. As you write, feel free to add new ideas or to leave out any of your original ideas that you feel don't work.

Tone

The tone of your letter is very important. You can check the tone by reading the letter out loud and listening to your voice. Does your voice sound angry and demanding? Revise the sentences until your voice sounds polite and sincere when you read them.

Be as positive as you can be, especially in your opening paragraph. Don't start out with a sentence like this: "I guess there's no hope that you'll agree to my proposal, but I just thought I'd mention it anyway." Such a negative approach just gives your reader an excuse to say no.

In your conclusion, you might mention that you would be happy to discuss the matter further on the phone or in person. This lets the reader know that you are willing to compromise if necessary.

By using a pleasant, respectful tone, you will earn the good will of your reader. And the reader's good will is something you need if you are to succeed.

161

POINTS TO REMEMBER

▷ As you write your first draft, add ideas or delete ideas as necessary.

▷ Keep the tone of your letter positive, polite, and sincere.

▷ End your letter with a statement that leaves the matter open for discussion.

Exercise Six   Now you are ready to write the first draft of your letter of persuasion. Use your outline as a guide, but feel free to depart from it if necessary.

Following is Walter's letter to Ms. Carter.

Dear Ms. Carter:

　　I am writing to get your support for a new extracuricular activity. I represent a bunch of students who would like to form a bowling team. We believe that it would do the school a lot of good.

　　We have many reasons for believing this. First, bowling is real fun, and its good exercise. It gives people a chance to get some exercise without straining or too tired. Second, bowling is one of the few sports that girls and boys can compete on an equal basis. This

means that our school could at long last have one sport that was truely coeducational. Third, bowling has no physical requirements of height or weight, almost anyone can do it. Thus, a bowling team might attract some of the students that don't go out for varsity sports.

We realize that the school has a limited amount of money to spend on sports. However, we believe that a bowling team wouldn't cost hardly anything. Athaletes All sporting goods store has offered to provide shoes and gloves. Team members can probaly buy their own shirts. The owner of Fast Lanes has agreed to let us practice free on weekday afternoons.

We can walk to Fast Lanes, and we know of some parents that are willing to drive us to meets with teams at other allies.

We would have no trouble finding a coach. John Grahams sister Judy has won several amature trophies and has offered to coach us for free.

I know that in the past some clubs and teams have faded away because of lack of interest. I believe, though, that a bowling team would have long-lasting support. Twenty-six students have allready signed a notice we put up for interested bowlers.

We hope you give some thought to our idea. We think a team would be a good thing for our school. If you would like to discuss the matter with me, I will be glad to come to your office at any time.

Sincerly,

Walter Landon

You may have noticed that Walter did not follow his outline exactly. First, he changed the introduction, leaving out the argument that a bowling team would not be expensive. He didn't want to draw attention to the question of expenses so early in the letter. He felt it would be better to discuss that issue later. Second, he decided not to mention the fact that other schools in the district had bowling teams. Ms. Carter, he told himself, was not the sort of person who would do a thing just because everybody else was doing it.

Walter made many mistakes in his first draft, but he succeeded in putting his main ideas into words. He knew that later, when he revised his letter, he would be able to correct problems in sentence structure, organization, word choice, tone, grammar, spelling, and punctuation.

Revise

Revising is an important part of the writing process. Few, if any, professional writers are satisfied with their first drafts. They write and revise, and write and revise until they're sure the work is as good as they can make it.

Each time you revise a piece of writing, you move it closer to the goal that you have set for it. Here are some questions you should ask yourself when you revise your letter:

☐ Have I included all the points that I need to mention in order to persuade my reader?

☐ Does my letter contain any unnecessary ideas that should be crossed out?

☐ Have I put the ideas in the best possible order?

☐ Have I expressed my thoughts clearly and precisely?

☐ Are my sentences varied in length and structure?

☐ Is the tone of my letter firm but courteous and pleasant?

Proofread and Edit

After you have revised your work for content and organization, look it over carefully for errors in grammar, punctuation, and spelling. Look up any words you are unsure of. Mistakes in writing will probably distract your reader's attention from your ideas. You want the reader to think about what you are saying, not how you are saying it. Mistakes may also make the reader think you wrote the letter carelessly. If your letter sounds careless, the reader may not take it seriously.

Exercise Seven   Read your letter a few times for content. Revise your first draft, using the questions above as a guide. When you are satisfied that you have written the best possible letter, proofread and edit your work for errors in grammar, spelling, and punctuation.

Turn to page 166 to see how Walter revised and corrected his letter.

This is Walter's revision of his letter to Ms. Carter.

Dear Ms. Carter:

I am writing to ~~get~~ _request_ your support for a new extracur~~i~~ricular activity.

I represent a ~~bunch~~ _number_ of students who would like to form a bowling
team. We believe that it would ~~do the school a lot of good.~~ _be a valuable addition to the school's athletic program._

We have ~~many~~ _several_ reasons for believing this. First, bowling is ~~real~~

fun, and it~~s~~ _'s_ good exercise. It gives people a chance to get some

exercise without straining or _becoming_ too tired. Second, bowling is one of the

few sports ~~that~~ _in which_ girls and boys can compete on an equal basis. This

means that our school ~~could at long last~~ _would_ have one sport that was

tru~~e~~ly coeducational. Third, bowling has no physical requirements of

height or weight, _so_ almost anyone can do it. Thus, a bowling team

might attract some of the students ~~that~~ _who_ don't go out for varsity

sports.

We realize that the school has a limited amount of money to

spend on sports. However, we believe that a bowling team ~~wouldn't~~
~~cost hardly anything.~~ _the school little or nothing._ Ath~~a~~letes ~~All sporting goods store~~ has offered

to provide shoes and gloves. Team members can proba~~b~~ly buy their

own shirts. The owner of Fast Lanes _Bowling Alley_ has agreed to let us practice free

on weekday afternoons.

We can walk to Fast Lanes, and we know of some parents ~~that~~ *who*

are willing to drive us to meets with teams at other ~~allies.~~ *eyso*⊙

We would have no trouble finding a coach. John Graham's sister

Judy has won several ama~~ture~~*eur* trophies and has offered to coach us

for free.

I know that in the past some clubs and teams have faded away

because of lack of interest. I believe, though, that a bowling team

would have long-lasting support. Twenty-six students have al*l*ready

signed a notice we put up for interested bowlers.

We hope you give ~~some thought~~ *serious Consideration* to our idea. We think *that* a *bowling* team

would be a good thing for our school. If you would like to discuss the

matter with me, I ~~will~~ *would* be glad to come to your office at any time.

Sincerely,

Walter Landon

Exercise Eight   When you finish writing your final draft, type or recopy it on a clean sheet of paper. Proofread your letter once more before you hand it in or send it.

Writing a Review

Italian director Federico Fellini directing on the set of a film, 1968
Mary Ellen Mark, Archive Pictures, Inc.

Writing a Review

magine that one afternoon you run across the following ad in your local newspaper.

Wanted: Reviewers for new teen magazine. Must possess high standards and a keen interest in books, movies, plays, or TV shows. Must also demonstrate an ability to write clearly. Prefer people who understand teenagers' tastes and interests. Write a review on topic of your choice, and submit along with resumé.

Well, you are definitely interested. But you are not sure what is meant by high standards. What are standards, anyway? What exactly does a reviewer do? And how do you go about writing a review?

Standards

A standard is a basic principle used to judge the quality of a particular work of art. Standards are a set of ideas about what makes something good.

Different people have different standards. If you ask two friends what they look for in a movie, you're likely to get two different answers. One may say that the plot must be believable and the characters must act and talk like real people. The other may say that a good movie has suspense, fast-paced action, and a surprise ending.

Reviewers

Reviewers (also known as critics) are people who offer the public their opinions on a variety of subjects. They may publish their reviews in a magazine, book, or newspaper, or they may broadcast them over the radio or on television. The people who read or hear the reviews are often strongly influenced by them. They may buy a book or stay away from a show because of what a critic said about it.

A good critic has clear standards that he or she uses in judging the quality of a particular work. But, no matter how clear the critic's standards are, and no matter how well he or she explains them, a review is still just one person's opinion. It deserves respect because it comes from an expert on the subject, but it cannot be considered fact.

Sometimes a reviewer identifies the standards he or she uses, but you can learn what they are without being told. The more you read or listen to the same critic, the better you understand his or her standards. And reading or listening to someone else's opinions of something you have seen or read or heard is also a good way of refining your own standards of judgment.

Reviews

Not only do different people judge the same thing differently, but the same person applies different standards to different things. Critics write reviews not only about books, movies, plays, and TV shows, but also about paintings, buildings, cars, concerts, ballets, clothes, recordings, restaurants, and sports events. Naturally, the standards used to evaluate a car are unlike those used to judge the food and service in a restaurant.

Reading reviews is a good way of keeping up with the cultural activities available in your area. A thoughtful review can help you decide how best to spend your time and money.

In this unit, you will learn how to write a review. You will learn how to discover your own standards for judging things, and how to back up your opinions.

P O I N T S   T O   R E M E M B E R

▷ A standard is a rule or a principle that gives you a basis for judging the quality of a particular product, performance, or work of art.

▷ Different people have different standards.

▷ There are different standards for judging different things.

▷ Reading or listening to a critic's opinions about something you have seen or read or heard is a good way of refining your own standards of judgment.

▷ Reading reviews is a good way of keeping up with the cultural activities available in your area.

Exercise One   Think about the last movie you saw or the last book you read. How did you happen to see or read it? Did you read a review of it beforehand? Did a friend recommend it to you? Did you simply stumble across it? Explain in a few sentences why you chose that particular book or movie, and tell whether or not it lived up to your expectations.

Set Your Goal

Choose a Topic

The first step in writing a review is to decide what you want to write about. You may want to pretend you are trying out for the new teen magazine described at the beginning of this unit. If so, you might write about a particular book, movie, play, or TV show.

Most reviewers are experts in a particular field. You, too, will want to select a topic that you know something about. Since you will be writing your review for other teenagers, you already have a good idea of your audience and your purpose. Your audience will be people your own age, and your purpose will be to present your point of view clearly and convincingly.

Exercise Two   It is time to choose a topic for the review that you will write in this unit. From the following general categories, select one that interests you. (If you wish, you may choose a category that is not on the list.) Make sure you are familiar enough with the category to name some specific members of it. For example, if you choose *fiction books*, you should be able to think of a particular book that you would like to review.

1. fiction books
2. movies
3. stage plays
4. TV dramas or comedies

173

P O I N T S   T O   R E M E M B E R

▷   A critic is supposed to be an expert, so review something about which you have quite a bit of knowledge.

▷   Your review should help the reader decide whether he or she might like the item you're writing about.

Make a Plan

Discover Your Standards

Discovering your own standards is the first step in writing a review that expresses your opinion. Although you may not have thought much about them, you undoubtedly do have standards for judging many things.

If you wanted to discover your own standards for judging books, for example, you could think of a book you like and one you do not like, and then list your reasons for liking the one and not liking the other.

Here is an example. Vicki has selected two books she recently read.

The Hound of the Baskervilles, by Arthur Conan Doyle

The reasons I like it:

1. It has plenty of action.
2. It is full of suspense and is scary.
3. The characters are interesting and quite believable.
4. The story ends happily.

Slime City, by Hugo Z. Fish

The reasons I don't like it:

1. It's too long.
2. It has too much unnecessary violence.
3. The characters are unrealistic.
4. The ending is depressing.

These two lists reveal some of the standards Vicki uses in judging books.

Exercise Three   From the category you chose in Exercise Two, list a title that you like and a title that you do not like. For each title, write four or five reasons for your opinion.

Exercise Four   Look over the lists of reasons you wrote for Exercise Three. Decide what standards they are based on. Write down these standards. You will find them to be important in writing your review.

Following are some of Vicki's standards for a good book.

1. plenty of action
2. believable, realistic characters
3. happy ending
4. no unnecessary violence
5. not too long

Exercise Five   Now choose a work to review. It should not be either of the ones you discussed in Exercise Three. It might be something you have seen or read recently, or something you can see or read especially for this assignment.

Additional Standards

You already have a list of standards from Exercise Four. But there may be other standards that would strengthen your review. To help yourself come up with additional standards, read the questions in the following checklists. The questions apply to works of fiction, either in print or on the stage or screen.

Plot

1. Was the plot believable? Why or why not?
2. Was the plot developed clearly, or was it confusing?
3. Were the transitions between scenes natural?
4. Did the work have a special feeling? Was it funny, sad, or exciting? Or did it have some other feeling?
5. Was the work always interesting, or was it boring at times? Why or why not?

Characters

1. Were the characters interesting or thought-provoking? Why or why not?
2. Were the characters believable? Why or why not?
3. Was there one character toward whom you felt especially sympathetic? Why?
4. Was the acting good or bad? Why?
5. Was there any one actor whose performance was better or worse than the others'? If so, name the actor and tell why his or her performance was superior or inferior.

Technical Quality

1. Were the camera angles and lighting interesting and effective? Why or why not?
2. Were the settings and costumes appropriate?

3. Did the music enhance the story, or was it distracting?

4. Did you have trouble at times hearing the dialogue?

5. Were there any special effects or unusual stunts, or was there anything remarkable about the costumes or makeup? If so, were they convincing?

6. Was the literary style appropriate to the subject of the book?

7. Was the writing imaginative? Did it help get you fully involved in the story?

Exercise Six   Go over the checklists again, answering the questions that relate to your topic. Ignore any questions that do not apply to the topic. Then use your answers to develop additional standards for judging the work you are reviewing. Write a few words to describe each of your standards.

Following is the answer Julie wrote to the question *Was the plot believable? Why or why not?* After her answer, she wrote down the standard she felt it revealed.

The plot of *Back to the Future* was farfetched. However, I didn't mind this. I like movies that are imaginative and funny, and contain fantasy and unusual adventures.

Standard: Prefer imaginative, funny movies that contain fantasy and unusual adventures

Using Specific Details

In your review, you will be telling your readers what you found funny, interesting, frightening, or boring in the work you have chosen to discuss. But simply making statements such as "the lighting was bad," or "the plot was silly" is not enough. Support your opinion with *specific details*. These details will make your review more useful to the reader.

Suppose, for instance, that you disliked the plot of the book you were reviewing because it didn't have enough action. If you took an example from a particularly slow part of the book, the readers of your review would understand your standard for judging a plot, and would be able to decide whether or not they agreed with you.

Exercise Seven   Look at the list of standards you wrote for Exercises Four and Six. Write a paragraph dealing with each of your standards.
The paragraph should follow this pattern:

1.   Write a sentence that refers to one of your standards—for example, fast-paced action.

2.   Next write several sentences that give details showing how the work you're reviewing does or does not measure up to your standard.

EXAMPLE: A comedy should have fast, funny action, and this one does. A new disaster strikes the bumbling hero, Alec, about once every two minutes. The trouble starts when he is shopping at a vegetable stand. He absentmindedly puts two ripe tomatoes into his jacket pocket and walks away without paying for them. Then these things happen in quick succession: He realizes that he "stole" the tomatoes. He hears a siren and thinks the police are after him. He collides with a fleeing murderer who crams a revolver into his pocket, crushing the tomatoes and leaving a bloodlike stain. He ducks into a manhole to hide. And he becomes trapped when a bus breaks down with one wheel on the manhole cover.

Summarizing the Plot

As you know, reading a review can often help you decide whether or not you would enjoy a particular work. But a review can also help you in another way: It can tell you what the work is about. A good review usually includes a *plot summary*.

The plot of a book, movie, play, or TV show is the series of events that make up the story. In other words, the plot is what happens. A summary is a brief description of the plot.

A summary doesn't include every detail of a plot. Telling everything that happens is boring and would spoil any surprises the story might have. To write a summary, follow these steps:

1.   Outline the major events.

2.   Be sure the events are in chronological order.

3.   Cross out any events that are not necessary to the reader's understanding of the plot.

4.   Be sure that you do not reveal the ending or any surprises along the way. You don't want to spoil the work for your reader.

Following is Julie's list of the major events of the movie *Back to the Future*:

1. Late at night, Dr. Brown shows Marty his time-travel car in a deserted parking lot.
2. Dr. Brown is killed by terrorists and Marty escapes by traveling back to 1955.
3. He meets his parents, who are teenagers and not yet married.
4. He jumps in front of a car to save his dad's life.
5. While recovering at his mom's house, he learns that she has fallen in love with him.
6. Marty meets Dr. Brown, who, of course, is thirty years younger. He tries to figure out a way to get Marty back to 1985.
7. Marty's mom wants *him* to take her to the dance.
8. He gets his dad to "save" her at the dance.
9. Dr. Brown discovers a way to send Marty back to 1985.
10. Marty returns to the future, where he finds that his parents have changed.

Julie used this list to write the following summary of the plot of *Back to the Future*.

Back to the Future, a film directed by Steven Spielberg, is about a seventeen-year-old boy who travels in a time machine back to 1955. Marty, played by Michael J. Fox, finds himself in the same town where he lived in 1985. He sees his parents, who are teenagers. He also sees Dr. Brown, the mad scientist who sent him time-traveling in 1985. Unless Dr. Brown can find a way to help him return, Marty will be trapped in the past. Marty really starts to worry when he interrupts his parents' first meeting. He realizes that he must act quickly to bring his parents together, or he and his brother and sister will never be born. Marty is in a race against time, to save the future and his own life.

Notice that the summary gives only enough details to let you know what the movie is about. It mentions, for example, that Marty travels back to 1955 and meets his parents, who, at that time, are in their teens. And it says that he interrupts their first meeting. But it doesn't give away the outcome of the movie.

Also, notice that present-tense verbs are used throughout the summary. When you summarize a plot, it is generally best to use verbs

in the present tense. They help the reader imagine that he or she is watching the story unfold right now.

Exercise Eight   Write a six- to ten-sentence summary of the plot of the work you have chosen. Use the guidelines given above for writing a summary. Include the title and the author or director, as well as any other information you think is important.

In reviews you write of movies, books, plays, television shows, or any other works that tell a story, it is useful to present a summary. The summary should probably appear early in your review—perhaps in the first or second paragraph—and should include the title of the work and its author or director. You may also want to list other books by the same author or, if the work is a film, a play, or a TV show, the actors appearing in the cast.

To decide on other information you might want to include in your review, refer to the following worksheet on movies. Julie filled in part of it with information about *Back to the Future.* You can also use this worksheet for TV shows, or adapt it for use with books and plays.

1. **Title:** *Back to the Future*

2. **Type of Work:** science fiction movie

3. **Credits:** Director, Steven Spielberg; actor, Michael J. Fox (Marty)

4. **General Information:** Teenager named Marty travels in a time machine invented by Dr. Brown back to 1955. He is in the same town where he started out in 1985, but he sees his parents and Dr. Brown as they were thirty years ago. Without meaning to, he interferes with the events that led to his parents' marriage. He must overcome many obstacles to arrange for their "falling in love" again. Then, with only moments to spare, he must get the Dr. Brown of 1955 to return him to the future.

5. **General Evaluation:** exciting, very enjoyable if you like fantasy

6. **Specific Evaluations:**

   plot: well constructed; events seem to develop logically, provided you accept the possibility of time travel.

   dialogue: realistic; uses the slang of the 1950's.

   characters: Marty, Dr. Brown good; others are stereotypes.

   performers: man who plays father makes character too goofy to be believed

   direction, photography, lighting: good use of special effects; crisp photography; dramatic lighting.

   sets, locations, costumes: convincing recreation of the time and place

   sound effects, music: effective use of rock music of 1950's

   theme, significance, psychological effect: thought-provoking: makes you wonder what might have happened if events had taken a different turn in the past. Also makes you wonder what kind of future will grow out of the present.

Write the First Draft

Now you can put together the information you have developed in this unit and the skills you have learned. As you write your first draft, concentrate on getting the information down on paper. Don't spend too much time worrying about minor details. Keep your ideas flowing. If you are unsure of something—such as punctuation, spelling, or grammar—put down what you think is right and move on. You can make corrections when you revise.

Exercise Nine   Here is an outline you can use as you write the first draft of your review:

1.   Begin with an introductory paragraph that summarizes the plot. You can use the summary you wrote in Exercise Eight.

2.   Treat each of your standards in a separate paragraph, telling how the work did or did not measure up to that standard. Include details to explain and support your opinion.

3.   Add a brief concluding paragraph in which you tell whether you would or would not recommend the work to your readers, and why.

POINTS TO REMEMBER

▷   Begin your review with a brief summary of the plot.

▷   Write a paragraph for each of the standards you are using.

▷   Include details to support and explain each of your opinions.

▷   Include a concluding paragraph that tells why you would or would not recommend the work.

It is tempting for beginning reviewers simply to recopy their first drafts and hand them in. But as all professional reviewers know, resisting this temptation is worthwhile. Take the time to make your review as good as you can.

Exercise Ten As you revise your review, correct your work by consulting the following checklist.

1. Does the review begin with a brief summary of the plot?
2. Are all the verbs in the summary in the present tense?
3. Does the review explain the standards used?
4. Does the review include details to support and explain the opinions expressed?
5. Does the review include a concluding paragraph that tells why you would or would not recommend the work?

Proofread and Edit

After you have written the second draft of your review, put it away for a day or two. Then read it again carefully to check for errors in punctuation, spelling, and grammar. Make sure you cross out any unnecessary words or thoughts, and correct any errors you may find. Finally, copy your finished review on a clean sheet of paper. It is important that you make the best impression possible.

You and your classmates might consider putting together a magazine to publish your reviews. It would probably be interesting to compare your standards to the standards of your fellow critics.

Writing an Autobiographical Narrative

Jesse Owens placing first for the United States in the 200-meter run at the 1936 Olympics, held in Munich, Austria
UPI/Bettmann Newsphotos

Writing an Autobiographical Narrative

D o you remember the last time you looked through an old family photo album? The pictures of your family's past probably reminded you of events and feelings that you had forgotten.

If you had a friend with you as you flipped through the album, you probably pointed out the snapshots that had a special meaning for you. You identified the people in each picture and explained when and where it was taken. Perhaps you told your friend a few stories similar to this one:

This is my brother Ted at the Two Flags Amusement Park last year. See that long string of tickets he's holding? He vowed that he would go on every ride in the park at least once. But he only used one of those tickets. The first ride we went on, the Ferris wheel, got stuck. Here's a shot of the wheel before we got on. We were swinging in one of those cars way at the top for two and a half hours! Was Ted ever disgusted —but at least he got all his money back.

When you tell the story behind one of the photos in your album, you are creating an *autobiographical narrative.* A narrative is a story, and it is autobiographical when it is based on the life of the person telling it.

In this unit, you are going to write an autobiographical narrative, a story about an event in your own life. What kind of event? It doesn't matter, just so it was important enough to you to leave a vivid memory in your mind.

Here is a short passage from "400 Mulvaney Street," an autobiographical narrative by Nikki Giovanni (*Scope English Anthology,* Level Four). It describes a visit with her grandmother after her grandfather's death. You can see that this visit made a strong impression on her.

We got up early Saturday morning, and Grandmother made fried chicken for us. Nobody said we were leaving, but we were. We walked down the hill to the car. We kissed. I looked at Grandmother standing there so bravely trying not to think what I was trying not to feel. I got in on the driver's side and looked at her standing there in her plaid apron and her hair in a bun, her feet hanging loosely out of her slippers. She was 63 years old. She was waving goodbye, and for the first time having to go into 400 Mulvaney Street without John Browne Watson.

. . . .

It is easy to understand why this event impressed the author deeply. The sight of her widowed grandmother facing loneliness so bravely made her heart ache with pity. Because the memory was meaningful to her, she was able to make it meaningful for her readers.

P O I N T S   T O   R E M E M B E R

▷ An autobiographical narrative tells about the writer's life.
▷ The incident you describe should be meaningful to you.

Set Your Goal

How do you sift through all the events in your life to come up with the right topic for an autobiographical narrative? To get an idea where to start looking, read the following list.

a difficult choice

an enemy who turns out to be a friend

a funny incident

an embarrassing situation

a dangerous situation

an incident that happened during a vacation

accepting disappointment

a news event that you will never forget

something that changed your life

You can also look through the journal you kept in Unit Four for ideas, or you can brainstorm. To brainstorm, relax and let your mind wander back over the events in your life. Let one thought lead to another. Don't evaluate the thoughts as you have them. Wait until later to do that. Just write down all the incidents and experiences that occur to you.

If an incident didn't mean much to you, it probably wouldn't interest your reader. For instance, read the following paragraph that Joanna wrote.

Last Saturday, my friend Christine came over to my house. We talked about what had happened in school that week. Then my grandmother drove us to our dancing lesson. My mother picked us up afterwards. When we got home, I made some popcorn, and we watched an old movie on TV.

Joanna's afternoon may have been enjoyable, but it was not especially meaningful. It makes pretty dull reading. To see whether a topic has meaning for you, answer the following questions about it.

1. Do you have strong feelings about the incident?

2. Did you learn something about yourself or others?

3. Did the incident lead to an important change in your life?

4. Did the incident have an unexpected result?

Exercise One　Using the suggestions on page 188, write down three incidents or experiences in your life that could be the basis of an autobiographical narrative.

Following is the list of possible topics that Seth wrote.

1. The day my brother got lost in the woods

2. The time I accused my best friend of taking my radio when I had misplaced it

3. The time our car ran out of gas in the Sonoran Desert

Plot

Now you have three ideas for an autobiographical narrative. You've made sure that the incidents are important to you. But there's more to a good story than an interesting topic. You need a plot, to transform a series of events into a story. A plot consists of four basic elements: *action, conflict, climax,* and *resolution.*

☐ The **action** is the events that take place in the story—what happens to the characters and what they do.

Let's look at Seth's first topic: the day his little brother got lost in the woods. Seth took his little brother Jonathan along on a picnic in the woods with his friends. While Seth and his friends played Frisbee in a small clearing, Jonathan wandered off. These events make up the action in Seth's story.

☐ A **conflict** is a clash, disagreement, or struggle between two opposing forces.

Here are some kinds of conflict that often occur in life and in stories:

1. **A conflict between people:** This might be an argument between you and a friend. Or it might be a conflict between you and your sister about who does which household chores.

2. **A conflict within a person:** If you notice that your teacher has accidentally left a copy of next week's test on her desk, you may feel a few moments of inner conflict, wanting to look at the test but feeling it would be wrong to do so.

3. **A conflict between a person and nature:** If you are caught in a blizzard in the middle of nowhere, you are in conflict with the forces of nature.

4. **A conflict between a person and society:** If you fight for a cause that most people disagree with, you are in conflict with society.

In Seth's story, he is in conflict with nature—the vastness of the woods that hide Jonathan. He is also in conflict with Jonathan, who created the problem by wandering off.

☐ The action and conflict in a narrative eventually reach a **climax.** The climax of a story is the point at which the most important event occurs, or a crucial decision is made. The climax is usually the turning point in the story and decides its outcome.

Finding Jonathan is the climax of Seth's narrative.

☐ The **resolution** of a story shows how the conflict was settled and how things turned out for the characters.

Exercise Two Examine the list you made in Exercise One. Copy each topic on a separate piece of paper. Below each one, write the major events that make up its action, conflict, climax, and resolution.

Following is an example taken from Seth's notes.

Action: The family's car ran out of gas while we were crossing the Sonoran Desert. My father and uncle disagreed about whether to wait for help or walk ahead to try to find a gas station. My uncle set out on foot with a tin can in his hand.

Conflict: Larger conflict between us and nature: broiling sun, freezing night to come. Smaller conflict between uncle and father.

Climax: Three hours later, a passing truck driver picked us up. We found my uncle ten miles down the road, ready to collapse.

Resolution: My uncle received medical attention and was fine the next day. The gas station manager in town gave my father a ride back to the car with some gas.

Exercise Three Choose the incident you feel has the best plot elements. This will be the basis of your autobiographical narrative.

Your choice does not have to be highly dramatic. As long as it contains some kind of conflict or problem—and as long as it's interesting and meaningful to you—it's a good topic.

P O I N T S   T O   R E M E M B E R

▷ An autobiographical narrative must have a plot.

▷ A plot consists of action, a conflict, a climax, and a resolution.

▷ Action consists of the events that take place and what the characters do.

▷ The conflict is a struggle between two opposing forces.

▷ The climax is the turning point in the story.

▷ The resolution of a story shows how everything worked out for its characters.

Make a Plan

A. Gather Ideas

You have chosen a topic for your autobiographical narrative and outlined its plot. Now it is time to focus on the particular events of the story.

Exercise Four   List all the events that took place in your story. Don't worry about the order in which they happened, or whether each event you jot down is important to the story. You can add or subtract events later, when you put them in order.

Once you have written down every event you can think of, reread your list. Put one star next to the event that marks the beginning of the conflict. Then put two stars next to the event that is the climax of your story.

Following is Seth's list of events. He put one star next to the third event, and two next to the eighth event.

1. I took my brother Jonathan along on a picnic in the woods with my friends.
2. Around five o'clock, we started gathering up everything to leave.
3. Suddenly I realized that Jonathan was nowhere to be seen.*
4. Ate sandwiches, cookies, etc., threw Frisbees.
5. Jonathan wandered through the trees.
6. I organized my friends into three search parties and sent each group in a different direction.
7. Vowed I'd never let Jonathan out of my sight on an outing again.
8. After half an hour of searching, Paula and Greg found Jonathan sitting behind some big rocks eating raisins.**
9. Jonathan explained that he'd gone there to be alone so that he wouldn't have to share his raisins.

Characters

The people in a story are called the characters. Part of your job as an author is to make your characters as lifelike as possible. Here are some questions that will help you think of details to use in describing characters.

1. What do your characters look like? Are they young, old, short, tall, bald, overweight, beautiful, or frightening? Do they have any interesting or unusual physical features?

2. What do they wear? Do they wear overalls, a fur coat, a business suit, a leather jacket, or an evening gown?

3. How do the characters speak? Are some voices high and squeaky and others low and rumbling? Does anyone stutter? Does someone have an accent?

4. How do they behave? Are they nervous, calm, full of energy, or tired? Are some lazy and others hardworking?

5. What habits do they have? Do they yawn, snap, kick the ground, pull on their hair, or fold their arms? Do they stand, sit, or walk in special ways?

You don't have to answer each of these questions for all the characters in your story. Only the most important people should be fully described. Too many details can slow down the flow of the story.

A skillful writer chooses the details that are the most interesting, important, or typical. A few strong, meaningful details will impress the reader more vividly than a long list of unimportant ones.

Exercise Five   On a clean sheet of paper, write the names of two or three main characters you want to include in your autobiographical narrative. Then write six to eight details to describe each character.

Setting

Another element of a story is the setting—the place or places where the events occur. The setting can help establish the mood of a story.

Setting is a more important element in some stories than in others. It forms the very basis of a story about running out of gas in the desert. It might matter very little, however, in a story that takes place entirely in one room.

As you learned in Unit Four, a good description uses sensory details—those that appeal to sight, smell, hearing, taste, and touch. When you describe the setting in your autobiographical narrative, you are recreating it from memory. So try to recall exactly the things that impressed you about the setting the first time you saw it.

Exercise Six   Each of the following sentences could begin a description of a story's setting. Choose two of them. Then use your imagination to picture the settings. For each one you choose, list six to eight details that could be included in a description of that setting. Try to appeal to all the five senses. After each detail, write the sense to which it appeals.

1. The auditorium was crowded with people eager to see and hear the greatest rock concert ever held in our town.
2. Watching the thunderstorm from a house overlooking a lake in the mountains was a breathtaking experience.
3. I hate shopping at the supermarket on a busy Saturday morning!
4. The abandoned farmhouse was a spooky place.
5. It was a hot, humid afternoon in August when the two baseball teams met on our school field to fight for the championship.

Exercise Seven   Think about the incident you chose in Exercise Three. Try to remember its setting as clearly as you can. List six to eight details to describe the setting. Use as many sensory details as possible.

Following is Seth's list.

1. muffled footsteps
2. sweet-smelling pine needles
3. bird darting through treetops
4. stillness broken by conversation
5. shadows growing longer
6. snapping branches

B. Organize Ideas

A good story has a beginning, a middle, and an end. In the beginning, the scene is set, the characters are introduced, and the nature of the conflict is explained. In the middle of the story, the conflict deepens and the action builds to a climax. At the end, the conflict is settled and the story is resolved.

Now that you have gathered ideas about the events that took place, about the setting, and about the characters, it is time to put those ideas in order.

The order in which a series of events actually happened is called *chronological order*. Writing a plot outline will help you organize the events of a story in chronological order.

Exercise Eight   Rewrite the events you listed in Exercise Four in the order in which they occurred, leaving at least one line of space between items. If you think of other things that should be added, put them in. Eliminate any items you don't think are important enough. Make sure you transfer the stars from your previous list to this one.

Then, under each appropriate event, make notes to indicate where you should introduce your characters and where you should discuss the setting.

Following is Seth's plot outline for his autobiographical narrative. The events are numbered according to the order in which they appeared in Seth's first list, so you can see how he moved them around.

1. I took my brother Jonathan along on a picnic in the woods with my friends. (Describe woods, quiet, pine needles, sunlight streaming through trees, birds.)

4. We ate sandwiches, cookies, and apples, and threw Frisbees while Jonathan wandered through the trees. (Jonathan always able to amuse himself.)

2. Around five o'clock, we started gathering everything to leave.

3. Suddenly I realized that Jonathan was nowhere to be seen. (woods now scary)*

6. I organized my friends into three search parties and sent each group in a separate direction.

8. After half an hour of searching, Paula and Greg found Jonathan sitting behind some big rocks, eating raisins.**

9. Jonathan explained that he'd gone there to be alone so that he wouldn't have to share his raisins.

Notice that Seth combined event 5 (*Jonathan wandered through the trees*) with event 4. He thought this would kep the reader from guessing too soon what was going to happen. He left out event 7.

Write the First Draft

You have outlined the plot of your autobiographical narrative and listed details describing the setting and the characters. Having done all this groundwork, you will probably find writing the first draft easier than you expected.

Dialogue

Before you put pencil to paper, however, there is another important ingredient of a good story that you should be aware of: *dialogue*. Dialogue is the exact words used in conversation between two or more people in a story. Here are some tips for writing dialogue:

1. Use tags—*he said, she asked, Bette declared*, and so on—to let the reader know who is speaking.

2. Start a new paragraph each time a new speaker begins to speak.

3. Vary the wording of the tags, as well as their placement. The following example shows that well-placed tags with varied wording can add a lot to a story.

   Petunia complained, "There's a fly in my soup."

   "I see it," said the waitress.

   "Well," demanded Petunia, "what's it doing there?"

   "The backstroke, I believe," the waitress answered.

4. If your tag is in the middle of a sentence of dialogue, be sure that the sentence is broken in a place that sounds natural. Following is an example of a poorly placed tag.

   "Here, take," screamed Petunia, "back the soup!"

Revised as you see below, the same sentence sounds much better. The words are the same as before, but the tag has been moved.

   "Here," screamed Petunia, "take back the soup!"

5. Make sure your dialogue sounds realistic. Test it by reading it aloud to yourself or a friend.

6. Try to make each line of dialogue fit the character who is speaking. If one of your characters is your five-year-old brother, for example, he should speak more childishly than a thirty-year-old bus driver.

Exercise Nine Look at the plot outline you made in Exercise Eight. Note one or more places in the outline where dialogue could appear.

Then, on a separate piece of paper, write at least five lines of dialogue that the characters actually spoke or could have spoken. Add tags, to make sure that the reader can tell who is speaking.

Write a Good Beginning

In addition to dialogue, an appealing beginning is important to a good narrative. Think about exactly how you will begin. Your narrative should capture your readers' interest from the outset—or they might not read more than a few sentences.

Seth at first decided to open his story with the following sentence, which simply states, in general terms, what the story is about.

> I took my brother Jonathan along on a picnic in the woods with my friends.

Compare Seth's first attempt with the one below. Which makes you want to read more?

> "I wish I'd see some lions and some tigers in these woods!" Jonathan declared in a loud voice. "And some elephants," he said. He trotted after me and my friends as we looked for a picnic spot. I had had to bring him along because our mother was visiting somebody in the hospital.

Both of Seth's beginnings give the same information, but the second one offers something extra: a vivid image of Jonathan, the main character. The reader can tell right away that Jonathan wants to do some exploring.

There are many ways to begin a story, and no specific rules on the best way to do so. If the setting of your story is particularly important for some reason, you might want to start with a description of it. Or you might prefer to begin by introducing one of your main characters. You could show the character doing something that is important to the plot.

Exercise Ten   Read over your plot outline. Then write at least three possible openings for your autobiographical narrative. After you have finished, look them over and choose the one you like the best.

Exercise Eleven   Now you are ready to write the first draft of your narrative. It should be two to four pages in length.

Remember that the point of a first draft is to get all your ideas down on paper. Don't worry about small mistakes or finishing touches now. You will have a chance to go back and correct your draft in the next step. As you work, refer to your plot outline.

Here is Seth's first draft:

"I wish I'd see some lions and some tigers in these woods!" Jonathan declared in a loud voice. "And some elephants," he said. He trotted after me and my friends as we looked for a picnic spot. I had had to bring him along because our mother was visiting somebody in the hospital.

Jonathan was the noisyest thing in the woods that afternoon. The rest of us kept our voices low. That was maybe so as to hear the birds singing and the pine trees sighing. Our feet were silent. They were muffled by the pine needles on the ground.

When we reached a small clearing, we laid out the blankets and ate our lunch. We had about a mountain of sandwiches, cookies, apples. Also a couple of gallons of homemade lemonaid. After lunch, some people threw Frisbees. Others sat and suned and talked. Jonathan wandered in and out of the woods. Probly looking for lions, tigers, and elephants.

We noticed our longer shadows, so I checked my watch. It was allmost five o'clock—time to start back. As we gathered the blankets and baskets, I sudenly saw Jonathan was nowhere to be seen. We all started calling him, but he didn't answer. The woods had been so peaceful. Now they seemed to threaten.

I suggested we organize into search parties. We divided into three groups and each started out in three different direction.

I had been so worried that Jonathan would spoil my day! I didn't want to waste my time watching him. And Jonathan was so good at amusing himself it was easy to forget all about him. Now he could be wondering around in circels, lost, crying. Or maybe he fell and hurt himself. My visions ran wild as we tramped thru the woods, calling Jonathan's name.

Then I heard a loud yell. Paula and Greg found Jonathan. He was sitting behind some big rocks, eating raisins.

"Why did you run away?" I asked. "Didn't you know we'd be worried?" I was shaking all over.

"I was afraid you big kids would want some of my raisins," Jonathan said. "I wanted them all myself, so I desided to hide here and eat them."

I opened my mouth to say "You selfish little pest"—but then I thought better of it. I was the one who was selfish.

"Okay big eater," I said. "Lets see how fast you can walk. Well have to hurry to get home before dark."

When you have finished the first draft of your autobiographical narrative, put it away for a while. Giving yourself time between writing and revising will help you see where your work needs improvement.

When you do look at your draft again, you might try reading it aloud to yourself. This will help you hear mistakes that you would have overlooked in a silent reading.

Exercise Twelve   Use the following checklist in revising your story. If the answer to any of the questions is "no," revise your narrative until the answer is "yes."

1. Is your narrative a story—not just a list of events? Does it have a beginning, a middle, and an end?
2. Does it contain a conflict, a climax, and a resolution?
3. Are the events told in chronological order?
4. Is it easy for the reader to follow what happens?
5. Have you used sensory details to describe the story's setting?
6. Have you used sensory details to help describe the important characters?
7. Have you used tags properly in your lines of dialogue?
8. Does the dialogue sound realistic? Does each new speaker begin a new paragraph?

Here is Seth's revised narrative:

"I wish I'd see some lions and some tigers in these woods!"

Jonathan declared in a loud voice. "And some elephants," he ~~said.~~ *added,*

~~He trotted~~ *trotting* after me and my friends as we looked for a *good* picnic spot. I

had had to bring him along because our mother was visiting

somebody in the hospital.

Jonathan was the noisiest thing in the woods that afternoon.

The rest of us kept our voices low, ~~That was maybe so as~~ ,perhaps because we wanted to hear the birds singing and the pine trees sighing in the breeze. Our feet were ~~(footsteps)~~ almost silent, ~~They were~~ muffled by the pine needles on the ground.

When we reached a small clearing, we laid out the blankets and ate our lunch. We had ~~about a~~ small mountain of sandwiches, cookies, and apples, ~~Also~~ and a couple of gallons of homemade lemon ade. After lunch, some people threw Frisbees, while ~~Others~~ others sat and sun ned themselves and talked. Jonathan wandered in and out of the woods, ~~Probly~~ probably looking for lions, tigers, and elephants.

After a while we ~~We~~ noticed that our ~~longer~~ shadows had grown longer, so I checked my watch. It was almost five o'clock—time to start back. As we gathered the blankets and baskets, I sudd enly ~~saw~~ realized that Jonathan was nowhere to be seen. We all started calling him, but he didn't answer. The woods had been ,which seemed so peaceful, ~~Now they~~ seemed ~~to~~ threaten ing. I suggested that we organize into search parties. We divided into three groups and each started out in ~~three~~ a different direction.

I had been so worried that Jonathan would spoil my day! I didn't want to waste my time watching him. And Jonathan was so good at amusing himself that it was easy to forget all about him. ~~Now he~~ "A"

¶ I was thoroughly scared. Jonathan—

wandering around in circle̸s, lost, ~~and~~ crying. Or maybe he ~~fell~~ *had fallen* and hurt

himself. My ~~visions~~ *imagination* ran wild as we tramped ~~thru~~ *through* the woods, calling

Jonathan's name.

Then I heard a loud yell. Paula and Greg *had* found Jonathan. He was

sitting behind some big rocks, eating raisins.

"Why did you run away?" I ~~asked.~~ *demanded when I reached the spot.* "Didn't you know we'd be

worried?" I was shaking all over, *with anger and relief.*

"I was afraid you big kids would want some of my raisins,"

Jonathan said. "I wanted them all myself, so I de̸cided to hide here

and eat them."

I opened my mouth to say, "You selfish little pest"—but then I

thought better of it. I was the one who was selfish. *(move "A" here)*

"Okay, big eater," I said. "Let's see ~~how fast you can~~ walk. *if you're also a* We̸'ll *ero*

have to hurry to get home before dark."

Proofread and Edit

You have made sure that your plot is easy to follow, that your sentences are clear and well-written, and that your characters are described completely. It's now time to edit and proofread your work. No matter how careful you are in revising, little mistakes often remain.

As you proofread, make sure that you have used correct punctuation, capitalization, and spelling. Also make sure you haven't used any sentence fragments.

Exercise Thirteen Proofread your autobiographical narrative. Then copy it neatly on a clean piece of paper and proofread it one last time.

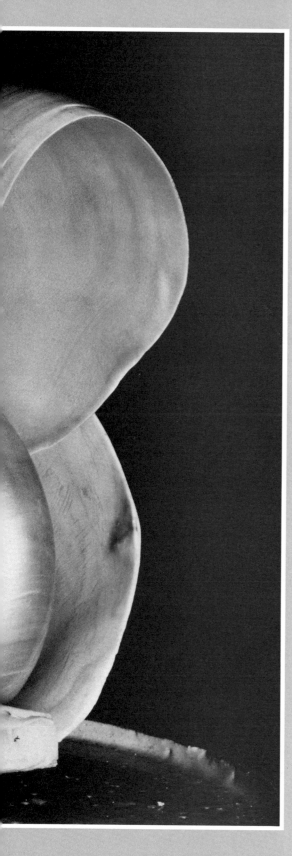

Improving Your Writing Style

Nautilus shells, 1927
Edward Weston
Arizona Board of Regents, Center for Creative Photography,
University of Arizona, Tucson

Improving Your Writing Style

Teach the same dance step to four different people, and each will do it in his or her own style. Ask several people to introduce themselves at a party, and each will do it in his or her own style.

Everyone has a personal style. But some people seem to have "more style" than others. For example, a famous singer not only has a well-trained voice but presents the song in a special way. Many of the stars we admire have this kind of style. It is the extra polish that grows out of knowledge, practice, and skill.

With practice, you can make your writing reflect your personal style. This is possible because most ideas can be expressed in several different ways. As you practice writing, you become more aware of what these different ways are. Your personality and your purpose in writing cause you to choose one way out of all the possible ways. The choices you make are your personal style.

To see how much difference writing style can make, read the following two paragraphs about long-distance swimming. The first paragraph is taken from "Mind Over Water" (*Scope English Anthology*, Level Four), by Diana Nyad, the famous marathon swimmer. The second paragraph contains the same ideas expressed in a different way.

MODEL......................................

At breakfast I have five or six raw eggs, a lot of cereal, toast and jam, and juice. For my feedings during the race from the boat, I drink a hot powdered liquid. It provides me with 1,300 calories and more protein per tablespoon than a four-ounce steak. It gets my blood sugar back up. In a race, my blood sugar drops below level in three minutes. A cup of this stuff every hour barely helps. Before the hour's up, my sugar is way down. I can feel it. I feel low. But if my protein level stays high, I'm not really in trouble.

. . . .

My meals are carefully planned to keep both my protein level and my blood sugar high. Of the two, the protein level is the more important. At breakfast before a race I eat five or six raw eggs, a large quantity of cereal, toast and jam, and juice. During the race I have one feeding every hour from the boat. It consists of one cup of a hot liquid made from a powdered concentrate, and it provides me with 1,300 calories and more protein per tablespoon than a four-ounce steak. Besides giving me vital protein, this concoction raises my blood sugar and gives me a psychological lift. But the psychological effect does not last long. In a race, my blood sugar drops below the normal level in three minutes. A cup of this liquid food once an hour helps only temporarily. Before the hour is up, my sugar is down again, and I feel low-spirited. However, if my protein level remains high, I am able to continue swimming.

As you probably noticed, the second paragraph is more formal than the first. Diana Nyad's original paragraph sounds relaxed and natural. She uses informal expressions, such as "a lot of cereal" and "this stuff." In the second version, these expressions have been changed to "a large quantity of cereal" and "this liquid food."

Diana Nyad also uses fairly short sentences in her paragraph. The second paragraph has longer, more complicated sentences. And the sentences are carefully arranged in a logical sequence. As a result, the second paragraph sounds almost like a textbook, whereas the first sounds like a friendly talk.

In this unit you will learn how you can vary your writing style to suit whatever purpose you have in mind. You will practice choosing words with just the right shade of meaning. And you will practice writing sentences of different lengths and structures.

P O I N T S   T O   R E M E M B E R

▷ There are many different ways to express the same idea.

▷ When you express an idea, you choose one way out of all the ways you know.

▷ The words you choose and the length and structure of your sentences are important elements of your writing style.

Set Your Goal

Choose a Topic

In this unit, what you say will be less important than how you say it. (Usually it's the other way around.) You will be trying out different ways of expressing the same thoughts, and almost any thoughts will serve for your experiments. This means that you should choose a topic that you won't have to think about very much. To find such a topic, you might try to recall a conversation you had recently with a friend. What did you talk about? Or, remember the last time someone asked you what you'd been doing lately. What experiences did you tell about?

It is especially important in this unit to choose a topic that interests you. You may be doing more rewriting than you usually do, and you will find the task more satisfying if you really like your topic.

Exercise One   Choose a topic about which you can easily write several paragraphs. Probably the easiest topic you could choose would be one that concerns your own life. You might write about a friend, a member of your family, or an activity that you frequently take part in (for example, singing, playing a musical instrument, dancing, a sport, a hobby, etc.). Your opinion on a controversial issue would probably *not* be a good topic because you would have to take time to develop logical arguments to support it. The following list may help you think of something interesting.

1.   what you did on your best day ever
2.   what you look for in a best friend
3.   what you would like to be doing in ten years
4.   something you are proud of
5.   something you wish you had done differently
6.   how you could improve things for those around you
7.   how you like to spend your leisure time
8.   a movie or TV show that you enjoyed
9.   a personal experience that you'd like to tell about

Make a Plan

A. Gather Ideas

If you chose a simple and familiar topic in Exercise One, gathering ideas on it should be easy. In fact, a few minutes of brainstorming may give you more ideas than you can use. However, don't stop writing your ideas down just because the list is getting long. It's good to have a large number of ideas to choose from.

If your ideas don't flow as fast as you'd like, you might try scheduling two sessions for gathering ideas. If you do, allow some time to pass between sessions. During that time, some good ideas may come to mind without any special effort on your part.

Exercise Two　　Jot down as many ideas as you can think of about your topic. You can write your ideas in the form of single words, phrases, or complete sentences. If possible, have two brainstorming sessions at least several hours apart, and make two separate lists of ideas. At the end of the first session, put your list aside, and do not reread it until after you finish your second list. Starting afresh in the second session may help you approach your topic from a different angle.

Donna decided to write about her idea of a best friend. Here are the notes she made in two separate brainstorming sessions.

First Session

a good listener

likes what you like

haven't had best friend since grade school

A best friend understands your feelings without being told.

fun to be with

sticks by you when you're in trouble

can keep a secret

always available for heart-to-heart talk

puts up with your faults

shouldn't pick friends just because of what they can do for you

Second Session

Friendship is a two-way street.

A best friend doesn't criticize or judge you.

doesn't try to change you

treats you as an equal

doesn't boss you around

helps you even when trouble is your own fault

has talents you don't have and vice versa

trusts you with his/her thoughts and secrets

B. Organize Ideas

If you had two brainstorming sessions for gathering ideas, you now have two lists. Your next step is to divide the ideas in the first list into groups. All the items in each group should relate to the same main idea. The main idea in each group will be a subtopic, or division, of the overall topic of your paper.

After you have divided your first list of ideas into subtopics, look at your second list (if you made one). Do any of the ideas on this list fit into the subtopics in your first list? If so, add them to the first list in the appropriate places. Then study the remaining ideas on the second list and group them into subtopics.

The example below shows how Donna grouped the ideas in her two lists. Notice that she numbered the groups and wrote each group's subtopic after its number. The result is not an outline, however. The numbers only reflect the order of the ideas in Donna's original lists.

First List

1. A best friend is someone you can talk to.

    is a good listener

    can keep a secret

    always available for heart-to-heart talk

2. A best friend shares your tastes and interests.

    likes what you like

    understands your feelings without being told

    fun to be with

3. I haven't had a best friend since grade school.

4. A best friend is loyal.

    sticks by you when you're in trouble

    puts up with your faults

    doesn't criticize or judge you

    doesn't try to change you

    helps you even when trouble is your own fault

5. You shouldn't pick best friend because of what he/she can do for you (get you into "in" crowd, etc.).

Second List

6. Friendship is a two-way street.

    treats you as an equal

    doesn't boss you around

    has talents you don't have and vice versa

    trusts you with his/her thoughts and secrets

Donna decided that three of the ideas in her second list belonged in group 4 of her first list. The remaining ideas clustered around a new subtopic: "Friendship is a two-way street." Evidently, Donna did some fresh thinking about friendship during the break between her two brainstorming sessions.

Exercise Three   Look over the ideas that you gathered in Exercise Two. Divide them into related groups, and write the main idea, or subtopic, of each group. Use Donna's list of subtopics as a model.

Donna decided to go one step further in organizing her ideas. She made a rough outline of her paper, based on her list of subtopics. She left out quite a few of the items on her original lists, and she also changed the order of some items.

1.   A best friend shares your tastes and interests.

     fun to be with

     likes what you like

2. A best friend is someone you can talk to.

    is a good listener

    can keep a secret

    does not criticize you when you confess something

3. A best friend is loyal.

    sticks by you

    helps you even when problem is your own fault

4. Friendship is a two-way street.

    treats you as equal

    respects your talents and good qualities

    doesn't boss you around

Exercise Four   Make a rough outline of your paper. You can base the outline on the work you did in Exercise Three.

C. Develop Word and Sentence Power

In the other composition units of this book, you go directly from organizing your ideas to writing the first draft of your paper (Step Three). In this unit, however, you are asked to pause and do some special exercises. These exercises focus on two important elements of writing style: word choice and sentence structure.

Word Choice

Perhaps you have noticed that general words often come to mind more easily than specific words. For example, if your clothing for this weekend's hiking trip includes a "garment for the upper body," you might refer to it as a *jacket.* That is probably the first word you would think of. It would probably take a little extra effort to think of a more specific word, such as *mackinaw, windbreaker,* or *parka.* It would be worth the effort, however, because specific words make your statements clearer and more interesting.

The following sentence illustrates this point.

The person entered the room and sat on a seat.

Whatever pictures come into your mind as you read this sentence, they are probably quite different from the ones your neighbor imagines. The words don't give enough information to enable a reader to form a vivid, detailed mental image. Therefore, each reader makes up a different picture out of images stored in his or her memory.

Here is another description of the same event:

The dancer skipped into the rehearsal studio and perched on the edge of a folding metal chair.

This sentence creates a more detailed picture because it uses words with more specific meanings. Therefore, readers are more likely to imagine the scene the way the writer does. As a writer, you can see the advantage in using specific words rather than general ones. Specific words give you more control over the reactions of your reader.

Exercise Five   On a sheet of paper, write the ten sets of words and phrases that follow. Arrange each set so that the most general term is first and the most specific term is last.

EXAMPLE: dessert, chocolate pie, food

food, dessert, chocolate pie

1. Navajo, Native Americans, people
2. S.S. *Titanic*, ship, ocean liner
3. painting, *Mona Lisa*, picture
4. performer, musician, tuba player
5. Empire State Building, building, skyscraper
6. novel, book, *Great Expectations*
7. pants, jeans, clothing
8. body of water, Mississippi River, river
9. milk, liquid, beverage
10. food processor, machine, kitchen appliance

Exercise Six   Rewrite each of the sentences below, replacing the vague, general words with words that are more specific. You may also add other words to make the picture clearer.

EXAMPLE: The animal went into a group of trees.

The tiger slunk into the dark, tangled forest.

1. Has the visitor seen our pet?
2. A child found something under a piece of furniture.

3. We spent time on an interesting hobby.
4. Have you seen him in his new clothes?
5. Something moved in the water.
6. She has vegetables and flowers in the backyard.
7. We watched television very late last night.
8. He hurt himself when he fell in the driveway.
9. One person watched the animal and made notes in a book.
10. Many people left the vehicle.

Connotation

As you know, synonyms are words that have the same general meaning but differ in their specific meanings. For example, a mackinaw and a windbreaker are both jackets, but a mackinaw is usually made of heavy wool, whereas a windbreaker is usually made of a light synthetic material. These two synonyms differ in *denotation*—that is, they differ in their precise dictionary definitions.

Synonyms can also differ in *connotation*. A word's connotation is the feelings that it arouses in the reader's or listener's mind. A word may have positive or negative connotations. For example, a person who works the land might be called a *farmer* or a *peasant*. But the word *peasant* has negative connotations. We associate it with the poorest, least educated members of society in undeveloped countries. The word *farmer*, on the other hand, has positive connotations. We think of farmers as independent, knowledgeable people who often own the land they cultivate.

Here is another example: Suppose you were writing about a group of revolutionaries. If you wanted to indicate approval, you might call them *freedom fighters*. If you wanted to indicate disapproval, you might call them *terrorists*. If you wanted to remain neutral, you could call them *revolutionaries, rebels,* or perhaps *guerrillas.* However, the word *guerrilla* is less "neutral" than the others because it calls to mind images of violence.

Exercise Seven   Write the following sets of words on your paper. Arrange each set so that the word with the most favorable connotation is first and the one with the least favorable connotation is last.

EXAMPLE: cheap, reasonable, inexpensive

reasonable, inexpensive, cheap

1. cowardly, cautious, timid
2. pompous, proud, dignified
3. smart, intelligent, sly
4. stubborn, mulish, firm
5. slow, sluggish, methodical
6. elderly, old, senior citizen
7. bookworm, student, scholar
8. information, slander, gossip

9. careless, relaxed, unconcerned

10. emotional, touchy, sensitive

Exercise Eight   Choose three pairs of words from Exercise Seven. For each word, write a separate sentence in which you use the word appropriately. Keep both the denotation and connotation of the word in mind. If you wish, you may change the form of the word to make it into another part of speech. For example, instead of *cautious,* you might use *cautiously* or *caution.*

EXAMPLE: cautious, cowardly

He walked toward the bull cautiously, staying close to the fence.

I was such a coward that I wouldn't go near the bull, even though there was a fence between us.

Sentence Style

The kinds of sentences you use and the order in which you arrange them determine the way your writing sounds. To see how sentence style affects rhythm and "tune," read the following two passages aloud. Both tell about one event in "The Enemy," by Pearl S. Buck (*Scope English Anthology,* Level Four). The second comes directly from the story. The first is an altered version that sounds quite different.

In the morning all the servants left. They had their belongings tied in large, square cotton kerchiefs. Hana got up and saw that nothing was done. The house was not cleaned. The food was not prepared. She knew what that meant. She was upset. In fact, she was terrified. But she was too proud to show it. She was the mistress of the house.

M O D E L ·

In the morning the servants left together, their belongings tied in large, square cotton kerchiefs. When Hana got up in the morning nothing was done. The house was not cleaned and the food not prepared. She knew what that meant. She was upset and even terrified, but her pride as a mistress would not allow her to show it.

· ·

Vary Sentence Structure

The most common English sentence pattern is this one:

John peeled the apple.

In this pattern the subject (*John*) comes first, the verb (*peeled*) comes next, and the complement (in this case a direct object, *the apple*) comes last. As you can see, it is a very simple pattern. Yet, even though you use it over and over in everything you write, the result does not have to be dull. You can add to this basic pattern to make a multitude of different kinds of sentences. Following are just a few examples.

After he had washed it carefully, John peeled the apple.

Noticing a wormhole in the apple, John decided to peel and core it.

John leaned his elbows on his knees and slowly peeled the apple.

The peel, hanging down in one long, thin spiral, almost reached the floor by the time John finished paring the apple.

The four longer sentences about John all follow the same basic pattern as the short original sentence. Yet they sound very different because words have been added to different parts of the basic pattern.

The following pairs of sentences illustrate another way to make a basic sentence pattern sound different. No new words are added; the words that are already there are simply rearranged to change the sentence opening. The first sentence in each pair starts with the subject. The second starts with a word, phrase, or clause that has been moved from elsewhere in the sentence.

Fran opened the door gently.

Gently Fran opened the door.

We saw the deer before they saw us.

Before the deer saw us, we saw them.

He braved the storm despite his illness.

Despite his illness he braved the storm.

The old man, remembering that happy day, smiled to himself.

Remembering that happy day, the old man smiled to himself.

Exercise Nine   The following sentences all begin with the subject. Rewrite them, changing the beginning of each sentence.

EXAMPLE: The girl rushed out the door, struggling into her coat as she ran.

Struggling into her coat as she ran, the girl rushed out the door.

1.   We gleefully told the class the news about the carnival.
2.   The game was canceled because of the snowstorm.
3.   A frog sat on a lily pad, patiently flicking its tongue.
4.   Marion waited in line for hours, hoping to buy tickets.
5.   We found a stray dog in the hall on the first day of school.

Avoid Choppy Sentences

Too many short sentences one after another make your writing sound "choppy." If two or more of these sentences are closely related to each other, you may be able to combine them.

One way to do this is to take part of one sentence and insert it into another sentence. Look at the following examples.

Kyle ran along the beach. Lani ran, too.

Kyle and Lani ran along the beach.

Kyle ran along the beach. Lani was close behind him.

Kyle ran along the beach, with Lani close behind him.

Another way to combine two short sentences is to put a connecting word between them. In the following example, the word *but* is used to join the sentences.

Rita was born in Albuquerque. Her parents moved to Boston the next year.

Rita was born in Albuquerque, but her parents moved to Boston the next year.

There are other words besides *but* that you can use to combine sentences in this way. They include *and, or, nor, yet,* and *so.*

They had saved a little money. They were not worried.
They had saved a little money, so they were not worried.

Still another way to combine two short sentences is to turn one of them into a sentence fragment and then join it to the other. Look at the following example.

The girl did a swan dive. She is my cousin.

The girl who did a swan dive is my cousin.

Notice that the writer turned the first of the original two sentences into a sentence fragment by removing the subject (*the girl*) and substituting the connecting word *who*. Then he inserted the fragment (*who did a swan dive*) into the other sentence. The list of other connecting words that you can use in this way includes *which, that, if, when, after, although, where,* and many more.

Here are three short sentences that can be combined to form a longer sentence. The connecting words *when* and *that* are used to turn two of the original sentences into fragments, so they can be joined to the third one.

Phil saw the long teeth. They came with the Dracula costume. He couldn't resist buying it.

When Phil saw the long teeth that came with the Dracula costume, he couldn't resist buying it.

You don't need to avoid short sentences completely, of course. In fact, a string of long sentences can be just as monotonous as a string of short ones. The idea is to have a variety of sentences in each paragraph, some long and some short.

Exercise Ten   Here are five sets of sentences. Combine each set to make one sentence. You will have to add, take out, or change some words.

1. There were many giant balloon figures in the Thanksgiving Day parade.
    Among them were Mickey Mouse, E.T., Rudolf the Red-nosed Reindeer, and Bullwinkle.
    There was also a friendly robot.

2. All scorpions can go for long periods without food.
    Some apparently never drink water.

3. Human beings cannot see ultraviolet light.
    They cannot see infrared light, either.
    Their bodies are affected by both, however.

4. We hung the wind chimes on the front porch.
   They were made of beautiful seashells.
   The seashells were from the Philippines.

5. People buy a lot of our special potato chips.
   These people are on a diet.
   Their diet must be salt-free.

Avoid Stringy Sentences

Reading a stringy sentence is like driving along a street that has no stop signs. You come to the end of a thought, but there's no period, so you roll right on to the next thought without a pause. Here is an example of a stringy sentence.

> The reason I think we should recycle our trash is that we are running out of places to dump it and burning it would pollute the air, and also our natural resources are getting scarcer all the time and we should try to conserve them.

In this example, the thoughts are loosely strung together with the word *and*. Since *and* doesn't mark a stop, it is hard for a reader to tell exactly where one statement ends and the next begins.

The best way to correct a stringy sentence is to break it apart and examine the pieces. Then you can decide how to put them back together. Here are the segments of thought that you would find in the sentence about recycling:

Main idea: We should recycle our trash.

Reasons why we should do this: We are running out of space to dump it. Burning it would pollute the air. Our natural resources are getting scarcer all the time.

These thoughts could be put together in many different ways. Here is one possibility:

There are two main reasons why we should recycle our trash. First, we have no other good way to get rid of it. We can't dump it much longer because we are running out of space. And, in my opinion, we shouldn't burn it because burning pollutes the air.

Second, we can no longer afford to throw away valuable materials after only one use. By constantly making new products of glass, paper, and metal, we are using up our natural resources too fast. We should recycle these materials as many times as possible.

In this version the thoughts are clearly separated from each other, and it is much easier to understand the writer's reasoning.

Exercise Eleven   Rewrite the following paragraph to correct the stringy sentences. The first sentence has been done for you as an example.

EXAMPLE: Many amazing stories have been told about lost animals that found their way home, and Lassie's story is one of the most amazing, and it's true, too.

Many stories have been told about lost animals that found their way home. Of these, the true story of Lassie is one of the most amazing.

Many amazing stories have been told about lost animals that found their way home, and Lassie's story is one of the most amazing, and it's true, too. Lassie was a mutt and not the famous film dog, and her owners left her behind on a small farm in Kentucky and they moved to California. Lassie didn't like her new owners, so she ran away and months later she appeared on the doorstep of her family's new home in Pacoma, California. Another dog, a collie named Bobbie, made a similar trip from Indiana to Oregon and that is two thousand miles, and he did it in the winter, and a lot of people gave him food and shelter along the way, so we know the story is true.

Write the First Draft

It's time now to write the first draft of the paper you planned in Exercises Two, Three, and Four. If several days have gone by since you did those exercises, you may have to spend a few minutes reviewing your lists of ideas and your rough outline.

"What about the exercises on writing style that I've done in the meantime?" you may ask. "Am I expected to apply what I've learned to my first draft?" The answer is "not necessarily." You should not make a conscious effort to improve your style while you are writing. If you did that, you might become tense. Later, when you revise your draft, you can make whatever changes are needed.

Here is the first draft of Donna's paper on the topic "My Idea of a Best Friend."

A best friend is fun to be with. He or she likes most of the things you like, so the two of you usually agree on how to spend your time together.

A best friend really listens to you and is sincerely interested in your thoughts and feelings. You can talk freely to your best friend because he or she knows how to keep a secret. You can have long, heart-to-heart conversations without fearing that your friend will turn around and tell everybody about your private business. You don't have to hide your faults and weaknesses, because your friend is not looking for a chance to criticize you or try to change you.

A best friend sticks by you through thick and thin. It doesn't matter whether your troubles come to you through no fault of your own or you cause them yourself. Your friend is always by your side, trying to help you.

A best friend knows that friendship is a two-way street. Each person looks on the other as an equal. Each one has talents or good qualities that the other respects. In some so-called friendships it seems as if one always leads while the other follows, or one is always belittling or putting down the other. I can't understand why the weak member of the pair puts up with such treatment. The strong, bossy one is certainly not my idea of a best friend.

Exercise Twelve   Review the outline that you made in Exercise Four. Since some time has probably passed since you made the outline, you may find that it doesn't reflect your latest thinking. If that is the case, bring your outline up to date. Then use it as a guide as you write the first draft of your composition.

In revising your composition, you will want to pay special attention to the elements of style that you have studied in this unit. These elements are listed in "Points to Remember," below.

POINTS TO REMEMBER

▷ When you have a choice between a general word and a specific word, use the specific word.

▷ When you have a choice between synonyms, consider both their denotations (dictionary definitions) and their connotations (pleasant or unpleasant associations).

▷ Try to avoid writing a series of sentences all of which start with the subject. If you do write a series of such sentences, rearrange the words in a few of them so that something other than the subject comes first.

▷ Vary the length of the sentences in a paragraph. Try to have some long, some short, and some of medium length.

Exercise Thirteen   Read the final version of Donna's composition, which appears on pages 226 and 227. Notice the differences between her final version and her first draft (page 223). Then revise your own paper, using the "Points to Remember" as a checklist.

Instead of just revising her first draft, Donna rewrote it. She did this because she had a sudden inspiration that changed her whole approach to the topic. She decided that her first draft was vague and unexciting because it kept referring to an abstract idea, "a best friend." Perhaps if she gave a name to this "best friend," she thought, the idea would seem more real. So she named her friend Betty Jean and began to imagine the good times the two of them would have. From then on, she felt as if she were describing a friendship that actually existed. So, with a little help from her best friend Betty Jean, Donna wrote a much livelier second draft.

Donna then revised her second draft to arrive at the final version of her paper.

My Idea of a Best Friend

To describe ~~My~~ idea of a best friend ~~is somebody like the imaginary one~~ *I am going to pretend* I have, *one named* ~~call her~~ Betty Jean. ~~I've only~~ known her *very long (just)* since I started writing this *haven't* paper, but there is ~~complete~~ *so much* sympathy between us, ~~It seems~~ *that I feel* as if we have been *best* friends for years.

Since we have similar interests and tastes, Betty Jean and I never have any trouble ~~deciding how we're going~~ *finding things to do* ~~to spend our time~~ together. ~~Some of the things~~ we both like to ~~do are to~~ *⊙We like to* *⊙We like to* go to basketball games and movies, bowl, rollerskate, swim, shop, sew *and* clothes, listen to records, and ~~playing~~ duets on ~~the~~ *her old upright* piano, *and* and lately *trying to* we've been ~~teaching~~ ourselves Yoga exercises out of a ~~library~~ book.

But what we like most of all is just *to* talking. Sometimes we will be in the middle of a conversation *when* ~~and~~ its time to go home, *so* I walk Betty Jean to her front door ~~and~~ then she walks me three quarters of the way *And all the time* ~~back~~ to my house ~~and~~ then I walk halfway back with her. ~~This is so~~ we *are* ~~can keep on~~ talking, *talking, talking* ~~as long as possible.~~

I feel safe talking to Betty Jean knows how to keep a secret. I can ~~safely~~ share my *inner* most *because she* ~~secret~~ thoughts with her. She asks questions and comments, but *makes* *she* ~~doesn't~~ *give me advice unless I ask for it* ~~try to force her advise on me, but~~ *do* if I ask for advise, she tries say something

hard to ~~be~~ helpful.

listen to

Some people like to ~~hear about~~ other people's secrets, but they

never share any of their own. My best friend is not like that. She tells me

and feelings as freely as I tell her mine. She even gives me

her thoughts, ~~I even get~~ a chance to advi~~z~~se her once in a while.

likes me

Betty Jean ~~thinks I'm just fine the way I am. I don't mean she thinks~~

accepts my   and

I'm perfect. She ~~knows I have~~ faults ~~but overlooks them. She~~ doesn't

If I get myself into trouble, she sticks by me.

criticize me or try to change me. She doesn't tell me ~~pleasant lies~~, but

make me   lie and   I'm right

she doesn't blame me, either. She just tries to help me, solve my problem.

an   I dreamed up. But

It's too bad that Betty Jean is only ~~my~~ idea ~~of a best friend and not a~~

I'm hoping that someday I'll meet a

real person, just like her.

Proofread

After you have revised your paper thoroughly, you will probably need to copy it onto a clean sheet of paper. Then you should proofread it carefully. It's a good idea to read it three times, once for grammatical errors, once for spelling errors, and once for punctuation errors.

Exercise Fourteen   Proofread the final version of your composition. You might like to ask a classmate to exchange papers with you, so each can have the benefit of a fresh pair of eyes. Correct any errors in your paper as neatly as possible. Look it over quickly one more time before you hand it in.

Preparing a Radio Talk

Boys listening to an adventure over a "wireless" (early radio), 1921
Culver Pictures, Inc.

Preparing a Radio Talk

I f you were to tune in to WLHS, Laurelton High School's own radio station, at 3:00 P.M. on a weekday, you would hear something like this:

"Good afternoon, and welcome to 'Sounding Off,' the radio show in which students air their opinions. This is your host, Howard Bender, coming to you live from our studio at Laurelton High School.

"Let me introduce our first guest. With me today is Elizabeth Quinlan, a sophomore, who is going to talk about something that concerns us all: exams. Elizabeth feels that the grades we get should depend less on exam scores and more on other academic activities. In a minute she'll tell us what activities she has in mind. She also thinks teachers should give more open-book exams, and she has some good arguments to back up that opinion. Here's Elizabeth Quinlan."

If you were in Elizabeth's shoes, about to deliver a talk over the radio, how would you feel? Nervous? Excited? You probably couldn't help being a little nervous. But there is a way to keep the tension under control: prepare your talk thoroughly in advance. The better prepared you are, the more relaxed you'll feel.

In this unit you are going to prepare the script for a short radio talk. You will follow the four steps of the writing process, but it will be important to remember that you will be delivering your composition out loud. Your audience will be listening rather than reading. This sort of verbal communication differs from writing in a number of ways.

For one thing, if they are confused by something you say, your audience can't return to a point you made earlier, as they could if they were reading a paper you wrote. Nor can they ask you to stop talking while they think about a statement you've just made. In addition, giving a radio speech is unique because you can't see your audience and they can't see you.

These special conditions affect the task of writing a radio talk. You'll need to use extra care in choosing a topic which you can explain in a brief time. You also need to organize your talk clearly and simply, since your audience will have only one chance to understand the points you make.

Finally, as you think about and prepare your talk, try to rely on simple and direct language. That way your listeners will grasp your meaning quickly and you won't run the risk of getting tongue-tied over a long word.

POINTS TO REMEMBER

▷ Prepare your radio talk thoroughly and well ahead of time, so you will be able to relax and enjoy the experience.

▷ You can follow the four steps of the writing process in preparing your radio talk.

▷ Pick a topic that can be explained clearly in a short time.

▷ Use simple, direct, conversational language in your radio talk.

▷ Remember that your audience has only one chance to understand what you tell them.

Set Your Goal

A. Choose a Topic

When you choose a topic, pick something which you know about already, or which appeals to you enough to learn about quickly. Your eagerness to communicate can be "transmitted" in a radio talk. Your listeners can hear and share your enthusiasm.

For a radio talk, simplicity is a key factor. Choose a topic which can be divided into two or, at the most, three subtopics. In other words, you should present no more than three main ideas in your two-minute talk. In her talk on exams and the grading system, for example, Elizabeth presented two subtopics. First, she discussed what was wrong with the present system. Second, she suggested ways to improve it.

Avoid choosing topics which need or require visual aids to be easily explained. Topics in which statistics play a crucial role should also be avoided. For instance, "How to Do Simple Algebra" is a poor topic for radio, as is "The Greatest Batting Averages of All Time." But "Babe Ruth's Greatest Home Runs" might do nicely.

Also to be avoided are topics which involve complex lines of reasoning or logical arguments. A simple radio talk on "James Madison: Architect of the Constitution" might be all right, but "Reexamining *The Federalist Papers*" sounds too complicated for radio.

Finally, be sure to choose a topic that you can cover in the time allowed. Whenever you are developing a radio talk, you will almost always have a time limit. In this unit, you'll be writing a talk to fill about two minutes, time enough to say only about 300-350 words.

Exercise One   People frequently give talks over the radio on topics that affect listeners' personal lives. From the list below, choose one topic that you would like to develop into a two-minute radio talk for the high school program known as "Sounding Off."

Topics:

1.   High School Students Can Help the Elderly
2.   How to Say "No"
3.   Why Teenagers Need to Exercise

4. Ten Ways Not to Get Your Driver's License
5. The Importance of Leisure
6. Dangers of Drinking and Driving
7. What It's Like to Be New in This School
8. Fighting Pollution in Your Hometown
9. A topic of your own choice

B. Define Your Purpose

You should have your purpose clearly in mind before you start writing your talk. You may intend to inform your listeners, to influence their opinions, feelings, or actions, or simply to entertain them. A clear statement of what you intend to accomplish will guide you as you select and organize your material.

Robert decided to develop a talk about how to say "no." He thought about several ways to state his purpose and decided on the following:

I want to convince others that saying "no" is important and that anyone can learn to do it.

While planning his talk, Robert used part of his statement of purpose as a working title: "Saying 'no' is something you can learn to do."

Exercise Two   Write a statement of purpose for your radio talk. You can use this statement as a temporary or working title.

Identify Your Audience

You have learned that when you write, it helps to identify your audience. When you prepare a radio talk, it is also important to tailor your material so that it will be appropriate to your listeners. Therefore, you want to consider the background of the people you expect to reach with your talk. You need to have some idea of how much they already know about your topic and how they feel about it.

In radio you usually hope to interest the widest possible group of listeners, even if some of them are not part of the specific audience you have in mind. For example, if you are talking to your school on "Freshman Dilemmas," you would want to write your talk in a way which interested not only freshmen but sophomores, juniors, seniors, and probably even teachers.

Exercise Three   Look at the topic you chose in Exercise One and consider the purpose you have developed in Exercise Two. Write down who your main audience will be. Then try to identify other groups who might listen.

Robert was writing his radio talk on "How to Say 'No.'" His main audience was the entire school body, but his listeners would also include teachers and administrators.

Make a Plan

A. Gather Ideas

Keeping your purpose constantly in mind, make a list of ideas about your topic. From this list choose two or three main points you want to make. For each main point, you should have one or more supporting details. These could take the form of examples, facts and figures, anecdotes, or quotations from experts.

Here is Robert's list of ideas.

TOPIC: How to Say "No"

PURPOSE: I want to convince others that saying "no" is important and that anyone can learn to do it.

NOTES:

Saying "no" not learned overnight.

Short term gains vs. long range goals.

If you are studying for a test when a friend calls you up to go somewhere, do you go?

Reasons it's hard to say "no": You want people to like you.

Also: you fear there won't be another time.

Standing up for yourself takes a lot of work and self-knowledge.

Satisfaction of saying "no."

Saying "no" can be crucial at some point in your life, but you have to learn in small ways first.

Sign of maturity.

Robert chose several of these ideas as the main ones he would work on. He thought about anecdotes which might fit his idea of "short term gains vs. long range goals." He also wanted to be able to illustrate the "reasons it's hard to say 'no.'"

Exercise Four   Gather information on the topic you have chosen. Decide which main ideas you will use, and try to think of anecdotes or examples that could be used to illustrate them.

B. Organize Ideas

A radio speech needs to have a simple organization that the audience can grasp even if they don't listen very carefully. The organization of your speech should give your listeners a mental framework on which they can position each idea as you state it. You can "build" this framework with key words and phrases as you go along.

Using his list of ideas, Robert sketched a basic framework for his radio talk by making three short lists:

Points to Make

Saying "no" not learned overnight.

A question of goals.

Importance of learning now for more important decisions later.

Examples

Study for a test when asked to a party.

My own problems with saying "no."

Key Words and Phrases

Short term gains

Long term goals

Mark of maturity

Using these lists, Robert borrowed from each to write a rough outline of his radio speech.

How do you learn to say "no"? Not overnight. A question of goals.

Example: You are studying for a test when asked to a party.

By not saying "no" you get short-term gains: A few hours of fun. But you may also get a failing grade.

By saying "no" you can satisfy long-term goals.

Example: My own problem saying "no."

Being able to say "no" a mark of maturity.

Exercise Five   Look at the notes you have gathered on the topic for your radio talk. Develop a framework by listing the points you want to make, and the examples, anecdotes, and factual information you want to use. Also include key words and phrases. Finally, write a rough outline.

Write the First Draft

Writing a radio talk is similar to writing other kinds of composition. You should write freely at first, without worrying about mistakes. Your talk will have three parts: an introduction, a body, and a conclusion.

Naturally, you want your radio listeners to remember what you said after you are "off the air." Therefore, you may want to repeat and emphasize key words and phrases in ways that will help listeners grasp the framework of your talk.

Also, since you are aiming for a conversational tone, you shouldn't be afraid to use the "second person" (the "you" form of address) in your talk. You might find it useful to speak out loud as you write, testing the phrasing and rhythm of your sentences.

Here are some other guidelines to help you.

Introduction

Try to capture your listeners' attention. You might want to begin with a straightforward statement about the purpose of your speech. Or you might want to lead the listeners into your subject by telling a story.

Body

Your rough outline should help give your talk order and unity as you write. Use it as you cover the main points. Remember the various ways you have learned to develop ideas in writing—describing; giving facts, reasons, and examples; telling an anecdote; comparing. Use whatever methods you think will help you reach your listeners.

Conclusion

Make a good final impression. Focus the listeners' attention on your main point one more time.

Exercise Six   Following the guidelines suggested above, make changes and additions to your rough outline. Refer to both your notes and the guidelines as you write the first draft of your talk.

When you write a composition, the major part of your work is finished once you get the first draft on paper. But after drafting a radio talk, you still have the actual presentation to look forward to. Many of the revisions you will make concern the way your writing sounds.

Think About Your Message. Put yourself in the place of your listeners. What is it like to hear your talk for the first time? Is there anything you need to emphasize? Do you need to repeat anything?

Does Your Talk Sound Natural? Are there any words that don't sound right or are difficult for you to pronounce? Are the rhythms of your speech lively and varied, or dull and repetitious? Are any of your statements unintentionally funny?

Is It the Right Length? Have a watch handy to time yourself as you read your radio talk aloud. Is it about two minutes long? If your talk is running short, you will need to add more details. If it's running long, you'll need to make some cuts.

Exercise Seven   Before you get back to work on the draft you made in Step Three, you might like to turn to page 240 and read the final version of Robert's radio talk. Then revise your own talk.

Delivering Your Radio Talk

When you have finished revising your talk, and have practiced it out loud, it is time to deliver it "over the air." Of course, your school may not operate a radio station or even broadcast programs like "Sounding Off" over the public address system. But you can always tape record your radio talk.

Tape recording has an advantage. It enables you to hear how you sound to others. You can revise your talk further if you or other people notice areas where it could be improved.

Exercise Eight   Deliver your radio talk over your school radio station or public address system, if possible. Or tape record your talk as though you were delivering it over the radio.

How and When to Say No

Is it difficult for you to say no? How do you give the right answer—when that answer is "Thanks, but no thanks"? I've been thinking about it.

Seriously, it's not something you learn overnight. But if you think about goals and gains and satisfaction and the long term, you can figure out how and when to say no.

Let's say tonight you're going to study. You've fallen behind in your work and you've got a test tomorrow, so tonight you're going to sit down and study.

Six-thirty. The phone rings. It's Jim McGiver. You've just met him and he's asking you to attend his birthday party that very evening. He's sorry he didn't ask you earlier but he just missed you at study hall. "It's going to be fun," says Jim. "Come on over."

You won't budge. At least you think you won't. "I've got to study, sorry." "Oh, come on," says Jim. "It's for a test," you say. "So come on," replies Jim. "It's only a test." He goes on to list the names of the students who are going to be there. They include some new people you don't know but want to meet. In short, everybody is going to Jim McGiver's birthday party.

You are feeling sick to your stomach. There's silence on the other end as Jim awaits your answer. Yes—or no?

If your goal is to pass a test and a friend calls you and wants you to change your goal—to having a good time—think about what you gain. You gain a few hours of fun and a failing grade in a course you should have passed. You gain a lot of pain because you have to take the course again.

When you give in to friends, you satisfy them. But when you satisfy your friends at the expense of your own long-range goals, you're making a mistake. I know. It was hard for me to learn to say no. The only thing that helped me was thinking about my long-range goals and remembering how important they are to me.

Well, maybe something else helped me, too. I knew I'd been hearing the word "no" from parents and teachers all my life. It must be a sign of maturity to say it. You don't learn to say it overnight, but I guess it comes to you more easily as you grow up.

II

COMMUNICATOR'S HANDBOOK

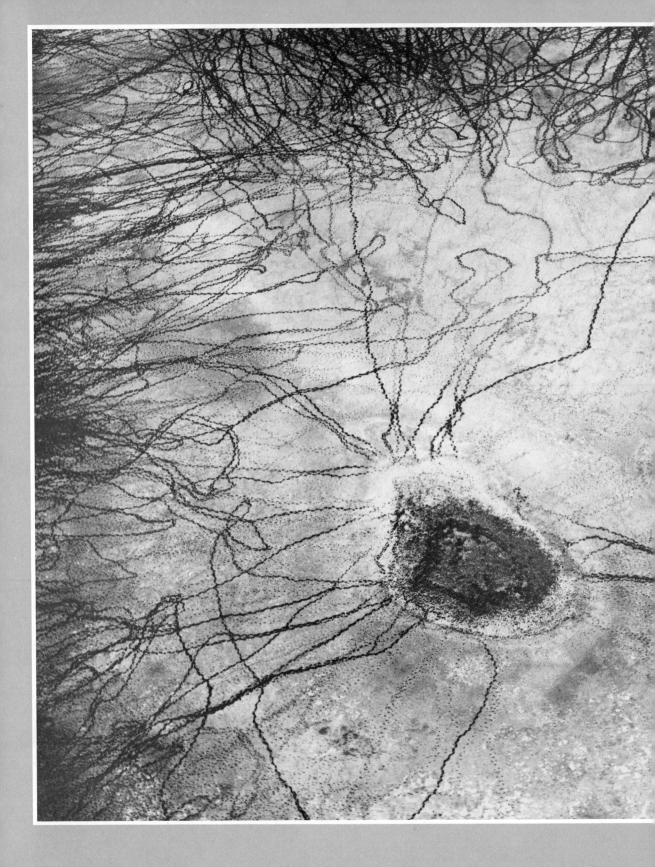

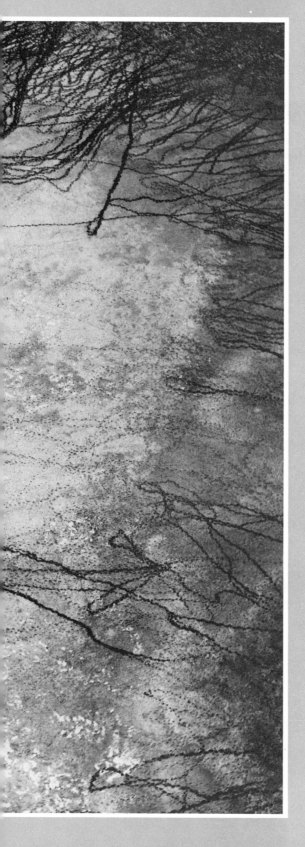

Vocabulary and Dictionary Skills

An aerial view of a watering hole on the Santa Fe trail in New Mexico, 1975. The lines radiating out from the watering hole are cattle tracks.
William A. Garnett

UNIT FOURTEEN

Vocabulary and Dictionary Skills

You have two vocabularies: a passive vocabulary and an active vocabulary. Your passive vocabulary includes all the words that you recognize or understand (either clearly or vaguely) when you hear or read them. Your active vocabulary, which is smaller, includes the words that you know well enough to use in your speaking and writing.

In this unit you will work to expand both of your vocabularies. You will learn how to figure out the meanings of unfamiliar words from their context. You will also learn how to guess the meanings of words by examining any Latin or Greek roots, prefixes, or suffixes they may contain. Then you will practice using new words in sentences.

Meaning From Context

Imagine that you're reading a detective novel and you come across these sentences:

> The detective said to Thora, "It was you who purloined the jewels. I've suspected you ever since I found them hidden in your room."

Suppose you don't know what the word *purloined* means. What do you do? You could forget about the word and hope it isn't important to the story. You could stop reading and look the word up in a dictionary. Or you could try to figure out the meaning of the word by studying its context.

The context of a word is the other words surrounding it. Often these offer clues to the meaning of the unknown word. Take another look at the context of the word *purloined*. How many clues can you discover?

There's an important clue in the word *jewels*. The detective says, "You purloined the jewels." He is saying that Thora did something to the jewels. What do people do to jewels? They buy them, sell them, steal them, wear them, admire them, lose them, desire them, and so on. But before you choose one of those meanings of *purloined*, see if you can find some more evidence.

The next sentence contains two clues: the words *suspected* and *hidden*. You suspect a person of doing something bad. And people often hide the things they steal.

Putting these three clues together, you will probably decide that *purloined* means "stole." And you will be right.

Here is another example:

> Jim was reticent because he saw that Carrie was within earshot. If she picked up information about his personal life, she might use it against him.

The word *reticent* may be unfamiliar to you. However, you can see that it describes Jim. The context tells you what the situation is. Jim is having a conversation with someone, and he is aware that Carrie is listening. Is Jim being talkative or loud? No, just the opposite. He is trying not to give any information that Carrie could use against him. From these context clues you can guess that *reticent* means "careful not to talk too much." This guess is quite close to the dictionary definition: "not given to speaking freely; secretive; uncommunicative."

Whenever you meet an unfamiliar word in your reading, look for context clues to its meaning. Often they will save you the trouble of thumbing through your dictionary.

Exercise One   Number your paper from 1 to 10. Each sentence below contains one word in italics. Following the sentence are four other words or phrases. Choose the word or phrase that is closest in meaning to the italicized word. Write your choice on your paper.

EXAMPLE: Because of her strange behavior, she was *ostracized* by the other club members, who refused to invite her to their parties.

a. welcomed   b. shunned   c. met   d. comforted

b. shunned

1. He did not say so directly, but he *insinuated* that I was not doing the job right.

   a. whispered   b. confessed   c. hinted   d. disproved

2. After ten years in the noisy, crowded city, the *tranquil* life of the country was a great relief.

   a. calm   b. dangerous   c. exciting   d. empty

3. The boy picked up a stout stick and *brandished* it threateningly.

   a. looked at   b. painted   c. waved   d. juggled

4. During our *nocturnal* walks, Uncle John would tell us about the stars and the planets.

   a. solitary   b. quiet   c. frequent   d. nighttime

5. Eager to find out what its new home was like, the puppy poked its nose *inquisitively* into every corner.

   a. safely   b. curiously   c. awkwardly   d. angrily

6. I didn't think you would be *gullible* enough to believe that story about the flying car.

   a. easily fooled   b. impatient   c. smart   d. old

7. Our cat, usually full of energy, seems *lethargic* today.

   a. drowsy   b. peppy   c. small   d. furry

8. Our club's *emblem* is a grinning snake sitting on a cloud.

   a. song   b. motto   c. idea   d. symbol

9. Felix often juggles his mother's best china plates to show how *dexterous* he is.

   a. stupid   b. clumsy   c. skillful   d. delighted

10. The crack in the bottom of the boat was barely *perceptible* to the naked eye.

   a. wet   b. noticeable   c. covered   d. rusted

Exercise Two   On your paper rewrite each sentence below, substituting a word or words of your own for each word in italics.

EXAMPLE: She spoke French *fluently* because she had lived in France for six years.

She spoke French well because she had lived in France for six years.

1. I hope you will not *squander* this money on things you don't need.

2. When the President of the United States arrived, I knew it was going to be a *momentous* occasion.

3. After hearing the terrible news, the child cheerfully repeated it to her doll; she was too young to realize its *significance*.

4. "If you would stop overfeeding this dog," the veterinarian said, "he would not be so *obese.*"

5. Since both sides seemed satisfied with the judge's decision, we can assume that it was *equitable*.

L E S S O N   T W O

Learning Prefixes, Suffixes, and Roots

Another way to build your vocabulary skills is to learn the meanings of some common prefixes and suffixes. Knowing these meanings can often help you figure out the meaning of a new word. For example, if you know that the prefix *in-* can mean "not," you probably have no trouble understanding such words as *insane, inaccurate, inactive,* and *incomplete.* If you know that the prefix *auto-* means "self," you can probably guess that an *autobiography* is the story of a person's life written by that person.

Prefixes

A prefix is an element that is added to the beginning of a word. Because a prefix has its own meaning, it changes the meaning of the word it is added to. Following is a list of some commonly used prefixes and their meanings.

Word With Prefix	Meaning of Prefix
antiwar	against
bicycle	two, twice
circumference	around
contain	with, together
companion	
cooperate	
contradict	against
depart	from, down
disagree	away, off
different	
expel	away from, out
inhuman	not
illegal	
immodest	
irregular	
international	among, between
introduce	inside, within
misplace	badly, wrongly
nonsense	not
postscript	after, following
preview	before
proceed	forward, before
recall	back, again
repeat	
semisweet	half
substandard	under
sustain	

Word With Prefix	Meaning of Prefix
superhuman	over, above, extra
television	far
transport	across
ultramodern	beyond, excessively
unhappy	not

Suffixes

A suffix is an element that is added to the end of a word. Some suffixes have their own meaning, which is added to the meaning of the word they are combined with. For example, -*less* added to *hope* makes a word that means "without hope." Other suffixes have only "grammatical meaning"; that is, they merely change the part of speech of the word they are added to. For example, if you add the suffix -*ish* to the noun *imp*, you get an adjective, *impish*. You can change *impish* into an adverb, *impishly*, by adding the suffix -*ly*. Following is a list of some commonly used suffixes and their meanings.

Word With Suffix	Meaning of Suffix
read**able**	able, fit for
terr**ible**	
marri**age**	process, state, rank
music**al**	pertaining to
toler**ance**	act, condition, fact
independ**ence**	
free**dom**	state, rank, condition
wood**en**	made of, like
broadcast**er**	doer, maker
play**ful**	full of, marked by
terr**ify**	make, cause to have
neighbor**hood**	state, condition
angel**ic**	dealing with, caused by
imp**ish**	suggesting, like
real**ism**	act, manner, doctrine

Word With Suffix	Meaning of Suffix
activ**ist**	doer, maker, believer
equal**ity**	state, condition
standard**ize**	make, cause to be
fear**less**	lacking, without
cow**like**	like, similar
establish**ment**	means, result, action
happi**ness**	quality, state
nerv**ous**	marked by, given to
fear**some** ⎤	marked by, given to
lone**some** ⎦	
east**ward**	in the direction of

Exercise Three   Following are ten prefixes. Copy each prefix, then write two words that contain the prefix. You may use a dictionary if you wish. Use one of the words in a written sentence of your own. You will write ten sentences.

EXAMPLE: semi-

semicircle

semiprivate

When Uncle Arthur was in the hospital, he had a semiprivate room.

1. re-		6. anti-	
2. inter-		7. pro-	
3. im-		8. ex-	
4. super-		9. trans-	
5. sub-		10. com-	

Exercise Four   Combine each of the following ten words with the suffix that follows it, to make a new word. Then use the new word in a sentence of your own. You may use a dictionary if you wish.

EXAMPLE: nation + al

national

The national anthem of the United States is ''The Star-Spangled Banner.''

1. sincere + ly
2. novel + ist
3. wonder + ful
4. like + able
5. lazy + ness
6. reck + less
7. carry + age
8. govern + ment
9. mystery + ous
10. free + dom

Roots

A *root* is one or more syllables that have been borrowed from a foreign language, usually Latin or Greek. A root can be combined with a prefix, a suffix, or both to form a word in English.

One root may grow into many words. For example, the Latin root *uni*, which means "one," is the basis of many English words. Among these are *union, universe, unicycle, uniform, university*, and *unity*.

Can you see how each of these words contains the idea "one"? A

unicycle has one wheel. A *union* is a joining of two or more people or things into one. *Universe* means "whole, entire"; it is everything that exists "turned into one." *Uniform* means "one form, type, or pattern for all." All the players on a baseball team, for example, wear the same type of clothing; they wear a uniform.

Following are some of the many Latin and Greek roots that are found in English words.

Root	Meaning	Sample Word
aqua	water	aquarium
aud	hear	audible
cogn	know	recognize
cred	believe, trust	incredible
duc, duct	lead	conductor
equ	equal	equation
fac, fact, fect, fic	do, make	factory
fer	carry, bear	transfer, fertile
frag, fract	break	fragment, fraction
junct	join	junction
jac, ject	throw, hurl	reject
loc	place	location
magn	large	magnificent
man	hand	manage
mit, miss	send	mission
ped	foot	pedestrian
pend	hang, weigh	depend
port	carry, bear	import
sci	know, knowledge	science
scrib, script	write	manuscript
ten, tain	hold	retain
tract	draw, pull	tractor
uni	one	union
vid, vis	see	visible
vit	life	vitamin

Exercise Five   Copy each of the following words below on your paper. Then use your dictionary to divide the words into prefixes, roots, and suffixes. Copy the meaning of each prefix and root. Copy one definition of each word. Then write a sentence using the word.

EXAMPLE: introduce

introduce

prefix: intro (inside)

root: duce (lead)

definition: to acquaint someone with someone or something

My uncle introduced me to trout fishing.

1. distract
2. magnify
3. export
4. supervision
5. container
6. describe
7. aqueduct
8. independence
9. transmission
10. inequality

Exercise Six   Following is a list of prefixes, suffixes, and roots. For each prefix, suffix, or root, write a word that contains it. Then write a sentence that contains the word. You may use your dictionary.

EXAMPLES: prefix: un-

unhappy The football players' strike made me very unhappy.

suffix: -ous

courageous It's part of a firefighter's job to be courageous.

root: aud

audience Speak loudly, so that everyone in the audience can hear you.

1. prefix: re-
2. prefix: ex-
3. suffix: -ness
4. suffix: -ful
5. root: cred

Using a Dictionary

A dictionary gives you many different kinds of information. Most of them are illustrated in the following sample entry.

> **neigh bor** (nā′ bər) *n* Also *chiefly British* **neigh bour. 1.** A person who lives near another. **2.** A person or thing that is near another. **3.** One's fellow human being. —*adj* Living or situated near another: *a neighbor state.* —*vt* To live near or be situated near to; adjoin: *Vermont neighbors New Hampshire.* [Old English *nēahgebūr:* from *nēah,* near + *gebūr,* dweller (*ge,* together + *būr,* dwelling).]

Word Meanings

The most important information included in a dictionary entry is the word's meaning. Many words in the English language have more than one meaning. If a word has several meanings for one part of speech, the definitions are usually numbered. Note that in the entry for the word *neighbor*, there are three numbered definitions for the word as a noun, and one definition each for the word as an adjective and a transitive verb. An entry for a word with multiple meanings, such as *neighbor*, often includes a sample phrase or sentence to illustrate one or more of the different definitions.

Usage Labels

Some words in the dictionary have usage labels. Following are some of the most common labels and their meanings.

☐ **archaic** The word is old-fashioned and is rarely used today. Words like *thou, thee*, and *ye* (for "you") and *aforetime* ("earlier, previously") are labeled *archaic*. They might still be found in books written long ago, but they are almost never used today.

☐ **obsolete** The word is no longer used at all. An example is the word *bellycheer*. As a noun, it referred to a plentiful, luxurious meal. As a verb, it meant "to feast."

☐ **colloquial** or **informal** The word or phrase is more commonly used in speech or informal writing than in formal writing. For example, you might say, "These shoes are *okay* for everyday wear." If you were writing, however, you would probably be more formal: "These shoes are *suitable* for everyday wear."

☐ **British** The word is used mainly in British English rather than in American English. For example, what we call a *subway* is called the *underground* in England. What we call an *apartment* the British call a *flat*.

☐ **dialect** The word or phrase is used by members of a certain group, or by people who live in a certain region. Here is an example from the Scottish dialect of English: *rumblegumption*. It means "common sense."

Word History

A dictionary entry includes the *etymology*, or history, of the word. In some dictionaries the etymology appears right after the pronunciation. In others it appears at the end of the entry.

The entry for *neighbor* tells you that the word comes from two Old English words, *neah* (near) and *gebur* (dweller).

Synonyms

Many dictionaries give lists of words that have similar meanings (*synonyms*) at the end of the entry. For example, in one dictionary the entry for *grant* ends with this list:

syn CONCEDE, VOUCHSAFE, ACCORD, AWARD

The exact meaning of each synonym is given, so you can choose the one that is best for the sentence you are writing.

Spelling and Pronunciation

A dictionary tells you the correct spelling, syllabication, and pronunciation of a word. The entry for *neighbor* offers two ways of spelling the word: *neighbor*, which is the preferred American English spelling, and *neighbour*, which is the British English spelling.

Words that have more than one syllable are divided into syllables: *neigh bor*. This tells you how to break up the word when you are hyphenating it at the end of the line. (You will learn more about hyphenation in Unit Twenty-eight.)

The pronunciation is given in parentheses, directly following the word. Dictionaries use special symbols to show how words are pronounced. Each dictionary has a pronunciation key, usually at the beginning of the book or at the bottom of each page. The pronunciation key explains the symbols used in that dictionary.

Look again at the entry for *neighbor* (page 248). There is an accent mark after the *nā* syllable: ′. It tells you to *stress*, or emphasize, that syllable when you say the word out loud. Many words that have three or more syllables have two accents. One is a strong accent (′) and the other a weak accent (′), as in *congregation:* con′ gri gā′ shən.

Notice the second syllable in the pronunciation spelling of *neighbor*. The upside-down *e* (ə) is called a *schwa*. The schwa stands for a weak vowel sound that resembles *uh*. Note that the word *con′ gri gā′ shən* also contains a schwa.

Grammatical Forms

A dictionary tells you the part of speech of a word. The part of speech is often abbreviated. Following is a list of the abbreviations most commonly used in dictionaries. Compare these abbreviations with the ones used in your dictionary.

n noun

pron pronoun

adj adjective

vb verb

vt transitive verb (takes a direct object)

vi intransitive verb (does not take a direct object)

adv adverb

prep preposition

conj conjunction

interj interjection

If you look again at the sample entry, you will see that *neighbor* is defined as a noun (*n*), an adjective (*adj*), and a transitive verb (*vt*).

If a noun has an irregular plural form, the dictionary will list it after the part of speech. Following is an example.

cri sis (krī′ səs) *n, pl* **cri ses**

If no plural form is given (as in the entry for *neighbor*), you know that the plural is formed in the regular way, by adding *s* or *es*.

If a verb is irregular, its principal parts will be listed after the part of speech. See the following example.

see (sē) *vb* **saw, seen, see ing**

Other Information Found in a Dictionary

Many dictionaries give facts about people and places. The entries for the people and places may be in the main alphabetical listing, or they may be in special sections in the back of the book. You might want to find out when Alexander the Great lived, or how many people live in Detroit. Of course there are other sources, such as encyclopedias, that will give you much more information. However, if you need just one or two basic facts, a dictionary is a good place to look.

Many dictionaries have special sections in the front or back where you can find lists of symbols for chemical elements, commonly used abbreviations, foreign words and phrases, and rules for spelling, punctuation, and capitalization.

P O I N T S   T O   R E M E M B E R

▷ A dictionary tells you what a word means. If a word has several meanings, all definitions are listed.

▷ A dictionary gives you the history of a word.

▷ A dictionary gives you the correct spelling, syllabication, and pronunciation of a word.

▷ A dictionary gives you the part of speech of a word.

▷ If a noun has an irregular plural form, the dictionary will list it after the part of speech.

▷ A dictionary lists the principal parts of irregular verbs.

▷ Many dictionaries have separate listings of biographical and geographical information, abbreviations, symbols, foreign words and phrases, and rules for spelling, punctuation, and capitalization.

Finding Words in a Dictionary

Words in a dictionary are arranged in alphabetical order, from A to Z. When words begin with the same letter, they are alphabetized according to their second letter. For example, *apple* comes before *art* because *p* comes before *r*. If the words are alike in their first two letters, the third letter determines their order. As you can see by studying the following list, it's the first different letter that decides which of two words will come first.

appeal

appearance

appetite

apple

appreciate

apricot

around

arrival

arrive

art

Guide words are the words that appear in boldface type at the top of each dictionary page. They help you to find words quickly.The guide word on the left side of the page tells you the first word defined on that page. The guide word on the right tells you the last word defined on that page. If the word you are looking for falls alphabetically between the two guide words, you know that it will be on that page.

Exercise Seven   Use a dictionary to answer the following questions. Write the answer to each question on your paper. Also write the number of the dictionary page where you found the information.

EXAMPLE: What is the population of Detroit?

1,670,144 p. 363

1. Who was Jupiter?
2. What is Jupiter?
3. From what language was the word *robot* borrowed?
4. List three very different definitions of the word *pen*.

5. When did Woodrow Wilson live?

6. The word *mine* can serve as several different parts of speech. Copy its part-of-speech labels from your dictionary. Then copy one definition of *mine* for each part of speech.

7. What do the initials CIA stand for?

8. What is the origin of the word *hansom?*

9. Find and write a synonym for *replica*.

10. Where are the Canary Islands?

Exercise Eight   Using a dictionary, look up each of the words below. For each one, write at least two definitions. Include the part of speech of each definition. Then write a sentence for each definition.

EXAMPLE: step

1. n   a movement made by lifting the foot

2. vb   to tread by intent or accident

Take one more step and you'll be sorry!

Did you step on the cat's tail?

1. charm   4. poison

2. upset   5. charge

3. stalk

L E S S O N   F O U R

Choosing the Exact Word

In Lesson One you practiced examining a word's context (other words nearby) to find clues to the meaning of the word. You were studying context from a reader's point of view. In this lesson you will approach the same skill from a writer's point of view. You will practice choosing words to fit the context of your own sentences and paragraphs.

As you know, a dictionary entry often includes one or more synonyms. A *synonym* is usually defined as a word that has the same meaning as another word. But, actually, synonyms hardly ever have exactly the same meaning. It's true that synonyms can often be substituted for one another in a sentence. However, each of the synonyms will give the sentence a slightly different meaning. Words with the same general meaning often differ in their shades of meaning.

For example, take the two words *stingy* and *thrifty*. Both describe someone who is careful with money. However, most people would rather be called thrifty than stingy. A thrifty person spends money but does not waste it. He or she buys only what is necessary and always tries to get the best value for the money. A stingy person tries not to spend money at all—particularly on other people! He or she finds it painful to give anything away.

Some sets of synonyms suggest different attitudes on the part of the writer. Suppose you are writing about motion pictures. If you call them *movies*, you are using the ordinary, everyday term. If you call them *films*, you suggest that you take them seriously and know quite a bit about them. If you refer to movies as *the cinema*, you make yourself sound like a highbrow critic!

Here is another set of synonyms that differ in important ways:

take	clutch
seize	snatch
grasp	grab

Take is the most common word in this set, and it has the most general meaning. It means to get something into one's possession or control.

Seize suggests a sudden, strong movement to get hold of something or someone.

Grasp suggests firmness in holding and keeping something.

Clutch suggests that the person grasps something anxiously, as though fearful of losing it.

Snatch suggests a quick, light movement.

Grab suggests a rough or rude movement.

The English language is rich in synonyms, so you have many choices to make when you write. Try to be aware of the many shades of meaning your words can have. Let your dictionary be your guide

Exercise Nine Choose the better word from each pair in parentheses in the sentences on page 263. Write the word on your paper next to the number of the sentence. Use your dictionary if you wish.

EXAMPLE: The movie was so (amusing, ironic) that the audience was laughing out loud.

amusing

1. Judy was in a hurry, so she only (skimmed, read) the newspaper.
2. The birds flew by so fast we could only (glimpse, examine) them.
3. As a child I was so (humble, meek) that I was frightened of meeting new people.
4. Will you ever learn to (handle, wield) a car?
5. The story moves me to tears because it is so (pathetic, dismal).
6. She told me about a family so (poor, meager) that they could not pay their fuel bills.
7. When the mayor boasted about his accomplishments, the crowd (jeered, sneered) loudly.
8. The dog (showed, demonstrated) its teeth and growled.
9. A light rain (dropped, fell) on the newly cut lawn.
10. He (took, grabbed) my arm and tried to pull me off the bike.

Exercise Ten   Below are five pairs of sentences. The first sentence in each pair has one italicized word. The second sentence in the pair has a blank. Find a synonym for the italicized word that fits in the blank. Write the synonym on your paper. You may use a dictionary.

EXAMPLE: This store sells both ladies' and men's *apparel*. I often buy _____ for myself and my family there.

clothes or *clothing*

1. The police jumped out of their patrol car and *pursued* the thief on foot. The puppy let out playful yips as it _____ its tail.
2. His decision was based on *erroneous* information. Trudy thought all her troubles were over, but she was _____.
3. The winds *diminished* toward evening, and the rain stopped. During the cold weather our fuel supply _____ so fast that we began to worry.
4. In 1863 President Lincoln signed a *proclamation* making Thanksgiving a national holiday. The _____ of a couple's engagement is usually made by the parents of the bride-to-be.
5. She refused to *divulge* the source of the money. He drew the curtain aside to _____ a secret door leading into a tunnel.

Speaking

The Great Sphinx at Giza, Egypt, built around 2550 B.C. The sphinx is a mythological creature with a lion's body and a human head. The face on this monument is believed to be a portrait of King Khafre, who reigned in Egypt at the time. Francis Frith, Victoria and Albert Museum, London, England

UNIT FIFTEEN

Speaking

For a person who's unused to it, speaking in public can be a frightening experience. But speaking is like everything else: the more you know about it and the more experience you have, the easier it gets. By the time you finish this unit, you will be both more knowledgeable and more experienced as a public speaker.

LESSON ONE

A Look at Speaking

One way to get over any self-consciousness you might have about speaking is to practice by yourself, or among close friends or family—people you know and are comfortable with. You might try talking out loud in front of a mirror when you are alone, or in the kitchen as your family gathers for dinner in the evening. The more you try speaking out loud in familiar settings, the less frightened you will feel at the prospect of speaking in unfamiliar settings. As you practice, pay special attention to *pronunciation, volume, tempo,* and *pitch.*

Pronunciation is how you say words. But it is more than whether you pronounce "route" as *root* or *rowt.* (By the way, both are correct.) It also has to do with how clearly and distinctly you speak each word.

Volume is the degree of loudness you use when you speak. Of course, you need to speak loudly enough to be heard by everyone in the group you are addressing. But above and beyond that, there might be times when you want to give special emphasis to a particular phrase by speaking more loudly—or, sometimes, more softly.

Tempo is the rate at which you speak. If you speak too slowly, people may become bored or distracted. If you speak too quickly, people may have a difficult time following what you are saying.

Pitch is how high or low your voice is. In general, the pitch of your voice lowers as you grow older. It can also change with your emotional state. For example, your voice might get higher when you are excited and lower when you are depressed.

A good way to learn more about speaking is to watch and listen to good speakers. Listen to radio announcers, for example. Watch television announcers. Pay attention to how they use their voices and bodies when they talk.

Just such a study of effective speakers produced the following *Guidelines for Speakers,* which you can use to make your own speaking more effective.

1. Speak in a pleasant voice—neither too loudly nor too softly.

2. Vary your pitch and intonation, so that your words sound fresh and spontaneous.

3. Speak at a constant, even rate, so that all your words can be heard and understood.

4. Enunciate words as clearly and distinctly as possible.

5. Use a varied vocabulary.

6. Do not use unnecessary words such as *like* or *you know* or *I mean,* or sounds such as *um* or *huh.*

7. Talk about subjects that you understand and know something about. The more you know about a topic, the more you will be able to communicate to your audience.

8. Use gestures that emphasize what you are saying, rather than gestures that betray uneasiness.

9. Establish eye contact with different members of your audience as you speak.

10. Sit or stand up straight so that you can project your voice fully.

Exercise One   Get together with a classmate. While he or she listens (or tape-records) and takes notes, talk about something that is familiar to you. Then listen or tape-record while your classmate talks, taking notes on his or her delivery. Each of you should use the guidelines for speakers to determine the other's strengths and weaknesses. After you've finished listening, give each other concrete suggestions for improving your speaking techniques.

Preparing for a Debate

The specific type of speaking you will be studying in this unit is a very formal one called debating. When you debate, you begin with a statement like the one that follows.

Resolved: Our school should build a new athletic field.

Do you support this view? Or do you disagree with it? Could you defend your point of view against students who are maintaining that the other side is right? That is what a debate is all about.

Here's how a debate works. First, a *proposition* is chosen. The proposition is a statement that may or may not be true. It is worded positively and uses straightforward, neutral language.

The proposition is not a statement of *fact* that can be *proved*, such as "The United States elects a President every four years." It is a statement open to discussion—both for and against.

Two teams are chosen to speak on the two sides of the question. Usually there are two speakers on each team. One team is called the *affirmative*. Its members will argue *for* the proposition. The other team, the *negative*, will argue *against* it. Each team will make two presentations. The first will be the members' *constructive speeches*, in which they will give the arguments that support their team's position. The second will be their *rebuttal speeches*, in which they will try to refute the other team's arguments. At the end of the debate, the judges will decide which team's performance was better.

Long before the debate, the members of each team get together to go over their ideas for either supporting or attacking the proposition. Ideas can come from many sources: books, magazines, newspapers, radio, television, interviews given by people in the community, conversations with classmates and family. Speakers should list every possible fact or quotation that supports their side. But these must be easy to present, as there are strict time limits on the speeches in debates.

Next, the team members work on what is called a *case*. They go over all their possible arguments and choose the strongest ones. They put these arguments in the order that they feel will be the most effective. Then they divide the arguments so that each team member will be stressing different points during the debate.

On the topic "Our school should build a new athletic field," for example, Brian will be the first speaker for the affirmative side. He might want to use statistics to describe the past and present use of the athletic field. Then he might conclude with statements by the school administration, local officials, and builders. The second speaker for the affirmative side, Janice, could talk about how much it would cost to build a new field and how the field could be used.

At the same time, the team members for the negative side are meeting to prepare their case. Ted and Rebecca sift through the evidence they have found and put together their best arguments for their constructive speeches. It is very important that all the figures and statistics used by both the affirmative and negative teams be carefully researched. Otherwise, each team can expect the other side to jump at the chance of showing these facts and figures to be incorrect.

After the members of both teams have decided on their own points, they should make another list of the arguments *they expect from the other side.* The lists of all their own arguments and the anticipated arguments of their opponents are together called a *brief.*

Sometimes a team is surprised by an unanticipated point that the other team comes up with. But usually, if the reasons supporting a proposition are known, it is possible to guess what people will say against it, and to plan a strategy based on those guesses.

For example, in the case of the athletic-field debaters, the team for the affirmative assumes the negative side will argue that the field has so far been good enough for thousands of students and that the sports played in school and the students' needs have not changed. The affirmative side also predicts the negative side will argue that a new athletic field would cost too much money and that citizens today are unwilling to pay higher taxes for things they think are unnecessary.

After each team has decided who will present what arguments, the speakers prepare their constructive speeches. They make notes to use during the debate. They print the notes clearly on index cards and number the cards, so that in their nervousness they won't mix them up. For example, three of Janice's cards contain the following information.

5. There should be all-weather surfaces on track and runways.

7. Students could help raise money: car washes, specially printed T-shirts.

8. Students could do some of the preparatory work on field.

After gathering and assigning the arguments, and writing them on cards, you should rehearse, both alone and with your debating partner. Offer each other helpful criticism. Rebecca and Ted, as you see below, were very frank with each other during one of their practice sessions.

"Rebecca, you're slurring your words again. And you've got to speak louder or they won't be able to hear you."

"Ted, you keep hemming and hawing, and saying 'you know' at the end of each sentence. It's distracting, and besides, it uses up too much time. And your voice would sound more commanding and project better if you stood up straight."

Paying close attention to the amount of time each person has is extremely important. In a debate, each speaker has a strict time limit, usually five minutes. During rehearsals, speeches must be timed. If they are too long, they must be cut; if too short, they must be lengthened.

Exercise Two   Organize debating groups in your class. For each group, you will need two people on the affirmative side and two people on the negative side. A good debater should be able to argue either side of a question.

Following is a list of propositions to debate. Each group in the class should either choose a proposition from the list or come up with one on its own.

Resolved: "The Star-Spangled Banner" should be replaced by a national anthem that is easier to sing.

Resolved: It should be against the law to eat foods that are not nutritious.

Resolved: Our school should ban football from the athletic program.

Resolved: There should be a national health care system in the United States.

Exercise Three   Now that you know what your proposition will be, and which side of the case you will be arguing, it's time to get together with your teammate to discuss the points you will want to make. Each of you should make a list of the possible arguments you come up with. Then divide the items on the list evenly between yourselves. Go to the library to research each of the items. (Your librarian may be able to help you if you have trouble deciding where to start. Also, consult Unit Seventeen of this book for tips on how to use the library.)

Exercise Four   Next, get together with your partner again. Outline your arguments, using your research to support them. Then decide which one of you will deal with which arguments, and in what order the arguments should be presented. Also outline the anticipated arguments of your opponents and divide those arguments between yourselves.

Make note cards clearly describing each separate point, and put them in the order in which you plan to use them. Don't forget to number the cards.

One reason you only make notes on your note cards rather than writing out your entire speech is that you don't want to read your speech during the debate. Instead, you want to establish a sense of immediacy that you cannot accomplish if your nose is buried in your notes. You want to address the audience and the judges directly, making eye contact as often as possible. At times you may even want to turn toward your opponents to emphasize a point.

Exercise Five You and your teammate should get together and practice delivering your constructive speeches. You'll need a stopwatch, or at least a watch with a second hand, so that you can make absolutely sure that each of your speeches is exactly five minutes in length. Also, be sure to advise each other on how to improve your delivery.

You may want to memorize the opening and the closing of your constructive speeches. The rest of the time you can refer to your numbered note cards for the major points that you want to make.

L E S S O N   T H R E E

The Debate

On the day of the debate, the four speakers and a chairperson, appointed or elected, sit on stage or at the front of the room. A panel of judges sits there, too.

The chairperson announces the topic:

Resolved: Our school should build a new athletic field.

The speakers are introduced. Facing Brian and Janice of the affirmative team are Rebecca and Ted of the negative team. The chairperson explains that each speaker has five minutes, and points to a watch or stopwatch. Brian is to speak first, for the affirmative. Then, Rebecca will speak for the negative. Janice will speak for the affirmative, and after that Ted will speak for the negative. This alternating pattern is the accepted one for a formal debate (Speaker A—Affirmative, Speaker B—Negative, Speaker C—Affirmative, Speaker D—Negative).

When each speaker has talked for four minutes, the chairperson says, "One minute," meaning "you have only one more minute to speak." In a debate, if the time limit is five minutes, that means *exactly* five minutes. If you are in the middle of a sentence when your time is

up, you may finish that sentence, but then you must sit down at once. If you were allowed a half minute extra, every other speaker would have to be allowed more time, too.

While your opponents talk, you can jot down brief notes. The notes and the list of arguments you *thought* the other team would make are ammunition for your *rebuttal*, in which you attempt to damage your opponent's position. (Obviously, you cannot memorize your rebuttal beforehand because you cannot be absolutely sure what your opponents will say.)

The rebuttal comes after all four speakers have finished their constructive speeches. It provides a chance for a good debater to shine, as he or she tears apart the other team's arguments.

If your opposing team has used arguments you anticipated, you're ready. If not, use the notes you've jotted down during their speeches to come up with new arguments. Don't feel you must attack every one of your opponent's positions, however. Unless you are sure you can really show that an argument is wrong, it's best not to try to do so. Concentrate instead on the faulty thinking you can clearly point out.

Rebuttal speeches are about half as long as the main speeches—two and a half minutes, if the main speech is five. As rebuttals are given, the chairperson keeping time with the watch will call out the one-minute warning, as he or she did in the earlier speeches.

Debaters "rebut" in this order: Speaker B—Negative, Speaker A—Affirmative, Speaker D—Negative, Speaker C—Affirmative. So, it will be Rebecca from the negative team who speaks first. Then, Brian will rebut for the affirmative team. Ted will finish for the negative and Janice for the affirmative.

In rebuttal, one speaker on each team will plan to "shoot down" certain points, the other speaker the rest. The debaters are trying to prove that their opponents' arguments are:

a. **inaccurate** For example: "Our opponents maintain that there are no new sports. But interviews with the coaches reveal that several sports have recently been added to the school program, and that these would benefit from a new athletic field. The new sports are field hockey, soccer, and ultimate Frisbee."

b. **illogical** For example: "Our opponents base their argument partly on what they call the need for more seats in the stadium. But the school population in this area is declining. The number of family members attending athletic events will decrease as well. So, fewer seats will be needed, not more."

c. **not as important as their team's** For example: "Our opponents accuse us of believing that the development of the body is not as important as that of the mind. On the contrary, we maintain that the development of a sound mind *and* a sound body is the goal of education."

How to Behave During a Debate

Although a debate is a competition, its rules require that you maintain respect toward your opponents. If you're in the audience, show respect for both teams and the chairperson. Never laugh in ridicule. Be courteous when others are speaking, as you want them to be when you're speaking.

When you are in a debate, make sure you pay attention to what your opponents are saying. You don't want to miss anything. Write down a word or phrase that later will remind you of each point you have heard.

Put a star beside each mistake that you catch in your opponent's speech, and jot down a note that will form the basis of your rebuttal. But don't write long messages to yourself. Also, avoid planning in elaborate detail what you are going to say and whispering at length about it to your teammate. If you do, you might miss some other important flaw in your opponent's argument.

How a Debate Is Judged

Most debates have an odd number of judges, usually three. They write their decisions on slips of paper. The chairperson totals the judges' votes and announces the winner of the debate.

But how do the judges determine who wins? The affirmative side has to prove that the change should be made. The negative side, on the other hand, has to prove that the change is unnecessary or unwanted. The judges decide which team has been the more convincing. In making this decision, they take into account not only the arguments each team has made, but the delivery of each speech. Don't forget to refresh your knowledge of speaking techniques before the debate takes place.

In general, the judges are looking for team members who do the following:

- ☐ present their arguments clearly and forcefully.
- ☐ back up every statement with convincing evidence.
- ☐ know the subject so well that the other team cannot catch them unprepared.
- ☐ effectively rebut their opponents' arguments while at the same time defending their own.

Exercise Six   Hold debates between the different groups in your class. To do this, elect or appoint judges and a chairperson who are familiar with the rules and know what to look for. Follow the format of the debate you have read about in this lesson.

A debate may be a serious activity, but it need not be grim. Debating is a good way to develop the ability to think on your feet and speak in public. Seasoned debaters can argue either side of a question. They display good humor toward themselves as well as their opponents. With practice, you too will be able to experience the challenge, excitement, and fun of debating.

Listening

Jazz dancing, August 22, 1917
UPI

Listening

Rebecca sat on the platform waiting for her turn to speak in the debate on building a new athletic field. Brian, her opponent, was speaking. As you probably remember if you read Unit Fifteen, "Speaking," Rebecca was a member of the negative team in the debate. She and her partner, Ted, were arguing against the proposition "Resolved: Our school should build a new athletic field."

Brian, the first speaker on the affirmative side, was giving his arguments in favor of the proposition. Rebecca was to speak next. She tried hard to listen to what Brian was saying, but she was nervous because this was her first debate.

"Maybe I wouldn't feel so jumpy if I took notes," she thought. She reached for her notepad and pencil and began to write what Brian was saying about how the students would benefit from a new field. She was in the middle of writing a sentence when she realized that Brian had moved on to another point. She had missed part of his argument.

"I'd better stop writing notes and just listen," she said to herself as Brian began to talk about the cost of a new field. That reminded Rebecca of the figures she had gathered. She began to go over the figures in her head, trying to decide how best to present them. Then she heard a ripple of applause in the auditorium. Brian had just made a very good point, and she had missed it completely! How in the world would she respond when her turn came?

Rebecca's problem was that she didn't listen well. The mistakes she made in listening caused her problems when she spoke. Failing to listen well can cause you problems too, not just in debates but in everyday life. If you don't listen well in class, you may miss facts that you'll need for a test. If you don't listen well in conversations, you may misunderstand information that a friend gives you. On a job you may miss important instructions. However, you can train yourself to be a good listener. The lessons in this unit will show you how.

Concentrating

Rebecca tried hard to concentrate on what Brian was saying, but she had trouble because she was nervous. It's not always easy to pay attention to what someone is saying. You may be distracted by your own feelings, as Rebecca was, or by noises, daydreams, or people around you. Sometimes you can even be distracted by a speaker who constantly fiddles with papers or with clothing or jewelry.

To help yourself concentrate, look directly at the speaker. Ignore other sights and sounds. If you have trouble paying attention, try the following tricks.

- ☐ Change your position. Sit up very straight, feet on the floor, head straight, eyes looking right into the speaker's eyes.

- ☐ Imagine that you are a judge scoring the speaker and decide how many points he or she is earning.

- ☐ If the speaker has a mannerism that bothers you, tell yourself that you will *never* do that when you speak. Then stop paying attention to it.

- ☐ Try keeping a list in your head of the speaker's main points. Each time you hear another one, quickly repeat the whole list to yourself.

- ☐ Make mental pictures of things the speaker is saying.

Like Rebecca, many people stop listening because they are thinking about what they are going to say when it's their turn to speak. If you do this, don't blame yourself; it shows that you want to plan your reply so it will be as effective as possible. However, you should wait until the speaker takes a short break before you start planning. Then you should quickly store in your memory the point that you want to make. The break may come when a teacher who is using notes pauses to turn a page. Or it may come when a friend you are talking to in the lunchroom stops to take a sip of milk. Be ready to listen again when the speaker starts talking again.

Exercise One   Try out your listening skills with a friend. Take turns reading aloud a few paragraphs from a textbook. When it's your turn to listen, try to concentrate on what your friend is saying. Try out each of the tricks described above to help yourself pay attention. (Your friend should do the same, of course.) When each of you has had several turns at listening, discuss which of the tricks worked best.

L E S S O N   T W O

Listening for Ideas

It's not enough to be sure you hear the speaker's words. You have to take in the ideas behind the words. As you listen, try to identify the speaker's main ideas. Then listen for details that support the main ideas. Following are some pointers that will help you "outline" a speech in your mind as you listen to it.

Introductions and Conclusions

When someone is speaking to an audience, he or she will often make "introductory" and "concluding" statements. Following are some examples.

"Today I will be covering the causes of the Civil War."

You know that the main ideas will concern those causes.

"Many people think of science as something that only professional scientists need to worry about. But I'm going to show you that this isn't true."

You know the speaker's main idea already—science is for everyone. Now you need to listen for the facts and reasons that the speaker will give to support the main idea.

"In conclusion, let me review the three main points I have made about Edward Field's poem 'Frankenstein.'"

You know that you are going to hear the three main ideas again.

Key Words and Phrases

Speakers often signal their main ideas with key words and phrases. Listen for expressions like the following.

"The important thing is . . ."

"There are three basic reasons for this."

"You may be surprised to learn that . . ."

"My opinion is . . ."

"Follow these steps . . ."

Speakers sometimes signal their main idea by asking a question, as in the following examples.

"Why do we need to build a new high school?"

"What caused General Washington to retreat?"

"Why do so many people love Shakespeare's plays?"

You know that the main idea is going to be the answer to the question.

Speakers often signal the supporting details for their main ideas with key words like *first*, *second*, *next*, or *last*. Here are some examples:

"The first reason is that it will cost too much."

"Second, General Washington's troops were badly outnumbered."

"The next thing you do is calculate the interest."

Taking Notes

Often you can help yourself listen better by taking notes. Because you have made up your mind to write down the main ideas and supporting details, you are alert and ready to catch each one. Of course, another advantage to taking notes is that they will help you remember the speech later.

If you do take notes, try to keep them very short. Don't write full sentences. Don't write the speaker's exact words unless they are very important. If Rebecca had kept her notes short, she wouldn't have missed part of Brian's argument.

Write down only the most important points. Here are the notes that a skilled listener might have taken while Brian was speaking.

Many benefits to athletes

    better playing surface

    more practice area

    better running track

More seats for fans (needed?)

Students can raise money. (?)

The comments in parentheses are questions that might have occurred to the listener. If Rebecca had taken notes like these during Brian's speech, she would have been better prepared to respond to it.

You may want to make some brief notes of your reactions to what a speaker says. If you do, try to keep each note brief.

Exercise Two   Do one or both the following activities.

1. Listen to a television news broadcast. For the first half of the broadcast, listen for main ideas and the details supporting them. For the second half, take notes on the main ideas and details. The next day, write a summary of the broadcast. Which half did you understand better as you listened? Which half did you remember better the next day? How does note-taking help you?

2. The next time you listen to a teacher giving directions or facts, write down all introductory or concluding statements, key words signaling main ideas or details, and questions signaling main ideas.

L E S S O N   T H R E E

Critical Listening

People often try to persuade others to do something or to agree with an opinion. Don't let yourself be swept along by everything a speaker says. Listen *critically*. Decide whether the speaker is giving you facts or appealing to your emotions. Listen for opinions disguised as facts, and be alert to errors in logic.

Suppose a friend tries to persuade you to skip doing your homework and go to a party. Your friend says, "Everyone is going to be there. It's the party of the year." Before you agree to go, think about what you have heard. Your friend is giving you an opinion and appealing to your emotions. Decide for yourself whether the party is really as important as your friend says. Also, ask yourself why your friend is so eager for you to go. Is he thinking about what is best for you or about his own convenience?

Suppose you hear someone say something like "That's the stupidest idea I ever heard." That speaker is appealing to your emotions. Listen for some facts before making up your mind.

Suppose you are listening to a debate on whether or not the school should continue to publish the school newspaper. One speaker says, "I don't know what the papers are like at other schools, but I'm sure ours is the best." Before you agree with that statement, notice that it

contains an error in logic. If the speaker hasn't seen any papers from other schools, how can she compare them with your school's paper?

By the way, listening critically doesn't mean that you have to criticize the speaker. It means that you should think about what you hear and should accept it only if it seems accurate and reasonable. If you disagree, you have a perfect right to express your opinion after the speaker has finished. Of course, you should do so politely.

Courteous Listening

It is every listener's duty to show good manners. Here are the basic rules of courteous listening.

- ☐ Pay attention to the speaker. Don't fidget.
- ☐ If you are one of a group of people listening to a speaker, don't talk or whisper to anyone else during the speech.
- ☐ Try not to interrupt. If you want to give your opinion or ask a question, wait until the speaker stops speaking.
- ☐ If you miss a point that you think might be important, wait until the speaker pauses for questions. Then politely ask him or her to repeat the statement.
- ☐ Don't hesitate to ask questions if you don't understand something you've heard. The speaker will welcome your questions because they show that you are interested.

Exercise Three   Do one or all of the following activities.

1. Practice critical listening. Listen to a television broadcast in which a speaker expresses his or her opinions. Afterward, make some notes on what the speaker said. Do you agree with what you heard? Why or why not?

2. For a day, keep count of the number of times someone (including you!) interrupts while someone else is speaking. Record your results. If possible, discuss the results with your classmates.

3. Work with a group of your fellow students. Pick a topic about your school to discuss. Each student should first write a sentence giving his or her opinion on the subject. Then practice courteous listening as you discuss the topic. Listen critically to what everyone says. At the end of the discussion, write a sentence giving your opinion now. Was it affected by what you heard? Why or why not?

Library and Research Skills

*Salt crystals, magnified with a scanning electron microscope
to 70 times their actual size, 1977
David Scharf, courtesy of Peter Arnold, Inc.*

Library and Research Skills

W hen your teacher asks you to write a research paper, do you panic because you don't know where to begin? When you go to the library to find a book, do you feel lost? If you answer yes to either of these questions, you're not alone. Many people feel uncomfortable in the library. They don't know how to find things quickly and easily.

In this unit you'll learn how to get the answers to thousands of questions from the materials in the library. You'll discover how to use the library to get information for a research paper. You'll find out how to get books for schoolwork and for your personal enjoyment. By the time you've completed the unit, you should feel comfortable in any library.

Exercise One   Complete the two following activities.

1. See if you can figure out where in a library you would look for each item on the left below. On your paper, match each item in the left-hand list to an item in the right-hand list.

something to read for fun	encyclopedia
music to listen to	dictionary
basic facts	cassettes
meaning of a word	book collection
news about recent sports events	newspapers
today's news	magazines

2. Make a list of all the questions you have about the library. You may want to know how to get started finding information for a paper. You may not know where the science books are located. You may wish to know how to get a back issue of a magazine. As you read the rest of the unit, keep your questions in mind. Many of them will be answered.

Fiction Books

Many people use libraries to find books to read for fun, about imaginary people, places, and things. They may read tales of adventure and romance, or realistic stories about people like themselves. Books like these are called *fiction*. Books about real people, places, and things are called *nonfiction*. Fiction and nonfiction are shelved in different sections of the library.

Here is what part of a shelf of fiction books might look like.

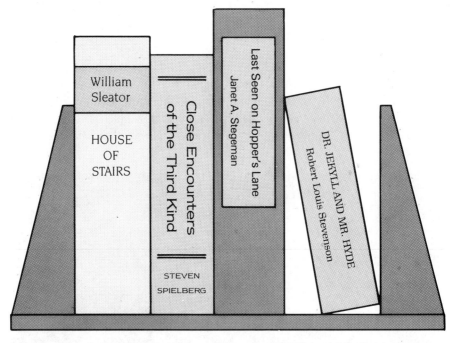

Notice that the books are placed on the shelf in alphabetical order according to the authors' last names. Remember the rules for putting words in alphabetical order: If the first letter in each word is the same, look at the second letter. If the first two letters are the same, look at the third, and so on.

Sleator, Spielberg, Stegeman, and Stevenson all begin with the letter *S*. The second letter in Sleator is *l*, whereas the second letter in Spielberg is *p*. You know that *l* comes before *p* in the alphabet, so you would look for Sleator nearer the beginning of the *S* section and Spielberg further on. Stegeman and Stevenson both begin with *St*. Since you know that *St* comes after *Sl* and *Sp* in alphabetical order, the Stegeman and Stevenson books would be further along in the *S* section. Stegeman and Stevenson share the first three letters *Ste*, so you need to look at the fourth letter to determine their correct alphabetical order. Since *g* comes before *v* in the alphabet, you would find books by Stegeman before books by Stevenson.

In the fiction section, the books by authors whose last names begin with *A* start on the upper left-hand shelf. To find a book by an author whose name begins with a letter that comes later in the alphabet, move your eyes to the right along the shelf. When you come to the end, drop your eyes to the left side of the shelf below, and move your eyes to the right along that shelf. Books are shelved in alphabetical order from left to right, and from top to bottom.

Some libraries have separate sections for special kinds of fiction, such as mysteries, science fiction, and books for young adults. The books in these special fiction sections are also arranged in alphabetical order according to the authors' last names.

Exercise Two   You will need to go to the library to complete the following activities.

1. Sketch a map of your library. Show the entrances, the librarian's desk, and the bookshelves. Find the main fiction section and label it on your map. Mark where the *A* books begin and where the *Z* books end. Show any special sections of fiction books.

2. Look on the library shelves for books by the following authors. On your paper, write down the title of each book you find by these authors.

    Pearl Buck

    Shirley Jackson

    J.R.R. Tolkien

    Mark Twain (may be under Samuel Clemens)

    Hannah Green

    Hermann Hesse

    William Styron

L E S S O N   T W O

Nonfiction Books

When you are looking for factual books for a research paper or for information on any topic you are curious about, you use nonfiction books. Nonfiction is kept on a different set of shelves from fiction, and it is not arranged alphabetically by the authors' last names. Instead, nonfiction books on the same subject are grouped together. This method of arranging books saves you time. You can look in one place and often find several books on the subject you are researching.

Most libraries use the Dewey Decimal system to arrange nonfiction books. In this system, each book is assigned a number from 0 to 999. These numbers are called *call numbers*. The books are arranged on the shelves in numerical order. Larger numbers are placed to the right of or below smaller numbers. Here is what part of a shelf of nonfiction books might look like.

457 A	458.35 P	458.6 J	459.01 T	459.176 Q	460 P

The letter in each call number is the first letter of the author's last name. Notice that librarians follow the rules for putting decimal numbers in order. For example, 458.6 is larger than 458.35, so it is placed after 458.35 on the shelf. (Think of 458.6 as 458.60, and you'll see that it is larger than 458.35.)

Following is a list of call numbers of different kinds of books. Don't memorize the list, but read it over to see what groups of books are placed together.

Numbers	Topic	Examples
000-099	General works	Encyclopedias, newspapers
100-199	Philosophy	People's thoughts, psychology, logic
200-299	Religion	History of religion, different religions
300-399	Social sciences	Politics, economics, law, education
400-499	Language	Dictionaries, foreign languages, English
500-599	Pure science	Chemistry, physics, biology, mathematics
600-699	Applied science	Medicine, farming, cooking, technology, engineering
700-799	Arts/recreation	Drawing, painting, music, games
800-899	Literature	Poems, plays, essays
900-999	History/geography	American and world history, travel, geography

Biographies

Books about people make up a special kind of nonfiction. If they are about one person but written by another, they are called *biographies.* If they are written by a person about himself or herself, they are called *autobiographies.*

Biographies and autobiographies are on a set of shelves separate from other nonfiction and from fiction. Each of the books has a *B* on its spine to indicate that it belongs in the biography section. The books are arranged on the shelves in alphabetical order according to the subject —the person the biography is about. A book about Albert Einstein by Ronald W. Clark would be found under *E* for Einstein. Books about Phil Donahue would come before books about Albert Einstein because *D* comes before *E* in the alphabet. When there is more than one biography of the same person, the alphabetical order of the authors' last names is used to decide the order of the books on the shelves.

Exercise Three   Complete the five following activities.

1. Fiction is arranged alphabetically by authors' last names. How is nonfiction arranged? Biography? Autobiography?

2. Look back at the list of Dewey Decimal numbers. What would be the range of call numbers for a book on China? What about a book on the solar system?

3. If you saw the call number 678.9 T on a book on the shelf, would you look to the left or to the right for a book with the call number 678.92 Q? Where would you look for a book with the call number 678.19 C?

4. A biography of W.E.B. Dubois would have a *B* (for biography) and a *D* (for the subject's last name) on its spine. What letters would be on a biography of Thomas Jefferson by Daniel Boorstin? What would the letters stand for?

5. If you saw a biography of Samuel Adams by Stewart Beach on a shelf, would you look to the right or the left for a book on John Brown by Oswald Garrison Villard? Why?

The Card Catalog

You can find a nonfiction book if you know its call number. You can find a work of fiction if you know the name of its author. You can find a biography if you know the subject and the author. If you don't know the call number or the author, where do you find the information? The answer: in the *card catalog*. The card catalog is a set of small drawers containing index cards. There are at least three cards in the catalog for every nonfiction book in the library. Here is what the three cards might look like for one nonfiction library book.

Getting into computers: a career guide to today's hottest new field

001.646   Brechner, Irv
B   Getting into computers: a career guide to today's
           hottest new field. New York: Ballantine Books,
           1983

001.646   Brechner, Irv
B   Getting into computers: a career guide to today's
           hottest new field. New York: Ballantine Books,
           1983

COMPUTERS — VOCATIONAL GUIDANCE

001.646   Brechner, Irv
B   Getting into computers: a career guide to today's
           hottest new field. New York: Ballantine Books,
           1983

The first card shown here is called the title card, because it has the title at the top. You could find the call number of the book if you knew the title. The call number is in the upper left-hand corner of each card. All the cards in the card catalog are in alphabetical order. So this title card would be found under *G* for *Getting into Computers.*

The second card is called the author card, because it has the author's name at the top. You could find out the title and call number of this book if you knew its author. You'd find the author card under *B* for Brechner.

The third card is the subject card. When you are searching for books for a term paper, you usually start by looking for subject cards in the catalog. The heading *Computers—Vocational Guidance* on a card tells you that this book is about jobs in the computer field. You'd find this card in the catalog under *C* for *Computers.*

This book has three cards because it is a nonfiction book. If it were fiction, it would have an author card and a title card but probably no subject card. It would not have a call number.

A book of biography, however, would have three cards. The subject card would have at the top the name of the person the book was about.

In most libraries, there is one card catalog for author and title cards and another for subject cards. Each drawer in each catalog is labeled with *guide letters*, which show the range of cards in the drawer. If the drawer in the illustration below was a subject drawer, for example, you'd look in it for the subject *Computers* because that word falls between the drawer's guide letters.

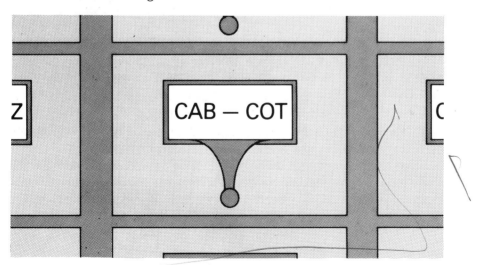

Suppose you were writing a paper on jobs in the computer field. Start with a subject drawer and look up your topic. If you don't find the topic as a heading, think of another way of saying the same thing. If you don't find the topic *Computers*, for example, look up *Data Processing*.

In the catalog there are often index tabs for main headings. Behind each main heading, there are index tabs for subheadings, like *Computers—Circuits* or *Computers—Games*. In the drawer shown below, you would look at the cards under *Computers—Vocational Guidance* for information on jobs.

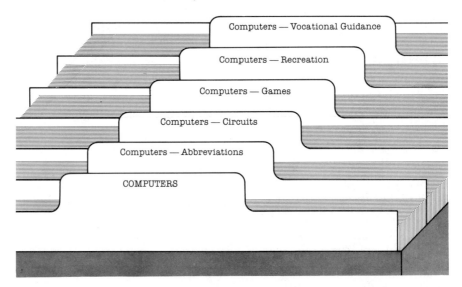

Copy the titles, authors, and call numbers of all the books that might have information on your topic. The card often gives a short description of the book to help you decide whether it contains information you need. Look also at the publication date of each book to see if its information is up-to-date. For a subject such as *space travel,* for example, you don't want a book from the 1960's. For a subject like the Civil War, however, the publication date is usually not important, because facts about past events do not usually change.

Check other headings in the card catalog as well. If you want books about jobs in computer programming, check the heading *Programming* in the catalog. If you are interested in jobs in microcomputers, check the heading *Microcomputers*. Copy the titles, authors, and call numbers of books that might be interesting. Then look for all the books on the shelves.

Some libraries no longer use index cards and drawers for their catalogs. Instead they store subject, author, and title information in books. Each book is like a drawer of the catalog, and its cover is marked with guide letters. You use the same skills whether the catalog is stored in drawers, in books, or even in a computer.

Exercise Four   Go to the library to answer the following questions.

1.   In the card catalog, find a book by Alvin Toffler. Which card catalog did you look in? What are the title and call number of the book you found?

2.   Find the book *Abraham Lincoln: The Prairie Years* in the card catalog. Which catalog did you look in? What kind of book is this? Who is its author? What is its call number?

3.   Find the book *Unsafe at Any Speed* in the card catalog. Who wrote it? What is its call number?

4.   Look up the topic *Computers* in the catalog. Which catalog did you look in? Copy three subheadings that you find under this main heading. Under which of the three subheadings would you look for books on jobs in the computer field?

5.   List two headings under which you could look to find books about jobs in another field. Look for each heading in the catalog. Copy the title, author, and call number of two books from each heading. Now look on the shelves for the books you have listed. Put a check mark next to each book you find. (Don't take the books off the shelf.)

L E S S O N   F O U R

The Parts of a Book

Once you've found a book on the shelf, you want to know whether it contains the information you need, and exactly where in the book the information can be found. By checking a few parts of a book you can usually determine whether the book will be useful to you. Most books are designed to help you find information quickly.

The *front cover* of a book usually displays its title and author. The same information, along with the book's call number, appears on the *spine*—the edge of the book that is exposed on the library shelf. Also, many books have a piece of paper folded around them called a *jacket*. The *back cover* and *flaps* of the jacket often have a description of the book and its author. Reading the jacket can help you decide whether the book will be useful to you.

Within the first few pages of the book is the *title page,* which shows the title, author, and publisher. On the back of the title page is the *copyright page*, which tells when the book was published.

Some books have a *dedication page,* on which the author dedicates the book to someone close to him or her. The dedication page is usually not important to you. The book may also contain a *preface* or *foreword*, in which the author discusses the contents of the book.

The *table of contents,* which also appears in the front of the book, is a listing of all the chapters. If the chapters have titles, a look at the table of contents will often tell you whether the book covers the subjects you are researching.

The *index* is a detailed alphabetical listing in the back of the book of all the topics covered and the pages on which they can be found. A glance at the index will reveal whether the facts you need are in the book.

The index and table of contents help you once you are reading the book as well. Use the table of contents to locate broad areas. Use the index to locate specific details.

Near the end, some books contain a *bibliography*—a list of other books on the same subject. You may want to look for some of these in the library and read them also.

Some books also have a *glossary*—a short dictionary of special words that have been used. A glossary would be very helpful in a computer book, for example.

Exercise Five   Please answer the following questions.

1. Where in a book can you find the date it was published? Would a book about computer programming published in 1970 be useful?

2. What kind of information might you find on the back cover and flaps of a book?

3. What kind of information is found in a glossary? In a bibliography?

4. In a book about computer jobs, where would you look to find out whether the book has information on job training? Where would you look to find out whether the book mentions IBM computers?

5. Why would you look at a book preface?

Using Reference Books

In addition to nonfiction, fiction, and biography, libraries have a group of books called *reference books*. These include *encyclopedias, dictionaries, almanacs,* and *atlases*. They are stored in a special reference section. There you can find facts on just about every subject imaginable. Reference books can be especially helpful to you when you are

writing a research paper, but they cannot be taken out of the library, so it's a good idea to bring a pencil and paper to take notes on the information you find in them.

Encyclopedias

When you start working on a research paper, a good place to look first is in an *encyclopedia*. Encyclopedias are sets of several books containing information on a multitude of topics. Each book in the set is called a *volume*. Encyclopedias only have space enough to offer basic information on a topic. They therefore offer a good place to begin research or to look for a major fact or statistic.

The articles in an encyclopedia are arranged in alphabetical order by topic. Each volume is labeled with a letter or guide letters. If you were looking for general information or statistics on Germany, for example, you would look up *Germany* in the volume labeled *G*.

If you cannot find your topic, or if you are unsure what topic to look under to find a fact, check the index, which is usually the last volume of an encyclopedia. It lists facts alphabetically, along with the volume and page where you can find them. Information on a topic often appears in more than one article. And some topics are not large enough to have their own separate, complete articles. Instead, information on those topics is included in one or more articles on broader subjects. The index will direct you to the correct heading, volume, and page.

When you use the index, think of the most general heading under which you might find information. Look at the subheadings listed under the main heading. The first article listed under a heading or subheading is the main article, but other articles may be more useful. Suppose you are looking for facts on computer jobs in the encyclopedia. You will look up *Computer* in the index. The main article will probably have information you don't need. You will find several subheadings under *Computer*, such as *Careers C 172L*. This entry tells you that there is information on *computer careers* on page 172L of the *Careers* article in Volume C. This article may be more useful than the main computer article.

When you use the index, look up all the headings and subheadings you can think of that might have entries related to your topic. For example, you might look up *Computer Programmer [career]* and find the listing *Ci 744C*. This is a volume and page number you didn't find under *Computer Careers*.

Exercise Six Use the *World Book Encyclopedia* to answer the following questions.

1. In what volume and on what page would you find information on John Kennedy?
2. Where would you find information on amusement parks?
3. Look up *Computer* in the index. Read the subheadings. Which subheading shows you where to look for information on robots?
4. What volumes and pages are listed under *Disney World* in the index? Which of these would be the best place to look for information if you were planning a trip to Disney World? Which might have information on how the park was planned? Look up the articles you chose. Were you right?

Dictionaries

To find information on how to spell a word, what it means, and how it came into the English language, you would use a *dictionary*. Most libraries have an unabridged dictionary—a huge, heavy dictionary that contains nearly every word in the English language. Smaller, abridged dictionaries contain only the most commonly used words. In both kinds of dictionary, words are arranged alphabetically.

Biographical Dictionaries

Biographical dictionaries are a good source of basic information on famous people. They contain short biographies, arranged alphabetically by last name. There are several different kinds of biographical dictionary. Each is useful for different kinds of people and different kinds of information.

A one-volume dictionary like *Webster's Biographical Dictionary* contains very short entries describing people of all times and in all fields. In *Webster's*, you can find facts about presidents, scientists, writers, and other very important people.

The *Dictionary of American Biography* is a twenty-volume set containing biographies of famous Americans of the past. It has no biographies of living people. The biographies are longer and more detailed than the ones in *Webster's*.

Another biographical dictionary is *Who's Who in America*. Updated every year, *Who's Who* has information on famous living Americans. It lists only basic facts, such as date of birth, names of family members, job, main accomplishments, and address. This is a good source of information about politicians, business people, sports figures, and other important living Americans.

Almanacs

Almanacs are books containing thousands of facts and figures. They provide population figures, world records, election results, sports scores, and other information on business, weather, and the earth. Almanacs are printed every year, so the information they contain is up-to-date.

To use an almanac, look in the index for the fact you want. Look under the most general heading you can think of, and check the subheadings under that heading. To find facts about how much rain fell in your state last year, for example, look under *weather* rather than *rainfall*. If you don't find a listing, try other ways of saying the same thing. If you don't find *weather*, for instance, try *climate*.

Atlases

An *atlas* contains maps. Some maps show the borders of countries and the locations of cities. Some show elevation or amount of rainfall. All of the maps in an atlas can help you answer questions about where a place is located or what a region is like.

The table of contents in the front of an atlas shows where each map is found. You would look there to find the page number for a map of Asia, for example. To find a map that shows a smaller area, such as a country or a city, use the index at the back. The index lists every place on every map in the atlas and gives the page number of the map on which the place appears. The index also gives you codes to help you find the place on the map. For example, *161 G6* tells you to turn to page 161 and find *G6* on the map. To find *G6*, trace one index finger down from the *G* at the top of the page and the other index finger across from the *6* at the side of the page. Where your two fingers meet is where you should start looking for the name of the place you want to find.

Exercise Seven   Go to the library to answer the following questions.

1. Look up George Washington in *Webster's Biographical Dictionary*. Then look up George Washington in the *Dictionary of American*

Biography. What differences do you notice between the two biographies?

2. Would you look for information on the current President of the United States in the *Dictionary of American Biography*? Why or why not?

3. For information on the governor of your state, would you look in *Who's Who in America, Webster's Biographical Dictionary*, or the *Dictionary of American Biography*? Explain your answer. Look up the governor in the reference book that you chose. When was he or she born?

4. Find a map of Africa in an atlas like the *National Geographic Atlas of the World*. How did you find out what page the map of Africa was on?

5. Find Kiev in the index of the same atlas. What page numbers and codes does it give? Where is Kiev?

6. Use a current almanac to find out what the flag of Bangladesh looks like. What heading did you look up in the index in order to find the information?

7. According to the almanac, what is the population of Calcutta? Under what heading did you find your answer?

8. Use the almanac to find the winner of the Academy Award for best actress in 1939. Who was she?

Magazines

When you write a research paper, it is often a good idea to look for information in magazines as well as books. Magazines have more up-to-date information than books or encyclopedias. They are the best source of information on events that have happened within the past year or so. And magazines often contain more colorful material than an encyclopedia.

General-interest magazines such as *Time* and *Newsweek* cover current events in many areas. Other magazines cover special interests like photography, cooking, or wildlife.

To find a magazine with information you need, look in the *Readers' Guide to Periodical Literature*. The *Readers' Guide* is published twice a month. Each issue is an index of all the articles published in magazines during the two weeks it covers. The articles are listed by subject.

Subjects are arranged alphabetically. Once a year the bimonthly guides are collected into a larger, hardbound volume.

To use the *Readers' Guide*, look for the most general heading for the information you want. Under that heading look for more specific headings on your topic. For example, to find information on computer jobs, you might look up *Computers*. Many articles are listed under that main heading. Many subheadings are listed as well. Here's an entry you might find under the heading *Computers*:

Study and Teaching

Computer training R.J. Goldfield *Work Woman* 9:60+ F '84

The *Readers' Guide* uses abbreviations. Keys in the front of the book tell you what the abbreviations mean. Using the keys, you can figure out what the above entry means.

Title: "Computer Training"

Author: R.J. Goldfield

Name of the magazine: *Working Woman*

Volume number: 9

Page number of the article: 60, plus later pages in the issue

Issue date: February 1984

Here's an entry under *Aids and devices*, a subcategory under the *Study and Teaching* subhead of the *Computers* heading.

A guide to computer training materials G. Blank il *Creative Computing* 10: S1-S16 Ag '84

The magazine in this entry is *Creative Computing*, a special-interest computer magazine. The article is illustrated.

To decide whether to read an article, look at its title and the name of the magazine in which it was published. Either of the articles on computers mentioned here might be useful to you. An article in *Working Woman* would have more general information on a subject like computers, whereas an article in *Creative Computing* would have more technical information.

To locate a magazine article in the library, first ask the librarian whether the library keeps back issues of the magazine. If so, copy the magazine's name, volume, and date from the *Readers' Guide*. The librarian will use the information to find the issue you need.

Exercise Eight   Use the *Readers' Guide* for March 1984 to February 1985 to answer the following questions.

1. Look at the keys in the front of the book to find out what *rev* means. Then find out what *N* means.

2. Look up the topic *Computers—Art use*. Copy the entry for the article "The computer as an artistic tool." Explain what each part of the entry means. Use the keys in the front of the book if you need help.

3. Look for an article on how to learn computer programming. What main heading did you look up? What subheadings under that did you look at? What is the title of the article you found?

4. Copy down the information the librarian would need in order to find the article you just looked up.

Study Skills

*Japanese family having a picnic in the foothills of Mt. Fuji, 1961
Burt Glinn, Magnum Photos, Inc.*

Study Skills

D arren decided to learn how to play the saxophone. At first, all he could make the instrument do was squeak and whine. It sounded awful, and Darren's little sister didn't hesitate to tell him so. But Darren was confident that he would get the hang of it eventually. He knew he just needed to practice. After a year of practicing every day, Darren auditioned for the school band, and made it. That accomplishment made all those hours of practice worthwhile. He was proud of his performance.

Learning how to study is like learning how to play an instrument. Your skills improve through practice. You just have to be patient and keep trying. In this unit, you will learn the specific study skills to practice, so that you, too, can be proud of your performance.

Understanding the Assignment

You may not think about it, but you follow all sorts of directions every day. From the moment the alarm clock goes off in the morning until you set it before you go to bed at night, there are hundreds of demands made on you. For example, you have to make sure the shower curtain is tucked inside the tub when you take a shower, so that you don't flood the bathroom. And when you cross the street, you know you should wait until the light turns green.

Following directions that aren't part of your daily routine require a little more attention. When your teacher gives you an assignment, you should listen carefully. Write it down on a memo pad or in a notebook. Make sure you understand what your teacher is asking you to do. If you don't understand, ask questions.

Read the following assignments.

1. Read pages 202 through 228.

2. Write a three-paragraph essay on your favorite food.

3. Complete problems 1 through 20, answering the even-numbered questions only.

These assignments may appear simple. But if you don't listen carefully and write them down when the teacher gives them, you may make mistakes. Suppose you tried to memorize the first assignment, but when you got home you couldn't remember if it was page 202 or 220. You could end up missing eighteen pages of reading. Suppose you thought that the second assignment asked for a three-*page* paper instead of a three-*paragraph* paper. You would be doing three times more writing than was necessary. It would be easy to remember to do problems 1 through 20, and easy to forget that only the even-numbered questions had been assigned. Doing the wrong assignment wastes time and leads to extra work for you.

Here is an assignment Mr. Martin gave his English class.

Mr. Martin: For Wednesday, please read the short story "The Telephone," by Dorothy Parker. Write a response from the telephone's point of view.

Sara: Mr. Martin, what page number is the story on in our textbook?

Mr. Martin: The story begins on page 125.

Arthur: Excuse me, but what exactly do you mean by "a response from the telephone's point of view"?

Mr. Martin: Good question. If the telephone had a mind of its own, how do you think it would react to the speaker in the story? What would it be thinking? What might it say to the woman in the story? Perhaps it would have suggestions or advice to give her. Maybe it would like to be unplugged and left alone. How do you think it feels? That would be the telephone's point of view.

George: Is it due this Wednesday or next?

Mr. Martin: This Wednesday, November 5.

Here is how Barbara wrote the assignment in her notebook:

English, Nov. 3

Read "The Telephone" pg. 125

Write response from telephone's point of view. (How tel. would feel.)

Due Wed., Nov. 5

P O I N T S   T O   R E M E M B E R

▷ Keep an assignment notebook.

▷ Write homework directions in your notebook when the teacher gives the assignment.

▷ If you have questions about the assignment, ask your teacher right away.

▷ Pay close attention when the assignment is being given.

Exercise One   Using the suggestions in Lesson One, write the following assignment in your own notebook. Beneath it, write three questions you could ask the teacher about the directions.

Read Eugenia Collier's story "Marigolds" in the *Scope English Anthology,* Level Four. Then do the following writing assignment: Pretend you are Lizabeth, the main character in the story. Write a letter to Miss Lottie, explaining why you ruined her marigolds and apologizing for your actions.

L E S S O N   T W O

Planning Time

Once you know what you have to do, you must figure out when you can do it. Organizing your time is important whether you are the president of a multimillion-dollar company, or a tenth-grader with a lot of homework and other responsibilities. Everyone starts out with the same twenty-hours in each day. How you use the hours is up to you.

Many people find routines helpful. Steven gets up, dresses, goes to school, comes home, does his homework, sets the table, eats dinner, watches TV, and goes to bed. Each school day is basically the same for him. But sometimes things come up unexpectedly (a baby-sitting job or an extra amount of homework, for example). Then Steven has to rearrange his basic schedule to make sure the most important things get done. Some days he has to give up watching TV or arrange for his brother to set the table, for example.

Many students find it helpful to consider the activities of other family members when they are working out a study schedule. Sally must do her homework early in the morning, before school starts. That is the only time her house is quiet enough for her to concentrate. Her friend Josh does his homework during study halls, and after school he goes to the library. When he tries to work at home, he is often interrupted and does a poor job on assignments, if he is able to finish them at all.

Making a timetable of your week can help you devise a good study schedule. Draw a calendar of a week. Label it with the days of the week and the hours of the day. Fill in classes, extracurricular activities, and any regular responsibilities. The empty spaces left on your timetable are periods when you can plan to do schoolwork.

Nancy made a list of assignments at the beginning of the school week:

For Monday:

    Math—chap. 5, problems 6-12

    Eng.—pp. 25-45, questions 1, 3, 5 at end of chap.

    Sci.—chap. 6

For Tuesday:

    Soc. Stud.—read newspaper article and write letter to editor

    Spanish—chap. 8, conjugate verbs on last page

    Art—sketch one household object

For Wednesday:

    Math—chap. 6, problems 1-8

    Eng.—pp. 50-65

    Sci.—quiz

For Thursday:

    Soc. Stud.—chap. 12

    Spanish—verb quiz

    Art—finished drawing of household object

For Friday:

    Math—test

    Eng.—book report due

    Sci.—chap. 7

Then Nancy made a schedule to make sure she would get all her assignments done on time. First, she carefully considered how much time she needed for each subject. Math, science, and Spanish are the subjects that are easiest for her. She needs less time for homework in these subjects than in others. She has track practice every day after school. On Wednesday she has a meet against another high school. On Monday she cooks dinner for her family. Tuesday and Thursday she cleans up after dinner. Her favorite TV show is on Thursday night at 8:00. On Friday she usually baby-sits for her next-door neighbor.

Here is the schedule Nancy devised for her week:

	MONDAY	TUESDAY	WEDNESDAY	THURSDAY	FRIDAY
7:00	Science homework	Spanish homework	Study for Science quiz	Art homework	Study Math
8:00	ENGLISH	ENGLISH	ENGLISH	ENGLISH	ENGLISH
9:00	SCIENCE	SCIENCE	SCIENCE	SCIENCE	SCIENCE
10:00	GYM	Study Hall English homework	GYM	Study Hall Study Spanish	GYM
11:00	Study Hall Math homework	ART	Study Hall Read Social Studies	ART	Study Hall English homework
12:00	LUNCH	LUNCH	LUNCH	LUNCH	LUNCH
1:00	MATH	MATH	MATH	MATH	MATH
2:00	SPANISH	SPANISH	SPANISH	SPANISH	SPANISH
3:00	Social Studies	Social Studies	Social Studies	Social Studies	Social Studies
4:00	TRACK	TRACK	Track Meet	TRACK	TRACK
5:00	Social Studies homework	Math homework	↓	Read Science Chapter	Free Time
6:00	Cook dinner	Free Time	Free Time	Begin Book report for English	↓
7:00	DINNER	Dinner & dishes	DINNER	Dinner & dishes	DINNER
8:00	Art homework	Study for Science quiz	Study for Spanish quiz	TV	Baby-sit for Grahams
9:00	TV			Finish Book report for English	
10:00	↓			↓	
11:00	↓	↓	↓	Study for Math quiz	↓

313

▷ Plan more time for assignments you think will be more difficult for you.

▷ Plan to do first the assignments that are due the earliest.

▷ Include rest breaks in your schedule. They help you stay fresh and alert.

▷ Use study halls to do your homework. That way you'll have more free time at the end of the day and on weekends.

Exercise Two　　In your notebook, make a study schedule for this week. See if planning your time carefully makes a difference in whether you complete your assignments on time. If you have trouble keeping to your schedule, try to figure out how you could change it to make it more effective. Did you give yourself enough time for difficult subjects? Did you plan ahead for long-term projects? Use what you've learned from this first schedule to make an even better schedule for next week.

L E S S O N　　　T H R E E

Choosing a Place to Study

Once you have a schedule, you need to find a place to work. Easy? Not always. This can sometimes be more difficult than it sounds. It certainly wasn't easy for Susan. Here's her story; see if any of the problems she had sound familiar.

Just as Susan sat down on the living room couch to study for her math quiz, the telephone rang. Her best friend, Ellen, had boyfriend troubles. Susan could tell Ellen was pretty upset. They talked for about half an hour. By then, Susan was sure that Ellen was feeling a little better. Susan returned to her books, but a few minutes later, her brother barged into the room to watch TV. Susan tried to continue studying, but she found it hard to concentrate with cartoons blaring in the background. Finally, she collected her books and moved into the kitchen. As soon as she had spread her papers out on the table, her mother came in

to cook dinner. Susan's mother was in a hurry, and she asked Susan to slice some carrots. She assured Susan it would take only a few minutes. By the time the clock struck six, Susan was in a bad mood. She had spent half the time she had planned to prepare for her math quiz. And she wouldn't be able to spend any more time studying for it that night because she had to write an essay for her English class.

Susan had a feeling she would not do her best on her math quiz. She promised herself that next time she would go to the library to study.

Here are some things to look for in a study space:

- ☐ Privacy
- ☐ Quiet
- ☐ A clean table or desk
- ☐ Good lighting

Here are some things to avoid:

- ☐ Friends and family
- ☐ The telephone
- ☐ TV and radio

Often it is helpful to discuss your study schedule with your family. Together you can establish a time and place for you to do your schoolwork. Once the members of your family know your routine, they will be less likely to interrupt you

If working at home seems too difficult, try studying at your school or public library. Some students prefer working in the library even when it is possible to study at home. The library is almost always quiet. There is good lighting. There are spacious tables to work on, and there are lots of reference books available if you need them.

Wherever you choose to study, it's helpful to have the following study tools on hand.

- ☐ a dictionary
- ☐ a one-volume encyclopedia
- ☐ appropriate textbooks
- ☐ your notebooks
- ☐ your assignment book
- ☐ pens and pencils
- ☐ an eraser
- ☐ extra paper

Exercise Three　　Imagine that you have an English test on Wednesday, and English is your toughest subject. You plan to prepare for it on Monday and Tuesday. But your older sister calls you on Monday after school, and asks you if you would baby-sit for your niece and nephew that night. You know that baby-sitting for them takes all your attention and every ounce of energy. What should you do?

a.　Say, "Sure." If you do poorly on this test, you can make up for it by studying extra hard next time. This one you will write off to family obligations.

b.　Tell your sister you'll be happy to baby-sit at a time when you don't have important school work to do.

c.　Tell your sister you have a lot of work to do, but you'll bring it along and hope to get as much done as possible.

Reading a Textbook

When you open a textbook, do you stare at the pages and think to yourself, "How can I possibly absorb and understand all this information?" If you do, you'll be relieved to know that reading a textbook doesn't have to be difficult. If you follow the suggestions in this lesson, you may find that reading a textbook is easier than you thought.

One approach you may find helpful when you read a textbook is to relate what you read to your own experience. This can help make the subject more understandable. In fact, the reason most information is included in a textbook is that it does have an important effect on your life, however unrelated the information may seem at first glance. As you read, try to figure out why the information was included, and how it relates to your life.

Here are some other tips to make your textbook reading more effective.

☐ Read the introduction of the assigned chapter. This usually tells you what kind of information will be discussed in the rest of the chapter.

☐ Read the conclusion. It summarizes the chapter and emphasizes the most important points. It helps to keep those points in mind when you read the chapter.

☐ Skim the assignment. This gives you a general sense of the subject matter it covers. Pay attention to headings and illustrations and the first sentence of each paragraph.

☐ Read the assignment carefully from start to finish. Keep in mind the points covered in the introduction and conclusion as you do so. Reread any sections that seem unclear.

☐ Take notes. Jot down important ideas and facts, as well as questions that you wish to ask your teacher about the material.

☐ Take the time to look up unfamiliar or technical words.

Exercise Four   Select a chapter you have not read in one of your textbooks. If you wish to use a current assignment, you may do so. Follow these instructions.

1. Read the introduction. In a sentence, write what you think the chapter will be about.

2. Read the conclusion. List the important ideas summarized there.

3. Skim the chapter, taking note of headings, illustrations, and the first sentence of each paragraph.

4. Carefully read the chapter from beginning to end. As you read, write down important facts, questions, and unfamiliar words in a notebook.

5. Look up the words you wrote down and write the definitions in your notebook.

6. Review the chapter. Try to find the answers to the questions you wrote down. Remember to ask your teacher the questions that aren't answered in your book.

Taking Notes

One of the best ways to remember information is to write it down. This is true whether you are going to the grocery store, driving to an unfamiliar city, or listening to a lecture on the American Civil War. The act of writing helps to plant information in your memory. Then if you need to refresh your memory later, you just have to look at your notes.

When you take notes in class, you have two goals. You want to write down all the information you need to remember. You also want to hear as much of the lesson or lecture as you can. It's hard to do both because writing takes your attention away from what you are hearing. That's why it's important to use shortcuts when you take notes.

One way to take notes faster is to write down only the most important points. This will help you save time, and your notes will be more useful because they will contain only what is really important. Using symbols can also save you time. Following are some common symbols that people use when taking notes. You can use these or invent your own.

=   same as; equal to; is

*   important

&, +   and

→   which leads to

Abbreviations are also helpful shortcuts. Some people write down the first few letters of words. Others write down the consonants and leave out the vowels. Any method that helps you to take notes quickly and legibly is a good method.

Here are some tips that may help you improve your note taking.

☐   Listen carefully for key words and phrases that relate to the subject you are studying.

☐   Don't try to write every word down.

☐   Read over your notes after class or after reading the assignment. Correct any errors immediately, and fill in any gaps in the information. The more often you read your notes, the easier it will be to remember the new information.

☐   Keep a vocabulary list of words and expressions you are not familiar with. Ask your teacher for the definitions or look them up in the dictionary after class.

Doug's science teacher, Mr. Barber, wrote the word *photosynthesis* on the board. He told the class that it would be the subject of the day's lesson. Following is part of what Mr. Barber said in class. As you read it, think of what notes you would take if you were in Doug's class.

Did you ever wonder how plants get their food? Well, green plants have a unique method of feeding themselves. They don't eat other plants or (with a few exceptions) animals. Instead, they produce their own food by a process called *photosynthesis.* This word comes from three Greek words which together mean "putting together with light." *Photo* means "light," *syn* means "together," and *thesis* comes from a word meaning "to put." The plant takes in light through its leaves. Then it combines the energy from the light with water and carbon dioxide to make food. Where does the plant get the carbon dioxide? Carbon dioxide is in the air. Every time you exhale, in fact, you are returning carbon dioxide to the atmosphere.

Here are the notes that Doug took during class:

Science, Nov. 2

Photosynthesis

    How plants get food?

    (don't eat)

    They produce own food by PHOTOSYNTHESIS.

    photosyn. = put together with light

    fr. Greek: photo = light, syn = together, thesis = put

    energy fr. light + H_2O + carbon diox. → food

carbon diox. in air (you exhale it)

Exercise Five   Practice taking notes in class. Choose a different class each day for a week. For that class period, concentrate on taking notes according to the suggestions in this lesson. (Refer to the tips on page 319.) Review your notes after a week to see which suggestions worked best for you.

Using Maps

Each map gives you a particular kind of information about an area. The kind of information it gives depends on the kind of map it is. For example, road maps show highways and roads within a state, between states, or running from one county or country to another. Street maps show you the streets within a smaller, more defined area: a city, town, or specific neighborhood. Street maps also indicate buildings, parks, and other local landmarks. Political maps show boundaries between cities, counties, states, and countries. Physical maps give information about an area's natural features, such as streams, lakes, rivers, mountains, plains, deserts, woodlands, and forests.

Below is a road map that shows the northeastern tip of the United States (part of Maine) and the southeastern tip of Canada, including all or part of the provinces of Nova Scotia, Prince Edward Island, and New Brunswick. The letters and numbers along the edges of the map help you to locate specific points. For example, suppose you wanted to find Bangor, Maine. First, you would look up Bangor in the index (not shown here). It would tell you to look for Bangor at the location E1. Using the letters and numbers along the edges, you would trace an imaginary line across from E and another down from 1. You would find Bangor somewhere near the point where the two lines meet.

The legend, located in the lower right-hand corner, indicates what each symbol on the map means. On this map a star represents a capital city; a dot represents a smaller city. The routes for ferries are indicated by dotted lines. Differently shaped emblems represent the various highways. Small arrows mark the mileage along these highways.

By using the scale on the map you can measure the distance between different cities. For this purpose you can also us the mileage markers. These arrows mark points along the roads where the mileage has been measured. The number that appears between each set of arrows tells you how many miles are represented. For example, the distance between Boiestown and Chatham is 64 miles.

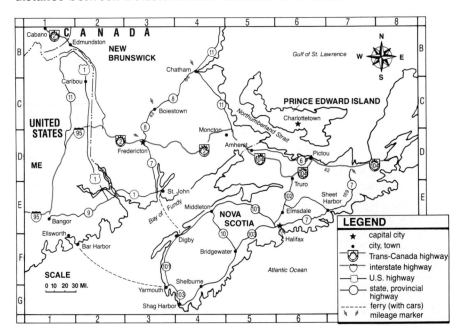

Use the map on page 322 to answer the following questions.

1. How many miles is it between Fredericton and Boiestown?
2. What is the shortest route from Bar Harbor to Yarmouth?
3. What is the capital city of Prince Edward Island?
4. What capital city is found at location E6?

L E S S O N   S E V E N

Reading Graphs and Tables

Graphs and tables help make facts and statistics easier to understand. They are generally used to show trends or changes over a period of time, or comparisons between different sets of information.

Graphs use bars, lines, or symbols to represent information. Bar graphs are used to compare information, usually amounts. The following bar graph shows how many electric blankets were sold at Jack's Appliance Palace during 1986. A quick glance tells you electric blanket sales peaked in January and again in June during the summer sale.

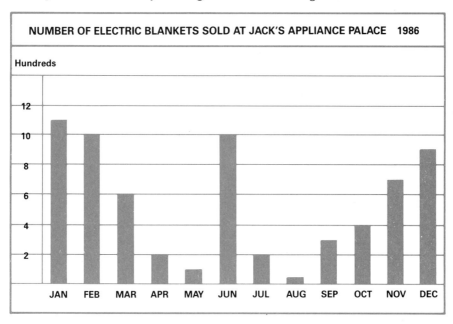

NUMBER OF ELECTRIC BLANKETS SOLD AT JACK'S APPLIANCE PALACE   1986

Hundreds

Circle graphs, also called pie charts, show percentages. The following graph illustrates the different modes of transportation that the students in Mr. Hunter's homeroom use to get to school. The graph tells you that more students travel by bus than any other method of transportation.

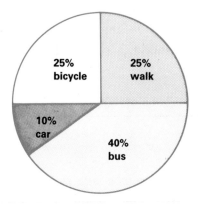

Line graphs generally show how something has changed over time. Line graphs can also show how one set of statistics compares to another. The line graph that follows compares the number of electric blankets sold at Jack's Appliance Palace in 1986 with the number of electric fans sold in 1986. The key at the bottom shows you what each line represents.

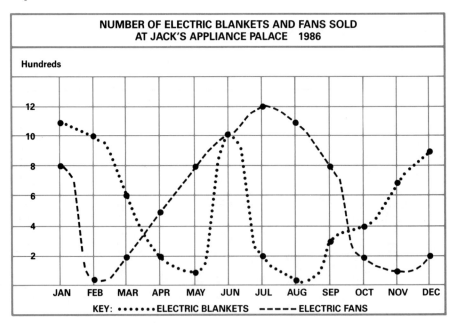

The information on a table is arranged in rows and columns. This format makes it easy for you to locate or compare the facts listed. The table that follows shows the different kinds of music that students in Ms. Tyson's class listen to during the course of an average week. As a group, Ms. Tyson's students spend more time listening to rock'n'roll than any other kind of music.

AVERAGE TIME SPENT LISTENING TO MUSIC (in hours per week)						
Students	Classical	Rock	Disco	Folk	Country	TOTAL
Mary	1	17	24	0	0	42
Steve	5	2	0	9	24	40
Nancy	8	1^1/$_2$	6	22	4^1/$_2$	42
Jonah	10	7	0	12	6	35
Susan	2	18	20	0	0	40
Matthew	0	24	5	0	15	44
Josh	30	8	2	9	0	49
Claire	0	22	8	0	0	30
TOTAL	56	99^1/$_2$	65	52	49^1/$_2$	322

Exercise Seven   Use the bar graph, circle graph, line graph, and table to answer the following questions:

1. In what month did Jack's Appliance Palace sell the most electric fans?
2. How many electric blankets were sold in that month?
3. In what month did Jack's Appliance Palace sell the same amount of electric blankets as electric fans?
4. What percentage of students in Mr. Hunter's homeroom walk to school?

5. What is the least common way for students in Mr. Hunter's homeroom to get to school?

6. What kind of music did Ms. Tyson's students listen to for the least number of hours?

7. Which of Ms. Tyson's students spent the most time listening to disco?

8. What kind of music did Josh spend the most time listening to?

L E S S O N   E I G H T

Taking Tests

Tests! Just the thought of a test makes Ellen feel queazy. She can't fall asleep the night before. During the test, she gets so nervous she sometimes forgets to put her name on the test paper. You probably don't fear tests as much as Ellen does. Most people don't. But most people feel some uneasiness, at the prospect of taking a test.

A good way to reduce test anxiety is to be as prepared for the test as possible. The more familiar you are with the material, the less likely you are to dread going to class the day of the test. In fact, if you know the information inside out, you may even *want* to take the test so that you can show your teacher how much you know.

Here are some tips to help you prepare for a test:

☐ Begin to study for a test well in advance.

☐ Review class notes and reading assignments.

☐ Make up practice tests for yourself. Try swapping practice tests with a classmate.

☐ If there is some material you have questions about, ask your teacher before you take the test. Don't be embarrassed to ask questions.

☐ Try to explain the information you are studying to someone else. Sometimes trying to teach the material can make it clearer to you.

Following are some tips to help you take a test.

- ☐ Arrive at the test early.
- ☐ Bring extra pens, pencils, and paper.
- ☐ Bring any suggested tools (compass, calculator, dictionary).
- ☐ If you are afraid you will forget something, write it on the test paper as soon as you sit down to take the test.
- ☐ Read over the entire test before you begin to answer the questions.
- ☐ Answer the questions you are sure of first.
- ☐ Use the process of elimination to narrow down the choices in multiple-choice questions. First, rule out any choices you know are wrong. Then look at the remaining choices, and use your best judgment to select the most likely answer.
- ☐ Before writing your answer, read the question carefully to make sure you understand exactly what is being asked.
- ☐ Check the clock occasionally to make sure you are pacing yourself well.

Exercise Eight   Answer the following questions.

1. *Multiple choice:* A good way to avoid getting nervous about taking a test is by _____.
   a. studying the material thoroughly. It takes time but almost always makes a difference.
   b. eating an enormous meal right before the test. Nourishment helps you think clearly.
   c. sitting next to someone who never gets nervous. Calmness has a way of rubbing off.
   d. not thinking about the test until the day before you have to take it.

2. *Short answer:* In a few sentences, describe how to answer a multiple-choice question.

3. *True or False:* It is important when taking notes in class to write out every word and to use perfect grammar and punctuation. T/F

4. *Fill in the Blank:* The best way to reduce test anxiety is to _____ for the test well in advance.

III
LANGUAGE SKILLS

The Parts of Speech

Horse, sheep, and goat, New Hampshire, 1985
Copyright Helen Levitt, courtesy of Daniel Wolf, Inc., New
York City

The Parts of Speech

Have you ever done a tangram puzzle? It's a kind of puzzle that was invented in China hundreds of years ago. You have seven cardboard pieces of different shapes and sizes. And you have a picture to look at. You are supposed to put the seven cardboard pieces together to form that picture. If you have a good eye for shapes—and quite a bit of patience—you can make hundreds of different pictures. To mention just a few—you can make a lighthouse, a high-heeled shoe, a kangaroo, a horse and rider, and two people in a boat.

In a way, the English language is like a tangram puzzle. You have seven different kinds of words called *parts of speech*. And you have an idea in your head that you want to express. You have to put the parts of speech together to form a sentence that matches your idea. Of course, there are many more English sentences than there are tangram pictures. The number of possible sentences is probably infinite.

The seven parts of speech that you have to work with are *nouns, pronouns, verbs, adjectives, adverbs, prepositions,* and *conjunctions*.

You may be saying to yourself, "But I thought there were eight parts of speech." You're right—there are *interjections,* too. However, an interjection is not really part of the sentence. It is an expression, like *oh* or *hey*, that is tacked on to the sentence. It shows how the speaker or writer feels, but it has no grammatical connection with the other words in the sentence. Nevertheless, in this unit you will study interjections along with the seven important parts of speech.

L E S S O N   O N E

Nouns

The following lines come from an old, familiar song. As you can see, eight words are missing. Can you fill in the blanks?

_____, _____,
Give me your _____, do!
I'm half crazy
All for the _____ of you!
It won't be a stylish _____,
I can't afford a _____,
But you'll look sweet upon the _____
Of a _____ built for two!

If you were able to fill in the blanks in that song, you used the following seven words: *Daisy* (you used this word twice in the first line), *answer, love, marriage, carriage, seat,* and *bicycle.* All seven of these words are examples of one part of speech. They are all *nouns.*

P O I N T S   T O   K N O W

A **noun** is the name of a person, place, or thing.

▶ A noun can be a person: *Daisy, athlete, woman, singer, George Washington.*

▶ A noun can be a place: *city, mountain, beach, Carson's Restaurant.*

▶ A noun can be a thing: *apple, rain, sidewalk, bicycle, marriage, freedom, success.*

As you probably noticed, some nouns name things that cannot be seen or touched. Things like *freedom* and *success* are ideas, not material objects. You can think about them and talk about them. But you cannot see them, although you may see the results of freedom or success in your life.

Common and Proper Nouns

The part of speech that we call nouns is a very large group, with hundreds of thousands of members. This large group can be divided into two smaller ones: *common nouns* and *proper nouns.*

Every noun is either **common** or **proper**.

A *common noun* refers to any member of a category of persons, places, or things. A *proper noun* refers to a particular person, place, or thing. It begins with a capital letter.

Common Nouns	Proper Nouns
athlete	Debbie Thomas
inventor	Eli Whitney
island	Oahu
country	France
movie	*Star Trek*
book	*Treasure Island*

In the list of nouns you have just read, there are four proper nouns that are made up of two words each. A proper noun may have two or more words in it. However, if it names one person, place, or thing, it is considered one noun. Following are some more examples.

Dr. Arthur Cabot	Golden Gate Bridge
Lake Michigan	*Sports Illustrated*

Singular and Plural Nouns

A noun is either *singular* or *plural* in number. You can usually tell by the form of the noun whether it is singular or plural.

▶ A noun that refers to one person, place, or thing is *singular*.

▶ A noun that refers to two or more people, places, or things is *plural*.

▶ Most nouns form the plural by adding *-s* or *-es* to the singular.

▶ Some nouns form the plural in different ways. For example, the plural of *child* is *children*, and the plural of *foot* is *feet*.

Here are some sentences containing singular and plural nouns.

Singular	**Plural**
My **sister** is a good **athlete**.	My **sisters** are good **athletes**.
The **canoe** tipped over.	The **canoes** tipped over.
The **man** swam toward the **boat**.	The **men** swam toward the **boats**.
The **mouse** is squeaking.	The **mice** are squeaking.

Collective Nouns

A **collective noun** names a group of people or things.

Here are some examples:

crew	herd
group	class
committee	pair
audience	team
band	family

Although a collection of people or things may have many members, the members often act together as a unit. When they do so, the collective noun is considered singular.

> The **crew** of the ship is well trained.
>
> The **herd** of cattle has broken through the fence.
>
> The **band** was playing my favorite song.

Compound Nouns

A **compound noun** is a combination of two or more words that work together as one noun.

Often a compound noun has a special meaning. It is not just the sum of its parts. For example, the two words *green house* refer to a house that is green. But when those two words are put together in a compound noun, the meaning changes. A *greenhouse* is a building where plants can be grown all year round.

Most compound nouns are written as one word, like *greenhouse*. However, some are written with hyphens (-) between the parts, and others are written with space between the parts. Here are examples of the three types.

bluebird	daughter-in-law	iron lung
pancake	teach-in	growing pains
playground	jack-o'-lantern	safety pin

Practice A   Identify singular and plural nouns.

Write the nouns from each sentence on your paper. Next to each noun, write *S* if it is singular or *P* if it is plural.

EXAMPLE: In April, George and his family went to New York City for a few days.

April—S; George—S; family—S; New York City—S; days—P

1. A collie with muddy feet jumped on the child in the pink dress.
2. Old Faithful is a geyser in Yellowstone National Park.
3. For his breakfast, Uncle Ned ate eggs and toast.
4. The intelligence of the dolphin is shown by the speed with which it learns.
5. I like to read stories about Nero Wolfe, a detective who grows orchids as a hobby.
6. Greece is called the birthplace of democracy.
7. Flocks of geese fly to Mexico for the winter.
8. It is against the law to pick wild flowers that are in danger of becoming extinct.
9. The Appalachian Trail goes from Georgia to Maine.
10. The president of the Booster Club asked for volunteers.
11. Lincoln was shot while watching a play in Ford's Theater.
12. The spectators gave a warm welcome to the team.
13. The month of August brought hot days and cool nights.
14. The terrifying tales of Edgar Allan Poe have thrilled readers for years.
15. This pair of shoes is too expensive.

Practice B   **Write common and proper nouns.**

Write a common or proper noun for each category listed below.

EXAMPLE: emotion (common)
happiness

1. body of water (common)
2. television show (proper)
3. language (proper)
4. kind of animal (common)
5. object in your locker (common)
6. person you like (proper)
7. occupation (common)
8. place in your community (proper)
9. place in your community (common)
10. group of people you belong to (common)
11. kind of book (common)
12. ruler (proper)
13. place you'd like to visit (common)
14. place you'd like to visit (proper)
15. body of water (proper)

Practice C   **Write sentences with nouns.**

Follow the directions for writing sentences.

EXAMPLE: Write a sentence about music that contains two proper nouns.
Ringo Starr played drums for the Beatles.

1. Write a sentence about food that contains three common nouns.
2. Write a sentence about history that contains two proper nouns.
3. Write a sentence about geography that contains a proper and a common noun.
4. Write a sentence about a vacation that contains a proper noun.
5. Write a sentence about sports that contains a collective noun.
6. Write a sentence about school that contains a common noun.

7. Write a sentence about animals that contains two collective nouns.

8. Write a sentence about a book that contains a proper noun.

9. Write a sentence about a hobby that contains a plural common noun.

10. Write a sentence about plants that contains a compound noun.

L E S S O N   T W O

Pronouns

The audience is waiting eagerly for the play to begin. The lights begin to fade, but the curtain does not go up. The star is sick.

What should the director say to the audience? Should she tell everyone to go home? Wait! Where is Dinah Drabble, that young beginning actress who memorized the star's part?

"Dinah, this is your chance," the director tells her. Into the star's costume goes Dinah Drabble. Up goes the curtain. Of course you know the result—the next day she's a star.

Dinah Drabble is what theater people call an understudy. An understudy must always be prepared to take the place of the regular performer.

Nouns have understudies, too. Words used as substitutes for nouns are called *pronouns*.

P O I N T S   T O   K N O W

A **pronoun** is a word that takes the place of one or more nouns. It refers to a noun that has already been stated or is understood.

Here is a paragraph with three pronouns:

When the actress walked on stage, **she** seemed nervous. The other actors supported Dinah wholeheartedly. **They** hoped **she** would succeed.

Nouns, of course, don't get sick. But readers can get sick of reading the same noun over and over. When that happens, they welcome the sight of any pronoun that can take the noun's place.

Read the paragraph that follows. When you finish it, you should be eager to hear more about pronouns.

Madeline picked up Madeline's glove from the bench. Madeline also picked up a ball and began to throw the ball to Madeline's friend Peter. Peter caught the ball in Peter's glove and said to Madeline, "Throw the ball harder." Madeline threw the ball to Peter with all Madeline's might. Peter caught the ball and then pulled off Peter's glove. "Don't throw the ball that hard," Peter said to Madeline. Peter returned the ball to Madeline. Peter rubbed Peter's sore hand and shook Peter's head as Peter waited for Madeline's next throw.

Let's bring in some pronouns for relief.

Madeline picked up **her** glove from the bench. **She** also picked up a ball and began to throw **it** to **her** friend Peter. Peter caught the ball in **his** glove and said to Madeline, "Throw **it** harder." Madeline threw the ball to **him** with all **her** might. **He** caught **it** and then pulled off **his** glove. "Don't throw **it** that hard," **he** said to **her**. Peter returned the ball to Madeline. **He** rubbed **his** sore hand and shook **his** head as **he** waited for **her** next throw.

In the second paragraph, the pronouns have taken the place of the nouns *Madeline, ball,* and *Peter* in some sentences.

▶ A noun that is replaced by a pronoun is called the *antecedent* of the pronoun.

Antecedent means "something that goes before something else." The noun usually goes before the pronoun that replaces it.

Madeline took off *her* glove. *She* also . . .

Peter rubbed *his* **hand** because *it* hurt.

▶ The antecedent of a pronoun may be another pronoun.

They were trying to push *their* car up the hill.

▶ Sometimes the antecedent of a pronoun is not stated but is understood by the reader or listener.

I hope you will be able to come to the party on June 10.

The reader knows that *I* refers to the writer.

On the next few pages you will find explanations of different kinds of pronouns. You don't have to memorize these pronouns. However, you do need to be able to recognize a pronoun when you see it.

Personal Pronouns

Look at these sentences.

> Jane gave George a present, and **he** thanked **her** for **it**.
>
> George gave **her** a present, and **she** thanked **him** for **it**.
>
> **They** opened **their** presents and put **them** on the table.

The words in boldface (heavy) type are called *personal pronouns* because each one is either "first person," "second person," or "third person." In addition, each pronoun is either singular or plural. The chart that follows shows the three persons and two numbers of the personal pronouns.

Persons	**Numbers**	
	Singular	*Plural*
First Person	the person speaking **I, me, my, mine**	the persons speaking or the person speaking and his/her associates **we, us, our, ours**
Second Person	the person spoken to **you, your, yours**	the persons spoken to **you, your, yours**
Third Person	the person, place, or thing spoken about **he, him, his, she, her, hers, it, its**	the persons, places, or things spoken about **they, them, their, theirs**

Certain forms of the personal pronouns are called *possessive pronouns* because they show possession or ownership. Here are the possessive forms of the personal pronouns:

	Singular	Plural
First Person	my, mine	our, ours
Second Person	your, yours	your, yours
Third Person	his, her, hers, its	their, theirs

That's **my** book on the desk.

The book on the desk is **mine**.

Is **your** car the red one?

Is the red car **yours?**

Her skates are on the shelf.

The skates on the shelf are **hers**.

Reflexive and Intensive Pronouns

There is a group of personal pronouns that end in the word *-self* or *-selves*. They are called either *reflexive pronouns* or *intensive pronouns*, depending on how they are used in the sentence. You will learn more about these pronouns in Unit Twenty-five. All you need to do now is to read the list of forms and look at the examples that follow.

	Singular	Plural
First Person	myself	ourselves
Second Person	yourself	yourselves
Third Person	himself, herself, itself	themselves

Here are examples of the reflexive and intensive uses of these pronouns:

I saw **myself** in the mirror.

He considers **himself** an expert in mathematics.

They treated **themselves** to ice cream cones.

I built this table **myself**.

The general **himself** fixed the car.

They catered the party **themselves**.

Interrogative Pronouns

An **interrogative pronoun** introduces a question.

The interrogative pronouns are *who, whom, which,* and *what.*

> **Who** came to the party?
>
> **Whom** did you see at the party?
>
> **Whose** present did Betty like best?
>
> **Which** is your present?
>
> **What** did Jessica give Betty?

As you can see, the antecedent of an interrogative pronoun is unknown. In fact, the purpose of the interrogative pronoun is to discover the antecedent. The antecedent is the answer to the question.

> **What** did Jessica give Betty? A record.

Demonstrative Pronouns

The word *demonstrate* means "to show or point out."

A **demonstrative pronoun** points to and identifies a person, place, or thing.

The demonstrative pronouns are *this, these, that,* and *those.*

> **This** is my brother.
>
> **Those** are the books I have read.

Relative Pronouns

A **relative pronoun** is used to introduce an adjective clause.

You will learn about adjective clauses in Unit Twenty-three. For now, just learn to recognize the relative pronouns: *who, whom, whose, which,* and *that.*

> The tennis player **who** wore the red headband won the match.
>
> The person to **whom** you were speaking is my sister.
>
> The man **whose** leg is in a cast is going to see a doctor now.
>
> The party, **which** will begin at eight o'clock, should be fun.
>
> The dog **that** just caught the Frisbee is mine.

Indefinite Pronouns

Indefinite pronouns refer to persons, places, or things that are not specifically identified.

Below is a list of indefinite pronouns. Notice that all of them involve the idea of number or quantity (for example, *many* and *much*).

all	each	little	none
another	either	many	no one
any	everybody	most	one
anyone	everyone	much	several
anybody	few	neither	some
both	someone	nobody	somebody

All left the party around midnight.

Everyone had a good time.

No one complained about the cake.

Many will arrive by train this afternoon.

Most didn't notice that the icing was made of yogurt.

One of the guests asked whether the cake was homemade.

Someone is always interested in food.

Several called the next day to thank us for the party.

Practice A   **Find pronouns.**

Number your paper from 1 to 15. Find the pronouns in each of the following fifteen sentences. Write the pronouns next to the number of the sentence.

EXAMPLE: She and I did the job for the fun of it.

she, I, it

1. Carla and Maureen wanted to work on their school newspaper.
2. They went to see Ms. Jordan, the adviser.
3. They wanted to discuss possible assignments with her.
4. They asked her to suggest several to them.
5. "Carla, you can write about the school's three-mile race," the adviser said to her

6. "Everyone is going to run in it," she added.

7. She told Maureen, "No one has been assigned to cover the Board of Education meeting."

8. "It should be covered by someone on the paper," she said.

9. "That should be an interesting story," Maureeen said.

10. Then she asked, "Is anyone writing about the new gym equipment?"

11. "The gym teachers have explained to us why they are so eager to get it," she added.

12. "That is a good idea," Ms. Jordan said.

13. "What will the school get?"

14. "I will find out," Maureen said.

15. Both left the office happy about the stories that they were going to write.

Practice B   Find pronouns and antecedents.

Each sentence below contains one pronoun. Copy the pronoun and its antecedent on your paper.

EXAMPLE: The swimmers thought the lifeguard was watching them.

them, swimmers

1. Pick the flower and put it in a vase.

2. Lou said he would help.

3. Beth left her books under the bleachers.

4. The dog that followed Gus home is a stray.

5. Don't buy the shoes if they don't feel comfortable.

6. The parrot has lost its voice.

7. The guests helped themselves to paper hats and noisemakers.

8. The person who led the hike is a photographer.

9. The Smiths advertised their yard sale in the local paper.

10. Joan made herself a sandwich.

Practice C   Add pronouns.

On your paper write pronouns that fit in the blanks in the sentences below. The word in parentheses after each blank tells you what type of pronoun to use. You may take pronouns from the lists on pages 340-343 if you wish.

EXAMPLE: _____ *(indefinite)* considers _____ *(demonstrative)* the best lake for fishing.

Everyone, this

1. Is _____ *(demonstrative)* the train _____ *(personal)* are taking?

2. Two robins built _____ *(possessive)* nest in the tree outside _____ *(possessive)* window.

3. _____ *(interrogative)* did Helen say about _____ *(possessive)* science project?

4. _____ *(personal)* and _____ *(possessive)* family went to the Grand Canyon on their vacation.

5. _____ *(demonstrative)* is the woman _____ *(relative)* gave _____ *(personal)* a ride to the game.

6. The child hurt _____ *(reflexive)* on the jungle gym.

7. _____ *(interrogative)* sneakers are _____? *(demonstrative)*

8. Is there _____ *(indefinite)* in the world _____ *(relative)* dislikes ice cream?

9. _____ *(personal)* looks like the cat _____ *(relative)* swallowed the canary.

10. _____ *(personal)* made _____ *(reflexive)* at home.

L E S S O N   T H R E E

Verbs

Are you a human being or a human doing? Probably you are both. Sometimes you do. You run, study, speak, wonder, wish, laugh, eat. Sometimes you simply are. You are happy, sad, angry, brilliant, a student, a mechanic, a cook.

Whether you are being or doing, the word that expresses your being or doing is a *verb*.

A **verb** is a word that expresses action, being, or state of being.

There are three kinds of verbs: *transitive, intransitive,* and *linking.*

▶   A *transitive* verb expresses action that affects someone or something mentioned in the sentence.

> Paul **borrowed** my bicycle for a day.

> A park ranger **found** the lost child.

The verb *borrowed* expresses an action that affects the bicycle. The verb *found* expresses an action that affects the child. The noun or pronoun that "receives" the action of a transitive verb is called the *direct object.* You will study direct objects in Unit Twenty-one.

▶   An *intransitive* verb may express either action or being. Even if an intransitive verb expresses action, however, there is no word in the sentence that receives the action of the verb.

> Janine always **arrives** early.

> A face **appeared** at the window.

The verbs *arrives* and *appeared* do not affect any other word in the sentence. They are intransitive verbs.

Here are some more sentences with intransitive verbs:

> Mangoes **grow** in a tropical climate.

> I **was** on my feet for the whole game.

> All day the snow **fell.**

▶   A *linking* verb joins (or links) two words in the sentence. The first word is always a noun or pronoun. The second word describes or renames the first word.

> The soda **is** cold.

The verb *is* links *soda* with *cold,* which describes the soda.

> Billy the Kid **was** an outlaw.

The verb *was* links *Billy the Kid* with *outlaw.*

Here are some more sentences with linking verbs. Can you tell which two words are linked?

The Yings **were** happy with our present.

I **am** the captain of the football team.

Nora **will be** tired after the race.

The crowd **grew** very still.

The most common linking verb is *be*. As you know, *be* has many forms: *am, is, are, was, were, will be, has been, is being*.

Here are some other linking verbs: *feel, look, seem, taste, appear, remain, sound, become, stay, smell, grow*.

Some of these verbs can also be transitive, intransitive, or both. It depends on how they are used in the sentence.

The science class **grew** vegetables.   (transitive)

The vegetables **grew** in a greenhouse.   (intransitive)

The carrots **grew** very large.   (linking)

If you are having trouble deciding whether a verb is linking or not, ask yourself whether it acts as an equal sign (=). Does it make two words "equal"?

I smell bread.   (Does *I* = *bread*? No, so *smell* is not a linking verb in this sentence. It is a transitive verb.)

The bread smells delicious.   (Does *bread* = *delicious*? Yes, so *smells* is a linking verb in this sentence.)

Verb Phrases

A verb may be one word or a group of words.

One word: **dances, ran, is, thinks**

Group of words: **is dancing, has been running, will think**

P O I N T S   T O   K N O W

A verb that is made up of two or more words is called a **verb phrase**.

▶ A verb phrase has one main verb and one or more helping (auxiliary) verbs. In the following examples, the main verb is in boldface type. The other words in the phrase are helping verbs.

has **done**

will have **finished**

may **seem**

could **happen**

was **trying**

Here are some common helping verbs:

be, been, am, is, are, was, were, have, has, do, does, did, shall, should, will, would, can, could, may, might, must

Sometimes a helping verb is separated from the main verb by other words. In these examples the verb phrase is in bold type.

I **did** not **say** that.

Will Josie ever **finish** that paper?

He **has** always **been** helpful.

Could you **have lost** your ticket?

Eva **can** usually **work** late.

We **have** often **written** to each other.

Principal Parts

As you have seen from the examples in this lesson, a verb can have more than one form.

P O I N T S   T O   K N O W

Every verb has four basic forms, which are called the **principal parts** of the verb. They are the **base form**, also called the **infinitive**; the **present participle**; the **past tense**; and the **past participle**.

Here are the principal parts of the verbs *wash* and *write*:

Base Form	Present Part.	Past Tense	Past Part.
(to) wash	(am) washing	washed	(had) washed
(to) write	(is) writing	wrote	(had) written

The present participle and the past participle are always used with helping verbs.

The children **are washing** the dog.

Kendra **has written** a letter.

You'll learn more about principal parts in Unit Twenty-six.

Practice A   Identify kinds of verbs.

Some of the words below are verbs. Some are not. If a word cannot be used as a verb, put an *X* next to the corresponding number on your paper. If the word can be used as a verb, use it in a sentence. Then say whether the verb is *transitive, intransitive,* or *linking*.

EXAMPLES: fly

We were flying kites all day.   transitive
baker   *X*

1. look
2. study
3. careful
4. sail
5. whistle

6. read
7. buyer
8. taste
9. are
10. anyone

Practice B   Identify kinds of verbs.

On your paper, write the verb or verb phrase from each sentence. Say whether it is *transitive, intransitive,* or *linking*.

EXAMPLE: The group camped in the woods for three nights.
camped   intransitive

1. Lorraine seems excited about her new job.
2. The squirrels took peanuts from our hands.
3. The manager has found the lost pocketbook.
4. I have been watching the clock for hours.

5. James exercises regularly at a gym.
6. This soup tastes too salty.
7. The woman in blue has been a pilot for three years.
8. The janitor will water the plants during vacation.
9. Every year the junior class raises money with a car wash.
10. The birds appeared suddenly.

Practice C **Write sentences with the principal parts of verbs.**

Below are the principal parts of five verbs. For each verb write four sentences, using a different principal part in each sentence.

EXAMPLE: take, taking, took, taken

Do you take cream in your coffee?

I am taking algebra this year.

My friends took me out to dinner.

Eloise has taken a vacation.

1. work, working, worked, worked
2. stay, staying, stayed, stayed
3. run, running, ran, run
4. talk, talking, talked, talked
5. grow, growing, grew, grown

L E S S O N   F O U R

Adjectives

Think about the word *car*. What picture do you have in your mind? Now think about a specific car that you are familiar with. You probably get a clearer picture in your mind when you think about a specific car. You can see what color it is, how old it is, whether or not it has dents, and so on. If you described the specific car to someone else, you would use *adjectives*.

An **adjective** is a word that modifies a noun or a pronoun.

> He drove a **new white compact** car.

The word *modify* means "to change." Have you ever seen a modified car? Someone has made it different from other cars by adding parts or changing parts. After being modified, the car is more individual and special.

An adjective modifies a noun or a pronoun by adding to its meaning and changing its meaning. Thus, an adjective makes the noun or pronoun more individual.

Take, for instance, the noun *car*. By adding different adjectives to that noun, you can describe two entirely different vehicles.

> a **dented, rusty, green** car
>
> a **new, sleek, powerful** car

Each adjective changes the meaning of the noun *car*.

Adjectives can describe many qualities, including size, shape, color, texture, inner qualities, and so on. Adjectives that refer to qualities are called *descriptive adjectives*.

> **large** dog
>
> **square** box
>
> **red** coat
>
> **smooth** hands
>
> **happy** person

There are other kinds of adjectives besides descriptive adjectives. These modify nouns in other ways.

▶ An adjective can answer the question *which one?* or *which ones?*

> She helped **those** people.
>
> **This** book will make you laugh.

▶ An adjective can answer the question *how many?* or *how much?*

> **Six** acrobats performed.
>
> We saved you **some** cake.

You have seen some of the adjectives in these examples before, in Lesson Two, on pronouns. Demonstratives (*this, that, these, those*) and indefinites (*any, some, most, all,* etc.) are pronouns when they take the place of nouns. They are adjectives when they modify nouns. The following examples show the difference between the pronoun use and the adjective use.

> **That** dog is unusual.   (adjective, modifies *dog*)
>
> **That** is an unusual dog.   (pronoun)
>
> Did Mel leave us **any** pie?   (adjective, modifies *pie*)
>
> Mel baked a pie. Did he leave us **any**?   (pronoun)

▶ An adjective can answer the question *whose?* The possessive pronouns *my, our, your, his, her, its,* and *their* precede the noun that they "possess." They act as adjectives modifying the noun.

> **Her** pen is on the desk.   (adjective, modifies *pen*)
>
> **Their** friends are waiting for them.   (adjective, modifies *friends*)

The possessive pronouns *mine, yours, hers, ours,* and *theirs* do not precede the noun that they "possess." Instead, they take the place of the noun and stand alone. Therefore, they are considered pronouns, not adjectives.

> The pen on the desk is **hers**.   (pronoun, takes the place of *her pen*)
>
> The friends who are waiting are **theirs**.   (pronoun, takes the place of *their friends*)

The possessive pronoun *his* sometimes precedes the noun it possesses and sometimes stands alone. Following are some examples.

> **His** dog is well trained.   (adjective)
>
> The dog is **his**.   (pronoun)

▶ Three adjectives that we use very frequently have a special name. The words *the, a,* and *an* are called *articles*. The following example contains all three articles.

> **The** radio has **a** built-in antenna and **an** earphone jack.

Adjectives From Nouns

Sometimes a word that is ordinarily a noun is used to modify another noun. In that case, it is considered an adjective. For example, *vegetable* is usually a noun, but in the following sentence it is an adjective.

> We have a **vegetable** garden in our backyard.

A proper noun, too, may be used to modify another noun.

> That **St. Bernard** puppy is enormous.

P O I N T S   T O   K N O W

▶ Some proper nouns change their forms to become adjectives. These adjectives are called *proper adjectives*.

> My sister loves **Japanese** food.

▶ A possessive noun acts as an adjective.

> **Frieda's** ambition is to be a chemist.

Adjectives From Verbs

Two of the four principal parts of a verb can be used as adjectives. These two parts are the *present participle* and the *past participle*.

P O I N T S   T O   K N O W

Following are some examples of present participles and past participles used as adjectives.

> That was an **exciting** movie.

Exciting is the present participle of the verb *excite*. In this example it acts as an adjective, modifying the noun *movie*.

> He called to us from behind the **locked** door.

Locked is the past participle of the verb *lock*. In this example it acts as an adjective, modifying the noun *door*.

▶ When verb forms like *exciting* and *locked* are used as another part of speech, they are called *verbals*.

Placement of Adjectives

An adjective usually comes before the word it modifies. However, it can also come right after the word it modifies.

> The dog, **frightened** but **hungry**, crept closer to the food.
>
> The baby, **smiling** and **happy**, played in the sandbox.

An adjective can follow a linking verb. In the following examples the linking verb is italicized.

> The students in the class *were* **happy** about the field trip.
>
> They *became* **quiet** after a while.

Practice A **Find adjectives.**

Copy each adjective from the following sentences on your paper. (For this exercise, do not copy articles—*the, a,* and *an*.)

EXAMPLE: Strange stories have been told about the old house.

strange, old

1. Many people know about the old Lovell house.
2. An English captain built it during the war for American independence.
3. Strange stories about the mysterious death of the first owner have been told.
4. Superstitious folks in the tiny town don't go by the huge house on dark nights.
5. My school friends have heard wild, scary noises that seemed to come from the deserted house.
6. On a November night, I decided to walk up the long, cracked sidewalk to the dark door.
7. I trembled from the cold, but I was brave.
8. Visions of pale ghosts and bony goblins filled my mind.

9. Suddenly I heard a chilling screech.

10. A broken door swung on two rusty hinges.

Practice B   Add adjectives.

The sentences below have no adjectives except articles. Rewrite each sentence, adding at least one adjective to modify each noun in italics. You may remove articles if you need to.

EXAMPLE: The *owner* fed the *puppy*.

The new owner fed the hungry puppy.

1. The players made the *team*.
2. People read *books* for information.
3. *Cars* and *trucks* crowd the highways.
4. The composer lifted a baton to conduct the *orchestra*.
5. The child cried as he looked at the *toy* he had broken.
6. The *radio* blared news and *music*.
7. *Jackets* on the rack will fit the students.
8. The *movie* starred a man as the villain.
9. The clock keeps *time* when the woman winds it.
10. The Constitution is a *document*.

Practice C   Write sentences with adjectives.

Below are ten nouns. Use each one in a sentence. Modify each noun with at least two adjectives, not counting articles.

EXAMPLE: bicycles

Stan has three old bicycles.

1. house
2. shoes
3. airplane
4. road
5. beach
6. school
7. drummer
8. car
9. sweater
10. music

Adverbs

Think of something you do every day, like eating. Do you always eat in the same way, in the same place, at the same time? Unless you are a robot, probably you eat in different ways, in different places, at different times. For example, you may eat *hungrily, quickly, absentmindedly, reluctantly,* or *slowly.* You may eat *early, late, often,* or *constantly.* You may eat *here, there, outdoors,* or *indoors.*

In the sentences you have just read, the italicized words that tell *how, when* and *where* you eat are *adverbs.*

P O I N T S   T O   K N O W

An **adverb** is a word that modifies a verb, an adjective, or another adverb. It answers the question *how?, when?, where?* or *to what degree?* about the word it modifies.

Following are some examples of adverbs in sentences.

Kam drove **carefully**.   (Modifies the verb. Tells *how,* or *in what manner,* Kam *drove.*)

They will deliver the new stereo **tomorrow**.   (Modifies the verb. Tells *when* they *will deliver* the new stereo.)

Father carried the chair **upstairs**.   (Modifies the verb. Tells *where* Father *carried* the chair.)

That color is **too** bright for my taste.   (Modifies the adjective *bright.* Tells *how bright* the color is, or tells *to what degree* the color is *bright.*)

The audience applauded **very** loudly.   (Modifies the adverb *loud-ly.* Tells *how loudly* the audience applauded, or tells *to what degree* the audience applauded *loudly.*)

Here are some more examples of adverbs that modify adjectives or adverbs. As you know, these are "adverbs of degree." They answer the question *how ____?* about the adjective or adverb they modify. They tell *to what degree* the adjective or adverb is true.

Adverbs Modifying Adjectives	Adverbs Modifying Adverbs
more expensive	**very** rapidly
rather chilly	**quite** late
extremely nervous	**far** ahead

▶ The words *how, when*, and *where* are adverbs, too. The word *not* is also an adverb. It modifies the verb by saying it is untrue.

> **How** can we solve this problem?
>
> **How** long have you lived here?
>
> **When** will the job be finished?
>
> **Where** do these birds spend the winter?
>
> They do **not** stay here.

▶ Adverbs can occur almost anywhere in a sentence. It is often possible to place an adverb in different positions in a sentence without changing the meaning of the sentence.

> **Suddenly** she raised her head.
>
> She **suddenly** raised her head.
>
> She raised her head **suddenly**.

Practice A   **Find adverbs.**

On a piece of paper, write the adverbs from the following sentences. After each adverb, write in parentheses ( ) the word or words that the adverb modifies.

EXAMPLE: I began the bicycle race very eagerly.

very (eagerly)   eagerly (began)

1. But I pedaled awkwardly.
2. The front wheel of my bicycle wobbled badly.
3. Hurriedly, I stopped at the equipment tent.
4. Some extremely helpful volunteers provided me with another wheel.
5. I changed the wheel quickly.

6. The new wheel ran more smoothly.
7. Now I could go faster.
8. I pedaled forward furiously.
9. I was trying very hard.
10. I was far behind.

Practice B   **Add adverbs.**

Rewrite each of the following sentences. Add at least one adverb to each sentence to modify each italicized word or verb phrase. You may use *not* as well as adverbs that tell how, when, where, or to what degree.

EXAMPLE: My legs were *tired.*

My legs were extremely tired.

1. The brakes on the bike *worked.*
2. I was *confident* of my ability.
3. I *approached* the pack.
4. I *got* my second wind.
5. I *looked,* and I *did see* many other racers.
6. I *might win.*
7. I was pedaling *rhythmically.*
8. My feet were *asleep* from the pinch of the pedal straps.
9. I *stood* on the pedals for the final lap of this close race.
10. I *won* the race by the width of my bicycle tire.

Practice C   **Write sentences with adverbs.**

Follow the directions for writing sentences. Use at least two adverbs in each sentence. Underline all the adverbs you use.

EXAMPLE: Write a sentence about a picnic.

The ants were very happy at our picnic yesterday.

1. Write a sentence about young children.
2. Write a sentence about preparing a meal.
3. Write a sentence about sports.
4. Write a sentence about an emotion.
5. Write a sentence about your ambitions.

6. Write a sentence about making something.

7. Write a sentence about music.

8. Write a sentence about a party.

9. Write a sentence about a vacation.

10. Write a sentence about working.

59

L E S S O N   S I X

Prepositions

Suppose you lost something important, perhaps your wallet. Where might you look for it? You might look

> **in** your locker
>
> **under** your bed
>
> **around** your room
>
> **behind** a door
>
> **on** your desk
>
> **beneath** the sleeping cat

Whether or not you found your wallet, you would certainly discover a lot of *prepositions*. The words in bold type above are prepositions.

P O I N T S   T O   K N O W

▶ A preposition is never used alone. It is always followed by a noun or pronoun. The noun or pronoun is called the *object of the preposition*.

under the **table**

▶ The object of the preposition may have one or more modifiers.

under the **small wooden** table

▶ The preposition, its object, and the modifiers of the object are called a *prepositional phrase*.

under the small wooden table

A **preposition** is a word that shows the relationship between its object and some other word in the sentence.

He found his wallet **under** the small wooden table.

The preposition *under* shows the relationship between its object, *table,* and *wallet.* If you removed *under* and substituted *on,* there would be a different relationship between *table* and *wallet.*

Here is a list of the common prepositions:

about	below	for	since
above	beneath	from	through
across	beside	in	to
after	besides	into	toward
against	between	like	under
along	beyond	near	until
among	by	of	up
around	concerning	off	upon
at	down	on	with
before	during	over	within
behind	except	past	without

Some prepositions consist of more than one word. For example:

out of	according to
on account of	in front of
because of	instead of
in addition to	next to

Some of the words in the list can also be used as adverbs. You can tell a preposition from an adverb easily. A preposition always has an object.

He came **in**.   (adverb)

He was carrying some flowers **in** a vase.   (preposition)

We looked **around**.   (adverb)

We looked **around** the park.   (preposition)

They sat **down**.   (adverb)

They rode **down** the street.   (preposition)

The bicyclists rode **by.**   (adverb)

The bicyclists rode **by** the school.   (preposition)

Practice A   **Find prepositions.**

On your paper, copy each preposition from the sentences below.

EXAMPLE: Have you heard about a sea monster in Scotland?

about, in

1. Until recent times, there was only one sea monster in the world.
2. That was the Loch Ness monster in Scotland.
3. Now there is another monster in addition to Nessie.
4. "Champ" is the American version of a lake monster.
5. Champ gets its name from the waters of its home.
6. This Yankee monster swims in Lake Champlain.
7. Lake Champlain forms the boundary between Vermont and New York.
8. Some local officials have written a law for the protection of Champ.
9. The law protects the monster from people who might shoot at it out of fear or curiosity.
10. The people around Lake Champlain take their monster very seriously.

Practice B   **Add prepositions.**

Rewrite each sentence, filling in the blanks with prepositions.

EXAMPLE: The man _____ the store rented them a canoe _____ ten dollars.

The man in the store rented them a canoe for ten dollars.

1. _____ an hour the two girls paddled their canoe.
2. They went _____ the center _____ the lake.
3. A thick mist slowly crept _____ the lake.

4. _____ a while, the girls began hearing a lapping noise _____ the canoe.

5. "What is that noise?" one girl said _____ the other.

6. The girls feared that they were _____ a lot _____ trouble.

7. They peered _____ the water and then looked _____ each other.

8. "Could Champ come up _____ us and overturn our canoe?" one said.

9. Finally they saw a rowboat _____ two people coming _____ them.

10. "We almost thought we were the first victims _____ the Lake Champlain monster," said one _____ the girls.

Practice C   Write sentences with prepositions.

Following is a list of pairs of prepositions. Use each pair in a sentence. If you wish, you may reverse the order of the prepositions in the pair. Remember that a preposition always takes a noun or a pronoun as its object.

EXAMPLE: near, without

I never go near the snake house without some fear.

1. into, for	6. about, until
2. through, over	7. past, up
3. unlike, like	8. on, from
4. beneath, during	9. down, upon
5. toward, of	10. after, behind

L E S S O N   S E V E N

Conjunctions

What is a pin? It's a small, pointed piece of wire that joins things together. What is a conjunction? It's a language "pin" that you use when you want to join words together.

A **conjunction** is a word that joins words or groups of words.

▶   A conjunction can join single words.

Joe **and** Angela went for a ride.

The engine coughed **and** sputtered **and** died.

▶   A conjunction can join groups of words.

Angela thought the problem was **either** in the battery **or** in the carburetor.

They waited for another car to pass, **but** none came along.

"This always happens **when** we're twenty miles from nowhere," said Joe.

There are three kinds of conjunctions: *coordinating, correlative,* and *subordinating.* In this lesson you will learn about the first two kinds. You will learn about subordinating conjunctions in Unit Twenty-two.

▶   The *coordinating conjunctions* are the ones with which you are most familiar: *and, but, or, nor, for, so,* and *yet.*

The children seemed busy **and** content.

We rang the bell, **but** no one came to the door.

The team will practice today **or** tomorrow.

I have not been invited, **nor** do I want to go.

She must be well, **for** we saw her at the party.

They are late, **so** we will go ahead.

He knows a lot, **yet** he doesn't boast.

▶   The correlative conjunctions are always used in pairs:

either . . . or

neither . . . nor

not only . . . but (also)

not . . . but

both . . . and

Either our puppy **or** our kitten has torn the upholstery.

Neither the peaches **nor** the plums are ripe.

Max plays **not only** the clarinet **but also** two different kinds of saxophones.

Not only did he do the dishes, **but** he **also** mopped the floor. (Notice that the word *he* comes between *but* and *also* in this sentence.)

On their hike they saw **not** one **but** three rare birds.

Both Jerry **and** his sister run in marathons.

Practice A **Find conjunctions.**

The sentences that follow contain coordinating and correlative conjunctions. Some sentences contain more than one conjunction. Write the conjunction(s) on your paper.

EXAMPLE: I am going to the city, but I shall be back soon.

but

1. Most sports make the body work hard, so most athletes perspire.
2. Many athletes aren't bothered by this, but for others it is a gripping problem.
3. Not only does the athlete have to catch a ball or swing a bat, but he or she has to do it with slippery hands.
4. Most baseball players put tar on the handles of their bats, for that gives them a better grip on the wood.
5. Baseball pitchers rub a special kind of swamp mud on baseballs, but few people know where the mud comes from.
6. One kind of goo or another seems to be used in all sports requiring a good grip.
7. Both baseball and football players often use sticky goos.
8. One football player was famous for his use of special goo, and he was the leading pass catcher for his team.
9. Neither the mud nor the tar nor the goos are illegal, yet many people think that the goos, at least, are unfair.
10. The answer may be not outlawing the goos but making rules to control their use.

Practice B   **Write sentences with conjunctions.**

Write five sentences. In each sentence use one of the following conjunctions.

EXAMPLE: neither . . . nor

She neither sings nor plays the piano.

1. and
2. but
3. or
4. both . . . and
5. yet

L E S S O N   E I G H T

Interjections

Everyone has heard the phrase "last but not least." You are about to learn about the last part of speech, the interjection. In this case, however, last *is* least. Interjections are the least used part of speech, probably because they are the least important.

P O I N T S   T O   K N O W

An **interjection** is a word or phrase that expresses emotion.

▶   The word or words used as an interjection stand alone. They have no grammatical connection to the rest of the sentence. Here are some examples of interjections:

oh	wow
well	my goodness
hurrah	good grief

▶   When an interjection shows very strong emotion, it is followed by an exclamation point (!). The first letter of the word following the interjection is capitalized.

▶ If an interjection shows only slight emotion, it is followed by a comma (,). The next word of the sentence is not capitalized.

Here are some examples:

Wow! Look at the stunt driver's car!

Oh, dear! She's going to crash!

Ah, ha! She's climbing out of the car and smiling.

Oh, we thought you had left.

Well, all of us feel the same way you do.

Oh, rats, did I misspell *calendar* again?

Practice   **Write sentences with interjections.**

Use each interjection below in a sentence.

EXAMPLE: hey

Hey, listen to this!

1. ouch
2. oh
3. ah
4. well
5. ugh

6. hurrah
7. oh, no
8. wow
9. ah, ha
10. my goodness

L E S S O N   N I N E

Determining Parts of Speech

Some tools are very versatile. Think of all the different things you can do with a knife, for instance. You can cut food such as meat and bread. You can spread butter or jelly. You can peel an apple or orange. You can open a package tied with string.

Certain words are very versatile, too. They can be used as several different parts of speech. For example, the word *dance* can be used as a verb, a noun, or an adjective.

They **dance** in contests all over the city.   (verb)

The **dance** will be held on Friday night.   (noun)

The **dance** class will give a recital.   (adjective)

A word's part of speech depends on how it is used in a particular sentence. If *dance* expresses action in a sentence, it is a verb in that sentence. If it names a thing, it is a noun. If it describes something, it is an adjective. Here are some more examples of words used as different parts of speech.

She has a light blue **telephone** in her room.   (noun)

I will **telephone** you soon.   (verb)

Where is the **telephone** book?   (adjective)

Today is my birthday.   (noun)

We arrive in Miami **today**.   (adverb)

The party is **over**.   (adverb)

The helicopter skimmed **over** our heads.   (preposition)

If heights make you dizzy, try not to look **down**.   (adverb)

We must climb **down** the ladder of the fire tower.   (preposition)

This is your best paper so far.   (pronoun)

This paper is well written.   (adjective)

The teacher brought crayons to her class and gave each child **some**.   (pronoun)

The teacher brought **some** crayons.   (adjective)

There is no one at **home**.   (noun)

It is time to go **home**.   (adverb)

Practice A   **Identify the parts of speech.**

Copy each italicized word onto your paper. Then write what part of speech the word is.

EXAMPLE: *They* stood *before* us.

they   *pronoun*

before   *preposition*

1. *Stand* when the *judge* enters.

2. *That plane* keeps flying *over* the house.

3. The *ocean* breeze smells *sweet* at this beach.

4. If we go to the *show*, I will bring my own *junk* food.

5. Did you *wind* the *watch* on *Thursday*?

6. Is *this* the *Omaha* train?

7. *After a long winter*, I get *spring* fever.

8. Must you have *motorcycle* insurance before you can *drive*?

9. We must pay the *telephone* bill *tomorrow*.

10. American blacksmiths used to *shoe horses* in their shops.

Practice B   **Write sentences using a word as a specific part of speech.**

Use each word in a sentence. Use the word as the part of speech given in parentheses.

EXAMPLE: paper   (adjective)

There are many ways to make a paper airplane.

1. plant	(verb)	6. yesterday	(adverb)
2. down	(adverb)	7. in	(preposition)
3. those	(pronoun)	8. help	(verb)
4. strike	(noun)	9. secret	(adjective)
5. light	(adjective)	10. play	(noun)

R E V I E W   E X E R C I S E S

I. Nouns On your paper, copy the nouns from each sentence. (Lesson One)

EXAMPLE: Mandy has a pet canary whose name is Arthur.

Mandy, canary, name, Arthur

1. The workers bought the drill at the Appliance Market.

2. The team travels to games in a van.

3. My sister donated a flute to the orchestra.

4. Elise found the brush in her red purse.

5. Paula Winters went to school and became a technician.

6. The family took a trip to the Blue Ridge Mountains.

7. An audience of several hundred people saw our class production of *Romeo and Juliet*.

8. The iron became so hot that it burned the silk shirts.

9. Vernon will travel to San Francisco by train.

10. The dollhouse that the woman bought in Europe was made by a group of crafts people.

II. Pronouns On your paper, copy the pronoun(s) from each sentence. (Lesson Two)

EXAMPLE: He gave me the book.

He, me

1. They invited us to dinner.

2. Those are the people who came with him to the dance.

3. The yoga teacher told me to look at myself in the mirror.

4. He offered all of us popcorn, but none of us wanted any.

5. Della's chocolate brownies are better than mine.

6. Which of them hit a home run for our team?

7. Both of them ran in the relay race.

8. To whom does that belong?

9. We are going to the park on Sunday.

10. They will let you take it home.

III. Verbs Copy the verb(s) from each sentence. If there is a verb phrase, put a check mark over the main verb and underline the helping verb(s). (Lesson Three)

EXAMPLE: They have been going to the park every day.

have been góing

1. The dog has been chasing cars again.

2. Andy was taking his friend to a show.

3. He sneezed loudly during the test.

4. For many years, Cynthia has been jogging along our road.

5. No one was kinder to me than Jane.

6. We should have arrived here sooner.

7. Erik sometimes becomes angry at the coach.

8. What are you bringing to the picnic?

9. Fran will call soon.

10. Bette seems quiet today.

IV. Adjectives Copy the adjectives from each sentence. Do not copy articles (*the, a, an*). (Lesson Four)

1. The young man sat on the wooden chair.

2. The sad child with blue eyes ran away from home.

3. The tall building in the middle of the French countryside surprised the American visitor.

4. Five mewing kittens and their mother appeared at the side door.

5. Rhode Island, our smallest state, is in the eastern part of the United States.

6. The blue electric typewriter belongs to the Brazilian diplomat.

7. The short man in the striped shirt had a brief interview with the English star.

8. My first visit to a Norwegian town took place on a snowy day.

9. A dangerous storm was forming on the distant horizon.

10. The broken cup belonged to our best set of china.

V. Adjectives and Adverbs Copy the adjective(s) and adverb(s) from each sentence. Do not copy articles (*the, a, an*). Label each one *adjective* or *adverb*. (Lessons Four and Five)

1. The officer talked kindly to the lost boy.

2. Gold is rarely found in this country.

3. On an exceedingly cold winter day, we counted fifty birds at the feeder.

4. Suddenly they were faced with an extremely difficult choice.

5. Fred spoke rudely because he was angry.

6. The jury will reach a verdict soon.

7. The riderless horse ran around in circles.

8. One could see the distant ship very clearly.

9. The tired racers pedaled home slowly and sadly.

10. The plate of tempting cookies was nearly empty.

VI. Prepositions, Conjunctions, and Interjections Copy the prepositions, conjunctions, and interjections from each sentence. Label each one *preposition, conjunction*, or *interjection*. (Lessons Six–Eight)

EXAMPLE: Inez and Maureen went to a movie about lions.

and   conjunction

to   preposition

about   preposition

1. At the dock we saw large and small boats.

2. Either a small bird or a large insect flew swiftly across the sky.

3. The game was canceled because of the storm, but it will be held on Saturday.

4. Well, you found an answer to that problem.

5. Stan was neither among the onlookers nor with the team.

6. After the game the cheerleaders ran off the field and into the gym.

7. Patty will stand in front of the man with the beard or next to the woman in pink.

8. Behind the shed there is a creek with both brook and rainbow trout.

9. Children need not only discipline from their parents but also affection.

10. Wow! Did you see that double play by Mendez and Corbett?

VII. Determining Parts of Speech Copy each italicized word. Then write what part of speech the word is. (Lesson Nine)

EXAMPLE: They crossed the *steel* bridge on their way home.

steel   adjective

1. At the fruit *stand* you can get delicious apples.

2. They *stand* on the sidelines and watch the game.

3. *Park* your truck in the driveway.

4. Andrew camped in the state *park*.

5. The *light* stayed on all night.

6. Harry carried a *light* package.

7. The *plants* grew a little taller each day.

8. She *plants* vegetables in her garden.

9. We are going to look *around*.

10. The theater is *around* the corner.

11. Bruce got a new *watch* for his birthday.

12. Will you please *watch* the baby?

13. Julie took me for a ride in her *boat*.

14. They stopped at the *boat* dock.

15. Ann just made a telephone *call*.

16. Will you *call* the store for me?

17. *That* is a wonderful story.

18. May we have some of *that* paper?

19. John has a *long* string on his kite.

20. I *long* for a pepperoni pizza.

VIII. Determining Parts of Speech For each word listed below, write a sentence using the word as the part of speech indicated. (Lesson Nine)

EXAMPLE: record   (adjective)

He works in a record store.

1. record	(noun)		6. city	(adjective)
2. hand	(verb)		7. place	(verb)
3. those	(adjective)		8. place	(noun)
4. back	(adverb)		9. car	(noun)
5. in	(preposition)		10. car	(adjective)

Using the Parts of Speech in Your Writing

In most sentences, you use at least two of the seven parts of speech— nouns and verbs. However, in many sentences, you use more than these two parts of speech. Whether you use few or many parts of speech, make sure each word you use is the best possible one to express your thoughts.

If you are writing about a person, try to find a specific noun that names that person. Is he or she a *librarian*, a *firefighter*, a *student*, or a *child*? Does that person simply walk into a room or does he or she *stroll, race, saunter*, or *hobble* into an *auditorium*, a *den,* or a *kitchen*?

If you use modifiers, choose vivid, exact ones. Don't write about red shoes if they are really *scarlet* or *crimson*. Don't write about a loud noise if it was a *piercing, thunderous,* or *earsplitting* one.

Since your purpose in writing is to communicate your ideas, choose the strongest, most lively words to achieve that purpose.

Practice   **Write sentences.**

Write a paragraph telling about something that has happened today. It could be something as ordinary as waking up to the alarm or eating cereal for breakfast. Or it could be something out-of-the-ordinary that occurred: you found a new route to school, you saw a strange sight, or you were chosen to be in the choir. After you finish your paragraph, look over each word. Make sure it is the strongest one possible.

Understanding Sentences

Picture postcard of Seabreeze, Florida, around 1890
Library of Congress

Understanding Sentences

L E S S O N   O N E

Sentences and Sentence Fragments

Imagine that you are playing a game of Frazzle with your friend Tom. You each have four tiles with words on them, which you have drawn from the "kitty" of tiles spread out, face down, on the table. The object of the game is to earn points by making sentences out of the words on the tiles. You must use all four of your tiles in any sentence you make. But, if you wish, at the beginning of your turn you can put one tile back into the kitty and draw another that you might like better. At the moment you have these four tiles: *the; a ladder; birds; building.*

It's Tom's turn. He discards a tile with the verb *were* on it. (Watch where he puts that tile—you might be able to use it.) He draws *discovered* and thinks he has a sentence:

the   wide   field   discovered

"That's not a complete sentence," you object. "It doesn't tell *what* the wide field discovered. You lose a point."

"No, wait," Tom answers. Hurriedly, he rearranges the four tiles. "How about this one?"

discovered   the   wide   field

"That's no good, either," you say. "It doesn't tell *who* discovered the wide field. You still lose a point, and it's my turn." You quickly discard *the* and pick up the tile that Tom discarded: *were.* Now you can make this sentence:

birds   were   building   a ladder

Your sentence isn't very convincing, but it is grammatically complete. It has a subject and a predicate. And it is worth five points in the game of Frazzle.

A **sentence** is a group of words that has a subject and a verb that shows tense. A sentence expresses a complete thought.

▶ A sentence always begins with a capital letter and ends with one of three punctuation marks—a period (.), a question mark (?), or an exclamation point (!).

▶ A group of words that lacks a subject or a verb, or does not complete the thought begun by the subject and the verb is called a *sentence fragment*. Here are some sentence fragments:

the young man standing in the doorway

their pet turtle crawling under the refrigerator

that they were going to the movies

she mentioned

parks cars at the restaurant

Jonathan and his brother found

The three sentences that follow each contain two of the preceding fragments.

She mentioned that they were going to the movies.

The young man standing in the doorway parks cars at the restaurant.

Jonathan and his brother found their pet turtle crawling under the refrigerator.

When you speak, you can use sentence fragments and still get your message across. That's because your listeners can fill in the gaps by asking questions. When you write, however, you want to be as complete as possible. The best way to express your thoughts completely is to write in complete sentences.

In the rest of this unit you'll study the parts that make up a sentence. Then, if you come across a fragment, you will know what is needed to make it a sentence.

Practice A   Identify sentences and fragments.

Following are fifteen groups of words. If a group of words is a sentence, write it as a sentence, beginning with a capital letter and ending with a punctuation mark. If a group of words is a fragment, write *fragment* next to its number on your paper.

EXAMPLES: was driving the other day

fragment

the highway was crowded

The highway was crowded.

1. a beautiful day
2. suddenly several cars pulled over
3. the shoulder crowded with vehicles
4. people getting out and throwing up their hands
5. I noticed a large truck ahead
6. something black from the back of it
7. spilled from an open bag by the tailgate
8. there was a thumping sound outside my car
9. now more and more cars by the edge of the road
10. suddenly the steering wheel fought against my hands
11. my front tires were both flat
12. thousands of spilled roofing nails were littering the road
13. the nails had disabled more than a hundred cars
14. many furious drivers along that road that morning
15. I was just one of the crowd

Practice B   Change fragments into sentences.

For each group of words you labeled *fragment* in Practice A, add words of your own to make the fragment into a sentence. Add the necessary capitalization and punctuation.

EXAMPLE: was driving the other day

I was driving the other day.

Subjects

If you have to write a composition, probably the first thing you ask is "What is the subject?" The subject is what the composition is about. Every sentence in the composition will have a *subject,* too.

P O I N T S   T O   K N O W

The **subject** of a sentence is who or what is doing something or what is being talked about.

In each sentence below, the subject is in boldface type.

> **Officer Pelagios** spoke to our driver education class.
>
> **He** talked about courtesy on the road.
>
> **All of the students in the class** enjoyed his talk.

Often, but not always, the subject is at the beginning of the sentence. Here are some exceptions:

> Did **the speaker** show slides?
>
> Tomorrow **the teacher** will give a quiz.
>
> In front of the class was **a poster about highway safety**.
>
> Outside the door stood **the principal**.

One way to find the subject of a sentence is to ask, "*Who* or *what* is doing something?" or "*Who* or *what* is being talked about?" For example, look again at the four sentences above and ask:

> *Who* did show slides?   Answer: the speaker
>
> *Who* will give a quiz?   Answer: the teacher
>
> *What* was in front of the class?   Answer: a poster about highway safety
>
> *Who* stood outside the door?   Answer: the principal

Simple and Complete Subjects

Perhaps you noticed that in one of the sentences on page 379 about the driver education class, the subject is one word.

He talked about courtesy on the road.

In another sentence, the subject is made up of several words.

All of the students in the class enjoyed his talk.

When a subject has more than one word, the most important word is called the *simple subject*. The whole group of words is called the *complete subject*.

P O I N T S   T O   K N O W

The **simple subject** is always a noun or pronoun.

The **complete subject** is a noun or pronoun and all its modifiers.

Of course, when a subject contains only one word, that one word (noun or pronoun) is both the simple subject and the complete subject.

I like many winter sports.

Here are some examples of simple and complete subjects. The complete subject is underlined. The simple subject is in boldface type.

My fondest childhood **memories** involve a skating pond.

All of the neighborhood children met at the pond daily in winter.

In late afternoon the whole **group** would gather around a fire built by older children.

Off came the **skates.**

Over the fire went our cold **fingers.**

Look again at this sentence:

All of the neighborhood children met at the pond daily in winter.

You may be tempted to think that *children* is the simple subject. However, *children* is the object of the preposition *of*. (See Unit Nineteen, Lesson Six.) The object of a preposition cannot also be a subject. The simple subject is the pronoun *all*. The prepositional phrase *of the neighborhood children* modifies the simple subject *all*. You will learn more about prepositional phrases later. For now, remember that an object of a preposition cannot be a subject.

Practice A   Find simple and complete subjects.

For each of the following sentences, write the complete subject on your paper. Then underline the simple subject.

EXAMPLE: The students in my home economics class made orange marmalade yesterday.

the students in my home economics class

1. The woman with the two Irish setters is a dog trainer.
2. Did the varsity basketball team win all of its games?
3. Marguerite went to every game this season.
4. In the middle of the night we heard a loud crash in the attic.
5. Up the stairs raced the whole family.
6. Most of the players looked tired after the game.
7. Will you watch my bicycle for a minute?
8. The audience gave the star a standing ovation.
9. Out of nowhere came a large red truck.
10. The New York skyline is beautiful at night.
11. My best friend is coming to my house for dinner.
12. The hungry kitten ate too quickly.
13. A famous writer is coming to speak at our school.
14. Karen's favorite food is spaghetti.
15. All of the students in the auditorium cheered.
16. A boy in my French class knows the Martins.
17. Young children must be accompanied by an adult.
18. We watched a great movie on television.
19. The best part of the movie was the end.
20. Did Jennifer's twin sister come to Al's party?

Practice B Add subjects and identify simple subjects.

Each group of words that follows needs a subject. Think of a subject you can add. Write the complete sentence on your paper. Underline the simple subject.

EXAMPLE: _____ ran around the track.

The gym class ran around the track.

1. _____ took a train across the country.
2. Fortunately, _____ was able to fix my stereo.
3. Will _____ need any equipment for the performance?
4. From a distance, _____ cannot see the young birds in a nest.
5. _____ appears at our local theater every summer.
6. _____ hardly said a word.
7. On top of the mountain was _____.
8. Have _____ ever gone skiing in Colorado?
9. In a large box _____ found a small puppy.
10. To the left of the house stood _____.

Practice C Write sentences.

Use each of the following words as the simple subject of a sentence. In at least five of your sentences include a complete subject of more than one word. Underline the complete subject of each sentence.

EXAMPLE: letter

A letter from my cousin arrived yesterday.

1. team	6. flowers
2. musicians	7. jeans
3. they	8. everyone
4. all	9. book
5. tent	10. peace

Predicates

Here are some complete subjects:

> the fishing boat from Denmark
>
> a forty-pound bluefish
>
> men in heavy wool jackets
>
> thousands of slithery fish

Even though these are complete subjects, they do not express complete thoughts. They are sentence fragments. After you read them, you have many questions. What about the fishing boat, the bluefish, the men, the thousands of fish? A complete subject needs a *predicate* to complete its meaning.

P O I N T S   T O   K N O W

The **predicate** of a sentence expresses some action done by or to the subject, or it expresses the state of being of the subject.

Every sentence is made up of a subject and a predicate. The words that are not part of the subject are part of the predicate. Here are some sentences divided into subjects and predicates.

Subject	Predicate
The fishing boat from Denmark	docked in our harbor.
A forty-pound bluefish	was the largest fish caught.
Men in heavy wool jackets	stood on the deck.
Thousands of slithery fish	filled the hold.

In the first sentence the predicate, *docked in our harbor*, tells what the subject, *boat*, did.

In the second sentence the predicate, *was the largest fish caught*, tells what the subject, *bluefish*, was.

Simple and Complete Predicates

The most important part of the predicate is the verb. The verb by itself is called the *simple predicate*. The *complete predicate* is the verb plus any words that go with it to make its meaning clear.

In each sentence below, the complete predicate is underlined, and the simple predicate, or verb, is in boldface type.

The captain **gave** the crew a night of shore leave.

The crew **was celebrating** a successful catch.

The captain **is** a skillful navigator.

Notice that in the second sentence the verb consists of two words, *was celebrating*. As you know, a verb that consists of more than one word is called a *verb phrase*. Thus, a simple predicate may be a one-word verb or a verb phrase.

Position of Subject and Predicate

In many sentences the subject comes first and is followed by the predicate. However, this is not always the case. Following are some exceptions. The complete subject is underlined and the complete predicate is in italics.

On the deck stood men in heavy wool jackets.   (The complete predicate comes before the complete subject.)

Tomorrow the ship *sails for its home port.*   (The complete subject separates two parts of the complete predicate.)

Have you *ever seen a commercial fishing boat?*   (Part of the verb phrase *have seen* comes before the subject.)

Does the captain of the boat *speak English?*   (Part of the verb phrase *does speak* comes before the complete subject.)

Since the subject and predicate can come in different places in the sentence, you cannot identify them by their position. Here is the best way to find the subject and predicate of a sentence. First find the verb (the simple predicate). Then ask *who?* or *what?* in front of the verb. The answer will be the complete subject. The rest of the words in the sentence are the complete predicate. For example:

   During a bad storm, the crew of the boat worked for twenty-four hours without sleep.

The verb is *worked*. Who worked? The answer is *the crew of the boat*. So, *the crew of the boat* is the complete subject. The complete predicate is all the other words in the sentence: *during a bad storm worked for twenty-four hours without sleep*.

Practice A   Find simple and complete predicates.

Write the complete predicate from each sentence on your paper. Then underline the simple predicate. Remember that the simple predicate can be a verb phrase.

EXAMPLE: Have the swallows returned to Capistrano?

have returned to Capistrano

1. Many birds travel south in the fall.
2. Some fly to South America in search of a good supply of food.
3. Have you ever seen flocks of geese in V formation?
4. In spring the birds return north.
5. On a beautiful, sunny day in April, my science class took a field trip to the New Jersey shore.
6. Overhead flew hundreds of hawks.
7. They were following the coastline north to Canada.
8. The Arctic tern is the greatest traveler of all the birds in the world.
9. Arctic terns fly from Antarctica to the Arctic and back.
10. The northern and southern hemispheres have opposite seasons.
11. The tilt of the earth causes this reversal of the seasons.
12. From April until September the northern hemisphere tilts toward the sun.
13. As a result, the days are longer than the nights.
14. Birds need long days for gathering food.
15. The length of the day tells birds when to fly north or south.

Practice B   **Write sentences.**

Use each of the following groups of words as the complete subject of a sentence. Add your own complete predicate. Write the sentence on your paper. Underline the verb.

EXAMPLE: thousands of runners

Thousands of runners <u>competed</u> in the Boston Marathon.

1. a large dish of delicious peach shortcake
2. a broken-down old car
3. my favorite song
4. all of the sophomore class
5. your friends
6. the last person in line
7. Siamese cats
8. my summer vacation
9. Molly's new dress
10. the waitress at the diner

Practice C   **Write sentences.**

Following are ten simple predicates. Use each one in a sentence. In each sentence you write, underline the complete predicate.

EXAMPLE: walked

The hiking club <u>walked through the state park.</u>

1. were
2. may win
3. will arrive
4. jumped
5. is carrying
6. flew
7. was working
8. lost
9. needs
10. are eating

Compound Subjects and Verbs

Some words just naturally go together. For example:

hamburgers and French fries

Often words like these not only go together but also work together in a sentence. For example:

Hamburgers and French fries are his favorite foods.

The two nouns *hamburgers* and *French fries* work together as the subject of the sentence.

P O I N T S   T O   K N O W

▶ A subject that is made up of more than one noun or pronoun is called a *compound subject*.

Here are some more examples of compound subjects:

Molly or Shanda will bake cookies for the party.

Vince, Mo, and Sue put up the decorations.

Some verbs go together too, such as *talk and laugh*.

We **talked and laughed** all night.

The two verbs *talked* and *laughed* make up the *compound verb* in this sentence.

▶ A compound verb is made up of two or more verbs that share the same subject.

Here are some more examples of compound verbs:

I **tried but failed.**

The player **dribbled, hesitated, and shot** a basket.

Practice   **Find compound subjects and verbs.**

Find the compound subject or verb in each of the following sentences. Write it on your paper. After each, write whether it is a *compound subject* or a *compound verb*.

EXAMPLE: Judd washed and waxed his car.

washed and waxed   compound verb

1. Nurses and doctors bustled around the operating room.
2. Marta, Cal, and Ray had an exhibit of their photographs.
3. The child swam, rested, and swam again.
4. At the sign, they stopped, looked, and proceeded with care.
5. The parents and children read and sang together.
6. Ezra and Jerry are studying for an exam.
7. The campers hiked and then rested.
8. I stood on the corner and waited for the bus.
9. The last few days and nights have been extremely cold.
10. Max and Jennie saw a movie and visited their grandparents.

L E S S O N   F I V E

Kinds of Sentences

Sentences can be classified by function. Some sentences make statements, others ask questions, some give orders or directions, and still others express strong emotion. Each of these four functions is expressed in a different kind of sentence: *declarative, interrogative, imperative,* and *exclamatory.*

P O I N T S   T O   K N O W

▶ A *declarative sentence* states an idea. It ends with a period.

Snow is falling heavily.

Honesty is a good policy.

▶ An *interrogative sentence* asks a question. It ends with a question mark.

>   Is snow falling heavily?

>   Is honesty a good policy?

▶ An *imperative sentence* gives an order or command. It ends with a period or an exclamation point.

>   Leave!

>   Take these books!

In most imperative sentences, the subject is not stated. It is understood to be "you."

>   Pick up that bag.   ("You" pick up that bag.)

However, in some imperative sentences, the subject is stated.

>   Will someone please turn off the lights.   ("Someone" is the subject.)

▶ An *exclamatory sentence* shows strong emotion. It ends with an exclamation point.

>   Are those mountains beautiful!

>   Can you sing!

Practice A   **Identify the kind of sentence.**

Following are ten sentences. Copy each on your paper. After each one, write the kind of sentence it is. Write *declarative, interrogative, imperative,* or *exclamatory.*

1. Henrietta is my friend.
2. Is she home today?
3. Answer the phone!
4. Will you stop by this afternoon?
5. We are planning to go shopping later.
6. I love shopping!
7. Some people enjoy playing board games.

8. Don't shout!

9. Where are my glasses?

10. What a wonderful day!

Practice B   **Write sentences.**

Write at least eight sentences of your own. Try to make them all about one subject. Make sure you include at least two examples of each of the four kinds of sentences.

R E V I E W   E X E R C I S E S

I. Sentences and Fragments Below are ten groups of words. Some of the groups express a complete thought. Others are sentence fragments. Rewrite the groups that express a complete thought so that each begins with a capital letter and ends with a punctuation mark. Add words to each fragment to make it into a complete sentence. (Lesson One)

EXAMPLE: everything at the yard sale
Everything at the yard sale was sold.

1. she looked out the window
2. the big, brown dog with the long tail
3. a large photograph on the table
4. during the loud thunderstorm
5. will someone please answer the door
6. jumped on the table
7. running up the street after the fire engine
8. to the store for some bread
9. after the game was rained out
10. rolled off the desk onto the floor

II. Complete Subjects and Predicates Each group of words below is either a complete subject or a complete predicate. Make each group of words into a complete sentence by adding words of your own. Write the complete sentence on your paper. (Lessons Two and Three)

EXAMPLE: the subway entrance near my house

The subway entrance near my house is always open.

1. will visit the park on warm spring days
2. the car with the broken windshield
3. lights up the western sky at sundown
4. the officer in the blue uniform
5. my worst day in school
6. passed the building with the strange statues in front
7. often leaves the dishes for me
8. all the members of my mother's family
9. my best birthday present last year
10. goes to a beach in Mexico for most of the summer

III. Simple Subjects and Predicates Make two columns on your paper. Label them *Simple Subject* and *Verb*. Write the simple subject and the verb from each sentence in the correct columns. (Lessons Two and Three)

EXAMPLE: The chair broke under the man's weight.

Simple Subject	*Verb*
chair	broke

1. The waves rippled over the rocks.
2. Eileen has called us twice today.
3. Do you know the plot of this play?
4. In spite of everything, I went back to the old house the next night.
5. Genette will take the dog to the veterinarian today.
6. My father almost always speaks in a low voice.
7. Have those girls talked to you yet?

8. The voice of the announcer sounds like a cracked bell.

9. The tree was lying on the ground.

10. Someone must have spilled ink on the desk.

IV. Compound Subjects and Verbs Each sentence below has a compound expression. Write the compound expression on your paper and tell whether it is a compound subject or verb. (Lesson Four)

EXAMPLE: Lorraine and I hardly ever fight.

Lorraine and I   compound subject

1. You may call or write for tickets.
2. The lindy and the Charleston are old dances, but they are fun.
3. The people in the marathon walked, ran, bicycled, or skated.
4. Every day Hal and Eileen get up early and exercise.
5. The teacher read and sang to the kindergarten children.
6. Peanut butter and jelly taste good together.
7. Clark ironed and wore his new blue shirt.
8. I stood and stared at the locked door for a long time.
9. Fresh fruit and vegetables can be bought at the supermarket.
10. Bob hums or sings in the shower.

V. Kinds of Sentences Copy the sentences below onto your paper. After each, place the correct end punctuation mark. Then tell what kind of sentence it is: *declarative, interrogative, imperative,* or *exclamatory.* (Lesson Five)

1. Where are my books
2. I haven't seen them anywhere
3. There they are
4. What luck
5. Please get them
6. Who put them there
7. I'm thrilled
8. How much would it have cost to replace them
9. What shall we do now
10. I think I'll read

Using Sentences in Your Writing

When you write, you want to communicate your ideas to your reader. In order to do this, you have to make your sentences both clear and interesting. Here are some suggestions for achieving these two purposes:

☐ Avoid using sentence fragments. They can be very confusing to your reader.

☐ Try to use different types of sentences.

☐ Try to vary the structure of your sentences. Use different combinations of single subjects, compound subjects, single verbs and compound verbs. Add modifiers to subjects and predicates to vary their length.

Each time you complete a writing assignment, take the time to look over your sentences. See if you can make any changes that will add variety. Have you used nothing but declarative sentences? If appropriate, change a sentence so it asks a question or makes an exclamation. Try to vary the lengths of your sentences, too. If possible, write some long sentences and some short sentences. If your sentences are varied, they will be more likely to hold your reader's attention.

Practice   **Write a paragraph, using a variety of sentences.**

Write a paragraph about what you think you might be doing five years from today. Include at least one example of each of the following in your paragraph:

1. compound subject
2. compound predicate
3. interrogative sentence
4. exclamatory sentence
5. imperative sentence

Complements

Coal trains on the Big Sandy River, Williamson,
West Virginia, 1979
Bill Burke, Archive Pictures, Inc.

Complements

A bride and groom can't make a wedding by themselves—they need a member of the clergy or a justice of the peace. A floor and four walls aren't enough to make a room—they must be finished off with a ceiling. A locomotive and a string of railway cars can't go anywhere unless they have a driver.

Some subjects and verbs need help, too: by themselves, they do not make a complete sentence. They need a *complement* to complete their meaning.

A complement is a word or words that follow the verb in a sentence and complete the meaning begun by the subject and verb.

In this unit you will learn about four kinds of complements: direct objects, indirect objects, predicate nominatives (nouns and pronouns), and predicate adjectives.

L E S S O N   O N E

Direct Objects

A complete sentence can be very short. For example:

Jorge sang.

This is a sentence. It has a subject and a verb, and it expresses a complete thought.

However, sometimes a subject and a verb by themselves do not express a complete thought. For example:

Mary pounded.

The shortstop grabbed.

The coach praised.

Each of these groups of words needs one or more additional words to complete its meaning. It needs a *complement*.

> Mary pounded her **bat** on the ground.
>
> The shortstop grabbed the **ball**.
>
> The coach praised **Mary**.

The words in boldface type are called *direct objects*. Some action verbs need direct objects to complete their meaning. A direct object is a type of complement. It is part of the predicate.

P O I N T S   T O   K N O W

A **direct object** is a noun or pronoun that receives the action of a verb. It answers the question *what?* or *whom?* after the action verb.

For example:

> Mary pounded *what?*   Answer: *bat*
>
> The coach praised *whom?*   Answer: *Mary*

The direct object is always a noun or a pronoun. If the noun or pronoun has modifiers, the modifiers are not considered part of the direct object. Look at the following sentences.

> Allison watched the baby.
>
> Tony worked carefully.
>
> Karen waited in the parking lot.

In the first sentence, *baby* is the direct object. It is a noun that answers the question *whom?* after the verb *watched*.

The second sentence does not have a direct object. *Carefully* is not a noun or a pronoun. It is an adverb. It does not answer the question *what?* or *whom?* It answers the question *how?*

The third sentence has no direct object, either. *In the parking lot* is a prepositional phrase. It acts as an adverb modifying the verb *waited*. It answers the question *where?*

Practice A   Find direct objects.

Some of the sentences that follow have direct objects, and some do not. On your paper, write each direct object next to the number of the sentence. If a sentence does not have a direct object, write *none* on your paper.

EXAMPLE: The magician tapped his hat with his wand.

hat

1. With a huge grin, he pulled a large white rabbit from his hat.
2. Several members of the audience gasped.
3. He observed them with amusement.
4. The rabbit hopped into the wings.
5. An assistant carried a table onto the stage.
6. The magician chose four volunteers from the audience.
7. He positioned a volunteer at each corner of the table.
8. A black velvet cloth covered the table.
9. No one could see the space under the table.
10. Each volunteer grabbed a corner of the cloth.
11. They all lifted the cloth at the same time.
12. Underneath the table sat a large family of rabbits.
13. The volunteers lowered the cloth for a count of five.
14. They lifted it again.
15. The rabbits were gone.

Practice B   Write sentences with direct objects.

Use each of the following words as the direct object in a sentence. Add at least one modifier to each direct object. Write the whole sentence on your paper. Underline each modifier.

EXAMPLE: pets

My friend keeps her larger pets in the backyard.

1. rhinoceros
2. dentists
3. note

4. clothes
5. bread
6. speech
7. banana
8. trick
9. movie
10. balloonist

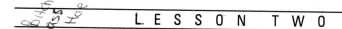

LESSON TWO

Indirect Objects

Can you find the direct object in this sentence?

Charles gave Ellen a silk scarf.

The noun that completes the meaning of the verb *gave* is *scarf. Scarf* answers the question *gave what?* Therefore, *scarf* is the direct object. Then, how is *Ellen* used in the sentence? *Ellen* is the *indirect object.* Certain special verbs can have both a direct object and a second type of complement—an indirect object.

POINTS TO KNOW

An **indirect object** is a noun or pronoun that comes before the direct object in a sentence. It answers the question *to whom?* or *for whom?* or *to what?* or *for what?* before the direct object.

My best friend gave **me** a silver pen for my birthday.   (*Me* tells *to whom* the friend gave the pen.)

Chris bought **Sophie** the largest valentine in the store.   (*Sophie* tells *for whom* Chris bought the valentine.)

Recently I built my little **sister** a kite.   (*Sister* tells *for whom* I built the kite.)

The teacher showed the **class** an experiment on the last day of school.   (*Class* tells *to whom* the teacher showed an experiment.)

Indirect objects are often found in sentences with the following verbs: *give, show, teach, send, promise, make, tell, buy, write, cost, pay,* and *offer.*

Another way to recognize an indirect object is by its position in the sentence. An indirect object always comes after the verb and before the direct object. This clue will help you tell an indirect object from the object of a preposition.

He showed the raccoon to us.   (*Us* is the object of the preposition *to.*)

He showed us the raccoon.   (*Us* is the indirect object of the verb *showed.* The indirect object comes before the direct object, *raccoon.*)

My brother baked a cake for the family.   (*Family* is the object of the preposition *for.*)

My brother baked the family a cake.   (*Family* is the indirect object of the verb *baked. Family* comes before the direct object, *cake.*)

Practice A   **Find indirect objects.**

Find the indirect object in each sentence. Write it on your paper.

EXAMPLE: Fran is sending her sister a clock radio.

sister

1. The Smiths offered Sam a ride to the hockey game.
2. The history teacher showed the class slides of ancient Greek buildings.
3. My brothers gave our dog a bath.
4. The exchange student taught us folk dances from her country.
5. The manager promised the angry customer a refund.
6. Did Mrs. Mercado pay you five dollars for baby-sitting?
7. The town council wrote the television station a letter.
8. That camera cost Hilary a week's salary.
9. The counselor told the young campers ghost stories.
10. In shop class I made myself a bookcase.
11. Please send me the photos if they are good.

12. The tourists asked their guide many questions.
13. Carl's Aunt Sophie brought him a croquet set.
14. You must show the guard your pass when you enter the building.
15. Promise you won't tell my father any of your bad jokes.

Practice B   Identify subjects, verbs, indirect and direct objects.

Make four columns on a piece of paper. Label the columns *Subject,*
Verb, Indirect Object, and *Direct Object.* In the appropriate columns,
write the subjects, verbs, indirect objects, and direct objects from the
sentences that follow. Not every sentence will have a word for all four
columns.

EXAMPLE: Dave Brubeck has given his audiences wonderful music.

Subject	Verb	Indir. Object	Direct Object
Dave Brubeck	*has given*	*audiences*	*music*

1. Dave Brubeck includes members of his family in his group.
2. One of Brubeck's sons showed his father the techniques of rock music.
3. Brubeck's own father once offered him a ranch manager's job.
4. Meanwhile, his mother taught her son classical piano.
5. In college, Brubeck failed his ranching courses.
6. Sadly he wrote his father a letter.
7. He explained his love of music to his father.
8. For three years, the music teachers at the conservatory gave Brubeck special attention.
9. Before graduation, a teacher gave Brubeck a music-writing test.
10. But Brubeck could not write the notes correctly.
11. No one had ever taught him this basic skill.
12. Would the school send its most promising student away without a diploma?
13. The dean made Brubeck an offer.
14. In exchange for his diploma, Brubeck gave the dean his solemn word.
15. He would never give anyone a music lesson.

Practice C   Add indirect objects.

Complete each sentence by adding an indirect object. You may also add modifiers for the indirect object. Write the sentence on your paper.

EXAMPLE: I will give _____ a bottle of perfume.

I will give my mother a bottle of perfume.

1. The toy store offered _____ a discount on old merchandise.
2. Helene baked _____ a pecan pie.
3. Mort promised _____ some help with the math homework.
4. After the successful fund-raising campaign, the club president wrote _____ thank-you letters.
5. The children's parents bought _____ a pet hamster.
6. Evelyn will never tell _____ a secret.
7. The speaker showed _____ the best way to make a fire.
8. The Sports Club awarded _____ a medal and the title "Athlete of the Year."
9. Will you bring _____ a surprise from the store?
10. The shortcut saves _____ a steep climb up a hill.

L E S S O N   T H R E E

Subject Complements

How many different ways can you complete this sentence?

I am _____.

Here are some words you might use to complete the sentence:

a girl, a boy, a student, a teenager, an athlete, a singer, a musician, an artist, a mechanic, a cook, happy, sad, bored, cheerful, angry

The words that might complete the sentence are either nouns or adjectives. They all identify or describe *I*, the subject of the sentence. These words are called *subject complements* because they complete the meaning of the subject.

A **subject complement** is a noun, pronoun, or adjective in the predicate that identifies or describes the subject.

A subject complement always comes after a linking verb. The linking verb "links" the subject with the subject complement. (For a review of linking verbs, see Unit Nineteen, Lesson Three.) The most common linking verb is the verb *be* in all its forms and combinations (*am, is, are, was, were, will be, is being, has been, have been, had been, may be, can be, should be, would be, could be,* and so on).

There are other linking verbs; for example: *become, seem, grow, appear, look, feel, taste, smell, remain, sound, stay.*

Here are some sentences with linking verbs and subject complements. The linking verbs are italicized. The subject complements are in boldface type.

> His brother *is* a **pilot**.
>
> Doris *became* a lab **technician**.
>
> The audience *is* very **restless**.
>
> The apples *grow* **larger** each day.
>
> The child *appears* **content** in her crib.
>
> You *look* **wonderful** in that color.
>
> Tina *feels* **excited** about the trip.
>
> The lemonade *tastes* **tart**.
>
> The garden *smells* **fragrant**.
>
> He *remains* **cheerful** in spite of his troubles.
>
> The rain *sounds* **heavier** now.

Some verbs can be used as both linking verbs and action verbs. Therefore, you cannot determine whether a sentence has a subject complement just by looking at the verb. The following sentences, for example, contain verbs that can be used as linking verbs. In these sentences, however, the verbs are used as action verbs with direct objects. The direct objects are in boldface type.

> The farmer grows spring **wheat**.
>
> The doctor felt my **forehead**.
>
> The cook tasted the **soup**.

Predicate Nominatives and Predicate Adjectives

A subject complement can be a noun, pronoun, or adjective. If it is a noun or pronoun, it is called a *predicate nominative*. If it is an adjective, it is called a *predicate adjective*.

Following are some examples of predicate nominatives.

> That man is a retired army **officer**.
>
> After graduation Tilly will become an **accountant**.
>
> The winner might be **anyone**.

Here are some examples of predicate adjectives.

> The question seemed **silly** at the time.
>
> He acts **pleased** with the gift.
>
> Jim grew **restless** waiting for the bus.

Practice A   **Find predicate nominatives and predicate adjectives.**

On your paper, write the predicate nominative or predicate adjective found in each sentence. Next to it, indicate whether it is a predicate nominative or a predicate adjective.

EXAMPLE: From a distance, the roar of the crowd sounded faint.

faint   predicate adjective

1. The lonely dog acted overjoyed at its owner's arrival.
2. The clouds grew darker by the minute.
3. Al has been an actor for four years.
4. Cigarette smoke is offensive to many people.
5. The biologist remained motionless while the rare bird perched on her windowsill.
6. This will be my last visit to the lake this year.
7. Grandmother may be disappointed if we don't call her.
8. The children grew sleepy as the night wore on.
9. At the beginning of the race, the runner felt nervous.
10. To our surprise, my sister became a jockey.

Practice B   Identify linking verbs and subject complements.

On your paper, make two columns. Label one column *Linking Verb*. Label the other column *Subject Complement*. For each sentence that follows, list the linking verb and the subject complement. Label each subject complement either *PN* (predicate nominative) or *PA* (predicate adjective).

EXAMPLE: Our school bazaar is the biggest event of the year.

Linking Verb   **Subject Complement**

is   *event*   *PN*

1. Work on the bazaar grows more intense from September until Thanksgiving weekend.
2. Each club is busy with plans for its booth.
3. The gymnasium becomes an indoor fairground.
4. This year the bazaar should be better than ever.
5. As usual, the entertainment will be live music by a country western band.
6. Its music always sounds right for a harvest celebration.
7. Last year my favorite booth was the one selling apple cider.
8. The fresh cider smelled tangy.
9. Crispy fried donuts tasted wonderful with the cider.
10. Other booths appeared ordinary next to the one shaped like a pumpkin.

Practice C   Add predicate nominatives and predicate adjectives.

Complete each of the following groups of words by adding either a predicate nominative or a predicate adjective. You may add other words also. Write the complete sentence on your paper. Underline the predicate nominative or predicate adjective that you have added. At the end of each sentence, write whether you added a predicate nominative (*PN*) or a predicate adjective (*PA*).

EXAMPLE: Music becomes

Music becomes more interesting when you know more about it.   *PA*

1. The waiter seemed

2. That tree is

3. After the game, the players looked

4. My friend is

5. This car will never be

6. Realizing his mistake, he felt

7. Your face has grown

8. Those children near the lion cage appear

9. This milk has turned

10. She always acts

L E S S O N   F O U R

Compound Objects and Subject Complements

Like subjects and verbs, objects and subject complements can be compound.

Here are some examples:

Compound Direct Object

The teacher put a **test booklet and pencil** on each desk.

Have you seen **Emmy, Dora, or Tim?**

Compound Indirect Object

The coach showed **Charlene and Gino** the gymnastics equipment.

Tell the **children, mothers, and fathers** the order of the program.

Compound Subject Complement (Predicate Nominative)

The best dancers are **Jim and Teresa.**

The members of the stage crew are **Jo, Raphael, and Curtis.**

Compound Subject Complement (Predicate Adjective)

The curtain is **red and gold.**

The weather will be **cloudy, windy, and cold.**

Any two or more nouns, pronouns, or adjectives can serve as a compound subject, object, or subject complement.

Practice A   Identify compound expressions.

In each of the following sentences, the compound expressions are in italics. On your paper, indicate how each compound expression is used. Use the labels *compound direct object, compound indirect object, compound predicate nominative,* and *compound predicate adjective.*

EXAMPLE: The weather is often *beautiful but chilly* in March.

compound predicate adjective

1. The peaches are *ripe and juicy.*
2. We were *sunburned and sandy* after our day at the beach.
3. At the end of the day the hikers felt *tired but content.*
4. The museum director showed the *teacher and class* a priceless ancient jewel.
5. The winners are *Syl, Cathy, and Belinda.*
6. The Potters prepared *us and themselves* a snack.
7. Do you see any *ducks or geese* on the pond?
8. The cloth for the costumes is *lavender, dark red, and silver.*
9. Aunt Ethel is *a singer, a storyteller, and a skilled musician.*
10. The park ranger gave the *hikers, picnickers, and campers* maps of the area.

Practice B   Add compound expressions.

For each sentence that follows, think of a compound expression that makes sense in the blank. Write the complete sentence on your paper.

EXAMPLE: For lunch we ate _____.

For lunch we ate cheese, bread, and fruit.

1. Joe invited _____ to a picnic.
2. The day was _____.
3. They brought _____.
4. The winners were _____.
5. Everyone felt _____.
6. We tossed _____ to the ducks.
7. Then we played _____.
8. Before we left the yard, we packed our _____.

9. The guests were all _____.

10. Everyone carried _____ into the basement.

R E V I E W   E X E R C I S E S

I. Direct Objects On your paper, write the direct object from each sentence below. Write only the noun that is the direct object; do not include the noun's modifiers. (Lesson One)

EXAMPLE: Harold broke the rod while fishing.   *rod*

1. Gary typed the letter for his sister.
2. They liked the teacher's ideas.
3. Michael nicked his finger with the knife.
4. Mr. Green gave no homework for the holiday.
5. I can read this book in an hour.
6. Kelly bought a new pair of shoes for the party.
7. Adam misses the kindness of his mother.
8. That boy threw a rock at the road sign.
9. Of all desserts, Mandy loves chocolate cake best.
10. Did I bring the right records to the party?

II. Indirect Objects Make two columns on your paper. Label them *Indirect Object* and *Direct Object*. Write the indirect and direct objects from the sentences below. (Lessons One and Two)

EXAMPLE: Tony gave me his favorite hat.

Indirect Object	**Direct Object**
me	*hat*

1. Marla showed her little brother the correct way to dive.
2. Mr. Brenzel taught the class something new today.
3. I promise you a rose without thorns.
4. Will you make me an offer on that car?
5. Eileen buys Greg a new jacket every year on his birthday.
6. He will tell you the time.

7. Paul wrote his friend a long description of his new home.

8. She handed the clerk her last ten-dollar bill.

9. Jack has told his parents the entire story.

10. Did anyone pay you a fee for your services?

III. Subject Complements On your paper write the subject complement from each sentence below. Indicate whether the word is a
predicate nominative or a *predicate adjective*. (Lesson Three)

EXAMPLE: The horn on that truck is too loud.

loud   predicate adjective

1. Karen acts old for her age.
2. Howie is a monster in the morning.
3. The leaves on that tree turn red in the fall.
4. A typewriter is a necessity for me.
5. Debbie has grown taller over the summer.
6. A saxophone sounds mellow compared with an oboe.
7. After our long jog, the lemonade tasted delicious.
8. During the fifth inning Robbie looked exhausted.
9. This painting is the work of a genius.
10. At sunset the sky is purple.
11. Debbie seemed surprised by her math grade.
12. The rock group's new record sounds different.
13. The person in the orange hat is a professional clown.
14. The speaker waited until the audience became quiet.
15. The water from the hot-water faucet felt cold.

IV. Compound Objects and Subject Complements Each sentence
below has a compound expression. Write the compound expression on
your paper and tell whether it is a *compound direct object, indirect
object,* or *subject complement.* (Lesson Four)

EXAMPLE: The day became sunny and warm.

sunny and warm   compound subject complement

1. We could see stars and planets through the telescope.

2. Picasso was a painter and sculptor.
3. Julie made ravioli and spaghetti for the party.
4. The owner of the store offered my brother and me good jobs for the summer.
5. He entertained the children and me for hours.

6. The flowers in the garden are red, white, and blue.
7. We fed the dog some bones and biscuits.
8. I sent my aunt and uncle an old photograph.
9. The day was sunny and warm.
10. Joey is giving Pete and Bill swimming lessons.

V. Complements In each sentence below there is an important part missing. For each sentence, think of a word or words which make sense in the blank and which complete the sentence correctly. Write the word or words on your paper after the number of the sentence. Then tell what part of the sentence you have added. Use these labels: *direct object, indirect object, subject complement*. (Lessons One to Four)

EXAMPLE: Inside the box Gail found _____.

a silver necklace   direct object

1. Aunt Mary promised _____ some homemade bread.
2. The best birthday present I ever received was _____.
3. Marshall took _____ to his sister in the hospital.
4. I bought _____ a magazine to read on the long train ride to Ottawa.
5. Lester has been very _____ lately.
6. The hungry dog ate the _____.
7. I will be extremely _____ if I pass the test.
8. The principal handed _____ a diploma.
9. The photographs of Saturn gave _____ many surprises.
10. Larry drew a(n) _____ in art class today.

Using Complements in Your Writing

As you know, not all sentences require complements. Some sentences are complete with only subjects and verbs:

Hilda is whispering.

Jake sings.

When sentences do require complements, make sure you choose the strongest, most precise words.

Read each pair of sentences below. Decide which one in each pair is stronger. Try to explain why.

Ina washed her dog.

Ina washed her Chihuahua.

David planted flowers.

David planted roses.

She is quiet.

She is calm and even-tempered.

These sentences can be made even better by adding details about the complement.

Ina washed her tiny, nervous Chihuahua, Bruno.

David planted American Beauty roses.

She is calm and even-tempered under pressure.

After you complete a writing assignment, look over your work. Be sure you have chosen the best words to express your ideas.

Practice **Write sentences with complements.**

Write a paragraph about something you enjoy doing. The activity could be cooking, playing Frisbee, riding your bike, skating, or anything else you like to do. When you finish, read over your work. Be sure you have created a clear picture of your ideas.

Clauses

Wailing Wall, Jerusalem, 1976
This wall is believed to be part of the original Temple of
Solomon (King Solomon reigned in the mid-10th century).
Since the 700's Jews have been accustomed to gather here
on the evening before their Sabbath to pray.
Ken Heyman

UNIT TWENTY-TWO

Clauses

LESSON ONE

Independent and Dependent Clauses

Below is a reporter's interview with a movie star. Which of the star's answers are incomplete?

Reporter: To what do you owe your success?

Star: Who taught me to set high goals.

Reporter: How did you get your start in films?

Star: While I was buying toothpaste in a drugstore.

Reporter: Did you always want to be famous?

Star: Although I rather enjoy it.

Reporter: What will you be doing in the future?

Star: Before I make any plans for the future.

Reporter: Do you have a favorite director?

Star: Who discovered me.

Reporter: What kind of role will you be playing in your next picture?

Star: Which you will have to find out for yourself.

Reporter: Do you spend a lot of money on clothes?

Star: Because my parents were poor.

Reporter: Well, this has certainly been an exciting interview. May we talk to you again when you return from Paris?

Star: So that he can arrange a meeting.

All of the star's answers are incomplete. Each answer contains some bits of information, but the bits do not add up to a complete thought. Instead of talking in sentences, the star talked in *dependent clauses*.

A **clause** is a group of words that contains both a subject and a verb.

There are two kinds of clauses, *independent* and *dependent clauses*.

▶   An *independent clause* expresses a complete thought and can stand on its own as a sentence.

▶   A *dependent clause* does not express a complete thought and cannot stand by itself as a sentence. Another name for this kind of clause is *subordinate clause*.

All the answers the star gave in the interview are dependent clauses. Can you make each of the star's answers into a complete sentence? To do that, you have to add an independent clause to each dependent clause.

▶   To make a dependent clause into a sentence, you must attach it to an independent clause.

Here is an example of an independent clause.

> I owe it to my parents.

This independent clause expresses a complete thought. If you add the star's first dependent clause to it, you get this sentence:

> I owe it to my parents, who taught me to set high goals.

The independent clause in a sentence like this is often called the *main clause*.

Can you think of independent clauses that would make the star's other statements into complete sentences? Following are some possibilities. The dependent clauses are in boldface type.

> A famous director noticed me **while I was buying toothpaste in a drugstore.**

> Fame was never my chief goal, **although I rather enjoy it.**

> **Before I make any plans for the future,** I am going to take a long vacation in Paris.

> Melvin LeMelvin, **who discovered me,** has always been my favorite director.

> That is a secret **which you will have to find out for yourself.**

415

Because my parents were very poor, I've always been careful with money.

Please get in touch with my agent **so that he can arrange a meeting.**

Notice the words that come at the beginning of these dependent clauses. There is a certain group of words that are used to connect a dependent clause to a main clause. Following are some of them.

after	so that	whereas	although
that	which	as	unless
while	because	until	who
before	when	if	where

You will learn more about these words and about dependent clauses in the rest of this unit.

Practice A   Find subjects and verbs within clauses.

Following are ten clauses. The independent clauses are written as sentences, with a capital at the beginning and a period or question mark at the end. The dependent clauses are written without a capital or end punctuation. Copy each clause on your paper. Underline the subject of the clause once, and underline the verb twice.

EXAMPLE: since you asked the question politely

since you asked the question politely

1. I will answer.
2. after Jim had eaten
3. when you finish the assignment
4. Who left early?
5. unless the rain stops soon
6. which surprised everybody
7. The flood drove many people out of their homes.
8. before you saw the movie
9. as we watched the parade
10. My brother applied for the job at Mr. Godwin's store.

Practice B   Identify independent and dependent clauses.

Each sentence that follows has a group of words in italics. Decide whether the group of words makes up an independent clause or a dependent clause. On your paper, write *independent* or *dependent* next to the number of the sentence.

EXAMPLE: *After they shook hands,* the girls talked about skiing.
dependent

1. *Before you go skiing,* you probably should take a few lessons.
2. I prefer downhill skiing, *although my sister likes cross-country skiing.*
3. While downhill skis are wide, *cross-country skis are extremely narrow.*
4. The tips of cross-country skis must have high, curled points *so that they can slide over hidden sticks.*
5. *A downhill ski run is short and swift,* whereas a cross-country ski trip is like a long, gliding walk.
6. Although lessons are very helpful, *you can learn cross-country skiing on your own.*
7. *If you live in open country,* you can do cross-country skiing in your own backyard.
8. People *who don't want to spend a lot of money* prefer cross-country skiing to the downhill variety.
9. After you have learned the correct leg and arm movements, *cross-country skiing is as easy as bicycling.*
10. You can ski at a relaxed pace *unless you want to test yourself by going at top speed.*
11. Because I am not an expert, *I usually ski cautiously.*
12. *When I first started downhill skiing,* I took a bad fall.
13. *Although I didn't hurt myself seriously,* it was a frightening experience.
14. *I decided to take lessons* so that I could prevent myself from getting hurt.
15. After I took lessons for a few weeks, *I felt confident enough to brave the slopes again.*

Practice C   Write sentences with dependent clauses.

Following are ten groups of words. If a group of words is an independent clause, write it on your paper as a sentence. Start the sentence with a capital letter and end it with a period or a question mark. If a group of words is a dependent clause, add an independent clause to it, to make it into a sentence. Write the sentence on your paper. (One of the groups of words can be used either as a dependent clause or as an independent clause [sentence] that asks a question.)

EXAMPLES: while he studied for the test
While he studied for the test, Paco ate a whole pizza.

who won the skiing event
Who won the skiing event?

or

Kendra is the girl who won the skiing event.

1. whose skis broke near the finish line
2. before they arrived
3. you can be proud of yourself
4. although he is only a beginner
5. take good care of your equipment
6. when I finish waxing my skis
7. because it is easy
8. unless the snow melts
9. if we can
10. both swimmers and skiers can get sunburned

L E S S O N   T W O

Dependent Clauses as Adjectives

In Lesson One you learned about two kinds of clauses: independent clauses and dependent clauses.

In this unit you will learn about two kinds of dependent clauses: *adjective clauses* and *adverb clauses*. Notice that the two kinds of dependent clauses are named after two of the parts of speech that you studied in Unit Nineteen. There is a good reason for this. A dependent clause is used as a part of speech in a sentence. Thus, an adjective clause does the same job as a one-word adjective. It modifies a noun or pronoun. (For a review of adjectives, see Unit Nineteen, Lesson Four.)

P O I N T S   T O   K N O W

An **adjective clause** is a dependent clause used as an adjective to modify a noun or a pronoun.

Look at these two sentences.

> The **friendly** stranger asked us for directions.
>
> The stranger, **who was friendly,** asked us for directions.

In the first sentence *friendly* is an adjective describing *stranger*. In the second sentence *who was friendly* is an adjective clause describing *stranger*. Both sentences say the same thing.

Here are some more examples of adjective clauses. Each adjective clause is in boldface type. The word in the independent clause that is modified by the adjective clause is italicized.

> The *woman* **who spoke to you** is my aunt.
>
> The *man* **whom I met on the train** was very talkative.
>
> The mechanic fixed my car *door*, **which had never worked properly.**
>
> May I borrow the *book* **that you bought?**
>
> There goes the *jockey* **whose horse fell down.**
>
> I remember the *time* **when you were lost in the woods.**
>
> Is that the *restaurant* **where they serve buffalo steaks?**
>
> The *day* **before we left on our trip** was hectic.

Relative Pronouns

The word that introduces an adjective clause is either a *relative pronoun (who, whose, whom, which, that)* or a *relative adverb (where, when, why, after, before)*. Both relative pronouns and relative adverbs connect, or "relate," the dependent clause to the independent clause.

In addition to being a connector, a relative pronoun does the work of a pronoun within the dependent clause. In Unit Nineteen, Lesson

Two, you learned that a pronoun takes the place of a noun or another pronoun. For example:

John ran.

He ran.

The pronoun *he* takes the place of the noun *John*.

▶ A *relative pronoun* takes the place of a noun or pronoun in the independent clause.

I met the singer **who won the Grammy award.**

The relative pronoun *who* refers to *singer*. The adjective clause *who won a Grammy award* modifies *singer*. Notice that the same idea can be expressed in two sentences by repeating the noun *singer*.

I met the singer. The singer won a Grammy award.

When you combine these two sentences, the relative pronoun *who* takes the place of the noun *singer* in the second clause. *Singer* is the antecedent of the relative pronoun *who*.

Uses of Relative Pronouns

In Lesson One of this unit you learned that a dependent clause has a subject and a verb. The relative pronoun of an adjective clause may be the subject of the clause. For example:

I met the singer **who won a Grammy award.** (The relative pronoun *who* is the subject of the adjective clause, and *won* is the verb.)

Relative pronouns can also serve as direct objects, objects of prepositions, and possessives in the dependent clause.

The hiker **whom the bear attacked is recovering.** (The relative pronoun *whom* is the direct object of the verb *attacked*.)

The child **for whom I baby-sit** is a genius. (The relative pronoun *whom* is the object of the preposition *for*.)

Maria, **whose uncle is mayor,** campaigns for him. (The relative pronoun *whose* shows possession.)

Relative Adverbs

Relative adverbs are also used to introduce adjective clauses. They are different from relative pronouns in that they do not replace a noun or pronoun. In the following examples the relative adverb is italicized.

The reason ***why* I was late** is very complicated.

The hospital ***where* I was born** is being torn down.

I'll never forget the summer ***when* my cousin came from Israel.**

The best event ***after* we arrived** was the water ballet.

The hours ***before* lunch was served** seemed endless.

A Review

Here is a review of the important information in this lesson about adjective clauses.

☐ An adjective clause is used as an adjective. The whole clause modifies a noun or pronoun in the independent clause.

☐ An adjective clause is introduced by a relative pronoun or a relative adverb.

☐ The relative pronoun takes the place of its antecedent, which is in the independent clause.

Practice A   Find subjects and verbs within adjective clauses.

Each of the following sentences contains an adjective clause in italics. Write the adjective clause on your paper. Underline the subject once and the verb twice. Then write the word in the independent clause that is modified by the adjective clause.

EXAMPLE: We walked in the garden, *which was full of roses.*

which was full of roses   garden

1. The workers *whose equipment broke* were given the day off.
2. The movies *that I like best* are science fiction.
3. Lil and I took Joe to a stream *where we had fished before.*
4. Fanny's letter arrived on the day *after I wrote to her.*

5. The team *that won most of the swimming events* was ours.
6. The hikers *who knew the trail best* led the group.
7. On our trip south we visited Knoxville, *where a world's fair was held in 1982.*
8. The student *whose painting is on the wall* won first prize.
9. The road, *which is unpaved,* will challenge your driving skill.
10. The dancer, *whom everyone admired,* performed several solos.

Practice B   **Combine sentences.**

Following are pairs of sentences. Combine the two sentences to make one sentence with an adjective clause.

EXAMPLE: Any dog can learn to do tricks.

The dog's owner has the patience to train it.

Any dog whose owner has the patience to train it can learn to do tricks.

1. The hall was decorated to look like a tropical island.
   The hall had been rented for the dance.
2. Do not believe the story.
   You heard the story from Lainie.
3. The woman is a marine biologist.
   The woman spoke about training dolphins.
4. The man was huffing and puffing.
   The man's hat had rolled down the street.
5. The club will hold a bake sale.
   The club is trying to raise money.
6. The saleslady was very apologetic.
   The saleslady was waiting on me.
7. The bus was modern and comfortable.
   I took the bus to Hartford.
8. The bird was outside my window this morning.
   The bird was not a robin.
9. Bring me some of the cookies.
   Karen baked the cookies for the club meeting.
10. Rob lives next door to me.
    Rob was named captain of the hockey team.

Dependent Clauses as Adverbs

You have just studied adjective clauses, which modify nouns and pronouns. Another kind of dependent clause is the *adverb clause.*

An **adverb clause** is a dependent clause that modifies a verb, an adjective, or an adverb.

He will play in a game **after he gets out of school tomorrow.** (The adverb clause modifies the verb *will play.*)

I was not as polite **as I should have been**.   (The adverb clause modifies the adjective *polite.*)

He practices harder **than his teammates do**.   (The adverb clause modifes the adverb *harder.*)

Here are some more examples of adverb clauses that modify the verb in the main clause. The adverb clause is in boldface type. The verb it modifies is italicized.

She *sings* **when no one is around.**

He *enjoys* soccer **because he is so good at it.**

He usually *makes* a goal **if the other team doesn't have a very good goalie.**

Although he is sometimes injured, he never *quits*.

Subordinating Conjunctions

An adverb clause is introduced by a *subordinating conjunction*. Here are some common subordinating conjunctions:

after	even though	till	although
except that	unless	as	if
until	as if	in order that	when
as long as	provided	whenever	as much as
provided that	where	as soon as	since

whereas	as though	so	wherever
because	so that	whether	before
than	while	even if	though

A subordinating conjunction is like other conjunctions. Its purpose is to join two groups of words. (For a review of conjunctions, see Unit Nineteen, Lesson Seven.) A subordinating conjunction joins the dependent adverb clause to the independent clause. Each subordinating conjunction expresses a certain relationship between the independent clause and the dependent adverb clause. In each of the three sentences that follow, the two ideas expressed in the independent and dependent clauses are the same. However, three different subordinating conjunctions give the three sentences three difference meanings.

> We sat on the beach **until** the sun came up.
>
> We sat on the beach **while** the sun came up.
>
> We sat on the beach **after** the sun came up.

Here is another example.

> I will go **if** you are going.
>
> I will go **because** you are going.
>
> I will go **unless** you are going.

Position of Adverb Clauses

An adverb clause that modifies a verb can be placed at the beginning, in the middle, or at the end of a sentence. In the following sentences the adverb clause modifies the verb *listened*. The adverb clause is in boldface type.

> **As she paddled her canoe down the river**, the girl listened for the sound of rushing water.
>
> The girl, **as she paddled her canoe down the river**, listened for the sound of rushing water.
>
> The girl listened for the sound of rushing water **as she paddled her canoe down the river**.

Notice that when an adverb clause comes at the beginning of a sentence, it is followed by a comma. When an adverb clause comes in the middle of a sentence, it is surrounded by commas. However, when an adverb clause comes at the end of the sentence, it usually is not set off by a comma.

The commas in the first two examples mark natural pauses in the sentences. If you were speaking instead of writing or reading, you would probably pause at those points in the sentences.

Practice A   Find subjects and verbs within adverb clauses.

Each of the following sentences has an adverb clause in italics. On your paper write the adverb clause from each sentence. Then underline the subject of the adverb clause once and underline the verb twice.

EXAMPLE: *If you ever think about carving your initials on a tree,* stop and consider the many useful products of trees.

if you ever think about carving your initials on a tree

1. *Before European settlers came to North America,* Native Americans made canoes from birch trees.

2. The early settlers made a dye from the husk of the butternut *since they could not always get dyes from Europe.*

3. *If you have ever put witch hazel on a mosquito bite,* you have used medicine from the hazel tree.

4. *When you eat maple syrup on pancakes,* you are eating the sap of the sugar maple.

5. Hickory wood, *when it is burned,* gives off a light, flavorful smoke useful for curing meats.

6. *Whenever you drink coffee or cocoa,* you are enjoying a tree product.

7. *Although cherry trees are grown mainly for their fruit,* they also give us fine wood for furniture.

8. *When you think of a chestnut tree,* you can almost taste those wonderful roasted nuts.

9. *Before the chestnuts appear,* the tree has beautiful white flowers.

10. The flowers point upward, *so that they look like candles.*

Practice B   Combine sentences.

Join each pair of sentences to make one sentence with an adverb clause. You may change some words in the sentence, but the meaning should remain the same.

EXAMPLE: I heard a key in the lock.

I was reading a murder mystery.

As I was reading a murder mystery, I heard a key in the lock.

1. I was not scared.
    I was alone in the house.
2. My parents use their key instead of ringing the bell.
    They come home late at night.
3. I turned and watched the door.
    It slowly swung open.
4. Then I let out a scream.
    There was no one there!
5. You do not believe my story.
    I will not blame you.
6. I realized what had happened.
    I started to laugh.
7. My father put the car in the garage.
    My mother unlocked the door.
8. She accidently dropped the keys in the bushes.
    She bent down to find them.
9. She jumped up.
    She heard my scream.
10. My mother was even more frightened.
    I was frightened.

Sentence Structure

Different kinds of buildings are constructed differently. An office building is different from a single-family house. A school is different from a bus station. All buildings have floors and ceilings and walls, but these parts are put together in different ways.

Sentences have different structures, too. As you know, sentences are made of clauses. However, these clauses can be combined in different ways. In this lesson you will study the four basic kinds of sentence structure: *simple, compound, complex,* and *compound-complex.*

P O I N T S T O K N O W

A **simple sentence** contains one independent clause.

Camping can be an enjoyable activity.

A simple sentence may have a compound subject, a compound verb, or some other compound part. However, it is still a simple sentence. (See Unit Twenty, Lesson Four, for a review of compound subjects and verbs.)

Here are some simple sentences with compound parts:

Modern **campers and hikers** can get excellent equipment.
(simple sentence with compound subject)

Most equipment is **lighter but stronger** because of new materials.
(simple sentence with compound predicate adjective)

A **compound sentence** contains two or more independent clauses.

The new kinds of fishing line stay clean longer, and **the knives come apart for cleaning.**   (two independent clauses)

My family went camping once, but **we did not have the right equipment,** and **the trip was a disaster.**   (three independent clauses)

In a compound sentence there is a comma after each independent clause except the last one. A coordinating conjunction may join each clause to the preceding one. In the examples above, the coordinating conjunctions are *and* and *but.*

Sometimes a coordinating conjunction joins only the last two clauses, as in this example:

We had no tent, our food was either cold or burned, and the mosquitoes ate us alive.

Also, the independent clauses in a compound sentence may be joined by a semicolon:

Graphite fishing poles are expensive; they can cost several hundred dollars.

A **complex sentence** contains one independent clause and one or more dependent clauses.

Here are examples of complex sentences. The dependent clauses are in boldface type.

People **who decide to go camping** should make careful plans. (complex sentence with one dependent clause)

After we got home from our camping trip, we discussed all the things **that had gone wrong.**   (complex sentence with two dependent clauses)

A **compound-complex sentence** contains two or more independent clauses and one or more dependent clauses.

The following example has two independent clauses (in italics) and one dependent clause (in boldface type).

We must make better plans **than we made last time,** or *my mother will not go camping again.*

Practice A   Identify kinds of sentence structure.

On your paper, indicate the structure of each sentence that follows. Use these labels: *simple, compound, complex, compound-complex.*

EXAMPLE: To my surprise, the tent weighed no more than a few ounces.

simple

1. Sylvia likes camping, but she likes talking even more.

2. She knows all about the latest camping gear.

3. The other day she gave me a lecture on the ways in which fishing has changed over the last twenty years.

4. The spinning reel, which was unknown before World War II, has made fishing easier, and the new type of fishing line needs less care.

5. The knowledge that we have gained from space travel has made a big difference.

6. New metals have been invented for use in space.

7. Fly rods, which used to be made of bamboo, are now made of metal or fiberglass.

8. Most campers used to buy their equipment at army surplus stores.

9. Nowadays, however, they can get equipment that is made especially for camping.

10. Sylvia gave me a lot of information that I could have lived without, but I am a patient listener when a friend is talking.

Practice B   Rewrite sentences to vary their structure.

All of the sentences in the following paragraph are simple sentences. On your paper, rewrite the paragraph so that it has a variety of sentence structures. You may combine sentences in any way you like. If you wish, you may leave some of the sentences as they are. There are many ways to revise this paragraph. When you have finished, you may want to compare your version with your classmates' versions.

The safety pin is one of the world's most useful inventions. Yet it took only three hours to make. It earned only four hundred dollars for its inventor. It was invented in 1849 by Walter Hunt. He also invented a sewing machine. Hunt made the safety pin for a reason. He owed another man fifteen dollars. The man kept asking him to pay it back. Hunt thought about his problem. He began to play with a piece of wire. He twisted the wire into different shapes. He had something. It looked very much like the safety pin of today.

I. Independent and Dependent Clauses Copy each dependent clause on your paper. If a sentence does not contain a dependent clause, write X after its number on your paper. (Lesson One)

1. While we ate lunch, we made plans for the afternoon.
2. We enjoyed the book, but no one liked the movie.
3. John hit the ball, and the ball broke a window.
4. As soon as they had eaten, they broke camp and started climbing again.
5. Henry took a break after he had finished the test.
6. Marge called Mary after the game.
7. Mrs. Gold likes to read a book when she spends an evening at home.
8. The paper, which won a prize, was about Beaver Island.
9. Mr. Klaus is a teacher whom everyone likes.
10. Is this the room where we are supposed to meet?

II. Adjective Clauses On your paper, write the adjective clause from each sentence. Then write the noun that the adjective clause modifies. (Lesson Two)

1. The dress that she likes is on sale.
2. The girl who made this cake is over there.
3. The school that won the championship is Germantown.
4. The house, which has been empty for almost fifteen years, is being repaired.
5. Is that the author whose books you like?
6. There has never been a time when Jack was scared.
7. He built houses that were made of wood.
8. This is the place where the park will be.
9. These are the ones that Janice likes best.
10. There is the woman who owns the store.

III. Adverb Clauses Copy each adverb clause from the sentences that follow. (Lesson Three)

1. The dog looked as if it hadn't eaten in a week.
2. If the telephone rings, Marcie will answer it.
3. Matt came home before he went to the game.
4. As soon as the show is over, I'm going to bed.
5. Put this box wherever you can find room for it.
6. We were late because the traffic was very heavy.
7. Whether or not Jeff comes to the party, you will have a good time.
8. The team sold pennants so that they could buy new uniforms.
9. Sandy will come, provided she does not have a baby-sitting job.
10. Even though she was hungry, Gloria would not eat.

IV. Adjective and Adverb Clauses In each sentence there is a dependent clause in italics. Decide whether the dependent clause is an adjective clause or an adverb clause. On your paper write *adjective clause* or *adverb clause* after the number of the sentence. (Lessons Two and Three)

EXAMPLE: Ballet dancing is an art *that has traveled widely.*

adjective clause

1. *Although it first appeared in Italy*, ballet soon found its way to France.
2. The first ballets were court entertainments *in which the king and the nobles took part.*
3. King Louis XIV of France, *who was called the Sun King*, often danced in ballets.
4. *Because there was such a demand for dance entertainments*, a class of professional dancers developed.
5. At the time *when Louis XIV was ruling France*, Peter the Great was Czar of Russia.
6. Peter, *who as a boy had lived near a colony of foreigners*, wanted his country to become "Westernized."

7. *Since the Russians had always loved dance*, Peter encouraged French-style dancing at his court.

8. Later the empress Anna brought a French dance teacher to Russia, *where he organized a ballet school.*

9. Today ballet is more popular *than it has ever been before.*

10. Television, *which can reach millions of people at a time*, has helped build a new audience for ballet.

V. Sentence Structure Number your paper from 1 to 10. Indicate the structure of each sentence that follows. Use these labels: *simple, compound, complex, compound-complex.* (Lesson Four)

1. The scent of flowers filled the air.

2. Delia was supposed to come, but she didn't.

3. The school that he attended was made of brick.

4. Barbara ate the asparagus even though she hated it.

5. We have chosen a band for the dance, and they have agreed to play for four hours.

6. The little boy broke the window with a ball, and then he ran away because he was scared.

7. Most schools offer many courses because of the wide range of student interests.

8. Jeffrey went to the store and bought groceries.

9. You can come to my house, or I can go to yours.

10. Through the window I can see the students.

In this unit, you have learned about four different types of sentence: simple, compound, complex, and compound-complex. Since you have four different sentence structures to choose from, you can put variety in your writing. You can mix the sentence types together in different combinations. You can make some sentences short and some sentences long, some easy and some complicated. If you do this, your paragraphs will never be as boring as the one that follows:

> We chose a campsite. It seemed deserted. My younger brothers made a dinner of burned hamburgers and cold canned beans. We sang songs around the campfire. My grandmother told ghost stories. Everyone got sleepy. We crawled into our sleeping bags. Soon we felt drops of rain. It quickly became a downpour. We had no tent. Finally we all slept sitting up in the car.

This paragraph is monotonous because all the sentences in it have the same structure. They are all simple sentences. Here is the same paragraph with a variety of sentence structures:

> We chose a campsite that seemed deserted. After my younger brothers made a dinner of burned hamburgers and cold canned beans, we sang songs around the campfire. Then my grandmother told ghost stories. When everyone got sleepy, we crawled into our sleeping bags. Soon we felt drops of rain, which quickly became a downpour. Since we had no tent, we all slept sitting up in the car.

Varying the sentence structure makes the story more interesting.

Practice   **Write varied sentences.**

Write a paragraph about something you did during a holiday. The holiday could be Christmas, Easter, Thanksgiving, Passover, Washington's Birthday, July 4th, or any other holiday. The event you write about could be a meal you ate, a parade you saw, a discussion you had, a game you played, or anything at all that you did. In your paragraph, try to vary your sentence structure. You should have at least one example of each of the four sentence types: simple, compound, complex, and compound-complex.

Phrases

"Children on Lawn," around 1910-1912
Samuel J. Castner
International Museum of Photography at George Eastman
House, Rochester, New York

Phrases

Imagine that you are a plainclothes detective. You are trying to catch the person who stole a painting from the museum last week. You think the thief may try to sell the painting to an art dealer in another city. One day you're in the art dealer's store when someone hands the dealer this note:

Stolen last week painting your bedroom furniture bright blue hidden carefully behind the times looking up and down glass and steel in terrible danger Elliot and Ralph living together peacefully Room at the Top.

It makes no sense, so it must be in code. To break the code, you have to divide the message into phrases. Find groups of words that seem to belong together. Then jot down the first word in each group. These words make up the secret message.

stolen last week

painting your bedroom furniture bright blue

hidden carefully

behind the times

looking up and down

glass and steel

in terrible danger

Elliot and Ralph

living together peacefully

Room at the Top

These groups of related words are called *phrases*. (Read the first words of the phrases in order, and you'll know where to find the stolen painting.)

A **phrase** is a group of related words that does not contain both a subject and a verb.

▶   A phrase is used as a single part of speech.

In this unit you will learn about several different kinds of phrases: *prepositional, participial, gerund, infinitive,* and *appositive.*

L E S S O N   O N E

Prepositional Phrases

Consider this sentence:

I ran.

Now think of some phrases you could add to tell where or when you ran. For example:

I ran **out the door.**
I ran **around the block.**
I ran **to the store.**
I ran **in the gym.**
I ran **across the bridge.**
I ran **after school.**
I ran **during the summer months.**
I ran **beside the lake.**

All the added phrases in boldface type are *prepositional phrases.*

A **prepositional phrase** is a group of related words that begins with a preposition and ends with a noun or a pronoun.

▶ The noun or pronoun that follows a preposition is called the *object of the preposition*. A prepositional phrase may also include words that modify the object. Following are some more examples of prepositional phrases

> The skydiver jumped **from the plane**.
>
> The insect **under my microscope** has two pairs **of wings**.
>
> The mail deliverers brought a package **for them**.
>
> The movers were carrying a very large sofa **through a very small door**.
>
> The mayor presented awards **to Louella and Steve**.

Notice that in the last example above there is a compound object of the preposition (*Louella and Steve*).

Here is a list of some commonly used prepositions.

about	beneath	into	through
above	beside	like	till
across	between	near	to
after	beyond	of	toward
against	by	off	until
along	down	on	up
among	during	onto	upon
around	except	out	with
at	for	over	within
behind	in	past	without
below	inside	since	

▶ Some prepositions consist of more than one word. Following are some examples.

out of	except for	instead of
in front of	because of	along with

▶ A prepositional phrase can be used as an adjective or an adverb.

Prepositional Phrases Used as Adjectives

As you learned in Unit Nineteen, Lesson Four, an adjective is a word that modifies a noun or a pronoun. Similarly, an adjective phrase is a phrase that modifies a noun or a pronoun.

► A prepositional phrase can function as an adjective modifying a noun or a pronoun.

The people **in the lobby** have tickets **for this show**.   (The prepositional phrase *in the lobby* modifies the noun *people.* The prepositional phrase *for this show* modifies the noun *tickets*.)

The woman **in the blue dress and red hat** is the mother **of the lead singer**.   (The prepositional phrase *in the blue dress and red hat* modifies the noun *woman.* The prepositional phrase *of the lead singer* modifies the noun *mother*.)

► A prepositional phrase used as an adjective can modify a noun or pronoun in another prepositional phrase.

The fishing tackle **in the box on the shelf** belongs to my uncle.   (*On the shelf* modifies the noun *box*, which is the object of the preposition *in*.)

Also, more than one prepositional phrase can modify the same noun.

The man **in the brown fur hat with the leather briefcase** is a gym teacher.   (*In the brown fur hat* and *with the leather briefcase* both modify the noun *man*.)

Prepositional Phrases Used as Adverbs

You learned in Unit Nineteen, Lesson Five, that a word that modifies a verb, an adjective, or an adverb is called an *adverb*. A prepositional phrase that modifies a verb, an adjective, or an adverb is called an *adverb phrase*.

The dog ran **up the stairs**.   She was faint **with hunger**.

▶ A prepositional phrase that functions as an adverb answers such questions as *when?, where?, how?,* and *why?*

The space capsule traveled **past Saturn and Mercury.** (*Past Saturn and Mercury* modifies the verb *traveled*. It answers the question *where?*)

I am always hungry **at bedtime.** (*At bedtime* modifies the adjective *hungry*. It answers the question *when?*)

We drove slowly **because of the rain.** (*Because of the rain* modifies the adverb *slowly*. It answers the question *why?*)

440

Practice A   Find prepositional phrases and identify how they are used.

On your paper write the prepositional phrases from the following sentences. After each phrase write *adjective* or *adverb*, to show how the phrase is used in the sentence.

EXAMPLE: The first marathon was run in 490 B.C. by a soldier in the Greek army.

in 490 B.C.   adverb

by a soldier   adverb

in the Greek army   adjective

1. The Greeks had just defeated an invading Persian army on the plain of Marathon.
2. Carrying news of the victory, the Greek soldier ran from Marathon to Athens, a distance of twenty-five miles.
3. Today one of the most famous marathons is held every year in Boston on April 19.
4. The name of Clarence DeMar is a part of the history of the Boston Marathon.
5. DeMar won seven Boston marathons between 1910 and 1930.
6. At the beginning of the second marathon, doctors discovered a murmur in DeMar's heart.

7. DeMar pleaded with the doctors.

8. In spite of their advice, DeMar ran.

9. He won his first Boston marathon with a record-breaking time.

10. In the following years DeMar won six more Boston marathons and many other races.

Practice B   **Add prepositional phrases.**

Write a prepositional phrase for each blank that follows, using the preposition in parentheses.

EXAMPLE: _____ dived the two clowns.   (into)

Into the tiny car dived the two clowns.

1. _____ several folk singers performed.   (at)

2. The blond woman sang a song _____.   (about)

3. The musicians were hidden _____.   (behind)

4. Everyone likes to sit _____.   (near)

5. I sat _____.   (between)

6. My favorite songs are the ones written _____.   (by)

7. The title _____ is "Midnight Blues."   (of)

8. I first heard it _____.   (on)

9. The Blue Mondays played it _____   (instead of)

10. It always reminds me _____   (of)

Practice C   **Write sentences with prepositional phrases.**

Choose one of the topics from the following list. Write five sentences about the topic. Include at least one prepositional phrase in each sentence. Underline the prepositional phrase or phrases.

EXAMPLE: Movies

I like movies about young people.

Topics:

1. Music

2. An athlete

3. Movies

4. A topic of your own choice

Participial Phrases

A person or an object that can do many different things is often described as "versatile." For example, a Swiss Army knife is versatile. You can use it to cut with a blade, scissors, or saw; to open a can or bottle; to remove a cork; to drive a screw; and to clean fish.

Certain words are versatile, too. Look at the word *arriving* in the following two sentences. It is used in two different ways.

The train will be **arriving** in five minutes.

Passengers from **arriving** trains can be met at Gate 7.

In the first sentence *arriving* is the main verb in the verb phrase *will be arriving*. In the second sentence *arriving* is used as an adjective to describe the noun *trains*.

Here's another example of a versatile word:

Margie has **carried** that heavy bag all day.

Carried away by the music, he began to dance around the room.

In the first sentence *carried* is the main verb in the verb phrase *has carried*. In the second sentence *carried* is an adjective describing the pronoun *he*.

Arriving and *carried* are forms of verbs called *participles*. (You learned about participles in Unit Nineteen, Lesson Three.) As you know, every verb has four principal parts, and two of those parts are the *present participle* and the *past participle*. Here are the principal parts of *arrive* and *carry*:

Base Form or Infinitive	Present Participle	Past Tense	Past Participle
arrive	arriving	arrived	arrived
carry	carrying	carried	carried

Base form: Please **carry** this box into the house.

Present participle: The boy **carrying** the flag is my brother.

Past tense: The man **carried** his small son on his shoulders.

Past participle: **Carried** along by the crowd, we followed the candidate.

▶ The present and past participles of verbs can be used with helping verbs to form verb phrases. They can also be used alone, as adjectives modifying nouns or pronouns. Here are some more examples of present and past participles used as adjectives.

> The **running** horses escaped from the corral.
>
> The **panting** boy gave up.
>
> The horses, **tiring,** gave up, too.
>
> **Looking** up, we saw a helicopter approaching.
>
> The **battered** old car still runs.
>
> The **abandoned** kittens grew healthy under our care.
>
> The athlete, **encouraged,** finished the race.

Like any other adjective, a participle sometimes follows a linking verb and refers to the subject. Then it is a subject complement (predicate adjective). (For a review of predicate adjectives, see Unit Twenty-one, Lesson Three.)

The following sentences contain participles used as predicate adjectives.

> The movie was **exciting**.
>
> That book looks **interesting**.
>
> After that big meal I felt **stuffed**.
>
> With dismay, I saw that my best skirt was **torn**.

▶ Be careful not to confuse a linking verb plus participle with a verb phrase (helping verb plus participle).

> The workers were **exhausted**.   (The past participle of the verb *exhaust* is used as an adjective to describe the noun *workers*. It means "extremely weary." *Were* is a linking verb.)
>
> More people came than we expected, so our supplies of food and water **were** soon **exhausted**.   (*Were exhausted* is a verb phrase meaning "were used up." It tells what was done to the supplies. *Were* is a helping verb.)

How Participles Become Phrases

A present or past participle used as an adjective may still behave like a verb in two ways. Like a verb, it may take an object, and it may have modifiers. Here is a participle that has a direct object:

I saw him **opening** *his locker door.*

Here is a participle that has modifiers:

Startled *by the sudden noise,* we turned and ran.

P O I N T S   T O   K N O W

A **participial phrase** is made up of a participle and its objects and modifiers.

Here are examples of participial phrases, in boldface. The noun or pronoun that is modified by the participial phrase is italicized.

In the park we saw *Jill* **reading a book**.   (The participle *reading* has a direct object, *book.*)

Glancing around nervously, *Tom* helped her up the steep hill. (The participle *glancing* is modified by two adverbs, *around* and *nervously.*)

Leaving her friends behind, *she* walked up the path to the haunted house.   (The participle *leaving* has a direct object, *friends. Behind* is an adverb modifying *leaving.*)

The two **evenly matched** *players* were engaged in a fierce battle for the championship.   (The participle *matched* is modified by the adverb *evenly.*)

Swinging from the branch, *Tarzan* gave a yell.   (The participle *swinging* is modified by the prepositional phrase *from a branch.*)

Our *friends,* **annoyed because we were late,** left without us. (The participle *annoyed* is modified by the adverb clause *because we were late.*)

From these examples, you can see that a participial phrase may come before or after the noun or pronoun it modifies.

Practice A   Find participial phrases and words they modify.

On your paper, copy the participial phrase from each sentence. Then copy the noun or pronoun that the participial phrase modifies.

EXAMPLE: I dream of a future filled with achievement.
filled with achievement   future

1. Hoping to get rich quick, I have decided to become an inventor.
2. A friend of mine, working with common materials, claims to have invented a new kind of winter coat.
3. The secret is in the tiny plastic bottles sewn all over the coat.
4. Filled with water, the bottles collect heat from the sun.
5. But, asked about the effectiveness of the solar coat, my friend pretends not to hear.
6. A flashlight powered by the sun seemed like a good idea to me.
7. Excited by the challenge, I bought the materials I needed.
8. Taking apart a cheap flashlight, I looked at all the pieces.
9. My friends found me seated at my work table, deep in thought.
10. Pointing out the uselessness of a flashlight in the sunshine, they advised me to forget the whole idea.

Practice B   Find participial phrases.

Copy the italicized group of words from each sentence. If the group of words is a participial phrase, write *yes*. If it is not, write *no*.

1. A fly has *landed on my nose*.
2. *Growling and showing its teeth*, the dog frightened us.
3. Visiting Valley Forge, we thought of the hardships *endured by Washington's army*.
4. They left the clean sheets *spread out on the grass*.
5. By six o'clock all of the guests had *left the party*.
6. A guide took them *up the river in a canoe*.
7. The newcomers were *interested in a tour of the island*.
8. *Singing and telling jokes*, the campers got acquainted.
9. *Snug in their sleeping bags*, the young campers giggled.
10. Her term paper had been *written but not typed*.

Practice C   **Combine sentences.**

Combine each pair of sentences below into one sentence by making one of the sentences into a participial phrase. Write the new sentence on your paper. Underline the participial phrase.

EXAMPLE: He tossed his hat into the air.

He gave a loud cheer.

Tossing his hat into the air, he gave a loud cheer.

1. The twins played happily.
    The twins splashed around in the mud puddle.
2. The forest was almost destroyed by fire last summer.
    The forest is beginning to show new growth.
3. The students were enjoying their trip to the museum.
    The students forgot about lunch.
4. The car was recently damaged in an accident.
    The car needs to be completely overhauled.
5. The skateboarders were protected by elbow and knee pads.
    The skateboarders did amazing tricks.

L E S S O N   T H R E E

Gerund Phrases

In the last lesson, you saw that the *-ing* form of a verb (the present participle) can be used in two different ways.

It can be the main verb in a verb phrase.

I am **baking** bread.

It can be used as an adjective.

The loaf **baking** in the oven is raisin bread.

The *-ing* form of a verb has a third use: it can be used as a noun. When it is used as a noun, it is called a *gerund*.

A **gerund** is the *-ing* form of a verb used as a noun in a sentence.

The following sentences show how gerunds are used as nouns.

Baking desserts is my favorite hobby.   (*Baking* is the subject of the verb *is.*)

The best part is the **eating** of all those cakes, pies, and cookies. (*Eating* is the subject complement, or predicate nominative, in the sentence.)

Everyone should try **baking**.   (*Baking* is the direct object of the verb *should try.*)

I learned about **baking** from my grandfather.   (*Baking* is the object of the preposition *about.*)

How Gerunds Become Phrases

Since a gerund is a verb form, it may have the same kinds of objects and modifiers that verbs can have.

A gerund with its objects and modifiers is a **gerund phrase**. The entire gerund phrase is used as a noun.

Here are some examples of gerund phrases:

Walking the dog is an adventure.   (The gerund *walking* has a direct object, *dog*. The gerund phrase is the subject of the sentence.)

I enjoyed **teaching Joe chess**.   (The gerund *teaching* has an indirect object, *Joe,* and a direct object, *chess*. The gerund phrase is the direct object of the verb *enjoyed*.)

The club's main activity is **tutoring children in math**.   (The gerund *tutoring* has a direct object, *children*, and is modified by an adverb phrase, *in math*. The gerund phrase is a predicate nominative after the linking verb *is*.)

Walking briskly is good for your heart.   (The gerund *walking* is modified by the adverb *briskly*. The gerund phrase is the subject of the sentence.)

Maureen likes **playing volleyball with her cousins.**   (The gerund *playing* has a direct object, *volleyball*, and is modified by the adverb phrase *with her cousins*. The gerund phrase is the direct object of the verb *likes*.)

We talked about **giving a party while our friends are in town.**
(The gerund *giving* has a direct object, *party*, and is modified by an adverb clause, *while our friends are in town*. The gerund phrase is the object of the preposition *about*.)

A Review

448

▶ The *-ing* form of a verb may be the main verb in a verb phrase.

Charles has been **working** for hours.

▶ The *-ing* form of a verb may be an adjective modifying a noun or a pronoun.

Working carefully, he weeded the whole garden.

▶ The *-ing* form of a verb may be used as noun. When so used it is called a gerund.

Working in the garden is a pleasure for him.

Practice A   Identify -ing words.

In each sentence one *-ing* word is in italics. On your paper, indicate whether the *-ing* word is a *main verb* in a verb phrase, an *adjective*, or a *gerund* (noun).

1. Suddenly the *ringing* of a telephone startled me.
2. *Jumping* up, I looked around.
3. A pay telephone right behind me was *ringing*.
4. I glared at the telephone, *willing* it to stop.
5. I was the only person *standing* up.
6. Everyone else was *watching* me.
7. *Answering* the telephone would be a public service.
8. The sound was *annoying* everyone in the room.
9. *Springing* to the phone, I picked it up.
10. I heard the dull *humming* of the dial tone.

Find gerund phrases.

Write the gerund phrase from each sentence on your paper.

1. Every summer I enjoy visiting my cousins in Chicago.
2. Last year my whole family tried going there by train.
3. We all got involved in making the plans.
4. The first hour of the trip was spent in looking out the window.
5. Observing other passengers was also fun for me.
6. One of my hobbies is making up mystery stories about strangers I see.
7. Eating meals in the dining car takes a certain amount of skill.
8. You must give getting the food into your mouth all your attention.
9. For me the best part of the trip was sleeping on the train.
10. The rocking of the train put me to sleep.

L E S S O N   F O U R

Infinitive Phrases

Here are some sentences with blanks in them. Can you fill in each blank with the same word?

> I like _____ eat ice cream on a hot summer day. The best place in town _____ buy ice cream is Dobson's. At Dobson's, customers are allowed _____ combine scoops of different flavors in one dish. _____ have only one flavor when you can have three different ones seems silly to me.

Notice that the word after each blank is a verb. Each verb is in the infinitive form. In Unit Nineteen, Lesson Three, you learned that the infinitive or base form is the first principal part of a verb. In a sentence the infinitive form is often preceded by the word *to*, which is called the "sign of the infinitive." If you put *to* in front of each verb in the sentences above, the sentences make sense.

▶ An *infinitive* can be used as a noun, an adjective, or an adverb.

On the following page you will find examples of each of these uses.

Infinitive as Noun

To dance is her greatest pleasure.   (*To dance* is the subject of the verb *is*.)

Dan likes **to paint**.   (*To paint* is the direct object of the verb *likes*.)

His goal was **to win**.   (*To win* is a predicate nominative after the linking verb *was*.)

Infinitive as Adjective

The movie **to see** is *Return of the Raiders*.   (*To see* modifies the noun *movie*.)

If you are making a summer skirt, cotton is the best material **to buy**.   (*To buy* modifies the noun *material*.)

Infinitive as Adverb

The band has come **to rehearse**.   (*To rehearse* modifies the verb *has come*.)

She seems glad **to help**.   (*To help* modifies the adjective *glad*.)

How Infinitives Become Phrases

Since an infinitive is a verb form, it may have objects and modifiers.

POINTS TO KNOW

An infinitive with all its objects and modifiers is an **infinitive phrase**.

Like an infinitive, an infinitive phrase may be used as a noun, an adjective, or an adverb. Here are some examples of infinitive phrases:

To answer letters promptly makes me feel businesslike.   (The infinitive *to answer* has a direct object, *letters*, and is modified by an adverb, *promptly*. The whole infinitive phrase is used as a noun and is the subject of the sentence.)

Joel plans **to give his dog a bath on Saturday**.   (The infinitive *to give* has an indirect object, *dog*, and a direct object, *bath*. It is modified by a prepositional phrase, *on Saturday*. The whole infinitive phrase is used as a noun and is the direct object of the verb *plans*.)

He is eager **to leave as soon as the performance is finished**. (The infinitive *to leave* is modified by an adverb clause, *as soon as the performance is finished.* The whole infinitive phrase is used as an adverb modifying the adjective *eager.*)

Her promise **to exercise for an hour daily** surprised us. (The infinitive *to exercise* is modified by an adverb, *daily*, and a prepositional phrase, *for an hour.* The whole infinitive phrase is used as an adjective modifying the noun *promise.*)

To is a sign of an infinitive if it is followed by a verb. However, if *to* is followed by a noun or a pronoun, it is a preposition.

Practice A   Find infinitive phrases.

Find the infinitive phrase in each sentence and write it on your paper.

EXAMPLE: There are many ways to become a writer.

to become a writer

1. Some writers live exciting lives for years and then retire to write about their adventures.
2. As a young man, Herman Melville went to sea to earn a living.
3. Later Melville decided to tell about his adventures in novels like *Moby Dick*.
4. Of course, Melville didn't write simply to tell stories.
5. He used his stories of the sea to express his philosophy of life.
6. Mark Twain also liked to write about his early experiences on the water.
7. One of his jobs was to pilot boats up and down the Mississippi River.
8. Unlike Melville, Mark Twain continued to travel in his later life.
9. To understand the human heart is the goal of many writers.
10. Emily Dickinson, who lived in one place all her life, was able to express much truth in her poems.

Practice B   Add infinitive phrases.

Each sentence below needs an infinitive phrase. Think of one that makes sense in the blank. Write the complete sentence on your paper.

EXAMPLE: His fondest wish is _____.

His fondest wish is to visit Alaska.

1. The kittens like _____.
2. _____ will be my good deed for the day.
3. The club members will be glad _____.
4. Saturday mornings are my time _____.
5. Her friend's birthday gave her a reason _____.
6. _____ is difficult.
7. This book explains the easiest way _____.
8. Tom's younger sister really likes _____.
9. _____ is a waste of time and energy.
10. I must study hard _____.
11. _____ has always been my dream.
12. Did Anthony teach you how _____.
13. My parents gave me permission _____.
14. Tuesday is the best day _____.
15. More than anything else, Jim wants _____.

L E S S O N   F I V E

Appositive Phrases

Which of these sentences gives you more information?

If you come across a deadly nightshade, be careful.

If you come across a deadly nightshade, **a poisonous plant,** be careful.

Of course the second sentence gives more information. That is because it contains an *appositive*.

An **appositive** is a noun or pronoun that follows another noun or pronoun and explains or identifies it.

Here are some more examples of appositives:

> The man on the left, **Mr. Snellings,** taught art at my school.

> The doctor, **a young woman,** checked the girl's eyes.

Appositives help you write more concisely. For example, you could use two sentences to tell about the doctor.

> The doctor is a young woman.

> The doctor checked the girl's eyes.

By using an appositive, you can give all the information in one sentence.

How Appositives Become Phrases

Since an appositive is a noun or a pronoun, it may have modifiers. It may be modified by an adjective, an adjective phrase, or an adjective clause.

An appositive with all its modifiers is an **appositive phrase**.

Here are some examples of appositive phrases:

> My uncle, **a wonderful storyteller,** always entertains us at family gatherings.   (The appositive *storyteller* is modified by the adjective *wonderful* and the article *a*.)

> *La Traviata*, **an opera by Verdi,** will be on television tonight.   (The appositive *opera* is modified by the article *an* and the prepositional phrase *by Verdi*.)

> I am reading a book by Charles Dickens, **an author who creates unforgettable characters**.   (The appositive *author* is modified by the article *an* and the adjective clause *who creates unforgettable characters*.)

Practice A   Find appositive phrases.

On your paper, copy the appositive phrase from each sentence.

EXAMPLE: Boyne City, a small town in Michigan, calls itself the mushroom capital of the world.

a small town in Michigan

1. I travel to work on my bicycle, an old balloon-tire model.
2. My favorite birthday present, a pocket calculator, was given to me by my aunt.
3. Our star pitcher, Valya Lubov, has won four out of five games.
4. We tiptoed around the sleeping animal, a large bulldog.
5. The class has planned a picnic for the last day of school, the fifteenth of May.
6. The car, a four-door sedan, was standing in the driveway.
7. We agreed to meet at a shopping mall, the Highway Buyway.
8. The All-Night Diner, a truck stop on Route 1, was used as the setting of a recent movie.
9. I like to read in the library, the quietest place in school.
10. My brother knows everything about lacrosse, a game invented by Native Americans.

Practice B   Combine sentences.

Combine each pair of sentences by making an appositive phrase out of the second sentence in the pair. Write the new sentence on your paper.

EXAMPLE: When my family visited the seashore, we attended a regatta.

A regatta is a series of boat races.

When my family visited the seashore, we attended a regatta, a series of boat races.

1. St. Augustine was founded in 1565.

    St. Augustine is the oldest city in the United States.
2. Sacajawea was most helpful as a translator.

    Sacajawea was a Shoshone woman who helped Lewis and Clark explore the Northwest.

3. Mt. McKinley was called Denali by native Alaskans.

   Mt. McKinley is the highest peak in North America.
4. We celebrated the summer solstice with an all-day party.

   The summer solstice is the longest day of the year.
5. You might like to try some sushi.

   Sushi is a Japanese dish made of raw fish.

R E V I E W   E X E R C I S E S

I. Prepositional Phrases On your paper, copy each prepositional phrase from the sentences below. Then write whether the phrase is used as an *adjective* or an *adverb*. (Lesson One)

1. The man in the brown coat is my uncle.
2. I ran across the tracks quickly.
3. John jumped over the hurdles.
4. Cheryl, the girl with red hair, is my friend.
5. Sharon fell against the post awkwardly.
6. Mark often listens to the radio.
7. The hammock on the porch is very comfortable.
8. Not every tree with needles is a pine tree.
9. Allison looked carefully at the painting.
10. Some people say the house beyond the field is haunted.

II. Participial Phrases Copy the participial phrase from each of the following sentences. Then write the word the participle modifies. (Lesson Two)

1. Running along the road, I met my friend.
2. The car leaving the driveway passed me.
3. Coming to school, Jen saw an accident.
4. Excited by the game, I almost fell.
5. The girl taking the test wants to be a detective.
6. The flowers left in the car had died.

7. The man drinking the soda asked me my name.
8. My bag, filled with books, was quite heavy.
9. The book lying on the table is a novel.
10. Tempted by the smell, I tasted the stew.

III. Gerund Phrases Copy the gerund phrase from each sentence below. (Lesson Three)

1. I enjoy knitting sweaters for friends.
2. I like listening to music while I think.
3. You scared the children by yelling at them.
4. Lou's favorite pastime is flying model planes.
5. Dave enjoys having parties at his home.
6. Betty wrote about traveling in Greece.
7. Elise was given a citation for rescuing the drowning swimmer.
8. The best part of the trip was singing in the bus on the way home.
9. Thomas loves playing basketball.
10. His hobby is cooking exotic foods.

IV. Infinitive Phrases Copy the infinitive phrase from each sentence below. (Lesson Four)

1. She tries to stay in shape.
2. Jack didn't have time to drive me to school.
3. We went to the gas station to check the oil in the jeep.
4. I promised to go to my brother's Little League game.
5. We want to hear the news and weather report.
6. She has always wanted to learn French.
7. Jeff plans to have a picnic tomorrow.
8. My career goal is to work in a hospital.
9. A sensible diet is the best way to lose weight.
10. Anne is working hard to improve her grades.

V. Appositive Phrases Copy the appositive phrase from each sentence below. (Lesson Five)

1. My uncle, a doctor in Milwaukee, is an expert in his field.
2. The women's 100-meter race was won by Fran, an excellent all-around athlete.
3. The teacher, a tennis pro during the summer, taught us to serve.
4. Erik, the tallest boy in school, can't play basketball.
5. The team, girls and boys from Lincoln High School, won the city championship.
6. We climbed Mt. Hunger, the highest peak in the area.
7. Nora's dog, the beagle with the black spots, always barks at me.
8. The photograph, a picture of my mother, was taken last year.
9. The television, an old black-and-white set, was given to us.
10. The car, a brown sedan, broke down.

VI. Phrases On your paper write whether the italicized phrase in each sentence is a *prepositional, participial, gerund, infinitive,* or *appositive phrase.* (Lessons One to Five)

EXAMPLE: *Helping others* is the best way to forget your own troubles.
gerund phrase

1. We went to the store *to buy fresh vegetables.*
2. *Looking for the perfect gift* took all afternoon.
3. The skiers, *speeding down the steep slope,* were a sight that took my breath away.
4. The person *to watch in the 100-meter race* is Liam Fogarty.
5. I am looking for a book *about buried treasure.*
6. We enjoyed the television show, *a special about the national parks system.*
7. The woman *in the pink straw hat* will show us some first-aid techniques.
8. *Startled by the loud noise,* we jumped up and ran to the window.
9. My ancestors, *pioneer settlers in Kansas territory,* suffered many hardships.
10. Josh often plays his saxophone *at parties.*

VII. Phrases Each of the following sentences contains an italicized preposition, participle, gerund, infinitive, or appositive. Add words to make the italicized word or words into a prepositional phrase, participial phrase, gerund phrase, infinitive phrase, or appositive phrase. Write the whole sentence on your paper. (Lessons One to Five)

EXAMPLE: *Whistling*, the carpenter sanded the door of the cabinet.

Whistling a cheerful tune, the carpenter sanded the door of the cabinet.

1. *Surprised*, I could not think of anything to say.
2. He comes *to see* almost every day.
3. *Shopping* is a chore that I try to avoid.
4. You will probably find her *in*.
5. Uncle Jim, *a fan*, watches every game on TV.
6. *Waving*, the flag welcomed us to Camp Watabassee.
7. She plans *to start* as soon as she gets out of college.
8. *Waiting* is a waste of time.
9. He stood quietly *behind* and listened.
10. The gym, *decorated*, was like a faraway, mysterious place where we had never been before.

Using Phrases in Your Writing

You naturally use phrases in your writing. When you are telling about the location of someone or something, you probably use a prepositional phrase: *in the locker, beside the pond, beyond the horizon.* However, phrases are useful for other reasons as well. Phrases can be used to vary your sentences and to add more information. Whenever you finish writing, look over your work. See if your ideas can be expressed more clearly and interestingly with gerund, participial, infinitive, or appositive phrases.

Practice   **Write sentences with phrases.**

Follow the directions below for writing sentences with phrases.

1. Write three sentences with phrases about sports. Begin each sentence with one of these groups of words: *Playing basketball, Thrilled with victory,* and *Practicing hard.*

2. Write three sentences about being late for school. Include these phrases in your sentences: *rushing as much as possible, hoping not to be scolded,* and *angered by my lateness.*

3. Write three sentences about after-school activities. Include these phrases in your sentences: *to practice for an hour, to have a snack with friends,* and *to take a walk.*

4. Write three sentences that include these appositive phrases: *a loyal friend, a wonderful book,* and *my favorite pastime.*

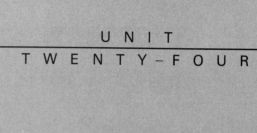

UNIT
TWENTY-FOUR

Agreement

Drottingholm, Sweden, 1967
Kenneth Josephson, The Museum of Modern Art, New York City

Agreement

L E S S O N   O N E

Agreement of Subject and Verb

Imagine that you are in the business of renting automobiles. Your company is rather unusual, however. You offer your customers only two choices. They can rent a tiny car with room for one person, or they can rent a huge double-decker bus. No, sorry—there's nothing in between.

If Mrs. Jones comes into your office alone, you rent her the tiny car. If Mrs. Jones comes in with a friend, you rent them the huge double-decker bus.

But wait a minute. Aren't you causing those two people to waste a lot of gasoline? Won't they feel silly driving around in that almost-empty bus? Is this any way to run a business?

Maybe not, but at least it makes your job easy. All you have to do is count noses. One nose—car. Two or more noses—bus.

Now imagine that you are writing a sentence. You want to make a statement about something that is happening now, in the present. Let's say the verb is *drive*. Your job is easy, because you have only two forms of that verb to choose from: *drives* and *drive*. Your choice depends on the subject of the sentence. If the subject is *Mrs. Jones* (one person—a singular subject), you choose *drives*.

Mrs. Jones **drives** away in the tiny car.

If the subject is *Mrs. Jones and her friend* (two people—a plural subject), you choose *drive*.

Mrs. Jones and her friend **drive** away in the bus.

or

The two women **drive** away in the bus.

As you can see, the business of deciding which verb form to use is easy. All you have to do is check the number of the subject.

A present-tense verb must agree with its subject in number.

Here are some more examples of this rule:

Peter **spends** a lot of money on records.

Some students **spend** a lot of money on records.

This jacket **fits** you quite well.

All three jackets **fit** you quite well.

The batter **watches** the pitcher closely.

The fans **watch** the pitcher closely.

Notice that a plural subject takes the base form of the verb:

Some students **spend** . . .

All three jackets **fit** . . .

The fans **watch** . . .

A singular subject takes the base form of the verb with -*s* or -*es* added:

Peter **spends** . . .

This jacket **fits** . . .

The batter **watches** . . .

The verb *have* is irregular. Instead of using *haves (have + s)* with a singular subject, you would use *has*:

David **has** six hockey sticks in his locker.

As you might expect, there are exceptions to this rule about subject-verb agreement. But, luckily, there are only two, and you know about them already.

▶ The pronouns *I* and *you* (singular), although they refer to one person, take the same verb form that a plural subject takes.

You **hope** and I **hope** and all the people on the earth **hope**.

▶ Unlike other verbs, the verb *be* has three forms in the present tense (instead of two). Also, unlike other verbs, *be* has two forms in the past tense (instead of one). The chart on the next page shows the present-tense forms of *be*.

I	am	we	are
you	are	you	are
he, she, it	is	they	are
the singer		the singers	

Here are the past-tense forms of *be*:

I	was	we	were
you	were	you	were
he, she, it	was	they	were
the singer		the singers	

You learned in Unit Nineteen that many verbs are not single words. Instead, they are groups of words—verb phrases. A verb phrase begins with a helping verb, and this helping verb must agree with the subject. Of course some helping verbs, such as *will* and *had*, agree with all subjects. But *have, has*, and the forms of *be* force you to make a choice. You must choose the form that agrees with the subject of your sentence.

▶ The first helping verb in a verb phrase must agree with the subject.

Following are some sentences that have verb phrases beginning with *have, has* or a form of *be*. Notice that sentences 1, 3, 5, and 6 have singular subjects and verbs. Sentences 2 and 4 have plural subjects and verbs.

1. My sister Amy *has won* several trophies in swimming meets.
2. She and her teammates *have been working* very hard.
3. Amy's coach *was beaming* with pride at the meet last night.
4. Our parents *were smiling* happily, too.
5. Amy *is going to be* an Olympic champion some day.
6. Excuse me; I guess I *am bragging* too much.

Practice A   Make subjects and verbs agree.

In each sentence choose the verb in parentheses that agrees with the subject of the sentence. Copy the verb on your paper.

EXAMPLE: Human beings often (seem, seems) to enjoy complaining.

seem

1. A favorite American pastime (is, are) telling stories about bad mail service.
2. Perhaps you (have, has) heard the one about the forty-year-old letter.
3. In this story a letter for Mr. Ben Carney (arrives, arrive) at the home of his niece.
4. The return address on the envelope (reads, read), "U.S. War Department."
5. This (surprise, surprises) the woman, since there hasn't been a War Department for many years.
6. She (glances, glance) at the postmark on the letter: "Aug. 12, 1940."
7. The letter (has, have) taken more than forty years to get here!
8. "But at least," she says to herself, "the post office workers (was, were) kind enough to include a note."
9. The note says: "Your mail is (is, are) important to you, and you have every right for it to be delivered in good condition."
10. The envelope (holds, hold) some old, unimportant government papers.

Practice B   **Add verbs that agree with subjects.**

Use each of the following groups of words as the subject of a sentence. Add a verb that agrees with the subject. Add any other words that are needed to make an interesting sentence. In each sentence, underline the subject once and the verb or verb phrase twice.

Note: The verbs you use should be in the present tense (except *was* and *were*, which you may also use).

EXAMPLE: Sometimes after school I . . .

Sometimes after school I travel on the bus to the art museum.

1. During gym class we . . .
2. At the approach of a stranger, our dog . . .
3. Every morning Joey . . .

4. Although a wonderful invention, the telephone . . .

5. Usually on Saturdays Pam and Rita . . .

6. Though rusty, this old car . . .

7. No matter what the weather, they . . .

8. When ripe and in season, apples . . .

9. Once in a while Henry . . .

10. While eating dinner, he . . .

Practice C   Write sentences.

Use each of the following ten verbs in a sentence of your own. Make sure the subjects and verbs agree in number. In each sentence tell something about the place where you live.

EXAMPLE: travel

Most people in my town don't travel far to get to work.

1. breathe	6. teach
2. is	7. argue
3. have	8. mix
4. try	9. likes
5. moves	10. meets

L E S S O N   T W O

Phrases and Clauses Between Subject and Verb

Have you ever tried to take a picture in a crowded place? You aim your camera at Uncle John but, just as you click the shutter, some stranger walks in front of him. Or, you're sight-seeing in Boston, and you want a photo of the Old North Church. You compose the picture carefully, press the button, and get a beautiful shot of a passing truck.

Something similar may happen when you write a sentence. You start the sentence with a certain subject. But before you get to the verb, another noun or pronoun comes along. This new noun or pronoun blocks your subject out of the picture and out of your mind. You take the new word as the subject and make the verb agree with it.

If you're lucky, the verb will also agree, accidentally, with the true subject. But if you're not lucky, the verb will disagree with the true subject, and your sentence will have an "error of agreement."

► No matter how many words come between the subject and the verb of a sentence, the verb must agree with the subject.

In each of the following examples, the subject is italicized and the verb or first helping verb is in boldface type.

The young man with twelve horses, three cars, two airplanes, and several boats **comes** home every weekend on the bus.

People who have lived in a big city **enjoy** the quiet atmosphere of our little town.

The shops near the entrance to the beach **sell** a lot of ice cream.

The girl throwing flowers and kisses **has** been elected Queen of the Tulip Festival.

The Browns' eldest son, a student with high grades in all his subjects, **does** well in sports, too.

You can write sentences like the preceding ones without making errors of agreement if you *kysim* until you get to the verb. *Kysim?* That's a word that was invented especially for this book. It means "Keep Your Subject In Mind."

To help yourself *kysim*, you might try this: Pretend that there are parentheses around the words that come between the subject and the verb. Then, in your mind, the subject and verb will be close together, and it will be easy to make them agree.

Here are the sample sentences with the extra words removed.

The young man **comes** home every weekend on the bus.

People **enjoy** the quiet atmosphere of our little town.

The shops **sell** a lot of ice cream.

The girl **has** been elected Queen of the Tulip Festival.

The Browns' eldest son **does** well in sports, too.

467

Practice A **Make subjects and verbs agree.**

Read each sentence. On your paper write the sentence *without* the words that come between the subject and the verb. Choose the verb in parentheses that agrees with the subject.

EXAMPLE: My two closest friends at camp last summer (is, are) going to visit Manhattan.

My two closest friends are going to visit Manhattan.

1. Readers of American history (knows, know) that Peter Minuit bought Manhattan Island from the Indians in 1626.
2. The students in my class at school (has, have) been learning about this purchase, too.
3. The price paid for this land, a part of New York City now worth billions of dollars, (was, were) only $24.
4. Minuit's purchase, according to most experts, (takes, take) the prize as the greatest bargain in history.
5. Our teacher, Mr. Twining, who knows a lot about money and saving banks, (likes, like) to imagine a slightly different story.
6. In his version, the Indian who receives the $24 (is, are) Mr. Twining himself in a former life!
7. The Indian, who happens to be standing near the Manhattan Bank for Savings, (decides, decide) to open a savings account with the $24.
8. That small sum over a period of 350 years (grows, grow) into a tremendous amount.
9. The heirs of that wise Indian, including Mr. Twining, of course, (shares, share) a fortune of four quadrillion dollars!
10. Unfortunately, his dream of riches (has, have) no chance of coming true.

Practice B **Write sentences.**

Following are five subjects of sentences. To each subject add a verb that agrees with it. Also add any other words that are needed to make an interesting sentence. Write the whole sentence on your paper. The verbs you add should be in the present tense (except *was* and *were*, which you may also use).

EXAMPLE: The man who sells tickets to the eager customers at the vampire movie . . .

The man who sells tickets to the eager customers at the vampire movie has long, sharp teeth!

1. The lectures about my laziness that I constantly get from Jane . . .
2. The car with white leather seats and new radial tires . . .
3. The students working on the microphone in the auditorium . . .
4. The hall, whose ceiling and walls are completely covered with mirrors, . . .
5. Martha's hobby of collecting stones and shells . . .

L E S S O N T H R E E

Indefinite Pronouns

Answer the following questions as best you can. (This is not a test.)

1. If you invited *everybody* in your class to come to your home, about how many people would you have in your house?
2. If you invited *nobody* to your home, how many visitors would you have in your house?
3. Would you let more people into your house if you let in *several* or *anyone*?

You can answer these question easily just by using your common sense. You probably gave thse answers:

1. 20-40 (depending on the size of your class)
2. none
3. anyone

But suppose you use your knowledge of grammar to answer those questions. Your answers will be quite different:

1. one
2. one
3. several

Here are the reasons for these strange answers.

The words *everybody, nobody, several*, and *anyone* are *indefinite pronouns*. Like all indefinite pronouns, they refer to number or amount. However, "number" in grammar is not always the same as "number" in real life. Take another look at the three questions.

1. If you invited *everybody* in your class to come to your home, about how many people would you have in your house?

In real life "everybody in your class" may mean thirty-five or forty people. But *everybody* as the subject of a sentence is singular.

> *Everybody* **has arrived** at my house.

2. If you invited *nobody* home, how many visitors would you have in your house?

In real life *nobody* has a value of zero. But as the subject of a sentence, *nobody* is a singular pronoun with a value of one.

> *Nobody* **has arrived** at my house.

3. Would you let more people into your house if you let in *several* or *anyone?*

When you're talking about how many people you are going to let into your home, *several* seems to mean a smaller number than *anyone*. Yet *several* is a plural pronoun, while *anyone* is considered singular.

> *Anyone* from the class **is** welcome, and *several* **are** here already.

To make matters worse, some indefinite pronouns can be either singular or plural. We will return to those later.

First, think about the word *everybody*. How could any word represent *more* people than the word *everybody?* How can that word be singular?

It makes better sense if you think of the word as two words: *every + body*. Imagine that you are writing a murder mystery. The detective says, "Every body has the same mark on the throat."

In other words, *everybody* does not mean "all people." It means "every *single* person." For that reason it is considered *singular*.

Here are the indefinite pronouns that are always singular. Notice that many of them end in *one, body*, or *thing*.

everyone	everybody	everything	each
anyone	anybody	anything	either
no one	nobody	nothing	neither
someone	somebody	something	another
one	little	less	much

Here are examples of these singular indefinite pronouns used as subjects of sentences:

Everybody in the store **wants** to buy something.

No one **seems** to like these polka dot shoes.

Neither **has** the size printed inside it.

Somebody here **is** wearing one blue shoe and one brown shoe.

The following indefinite pronouns are always plural:

both	few	several
many	fewer	two, three . . .

Here are examples of plural indefinite pronouns in sentences:

Both of the women **have** good eyesight.

Many **see** better in clean air.

Few **know** much about eyesight.

Several of these books **tell** more about it.

Some indefinite pronouns can be either singular or plural, depending on their use in the sentence. These changeable pronouns are:

all	any	none	more
most	some	enough	plenty

These pronouns are singular when they refer to an amount of something. They are plural when they refer to things that can be counted. Study the following examples:

Singular Uses

All of his writing **is printed** on yellow paper.   (All of one thing *is*.)

Most of the country **has voted**.   (Most of one thing *has*.)

Is *any* of this land for sale?   (Any part of one thing *is*.)

None of his work **deals** with his life.   (No part of one thing *deals*.)

471

Plural Uses

All of these pages **are** yellow.   (All of a number of things *are*.)

Most of the votes **have been counted**.   (Most of a number of things *have*.)

Are *any* of these building lots for sale?   (Any of a number of things *are*.)

None of his books **deal** with his life.   (None of a number of things *deal*.)

Practice A   Make subjects and verbs agree.

On your paper, copy each of the following sentences. Choose the verb in parentheses that agrees with the subject.

EXAMPLE: If life is a drama, all of us (is, are) actors.

If life is a drama, all of us are actors.

1. Everybody in the world (plays, play) some kind of role.
2. According to a British scientist, all of the members of a group (has, have) to perform a role.
3. Some of us (doesn't, don't) know how important these roles are.
4. Few of the parents in the world (thinks, think) of fatherhood or motherhood as a role in a drama.
5. However, both of the parents of a child (has, have) strong ideas about what family life should be like.
6. Most of their ideas about family life (comes, come) from their own childhood.
7. All of their experience (tells, tell) them that fathers and mothers should behave in certain ways.
8. Each of the parents (wants, want) to give the children a safe and loving home.
9. Several of the people in our neighborhood (treats, treat) all children with great respect.
10. No one among them (refuses, refuse) to listen to the ideas and opinions of the children.

Add verbs that agree with subjects.

On your paper, copy each of the following groups of words. Each group of words contains the subject of a sentence that you will write. Add a verb in the present tense (or *was* or *were*), plus any other words you need to make a complete sentence.

EXAMPLE: Somebody in my home town . . .

Somebody in my home town has an invitation to a party at the White House.

1. All of those people near the door . . .
2. Anyone who has these important skills . . .
3. Most of the toys on this shelf . . .
4. Each of the stars and stripes . . .
5. All of this lesson on the history of hubcaps . . .
6. None of the baseballs hit by Mickey Mantle . . .
7. Few who leave this house . . .
8. No one holding an orange ticket with six green dots . . .
9. Neither of the students, who are arriving on two separate planes, . . .
10. None of the luck that my mother was famous for . . .

473

L E S S O N   F O U R

Agreement With Compound Subjects

Have you ever worked for two or more bosses at the same time? If you have, you know that it's not always easy. Boss number one may tell you to do the job in a certain way. But then along come bosses two and three, and they want the job done differently. You have to figure out a way to please them all.

When the subject of a sentence is compound, the verb has the same problem. It has to agree with the compound subject, even when the members of the compound differ in number.

As you learned in Unit Twenty, a compound subject is made up of two or more subjects that share the same verb. The members of the compound are joined by the conjunction *and, or,* or *nor.* As far as the subject-verb agreement is concerned, the conjunction is the most important word in the compound. You have to look at the conjunction to see whether the compound subject is singular or plural.

POINTS TO KNOW

Here are the rules you should follow when you write sentences with compound subjects:

▶ A compound subject whose members are joined by *and* must have a plural verb.

> *Cats and dogs* **are** rarely friends.

> However, *this cat and this dog* **are** friends.

▶ A compound subject with singular members joined by *or* or *nor* takes a singular verb.

> *Either the red car, the yellow station wagon, or the green van* **is** available.

Note the meaning of this sentence: Only one of the three autos is available. Either the red car is available, or the yellow station wagon is available, or the green van is available.

▶ A compound subject with plural members joined by *or* or *nor* takes a plural verb.

> *Neither red cars, yellow station wagons, nor green vans* **are** available.

▶ If the members of an *or* or *nor* compound differ in number, the verb agrees with the part that is closest to the verb.

> *Either the bicycle or the skates* **are** yours for the asking.

> *Either the skates or the bicycle* **is** yours for the asking.

> *Neither my cousin nor I* **am** afraid of snakes.

Notice that, in this last example, the verb agrees in number with both members of the compound subject. But the verb agrees in person with only the member closer to it. Both *cousin* and *I* are singular, but *cousin* is a third-person subject, while *I* is a first-person subject. The verb agrees with *I* because it is closer.

Note: There is one exception to the rule about compounds whose members are joined by *and*. If the members of the compound make up a single item, the compound is considered singular.

The **rod and reel** is broken.   (The rod and the reel make up a single tool for fishing.)

Rhythm and blues is the only music I ever hear on that radio station.   (The two words make up the name of a type of music.)

Pancakes and syrup is my favorite breakfast.   (The two foods make up a single dish.)

Practice A   Make subjects and verbs agree.

Number your paper from 1 to 10. In each sentence choose the correct verb from the two in parentheses. Write the verb on your paper.

EXAMPLE: Neither he nor his brother (has, have) a driver's license.

has

1. Both the newspaper and the radio (gives, give) news about the weather.
2. Either you or somebody else (has, have) to do this job.
3. The coach or the volleyball players (has, have) the new net.
4. Bacon and eggs (is, are) served at the firehouse every Sunday.
5. Neither the robbers nor the bank clerk (was, were) injured.
6. Pride and boastfulness (is, are) two different things.
7. Neither Sheila nor her parents (accepts, accept) telephone calls during dinner.
8. Either two cars or a station wagon (is, are) needed to carry this load.
9. Neither Harry's brother nor his sister (has, have) seen him.
10. Food, water, and shelter (is, are) the three basic needs in human life.

Practice B   Add verbs that agree with subjects.

Copy each of the following groups of words onto your paper. Make each group of words into a sentence by adding a verb plus any other words you need. The verbs you use should be in the present tense (except for *was* and *were*, which you may also use).

EXAMPLE: Neither the music nor the musicians on this record . . .

Neither the music nor the musicians on this record are the kind I like.

1. The Haroldsons and their son . . .
2. Neither the other customers nor the clerk . . .
3. Either you or the other members of the team . . .
4. Either Nicholas, Francesca, or the Cobb sisters . . .
5. Neither the house nor the garden . . .
6. Neither my ambitions nor my experience . . .
7. Either the two students or a teacher . . .
8. The gym in our school and the one in yours . . .
9. Either a heavy overcoat or three sweaters . . .
10. Neither my brothers nor their dog . . .

L E S S O N   F I V E

Special Problems in Agreement

Congratulations are in order. Agreement is a tricky subject, and you have made it through the hardest part.

What remains is a small number of odds and ends. Since you have learned the basic rules, these special problems shouldn't give you any trouble. In this lesson, you will learn about the following problems in agreement: collective nouns; nouns of measurement; reverse word order; one of those who . . .; doesn't and don't; and the expressions "more than one," "every" and "many a . . ."

Collective Nouns

A **collective noun** is the name of a group of people, places, or things.

Here are some examples of collective nouns:

group	audience	collection	crew
team	faculty	flock	public
club	jury	family	orchestra
committee	crowd	cast	class

P O I N T S   T O   K N O W

▶ When a collective noun is used as the subject of a sentence, it is usually considered singular.

This rule applies whenever the members of a group act together as a unit. For example:

> The *family* **has** moved out of the house next door.
>
> The *crowd* **was** turned away by the ticket sellers.
>
> This *group* of chess players **wants** to challenge the other group.
>
> No other *team* in the history of our school **has** had such a fine record.

▶ When the members of a group act separately, as individuals, the collective noun is considered plural.

Look at the following examples:

> The *family* **are** putting on their costumes for the party.   (Each member of the family is putting on his or her own costume.)
>
> The *committee* always **vote** according to their consciences. (Each member of the committee has his or her own conscience.)

Sometimes treating a collective noun as a plural results in an awkward sentence. The sentence about the committee is an example. Still, treating *committee* as a singular noun also results in an awkward sentence:

> The *committee* always **votes** according to its conscience.

The best thing to do with a sentence like this is to rewrite it so that the collective noun is no longer the subject. Here is the same idea expressed in two other sentences:

The committee *members* **vote** according to their consciences.

Each committee *member* **votes** according to his or her conscience.

Nouns of Measurement

A noun of measurement is a noun that refers to an amount or quantity of something. The nouns of measurement are in boldface type in the following examples.

two **cups** of sugar

seven **yards** of cloth

P O I N T S   T O   K N O W

▶ A noun of measurement is singular if it refers to an amount of something.

Look at these examples:

Twenty-five *cents* **is** a high price for a glass of water.   (Twenty-five cents is a single amount of money.)

Six *months* of school without a break **is** a long time.   (Six months is a single period of time.)

Two *pounds* of fish **feeds** four people.   (Two pounds is a single amount of fish.)

Fourteen *acres* **comes** with the house.   (Fourteen acres is a single area of land.)

Two *thirds* of my money **goes** for movies.   (Two thirds of my money is a single amount.)

▶ A noun of measurement is plural if it refers to the individual units in an amount.

Twenty-five *cents* **were** stacked on her desk.   (There were twenty-five individual coins.)

The last six *months* **have** seemed longer than usual.   (Six individual months have each seemed longer than a month usually does.)

The thirty-two *miles* from Lilith to Belleville **are** marked with mileposts.   (Thirty-two individual miles are each marked with a milepost.)

Two *thirds* of the students **have** finished the test.   (A number of individual students have finished the test.)

Reverse Word Order

In most sentences the subject comes before the verb. However, there are three kinds of sentences in which the verb, or part of the verb phrase, comes before the subject. They are sentences that ask a question, sentences that begin with *Here is/are* or *There is/are/was/were,* and change-of-pace sentences.

As you know, the verb must agree with the subject no matter which comes first in the sentence. When the verb comes first, you have to think ahead to the subject and decide whether it is going to be singular or plural. Then you have to make the verb agree.

In the following examples the subject is in italics and the verb or helping verb is in boldface type.

Sentences that ask a question:

Are *we* late?

Doesn't *your friend* want to stay for lunch?

How **is** *your mother* today?

Where **does** *he* live?

Sentences beginning with *Here is/are* or *There is/are/was/were:*

Here **is** *the report* on the storm.

There **are** *two storm systems* coming our way.

There **were** *an eraser, a comb, and a stick of gum, but no pencils,* in Rita's pencil box.

Note: The contractions *here's* and *there's* cannot be used with plural subjects. The examples on the following page are incorrect.

Here**'s** *my friends.*

There**'s** *the horses.*

These examples are incorrect because *'s* takes the place of the word *is*. You wouldn't say:

Here **is** *my friends.*

There **is** *the horses.*

You would say:

Here **are** *my friends.*

There **are** *the horses.*

Following is an example of a change-of-pace sentence.

Through the door **bursts** *Ed,* yelling, "Hey, everybody, I'm home!"

This sentence could have been written with the usual word order:

Ed **bursts** through the door, yelling, "Hey, everybody, I'm home!"

There was no need to put the verb before the subject. Then why did the writer choose to do so? Probably he or she thought it was time for a change of pace. The unexpected word order, coming after a long string of "regular" sentences, helps break the monotony. However, this trick works only when it surprises the reader. If it is used too often, it loses its effect.

One of Those Who . . .

So far in this unit you have been studying agreement of subjects and verbs in independent clauses. However, as you know from your reading of Unit Twenty-two, dependent clauses also have subjects and verbs. These clauses follow the same rules of agreement that independent clauses do. There is just one extra problem that you should know about. It's a problem you sometimes face when you write a dependent clause beginning with *who*. Which verb is correct in the following example?

Mrs. Bates is one of those teachers who rarely (loses, lose) patience.

The verb in the dependent clause (*loses* or *lose*) must agree with the subject of the clause. This subject, of course, is *who*. Is *who* singular or plural? To find out, check the antecedent of *who* in the main clause. The antecedent is *teachers*, which is plural. Therefore, *who* is plural. *Lose* agrees with the plural subject, *who*:

> Mrs. Bates is one of those teachers *who* rarely **lose** patience.

The same rule applies when the dependent clause starts with *that* instead of *who*.

> Kelly wants one of those wristwatches *that* **are** waterproof and shockproof.   (The antecedent of *that* is *wristwatches*.)

Doesn't and Don't

Many writers and speakers have trouble using *doesn't* and *don't* correctly. But the solution to the problem is really very simple. Just keep reminding yourself that *doesn't* and *don't* are contractions. They agree with their subjects just as if they were fully spelled out.

P O I N T S   T O   K N O W

▶ *Doesn't* is a contraction of two words: *does* and *not*. Therefore, you should use *doesn't* only with subjects that agree with *does*.

▶ *Don't* is a contraction of *do* and *not*. Therefore, you should use *don't* only with subjects that agree with *do*.

Doesn't and *don't* are used correctly in these examples:

> I **don't** remember the words to that song.
> **Don't** you work at the shoe store?
> That boy **doesn't** look at all like Ramon.
> We **don't** play chess anymore.
> You girls **don't** have to wait for me.
> They **don't** know anything about training dogs.

"More Than One," "Every," and "Many a . . ."

When the expression "more than one," "every," or "many a . . ." modifies the subject of a sentence, the subject is always singular.

The subject of each of the following sentences is in italics. The verb or helping verb is in boldface type.

More than one student **has** protested, "But these expressions sound plural!"

And *more than one teacher* **has** replied, "Nevertheless, it is the custom to consider them singular."

Many a sailor **gets** seasick from time to time.

Every bird, bear, and bee **enjoys** the start of warm weather.

Practice A   Make subjects and verbs agree.

In each sentence choose the correct verb from the two in parentheses. Write the verb on your paper.

482

1. A herd of wild horses (lives, live) in this valley.
2. There (is, are) a sandwich and an apple in the lunch pail.
3. The team (stands, stand) at attention with their helmets off as the national anthem is played.
4. Where (has, have) your brother's guests gone?
5. Many a shout of "go, team, go!" (has, have) echoed from these walls.
6. There (has, have) been more than one serious accident at this corner.
7. Three fourths of the experiments (has, have) been completed.
8. Two thirds of her allowance (goes, go) for food for her raccoon.
9. Every glass, dish, and cup (was, were) broken during the earthquake.
10. Mr. Warner is one of those referees who never (misses, miss) anything.
11. George (doesn't, don't) care if he hurts other people's feelings.
12. Sitting on the hood of our car (was, were) the lion that had escaped from the circus.
13. Many a great writer (has, have) come from South America.
14. From our past (comes, come) the clues to our future.
15. Four teaspoons of vanilla (is, are) a lot for a cake of this size.

Practice B   **Make subjects and verbs agree.**

Read the following sentences. If a sentence has a mistake in agreement, rewrite it correctly on your paper. If a sentence is correct as it stands, write *C* beside its number on your paper.

1. Down the street comes two elephants advertising the circus.
2. Don't anybody go to the circus anymore?
3. Every man, woman, and child in America has probably seen at least one circus.
4. At the circus many a youngster have seen tigers and lions for the first time.
5. For a dignified adult like me, there's less thrill in the circus than there used to be.
6. The audience always enjoy seeing the acrobats and clowns.
7. However, the crowd don't seem to be as big these days.
8. Fifty dollars to take the family to the circus are a lot of money.
9. Also, there's many other ways to be entertained.
10. Television is one of the other amusements that keeps people away from the circus.
11. People simply doesn't go out as much as they used to.
12. Some experts think that the American public spends too much time watching TV.
13. Recently our class has been trying an interesting experiment.
14. Every boy and girl in the class have to promise to give up television for two full weeks.
15. Already we've found out that two thirds of our class is unable to keep themselves away from the TV set!

R E V I E W   E X E R C I S E S

I. Agreement of Subject and Verb   Number your paper from 1 to 10. In each sentence choose the correct verb from the two in parentheses. Write the verb on your paper. (Lesson One)

1. Doris (has, have) been taking driving lessons from her aunt.

2. Many people (thinks, think) only of themselves.
3. Alice (is, are) planning to come over after school.
4. I (am, are) a good worker.
5. Larry (was, were) late, as usual.
6. He (answers, answer) the phone politely.
7. A recent news article stated that caffeine (is, are) bad for you.
8. The trees (is, are) growing rapidly.
9. That shirt (was, were) my favorite.
10. They (has, have) just returned from their vacation.

II. Phrases and Clauses Between Subject and Verb Number your paper from 1 to 10. In each sentence choose the verb in parentheses that agrees with the subject of the sentence. Write the verb on your paper. (Lesson Two)

1. That girl who is sitting between the soldiers (looks, look) like my sister.
2. The boy chasing the horses (is, are) a champion rider.
3. Viewers of that program (has, have) written many letters to the TV station.
4. Those pictures on the dresser (shows, show) how skinny I used to be.
5. California, which has the largest population of all the states, (is, are) on the West Coast.
6. The players on the team (seems, seem) tired.
7. Singers who performed at the concert (was, were) invited to supper afterwards at the mayor's house.
8. The young man with the field glasses (watches, watch) the swimmers.
9. Swimmers who go far beyond the pier (risks, risk) meeting a shark.
10. The outer rings of the target (was, were) hit by several people.

III. Agreement with Indefinite Pronouns Number your paper from 1 to 15. In each sentence choose the verb in parentheses that agrees with the subject of the sentence. Write the verb on your paper. (Lesson Three)

1. I wonder whether any of the food (tastes, taste) good enough to eat.
2. Both of the kittens (has, have) their own toys.
3. Neither of the children (is, are) able to lift the couch.
4. All of the animals (is, are) in the barn for the night.
5. None of the teachers (knows, know) how to speak German.
6. Few of the people (thinks, think) the law should be changed.
7. Most of the reporters (wants, want) to interview the visitors from outer space.
8. Some of these books (is, are) excellent mysteries.
9. The host announces a topic—for example, jogging—and each of the guests (tells, tell) a joke on that topic.
10. Most of the corn (was, were) ruined by the storm.
11. Many a dog (has, have) learned to fetch a ball.
12. The bowling ball (doesn't, don't) belong in that closet.
13. Seventeen dollars (is, are) a good price for that dress.
14. Three fourths of my salary (goes, go) into the bank.
15. Two years without a vacation (is, are) a long time.

IV. Agreement with Compound Subjects Number your paper from 1 to 10. In each sentence choose the verb in parentheses that agrees with the subject of the sentence. Write the verb on your paper. (Lesson Four)

1. Bacon and eggs (is, are) my favorite food.
2. Either the cat or the dog (stays, stay) outside tonight.
3. The red skates or the blue skateboard (is, are) the perfect gift.
4. Oil and vinegar (was, were) the only salad dressing on the table.
5. Janet and the other people in her car pool (takes, take) turns paying for gas.
6. Either a pen or a pencil (is, are) fine to use for the test.
7. The parakeet and the rabbit (has, have) been playing together.
8. The boys or their sister (delivers, deliver) the newspaper to us every day.
9. Either Leo or I (has, have) to tell Richard the bad news.
10. Lisa and her two friends (walks, walk) to town.

V. Special Problems in Agreement Number your paper from 1 to 10. In each sentence choose the verb that agrees with the subject. Write the verb on your paper. (Lesson Five)

1. The first group (is, are) dismissed for lunch at 11:55.
2. A committee of teachers (decides, decide) the rules.
3. That herd of cows (belongs, belong) to the Westland brothers.
4. Is that one of those fish that (gives, give) a strong electric shock?
5. The family (is, are) going out for dinner tonight.
6. Here (comes, come) the drummers for the parade.
7. There (goes, go) Timmy, his sister Jill, and her college roommate.
8. When (is, are) the guests arriving?
9. Seven pounds of beef (is, are) a lot of meat.
10. Where (does, do) this chair belong?

VI. Agreement Review Number your paper from 1 to 10. In each sentence choose the verb that agrees with the subject. Write the verb on your paper. (Lessons One to Five)

1. The computers that our math class uses (is, are) located in the Media Room.
2. Each of the math students (reserves, reserve) some time on a computer each week.
3. Are you one of those who (has, have) signed up to use a computer this afternoon?
4. "Show and tell" (is, are) a favorite activity of the children in the kindergarten class.
5. Neither the Scout leader nor the members of the troop (believes, believe) that the creature they saw was Bigfoot.
6. Our city and a Japanese city of about the same size (is, are) going to become "sisters."
7. There (is, are) enough extracurricular activities in this school to keep you very busy.
8. Among the winners (was, were) Randy Carson and his partner.
9. If the state legislature (passes, pass) this bill, litterers will pay a heavy fine for each offense.
10. One hundred dollars (is, are) a lot of money for most people.

Using Agreement in Your Writing

Imagine that you come across the following sentence in your reading.

> The painting of the oranges cost $1,000.00.

Since common sense tells you that oranges would never cost $1,000.00, you figure out that the subject of the sentence must be *painting,* and that the writer of this sentence made an error in subject-verb agreement. But you probably have to read the sentence twice to understand what it's trying to say.

Using agreement in your sentences shows that you have mastered some of the rules of our language. Rules are agreed-upon ways of proceeding, whether it be in writing or in some other discipline. In baseball, for example, you can't run from first base to homeplate and declare that you have scored a home run. That's because the rules state that you must run from first base, to second, to third and then home plate before you score a run.

In grammar, as in baseball, we follow rules. These rules establish the correct way to write, and they help insure that our thoughts will be understood easily.

The following exercise will give you practice in writing sentences with subjects and verbs that agree.

Practice **Write sentences.**

Follow each numbered set of directions for writing sentences. Make sure that all the verbs agree with their subjects.

1. Write a sentence in the present tense about yourself that begins with the pronoun "I."
2. Write a sentence in the present tense that begins with the words "Some people."
3. Write a sentence in the present tense that begins with the words "The records on the shelf."
4. Write a sentence in the present tense that begins with the words "A student in my class."
5. Write a sentence in the present tense with a singular verb that begins with the word "Some."

Using Pronouns Correctly

"The Loneliest Job in the World," 1961
This photo of President Kennedy in the Oval Office was taken for an assignment entitled "A Day in the Life of the President." It shows the President in a typical pose, leaning forward with his weight on his hands and shoulders. He would do this to rest his back, which had been injured during World War II.
George Tames, The New York Times

Using Pronouns Correctly

Pronouns and Antecedents

Are you good at doing imitations of other people? Even if you think you're not, try this experiment: Write down the name of someone who is well known to all your classmates. Then pretend that you are going to perform the role of that person in a play.

Ask yourself what traits or habits make the person different from other people. Does he or she stand or walk in special way? Or have an unusual voice? Or always dress in a certain way? Or always carry a certain thing, like a stopwatch or a slide rule? Or have some habit, like staring at the ceiling when thinking hard? Write down two or three traits that you can show or act out. If you've chosen well, your audience will know right away who you are pretending to be.

As you know, personal pronouns play roles, too. A personal pronoun takes the place of a noun or a pronoun that has been mentioned earlier or is understood. This earlier noun or pronoun is called an *antecedent*. (*Antecedent* means "going before.") The pronoun has the same "traits" as the antecedent and does the job of the antecedent in the sentence.

P O I N T S   T O   K N O W

▶ A personal pronoun must agree with its antecedent in person and number.

The two traits that the personal pronoun must imitate are *person* and *number*. If the antecedent is first-person singular (*I*), the pronoun must also be first-person singular (*I, me, my, mine*). If the antecedent is third-person plural (*the men*), the pronoun must also be third-person plural (*they, them, their, theirs*).

In Unit Nineteen you learned that personal pronouns have forms for three persons. You also learned that they have singular forms (referring to one person, place, or thing), and plural forms (referring to two or more persons, places, or things). You can review these forms by looking at the following chart.

PERSON		NUMBER
	SINGULAR	PLURAL
First Person	the person speaking **I, me, my, mine**	the persons speaking, or the person speaking and his/her associates **we, us, our, ours**
Second Person	the person spoken to **you, your, yours**	the persons spoken to **you, your, yours**
Third Person	the person, place, or thing spoken about **he, him, his, she, her, hers, it, its**	the persons, places, or things spoken about **they, them, their, theirs**

Here are some examples of agreement in person and number. In each sentence the pronoun is in boldface type, and its antecedent is in italics.

When *John* looked closely at the dish, **he** saw a tiny crack near the edge.

My brother and I never argue except when **we** go shopping together.

The girls rested for a while, and then **they** went back to work.

Please tell **me** which coat is **yours.**   (The antecedents of *me* and *yours* are not stated, but they are understood).

Glancing back over **her** shoulder, *Carol* saw Ben drop the note into the wastebasket.   (Notice that the antecedent comes *after* the pronoun in this sentence.)

Why hadn't **he** torn the note up?   (The antecedent of *he*—the noun *Ben*—is in the preceding sentence.)

Reminder: You learned how to tell the number of a compound subject in Unit Twenty-four. Follow the same rules to tell the number of a compound antecedent. Here are some examples:

> *Either Irving or Perry* will lend you **his** bike.

> *Neither Greta nor her sisters* seem to be enjoying **themselves**.

All these examples make agreement between pronoun and antecedent look easy. However, there is one problem that you have to face quite often when you are writing. A third-person-singular personal pronoun has different forms for the three genders: masculine (*he*), feminine (*she*), and neuter (*it*). You must pick the form that matches the gender of the antecedent.

▶ A third-person-singular personal pronoun must agree with its antecedent in gender.

Some antecedents are clearly masculine. For example, *man, husband, father, son, boy, king, emperor, duke, headmaster, tenor, bull, gander,* and *stallion* are masculine because they refer to males.

Some antecedents are clearly feminine. For example, *woman, wife, mother, daughter, girl, queen, empress, duchess, headmistress, soprano, cow, goose,* and *mare* are feminine because they refer to females.

Antecedents that are neither masculine nor feminine are neuter; for example, *house, rock, tree, train, book, spoon, justice, movie,* and *surprise.* Nouns that refer to animals may be considered neuter when the sex of the animal isn't known or is not important. For example, you might say, "The dog kept scratching *its* ear."

A problem arises when the gender of the antecedent isn't known but is important. Many nouns can refer to a person of either sex; for example, *teacher, driver, friend, cousin, employee, typist, neighbor, boss, clerk,* and *student.*

Many of the indefinite pronouns, too, can refer to a person of either sex. So can the interrogative and relative pronouns. Agreement in gender can be a problem when the antecedent is a word like *everybody, anybody, someone, who, which,* or *that.*

If the gender of the noun or pronoun is made clear by other words nearby, your problem is solved. Look at these examples:

> Has *anyone* invited **her** father to the father-daughter banquet yet?

> *One* of the Boy Scouts received **his** Eagle badge yesterday.

Which of the sopranos left **her** music under **her** chair?

▶ If the gender of the noun or pronoun is not made clear by other words nearby, you have two choices.

1. You can use both the masculine and the feminine pronoun, as in these examples:

   Someone dropped **his or her** wallet in the hall.

   If a *student* would like to earn extra credit, **he or she** can get a special assignment from the teacher.

2. You can rewrite the sentence to avoid the problem.

   Someone dropped this wallet in the hall.

   Any *student* who would like to earn extra credit can get a special assignment from the teacher.

   If any *students* would like to earn extra credit, **they** can get a special assignment from the teacher.

Practice A   **Choose the correct pronoun.**

On your paper, copy each sentence below. Choose one of the words or phrases in parentheses to complete the sentence.

1. Neither Sidney nor my father likes (his, their) soup cold.
2. Someone in the girls' dormitory has (her, their) own phone.
3. Several of the teacher's old friends sent (his, their) regrets.
4. One of the waitresses says (she, they) served the rock star and was given a large tip.
5. Either Slim or Jake can sign (his, their) name on this check.
6. One of the women gave us (her, their) personal opinion.
7. Everyone in the band must buy (his or her, their) own uniform.
8. Both the male teachers and the female teachers agreed to hold (his or her, their) meeting on Thursday.
9. Each of Doreen's dogs has (his or her, its, their) special place in her heart.
10. Every student must decide (his or her, their) own future.

Practice B   **Rewrite sentences with pronouns.**

Each sentence that follows contains the expression "he or she," "him or her," or "his or her." On your paper, rewrite the sentence without that expression. Be careful not to change the meaning of the sentence.

EXAMPLE: Everyone in our school has passed his or her exams.

All the students in our school have passed their exams.

1. Someone at the business luncheon left his or her briefcase under the restaurant table.
2. Everybody I know is happy when he or she receives gifts.
3. If a person wants to audition for a part in the spring play, he or she must pick up a script in the theater office.
4. We honored each cheerleader by giving him or her a school sweater.
5. An employee may be promoted after he or she has worked there for a year.

L E S S O N   T W O

Subjective and Objective Pronouns

Question: Which are stronger, nouns or personal pronouns?

Answer: Nouns are stronger. They never change, no matter what happens to them. Here's proof:

> **Ed** walked into the room. The teacher gave **Ed** a disapproving look and said, "You're late!"
>
> Then the wastebasket got in the way and tripped **Ed**. "Quiet!" the other students yelled at **Ed**. "The **class** is trying to do some work. The teacher has just given the **class** a written test."

The nouns *Ed* and *class* remain the same whether they do something or have something done to them. But look how personal pronouns behave in the same situations:

> **He** walked into the room. The teacher gave **him** a disapproving look and said, "You're late!"
>
> Then the wastebasket got in the way and tripped **him**. "Quiet!" the

other students yelled at **him**. '**We** are trying to do some work. The teacher has just given **us** a written test.''

In the first sentence the pronoun *he* is in the subjective case because it is the subject of the sentence.

In the second sentence *he* changes to *him*, the objective case, because it is the indirect object of the verb *gave*.

In the third sentence *him* is the direct object of the verb *tripped*.

In the fourth sentence *him* is the object of the preposition *at*.

In the last two sentences the first-person-plural pronoun occurs in two forms. *We*, the subjective form, is the subject of the sentence. *Us*, the objective form, is the indirect object of the verb *has given*.

▶ A personal pronoun is in the *subjective case* when it is the subject of a verb. A personal pronoun is in the *objective case* when it is the direct or indirect object of a verb or the object of a preposition.

Here are the subjective and objective forms of the personal pronouns. As you know, the pronouns *it* and *you* are the same in both cases.

	Singular	
	Subjective	*Objective*
First Person:	I	me
Second Person:	you	you
Third Person:	he, she, it	him, her, it
	Plural	
	Subjective	*Objective*
First Person:	we	us
Second Person:	you	you
Third Person:	they	them

People rarely use the wrong form of a pronoun in easy sentences like the following:

They are tired from playing in the hot sun.   (subject)

Please take **them** into the house.   (direct object of verb *take*)

Give **them** some cold lemonade.   (indirect object of verb *give*)

Look after **them** until dinnertime.   (object of preposition *after*)

However, people sometimes use pronouns incorrectly when the sentence is more complicated. In the following examples the personal pronoun is part of a compound subject or object. Which form is correct in each?

Fred, Linda, and (I, me) explored the island.

Fred and (she, her) walked over to the north side.

(We, Us) and our dog were the only living beings on the island.

Pete says you can trust the Carey brothers and (he, him) to do a good job.

Would you please lend Samantha or (I, me) the lawn mower?

Mr. Wilson is making barbecued spareribs for his family and (we, us).

▶ A pronoun that is part of a compound subject is in the subjective case. A pronoun that is part of a compound object is in the objective case.

In the first three examples above, the pronoun is part of a compound subject. Therefore, it is in the subjective case.

Fred, Linda, and **I** explored the island.

Fred and **she** walked over to the north side.

We and our dog were the only living beings on the island.

In the other three examples the pronoun is part of a compound object. Therefore, it is in the objective case.

Pete said you can trust the Carey brothers and **him** to do a good job.   (The compound *the Carey brothers and him* is the direct object of the verb *trust*).

Would you please lend Samantha or **me** the lawn mower?   (The compound *Samantha or me* is the indirect object of the verb *would lend*).

Mr. Wilson is making barbecued spareribs for his family and **us.** (The compound *his family and us* is the object of the preposition *for*).

There is an easy way to make sure your pronouns are correct in sentences like these. Just remove the other words in the compound so that the pronoun stands alone. If you do this with the six examples on the previous page, they will read as follows:

I explored the island. (You would never say, *"Me* explored the island." So you know that *I* is correct in the compound subject.)

She walked over to the north side.

We were the only living beings on the island.

Pete says you can trust **him** to do a good job. (You would never say, ". . . you can trust *he* to do a good job." So you know that *him* is correct in the compound object.)

Would you please lend **me** the lawn mower?

Mr. Wilson is making barbecued spareribs for **us.**

▶ A pronoun that is used as a subject complement should be in the subjective case.

Here are two examples of subject complements.

Which woman is your **aunt?**

That's **she** in the army uniform.

In the first example the subject is *woman* and the complement is *aunt*. The subject complement follows the linking verb *is*.

In the second example *that* is the subject and *she* is the subject complement. It follows the linking verb *is* (shortened to *'s* in the contraction *that's*). Notice that the subjective form of the pronoun *(she)* is used. The subject complement must be in the same case as the subject. It would be incorrect to say, "That's *her*," because *her* is the objective case form.

Here are more examples of pronouns used as subject complements:

I'm afraid it was **I** who gave away your secret.

If you were **he**, wouldn't you do what he's doing?

Although the Harrises were poor, it was **they** and not our rich neighbors who helped us.

You have probably heard people say, "It's me," or "It's us." In fact, you may often use those expressions yourself. They are perfectly all right in everyday conversation. However, when you are writing a paper or business letter, or giving a formal speech, it is best to follow the rule. Use the subjective form of the pronoun and say, "It's I" and "It's we." Try to avoid *it's her, it's him*, and *it's them* at all times.

If you feel that following the rule makes your sentence sound stilted, you can rephrase it. Look at the following examples.

> I'm afraid I'm the one who gave away your secret.

> If you were in his place, wouldn't you do what he's doing?

> Although they were poor, it was the Harrises, and not our rich neighbors, who helped us.

▶ When a pronoun is used as an appositive, the pronoun is in the same case as the word it is in apposition to.

No doubt you remember studying appositives in Lesson Five of Unit Twenty-three. There an *appositive* is defined as "a noun or pronoun that follows another noun or pronoun and explains or identifies it."

In the examples on the next page, each boldface pronoun is part of a compound appositive, which is underlined. The compound appositive explains or identifies the italicized noun.

> The best *players*, <u>Stella, Tom, and **I**</u>, are going to be honored at a banquet.   (The noun *players* is the subject of the verb *are going to be honored*. Therefore, the pronoun in apposition, *I*, must be in the subjective case.)

> We could not get along without the *librarians*, <u>Bill and **her**.</u>   (The noun *librarians* is the object of the preposition *without*. Therefore, the pronoun in apposition, *her*, must be in the objective case.)

▶ A noun in apposition to a pronoun does not change the case of the pronoun.

Here are some examples of this rule:

> **We** juniors are trying to raise money for our class trip to Washington, D.C.

> Don't go into the jungle without one of **us** guides.

It's easy to test sentences like these for correctness. Just take out the appositive noun (*juniors, guides*) and see if the pronoun sounds right.

We are trying to raise money for our class trip.   (You wouldn't say,
"*Us* are trying to raise money.")

　　Don't go into the jungle without one of **us**.   (You wouldn't say,
"Don't go . . . without one of *we*.")

Practice A　　**Add personal pronouns.**

Copy each sentence onto your paper. Add one or two personal
pronouns to complete the sentence. The person and the number of
each pronoun are indicated in parentheses.

EXAMPLE: My family and _____ run an unusual business.
(first-person singular)

My family and I run an unusual business.

1. _____ say you can't argue with the phone
   company. (third-person plural)
2. _____ four members of the Kaufman family can argue with
   our phone company because we run it.   (first-person plural)
3. The four people in the family are my mother, my dad, my sister
   Janice, and _____.   (first-person singular)
4. Of course, _____ Kaufmans rent most of our lines from a
   bigger company.   (first-person plural)
5. You can call my mother or _____ if a phone goes on the
   blink.   (first-person singular)
6. _____ or I will send either Dad or Janice to fix it.
   (third-person singular)
7. The repair work usually keeps _____ and _____ pretty
   busy.   (third-person singular, third-person singular)
8. All four of _____ Kaufmans like running our own business.
   (first-person plural)
9. When people ask how we make a living, we enjoy telling
   _____.   (third-person plural)
10. Our parents are fond of saying that _____ and _____
    "kids" make a perfect team.   (third-person plural, first-person
    plural)

Practice B   **Add personal pronouns.**

Copy the following sentences on your paper. Complete the sentences by adding a personal pronoun for each blank shown. Do not use the pronoun *it* or *you* in any answer.

EXAMPLE: Meade and _____ wanted to learn how to play rugby.

Meade and I wanted to learn how to play rugby.

1. All _____ knew was that the game had begun at a school in England called Rugby.

2. Neither Meade nor _____ realized how rough the game was.

3. We found out when our coach invited _____ two beginners to play a practice game with the team.

4. Early in the game Meade passed the ball to _____ .

5. Then he ran alongside _____ as _____ tried to get away from other players.

6. But nothing could stop _____ from tackling both of _____ as hard _____ could.

7. That play was enough for _____ for a while, and _____ asked for a time-out.

8. But there was a little disagreement between the coach and _____ about taking a rest.

9. _____ told _____ that each half was forty minutes long!

10. Several of the other players laughed at _____ , but _____ told _____ and the coach that _____ had had enough.

Practice C   **Rewrite sentences, changing pronouns to the right case.**

Each sentence below contains one or more pronouns in the wrong case. Rewrite each sentence, changing the pronoun(s) to the right case.

EXAMPLE: She and him have just met.

She and he have just met.

1. The two soloists, Connie and me, were at the front of the stage, and the chorus stood behind us.
2. Most of us went along with she and he.
3. Clyde and them brought us the news.
4. The winners were Doug and her.
5. There was nothing they could do for him and I.
6. Please show her and we how the machine works.
7. How well do you know they and her?
8. I've never said a word against either her family or she.
9. No one wants to talk to them about he and I until tomorrow.
10. It was probably him who called while you were out.

L E S S O N   T H R E E

Who and Whom

You've probably used or at least heard of *Who's Who*. It's a book that gives facts about famous or successful people living today. You may also have heard of *Who Was Who*, a book about important people of the past. But chances are you have never heard of the following:

Who "Hoos"   (a book about famous owls)

People Whom No One Remembers   (a book of blank pages)

Let's Hum Along With "The Whom"   (a book of songs by an unknown rock group)

The Ho-Hum Book About Who/Whom   (an exciting book about the subject of this lesson)

Who is the only other word besides the personal pronouns that changes when it is an object. As you know, *who* is the subjective form, and *whom* is the objective form. Few people pay attention to the difference when they are speaking informally. However, many people do try to follow the *Who/Whom* rules when they write. You should understand the difference between *who* and *whom* so that you can use them correctly when you want to.

▶   Use *who* when the pronoun is the subject of the verb in a question. Use *whom* when the pronoun is the object of a verb or preposition in a question.

Who is knocking on the door?   (*Who* is the subject of the verb *is knocking*).

Who told you that the soup was too salty?   (*Who* is the subject of the verb *told*).

Whom did Kitty ask to the party?   (*Whom* is the object of the verb *did ask*).

To **whom** is the letter addressed?   (*Whom* is the object of the preposition *to*).

Take another look at that last example. Even if you were speaking instead of writing, you would have to say, "to *whom*." "To *who* is the letter addressed?" would sound strange to most people. However, you could use *who* if you moved the preposition (*to*) away from the pronoun. You could say, "Who is the letter addressed to?"

There is an easy way to figure out which form is correct in a question. Just answer the question and substitute a personal pronoun for *who* or *whom*. If the personal pronoun is in the subjective case (*he, she, they*, etc.), you know that *who* is correct. If the personal pronoun is in the objective case (*him, her, them*, etc.), you know that *whom* is correct.

She is knocking on the door.   (Therefore, *who* is correct in the question.)

They told you that the soup was too salty.   (Therefore, *who* is correct in the question.)

Kitty asked **him** to the party.   (Therefore, *whom* is correct in the question.)

The letter is addressed to **me**.   (Therefore, *whom* is correct in the question.)

▶   Do not let an interrupting phrase, such as "do you think" or "did he say," confuse you.

In the following examples the interrupting phrase is italicized. Notice that it has no grammatical connection with the other words in the sentence.

Therefore, it does not affect your choice of *who* or *whom*.

> **Who** *did you say* gave you this rubber snake?

> **Who** *does she think* will win the diving championship?

▶ Use *who* when the pronoun is the subject of the verb in an adjective clause. Use *whom* when the pronoun is an object of a verb or a preposition in an adjective clause.

In the following examples, the adjective clauses are in bold type.

> The violinist **who will play next** has been studying since the age of seven.   (*Who* is the subject of the verb *will play* in the dependent clause. The dependent clause acts as an adjective modifying the noun *violinist* in the main clause.)

> She is a person **whom everybody likes**.   (*Whom* is the object of the verb *likes* in the adjective clause. The clause modifies the noun *person* in the main clause.)

> He is the chef **about whom I told you**.   (*Whom* is the object of the preposition *about* in the adjective clause.)

To make sure the pronoun (*who* or *whom*) is correct, use the same test you used before. Substitute a personal pronoun for *who* or *whom* in the dependent clause.

> The violinist **who will play next** has been studying since the age of seven.   (*He* will play next.)

> The violinist **whom you will hear next** has been studying since the age of seven.   (You will hear *him* next.)

> She is a person **whom everybody likes**.   (Everybody likes *her*).

> He is the chef about **whom I told you**.   (I told you about *him*).

Practice A   Choose the correct pronoun.

Number your paper 1 to 10. Decide which form of the pronoun, *who* or *whom*, is correct in each question. Write the pronoun on your paper.

1. (Who, Whom) did Mrs. Talbot sell your house to?
2. For (who, whom) are you working at the present time?
3. (Who, Whom) did Rhonda say taught her to repair clocks?

4. When experts disagree, (who, whom) can you believe?
5. (Who, Whom) was elected chairperson of the committee?
6. (Who, Whom) does Lawrence plan to give this painting to?
7. (Who, Whom) among us can afford those prices?
8. When we get there, (who, whom) is going to help unload the car?
9. (Who, Whom) did you see sneaking out the back door?
10. (Who, Whom), pray tell, is going to clean up this mess?

Practice B   Choose the correct pronoun.

On your paper copy the adjective clause in each sentence. Choose the correct word in parentheses to complete the clause.

EXAMPLE: That's the man to (who, whom) you should speak.

to whom you should speak

1. I'm looking for someone (who, whom) will give me a job.
2. Do you know anyone (who, whom) has a good job for me?
3. I am a person (who, whom) everyone gets along with.
4. A woman (who, whom) hired me last summer hated to see me go.
5. There was no one else in the store to (who, whom) she could give my job.
6. I'd like to meet the person (who, whom) replaced me.
7. I am a worker (who, whom) has never quit a job, except to go back to school.
8. Employers want workers (who, whom) are reliable.
9. I know people (who, whom) can work well when they want to.
10. However, they aren't the kind (who, whom) you can count on to do anything extra.

Practice C   **Add dependent clauses.**

Complete each sentence by adding a dependent clause. Begin the clause with the pronoun given. Write the sentence on your paper.

EXAMPLE: The people whom . . . told us to take Route 92.

The people whom we asked for directions told us to take Route 92.

1. I like teachers who . . .
2. Everyone whom . . . gave their money or their time.
3. People who . . . make the best friends.
4. A leader is someone whom . . .
5. Hundreds of people whom . . . came to the crafts fair.
6. Reckless drivers are usually people . . .
7. The player whom . . . got a free throw, and Sandra was ordered off the floor.
8. I do not like to go anywhere with a person who . . .
9. The members who . . . asked the others to wait outside.
10. The window-washer, who . . . looked down on the crowds far below.

L E S S O N   F O U R

Special Problems in Pronoun Use

As you may know, the fourth batter in a baseball lineup is called the "cleanup" batter. That person, the fourth hitter, is usually the best batter on the team. If things have been going well, there are three runners on the base when the fourth hitter comes to the plate. The fans rise to their feet with a roar. And now the windup, the pitch, a mighty swing—it's a home run! The batter "cleans up" the bases by bringing all three runners home to score.

Have you guessed where this talk about baseball is leading? That's right—you are about to read the fourth lesson, the "clean up" lesson, of this unit. It will take care of three pronoun problems that are left over from earlier lessons. These problems may not come up very often in your writing. But when they do come up, you should know how to make them score in your favor.

Pronouns in Comparisons

Two words that are often used in comparisons are *as* and *than*. These words are always followed by a noun or pronoun. When they are followed by a pronoun, the case of that pronoun is important. Often it decides the meaning of the sentence. Look at these examples:

We helped her brother as much as **she**.

We helped her brother as much as **her**.

In each sentence there are some words missing after the pronoun (*she* or *her*). Without these words, the clause that begins with *as* is incomplete. Such a clause is called an *elliptical clause*.

P O I N T S   T O   K N O W

An **elliptical clause** is a clause from which one or more words are missing.

When you read an elliptical clause, you mentally fill in the missing words. How do you know what words to fill in? The pronoun tells you.

We helped her brother as much as **she** *helped him*.

We helped her brother as much as *we helped* **her**.

Here is an elliptical clause beginning with *than*.

People visit Vito more than **I**.

You mentally complete the sentence this way: "People visit Vito more than I do," or "... more than I visit Vito."
Change the pronoun and you change the meaning:

People visit Vito more than **me**.

Now the sentence means, "People visit Vito more than they visit me."
In some sentences you do not have a choice of pronoun cases. Only the subjective case fits in this example:

Katherine usually gets better grades than **I**.   (get)

▶   To decide which case of a pronoun to use in an elliptical clause, just fill in the missing words.

Reflexive and Intensive Pronouns

English has a handy set of pronouns that end in *-self* or *-selves*. There are eight of them. Here are the eight reflexive and intensive pronouns.

Singular	Plural
myself	ourselves
yourself	yourselves
himself	
herself	themselves
itself	

Note: Always say *himself* (not *hisself*) and *themselves* (not *theirselves*).

These pronouns are called either *reflexive* or *intensive*, depending on how they are used.

507

P O I N T S   T O   K N O W

▶ A *reflexive pronoun* shows that the action performed by the subject is reflected back onto the subject.

Steve grabbed the rope and pulled **himself** out of the water. (Steve performed the action of pulling and also received the action of pulling.)

Give **yourself** a pat on the back for a job well done.   (You give the pat and you also receive the pat.)

▶ An *intensive pronoun* adds emphasis to a noun or another pronoun in the sentence.

Compare these two sentences:

They always do the work.

They always do the work **themselves.**

The first sentence just states a fact, without emphasis. The second sentence emphasizes the fact that they, and no one else, always do the work. The intensive pronoun *themselves* draws attention to the subject, *they*.

Here is another pair of examples:

Nanette tested the engine.

Nanette tested the engine **herself**.

The intensive pronoun, *herself*, emphasizes the noun, *Nanette*.

Possessive Pronouns Before Gerunds

In Lesson Three of Unit Twenty-three you learned that a *gerund* is the *-ing* form of a verb used as a noun. A *gerund phrase* is a gerund plus any modifiers and objects it may have. Here are some examples, to refresh your memory.

Knitting is my sister's favorite pastime.   (The gerund *knitting* is the subject of the sentence.)

Shirley enjoys **skiing**.   (The gerund *skiing* is the object of the verb *enjoys*).

Since a gerund is a noun, it can be "possessed" by another noun or pronoun. In the following examples the gerund is in italics and the possessive noun or pronoun is in boldface type.

Her *laughing* at his mistake was not very kind.

Bill's *practicing* the piano all day is getting on my nerves.

Their constant *fighting* kept the family in an uproar.

I was amazed at **his** *getting* the right answer.

I was amazed at the **student's** *getting* the right answer.

Their *being* with me was enough.

My **friends'** *being* with me was enough.

Practice A   Choose the correct pronoun.

Choose the correct form in parentheses to complete each sentence. Write the whole sentence on your paper. One sentence is correct with either pronoun.

1. (Us, Our) finding the balloon with the message tied to it was the beginning of an adventure.

2. The students (theirselves, themselves) say that they are learning a lot in the course.
3. (Rachel, Rachel's) making friends with the Stewarts should not bother you.
4. She still gives much more of her time to you than (they, them).
5. One boy in our class has taught (hisself, himself) to be a ventriloquist.
6. Our teacher doesn't object to (him, his) "throwing his voice around" once or twice a day.
7. Yesterday several people found (theirselves, themselves) being scolded by a voice that came from the pencil sharpener.
8. No one deserves a good mark more than (we, us).
9. Have you heard about (me, my) getting my foot caught in the bus door?
10. It's too bad that everyone isn't as good-natured as (he, him.)

Practice B   Identify pronouns.

Number your paper from 1 to 10. Each sentence that follows has a word or words in italics. Decide whether the italicized word or words are an example of an *elliptical clause*, a *reflexive pronoun*, an *intensive pronoun*, or a *possessive before a gerund*. Write your answer on your paper after the number of the sentence.

EXAMPLE: I know a few people who take *themselves* too seriously.

reflexive pronoun

1. We congratulated him on *his* staying calm while everyone else panicked.
2. I am going to do the job *myself*, to make sure it is done right.
3. The two runners thought that no one else in the school was as fast *as they*.
4. The boss has been complaining about *your* being late almost every day.
5. Let's test *ourselves* to see whether we remember what we've learned so far.
6. *Frank's* winning the contest gave our morale a boost.
7. Loud noises seem to bother you more *than me*.

8. If you eat candy, you will make *yourself* sick.

9. You have just as much right *as I* to express an opinion.

10. He said *himself* that the ladder wasn't safe, but he still used it.

R E V I E W   E X E R C I S E S

I. Pronouns and Antecedents Number your paper from 1 to 10. In each sentence, choose the pronoun or pronouns that agree with the antecedent. Write the pronoun(s) on your paper. (Lesson One)

1. Somebody forgot to wash (his or her, their) dishes.
2. Neither the boy nor the two girls ate (his or her, their) pie.
3. Each person has (his or her, their) own set of standards.
4. Both the boy and his uncles bring (his, their) own fishing poles.
5. Every animal has (his or her, its, their) place in the world.
6. Sue and Dick will ride (his or her, their) bikes to the parade.
7. One of the puppies has a white spot on (its, his, their) forehead.
8. Everybody has (his or her, their) favorite food.
9. Either Dora or Ellen will have to lend June (her, their) tennis racquet.
10. None of the students left (his or her, their) jackets in school.

II. Subjective and Objective Pronouns Number your paper from 1 to 10. In each sentence, choose the correct pronoun or pronouns from those given in parentheses. Write the pronoun(s) on your paper. (Lesson Two)

1. The horse belongs equally to his sister and (he, him).
2. Why doesn't somebody ask (we, us) artists to decorate the halls?
3. Was it (she, her) who did the shopping last week?
4. (Her, She) and I watched the parade for a half hour.
5. You and (me, I) are the best of friends.
6. (Us, We) baseball fans are going to the game.
7. We often stop and talk to the officer on duty, Lt. Mary Tompkins or (he, him).

8. It was (they, them) who found the lost dog.

9. The boy standing by the fence is (he, him).

10. I did not see either (he or she, him or her) at the dance last night.

III. *Who* and *Whom* Number your paper from 1 to 10. In each sentence, decide whether *who* or *whom* is correct. Write the correct pronoun on your paper. (Lesson Three)

1. To (who, whom) am I speaking?

2. (Who, Whom) is coming to the party?

3. That is the person with (who, whom) I sat.

4. I know someone (who, whom) would like to meet you.

5. (Who, Whom) was that story about?

6. Mr. Anderson, (who, whom) is my teacher, is from Norway.

7. He was a man (who, whom) everyone respected.

8. Do you know (who, whom) might have left these bowling shoes here?

9. The parents (who, whom) the teacher asked to help said they would be glad to.

10. I like people (who, whom) can take responsibility.

IV. Special Problems in Pronoun Use Number your paper from 1 to 10. Each sentence that follows has a word or words in italics. Decide whether the italicized word or words are an example of an *elliptical clause*, a *reflexive pronoun*, an *intensive pronoun*, or a *possessive before a gerund*. Write your answer on your paper after the number of the sentence. (Lesson Four)

1. I see you both bought *yourselves* some new clothes.

2. There were many skaters at the rink today who were better *than we*.

3. I *myself* was fooled by his tricks for a long time.

4. *Your* offering to help him restored his faith in human nature.

5. The people who opposed them are just as intelligent *as they*.

6. She *herself* admits that she should have planned more carefully.

7. We were insulted at *their* refusing our gift.

8. Gregory should not be so quick to blame *himself* every time something goes wrong.

9. We see him more often *than her*.

10. Does the weather affect animals as much *as us*?

V. Using Pronouns Correctly Number your paper from 1 to 10. In each sentence, choose the correct pronoun or pronouns from those given in parentheses. Write the pronoun(s) on your paper. (Lessons One - Four)

1. I admire anyone who makes (his or her, their) own clothes.
2. Either Mrs. Leonard or her son Jack left (her, his) umbrella at our house.
3. George, Henry, and (I, me) are planning a trip to Europe.
4. You promised that you would take (he, him) to the library.
5. Grandpa built this bookshelf for you and (I, me) to share.
6. It couldn't have been (she, her) who mowed the lawn.
7. (Who, Whom) did Frank invite to the spring dance?
8. The baby-sitter (who, whom) they hired is very reliable.
9. Nobody practices the piano as much as (he, him).
10. My father prefers to repair the appliances (himself, hisself).

Using Pronouns Correctly in Your Writing

In most of your writing, you use pronouns correctly. For example, you probably never write, "*Me* went to the store" or "I bought *she* a gift." Instead, you write "*I* went to the store" and "I bought *her* a gift." However, the rules for using English pronouns are so complicated that you may occasionally use a pronoun incorrectly. You may write, "Jim and *me* went fishing" or "Terry gave Georgia and *I* some old magazines." In those two examples, the pronouns in italics break two of the rules that you learned in this unit. Now you know how to correct those sentences: "Jim and *I* went fishing" and "Terry gave Georgia and *me* some old magazines."

Sometimes the wrong pronoun can change the meaning of your sentence, as in the case of elliptical clauses (see Lesson Four). Look at the following examples.

Wendy likes her cat more than *me*.

Wendy likes her cat more than *I*.

The first sentence means that Wendy likes her cat more than she likes me. The second sentence means that Wendy likes her cat more than I like her cat. As you can see, the choice between *I* and *me* can make a big difference in meaning.

Whether your aim is to avoid confusion in your writing, or simply to be correct, it is important to choose the correct pronoun. The following exercise will give you practice in writing with pronouns.

Practice   **Write a paragraph with pronouns.**

Write a paragraph describing a game that you played with two or more friends. It could be a board game, card game, ball game, or any other type of game. Use the pronouns listed below in your paragraph. Of course, you may use other pronouns that you choose in addition to the ones listed. As you write, make sure that each pronoun agrees with its antecedent, and that each pronoun is in the correct case.

he	me	their
whom	our	themselves

Using Verbs Correctly

"Tractored Out," Childress County, Texas, 1938
Dorothea Lange, Culver Pictures, Inc.

Using Verbs Correctly

L E S S O N   O N E

Irregular Verbs

In the following passage there are ten verbs that are not used correctly. Can you find them?

We seen our old friends, the Morrisons, on Saturday. "My, how you've growed!" Mrs. Morrison said to me.

"Well, he has practically ate a horse every day this year," my mother told her friend. "He has always getted a lot of exercise, too," my mother bragged. "He must have swimmed thirty miles a week last summer."

I becomed embarrassed. "I never done that," I whispered. Mr. Morrison give me a wink. "Some people can't stand praise," he said, and bursted out laughing.

The errors in this passage all come from one problem: not knowing the principal parts of irregular verbs.

Principal Parts of Verbs

Every verb has four principal parts, as you learned in Unit Nineteen, Lesson Three. All forms of the verb are made from these four principal parts.

P O I N T S   T O   K N O W

The **principal parts** of a verb are the infinitive or base form, the present participle, the past tense, and the past participle.

On the following page are the principal parts of some familiar verbs.

Base Form or Infinitive	Present Participle	Past Tense	Past Participle
lift	lifting	lifted	lifted
need	needing	needed	needed
change	changing	changed	changed
smile	smiling	smiled	smiled
make	making	made	made
sing	singing	sang	sung

▶ The present participle always ends in *-ing*.

▶ When the present participle is used as the main verb in a verb phrase, it is always accompanied by a helping verb. The helping verb is a form of *be*.

> He **is waving** at us.
>
> They **were smiling** mysteriously.

▶ The past tense is always used alone as a main verb.

> He **lifted** the heavy bundle slowly.
>
> They **smiled** mysteriously.

▶ When the past participle is used as the main verb in a verb phrase, it is always accompanied by a helping verb. The helping verb is a form of *have*.

> He **has lifted** heavy bundles for me many times.
>
> I **have made** a pecan pie.

Regular Verbs

Notice that in the list of principal parts above, the first four verbs follow the same pattern in forming the past tense and past participle. They are all *regular verbs*.

Regular verbs form the past tense and past participle by adding *-ed* or *-d* to the base form.

Irregular Verbs

Irregular verbs, as their name suggests, do not follow one particular pattern. They form the past tense and past participle in many different ways. This means that you have to learn each irregular verb separately. However, most irregular verbs are used so often in everyday speech that you already know their principal parts.

   The list that follows will help you review the irregular verbs you know and learn any others that you don't know. The verbs are arranged in groups according to the way they form the past tense and past participle. This should make it easier for you to remember the correct forms.

Base Form	Past Tense	Past Participle
drive	drove	driven
ride	rode	ridden
rise	rose	risen
write	wrote	written
begin	began	begun
drink	drank	drunk
ring	rang	rung
sing	sang	sung
swim	swam	swum
fly	flew	flown
blow	blew	blown
grow	grew	grown
know	knew	known
throw	threw	thrown
draw	drew	drawn
take	took	taken
shake	shook	shaken
give	gave	given
fall	fell	fallen
eat	ate	eaten
see	saw	seen

come	came	come
run	ran	run
freeze	froze	frozen
break	broke	broken
speak	spoke	spoken
steal	stole	stolen
choose	chose	chosen
wear	wore	worn
tear	tore	torn
bite	bit	bitten
bring	brought	brought
catch	caught	caught
creep	crept	crept
get	got	got or gotten
lead	led	led
lend	lent	lent
lose	lost	lost
say	said	said
sit	sat	sat
stand	stood	stood
sting	stung	stung
swing	swung	swung
burst	burst	burst
put	put	put
beat	beat	beat or beaten
set	set	set
be	was, were	been
do	did	done
go	went	gone

Practice A   Choose the correct verb form.

Number your paper from 1 to 10. In each sentence below you are asked to choose the correct form of one or more verbs. On your paper write the verb(s) from each sentence.

1. Just as I (bited, bit) into the apple, the chocolate cake (catched, caught) my attention.
2. Our class has (wrote, written) a letter to the city council.
3. Beryl had (took, taken) the exam earlier that day, and she (knew, knowed) that she had (did, done) well.
4. In honor of the town's three-hundredth birthday, the church bells were (rang, rung) from noon till one o'clock.
5. The pitcher (threw, throwed) the batter out at first base.
6. Last winter it was so cold that the harbor (freezed, froze) over.
7. Have you ever (flew, flown) across the continent?
8. By the time we had (ate, eaten) the salty meal, everyone had (drank, drunk) three glasses of water.
9. I would have (wore, worn) old clothes if I had (knew, known) we were going to work.
10. We (drove, drived) miles out of our way before we (came, come) to a sign.

Practice B   Write the correct verb form.

In each sentence that follows you are given, in parentheses, the base form of one or more verbs. Decide which form of each verb (past tense or past participle) is correct. Write the verb(s) from each sentence next to the number of the sentence.

EXAMPLE: I had never (speak) in front of an audience before.

spoken

1. The child is crying because he has been (sting) by a bee.
2. Cars (be) not allowed to cross the parade route except when the police stopped the marchers.
3. For the junior prom, the decorations committee (blow) up hundreds of balloons.
4. Whoever (lose) that ring will be back to look for it.

5. As we (stand) on the steps of the haunted house, our friends (creep) up behind us.
6. The national anthem was (sing), and the game (begin).
7. The artist (draw) a sketch as the autumn leaves (fall).
8. Everyone has (bring) something for the barbecue.
9. They have (sit) in their seats and (say) nothing all evening.
10. The dog (shake) water all over us.

Practice C   **Write sentences with the principal parts of verbs.**

Write ten sentences. In each sentence use one of the verbs below in the form indicated in parentheses.

EXAMPLE: catch   (past participle)
They have caught three fish.

1. break   (past tense)
2. take   (past participle)
3. run   (past participle)
4. eat   (past tense)
5. wear   (past tense)
6. set   (past participle)
7. lead   (past tense)
8. speak   (past participle)
9. break   (past participle)
10. rise   (past participle)

L E S S O N   T W O

Verb Tenses

Have you ever wanted to travel backward or forward in time, like the characters in H.G. Wells' *The Time Machine*?

The fact is that you do travel around in time, at least mentally, when you talk about past events or future plans. Verb tenses are your time machines.

Verbs do two jobs at once. They express action or being, and they show when the action or being takes place. Verbs have different tense forms to show different times. There are six tenses: the *present tense*, the *past tense*, the *future tense*, the *present perfect tense*, the *past perfect tense*, and the *future perfect tense*.

▶ The present tense shows that the action or being is taking place now or takes place regularly or always.

> Margaret **seems** nervous.   (now)
>
> The workers **clean** their tools at the end of the day.   (regularly)
>
> Cucumbers **need** more heat than most vegetables.   (always)

The present tense form of a verb is the same as the infinitive or base form for all subjects but one. If the subject is third person singular, -s or -es is added to the base form. Here are the present tense forms of the verb *write*:

Present Tense

Singular	*Plural*
I write	we write
you write	you write
he, she, it writes	they write

▶ The past tense shows that the action or being took place before the present moment.

> We **spoke** to him a few minutes ago.
>
> Last year I **studied** algebra.
>
> Marilyn **bought** three records.

The past tense form is one of the four principal parts of the verb.

Past Tense

Singular	*Plural*
I wrote	we wrote
you wrote	you wrote
he, she, it wrote	they wrote

► The future tense shows that the action or being will take place in the future.

The train **will arrive** at six o'clock.

The movie **will start** soon.

I **shall be** happy to see my friends.

The future tense form is a phrase. It consists of the helping verb *will* or *shall* plus the base form of the main verb.

Future Tense

Singular	*Plural*
I will (shall) write	We will (shall) write
you will write	you will write
he, she, it will write	they will write

► The present perfect tense shows that the action or being is complete ("perfect") as of the present moment.

They **have** already **left**.

We **have asked** the owner for his permission to use his basement.

I **have finished** my homework.

► The present perfect tense can also be used when the action or being is still going on.

We **have waited** long enough.   (We are still waiting.)

You **have come** to my house for the package.   (You are still here.)

The Stewarts **have lived** in that house for forty years.   (They still live there.)

The present perfect tense form consists of the helping verb *has* or *have* plus the past participle of the main verb.

Present Perfect Tense

Singular	*Plural*
I have written	we have written
you have written	you have written
he, she, it has written	they have written

▶ The past perfect tense shows that the action or being was complete ("perfect") at a certain time in the past. It refers to an event that was over by the time another event happened.

> He **had planned** the trip so well that nothing was left to chance.

> We could not find the kittens because the cat **had hidden** them.

The past perfect tense form consists of the helping verb *had* plus the past participle of the main verb.

Past Perfect Tense

Singular	*Plural*
I had written	we had written
you had written	you had written
he, she, it had written	they had written

▶ The future perfect tense shows that the action or being will be complete ("perfect") by a certain time in the future. It refers to a future event that will be over by the time another future event happens.

> By noon I **shall have left**.

> The team **will have become** more confident by the end of the season.

The future perfect tense form consists of the helping verbs *shall have* or *will have* plus the past participle of the main verb.

Future Perfect Tense

Singular	*Plural*
I will (shall) have written	we will (shall) have written
you will have written	you will have written
he, she, it will have written	they will have written

Continuous Forms

All six verb tenses have *continuous forms*.

▶ The continuous form is used to show that the action or being expressed by the verb is going on or continuing at a certain time.

I **am listening**.   (The action of listening is going on at this moment.)

The last time I saw him he **was working** at the bank.   (The action of working was going on at a certain time in the past.)

Next year they **will be living** in their new house.   (The action of living will be going on at a certain time in the future.)

The continuous form of any tense is made up of a form of the verb *be* in that tense plus the present participle of the main verb. Here are some more examples of the continuous forms:

They **are giving** us the signal.   (present continuous)

I could see that you **were dialing** the wrong number.   (past continuous)

She **will be taking** the test during the first period tomorrow. (future continuous)

Mike **has been reading** the same book for weeks. (present perfect continuous)

We **had been waiting** for two hours when my plane finally landed.   (past perfect continuous)

He **will have been working** here for thirty years by the time he retires.   (future perfect continuous)

Note: Some people have a different name for the continuous forms. They call them the *progressive* forms.

Helping Verbs

You have seen that helping verbs are used in verb phrases to express certain meanings. The helping verbs *will* and *shall* indicate future time. The helping verb *have (has, had)* helps form the perfect tenses. The helping verb *be* helps make up the continuous forms.

Another helping verb—*do (did)*—is used to show emphasis, to ask a question, or to express a negative idea.

You **do make** the best cakes!   (emphasis)

Did you **put** any sugar in this one?   (question)

I **do** not **have** time.   (negative)

There are other common helping verbs that help express the speaker's mood or attitude. These helping verbs are called *modal auxiliaries*, or just *modals*. Here are the most common modals and the "moods" or attitudes they express:

1. may, might   (permission, possibility)
   You *may use* my bicycle this afternoon.   (permission)
   However, it *might rain* later.   (possibility)

2. can, could   (ability)
   Can you *take* the bus instead?
   Your brother *could drive* you home from the theater.

3. should   (obligation)
   You *should be* grateful for the ride.

4. must   (necessity)
   You *must fix* your own bicycle.

5. would   (inclination)
   I would help you if I had time.

Special Uses of the Present Tense

The present tense has some special uses. It is sometimes used to express actions that will take place in the future. However, future time is always indicated by another word in the sentence.

Tomorrow we call the Johnsons.

We give blood **next week**.

The wedding takes place **this coming Sunday**.

Occasionally the present tense is used to express past time. You sometimes use it this way when you are telling a story and want to make it more exciting. For example, suppose you are telling about something that happened last night. The action will seem to be happening right now if you say:

So I get to Marcie's house at seven o'clock. Her brother is watering the lawn. I yell at him, and he swings around holding the hose. Before I know it, I'm getting a cold shower.

The use of the present tense is called the *historical present.* It can become very tiresome if it is used too much. However, the historical present is effective when used just once in a while to highlight important action.

Keeping Tenses Consistent

In your writing you should change tenses only when you want to show a change in time. Look at the unnecessary changes of tense in this paragraph:

> He **comes** to see me and immediately **asked** if he could use my telephone. *I said*, "Help yourself." He **dials** the number and **talks** on the phone for forty-five minutes. I **had begun** to get annoyed. Finally he **hangs** up and **says** to me, "I can't visit with you now; I'm in a hurry." Then he **walked** out.

This paragraph contains five unnecessary shifts in verb tense. It goes from present to past to present to past perfect to present to past. Here is a corrected version of the paragraph:

> He came to see me and immediately asked if he could use my telephone. I said, "Help yourself." He dialed the number and talked on the phone for forty-five minutes. I was beginning to get annoyed. Finally he hung up and said to me, "I can't visit with you now; I'm in a hurry." Then he walked out.

Practice A   **Identify verb tense.**

On your paper copy each italicized verb. (The verb may be one word, or it may be a phrase.) Then tell what tense the verb is in.

EXAMPLE: For years people *have asked* my uncle to make cakes for special occasions.

have asked   present perfect

1. Many years ago he *was* an art student with very little money.
2. He *had* always *enjoyed* baking.
3. A friend *was moving* to Alaska.
4. My uncle thought, "I *will give* him a going-away party."
5. My uncle *baked* a cake in the shape of an igloo.

6. People who *had attended* the party began to call him with requests for special cakes.

7. After his graduation from art school, he *needed* a business to support his art work.

8. Because he *had made* a reputation for himself as a cake decorator, he *decided* to bake for profit and paint for fun.

9. By the end of this year he *will have decorated* more than five thousand cakes.

10. He *will design* a cake in the shape of an old-fashioned airplane for my graduation from pilot school.

11. He *has made* his favorite cakes for special events.

12. He never *knows* what assignment he will get next.

13. He *claims* that soon he will have decorated cakes for every holiday on the calendar.

14. He *has made* cakes in the shape of trees for Arbor Day, flags for the Fourth of July, and turkeys for Thanksgiving.

15. Next year he *will travel* to Europe to give courses on cake decorating at a famous cooking school.

Practice B   **Find verb phrases.**

Each sentence below contains one verb phrase. On your paper write the verb phrase after the number of the sentence.

EXAMPLE: You might not have seen the highway exit in the dark.

might have seen

1. Ethel will be doing that assignment for hours.
2. Did you read the magazine article about solar power?
3. When the grand marshal gives the signal, the parade will begin.
4. Can cats really see in the dark?
5. He should have stopped immediately.
6. Had the audience been waiting long for the speaker?
7. By tomorrow he will have finished most of the painting.
8. The rain may stop later in the afternoon.
9. That does not seem like a good idea to me.
10. Donald will have been practicing all afternoon.

Active Voice and Passive Voice

What is the difference between these two sentences?

> A man in a pink satin jacket delivered the message.

> The message was delivered by a man in a pink satin jacket.

There is no difference in meaning between the two sentences. They both give the same information. However, there is a difference in emphasis. In the first sentence the man is mentioned first. In the second sentence the message is mentioned first.

A transitive verb—an action verb that has a doer of the action and a receiver of the action—can be expressed in two different ways. The two ways are called the *active voice* and the *passive voice*.

P O I N T S   T O   K N O W

A verb is in the **active voice** when the subject is the doer of the action and the direct object is the receiver of the action.

> The quarterback **caught** the ball.   (The subject, *quarterback*, is the doer of the action. The receiver of the action is *ball*, the direct object.)

> Ellen **brought** the cookies.

> The dog **chewed** the furniture.

A verb is in the **passive voice** when the subject is the receiver of the action.

> The ball **was caught** by the quarterback.   (The subject, *ball*, is the receiver of the action.)

> The cookies **were brought** by Ellen.

> The furniture **was chewed** by the dog.

In the passive voice, the doer of the action may be mentioned in a phrase beginning with *by*. In the three examples above, the action is done *by the quarterback, by Ellen*, and *by the dog*.

In the following two examples the doer of the action is not mentioned:

At noon the winner **will be announced.**

The window on the driver's side **had been smashed.**

How the Passive Voice Is Formed.

To put a verb in the the passive voice, you combine some form of the verb *be* (*am, is, are, was, were, been,* etc.) with the past participle of the main verb. If the verb phrase in an active-voice sentence contains helping verbs, these must be included when the sentence is put into the passive voice.

Active: He **won** the race.

Passive: The race **was won** by him.

Active: Frank **will drive** my car.

Passive: My car **will be driven** by Frank.

Active: Jane **has fed** the children.

Passive: The children **have been fed** by Jane.

When to Use the Passive Voice

As a general rule, your sentences will be more direct and forceful if you use the active voice. However, there are two situations in which you can use the passive voice to good advantage.

▶ You can use the passive voice when you do not know who performed the action.

The drawings **were made** in ancient times.   (You don't know who made the drawings.)

The package **had** already **been delivered** when I got home.   (You don't know who delivered the package.)

▶ You can use the passive voice when you want to emphasize the receiver of the action. The subject of a sentence ranks above the direct object in importance. Therefore, one way to emphasize the receiver of the action is to let it be the subject. Of course, when the receiver of the action is the subject, the verb is in the passive voice. Notice the difference in emphasis in these two sentences:

The Red Cross **fed** thousands of refugees.   (active voice)

Thousands of refugees **were fed** by the Red Cross.   (passive voice)

In the first sentence the emphasis is on the Red Cross. In the second sentence the emphasis is on the refugees.

Practice A   Identify active and passive voices.

On your paper write the italicized verb in each sentence below. Then indicate whether the verb is in the *active* voice or the *passive* voice.

EXAMPLE: The dog *has been scolded*.

has been scolded   passive

1. All of my friends *are coming* to the craft show.
2. The macrame hangings *were made* by our neighbors.
3. Visitors to the show *will buy* tickets at the door.
4. The entrance to the show *will be* closely *guarded*.
5. Some of the pottery is *being unwrapped now*.
6. Ramon *has won* several prizes in the past.
7. His jars and clay figures *can be seen* in the north corner of the hall.
8. The silver jewelry *was made* by a newcomer to town.
9. She *will be opening* a shop next month.
10. The shop *will be shared* by the silversmith, a woodcarver, and a weaver.
11. The wood carver *was instructed* by a famous craftsman.
12. The weaver *taught herself* how to make rugs.
13. We hope the show *will receive* enough patronage.
14. I *will be handing* out name tags at the entrance.
15. You *were* already *given* a free pass to the show.

Rewrite sentences, changing the voice.

Rewrite the ten sentences below, changing the voice of each verb. If a verb is in the active voice, make it passive. If a verb is in the passive voice, make it active. Make any other changes that are needed in the sentence.

EXAMPLE: We were shown to our seats by an usher.

An usher showed us to our seats.

1. The operator put the call through for me.
2. Rain was predicted by the weather forecaster.
3. Dinner was prepared by the home economics classes.
4. Someone had opened the window to let in air.
5. The batter smacked the ball over the fence.
6. Someone will leave a package for me.
7. The dog has been groomed for the show by its owner.
8. After the storm the hotel manager reset all the clocks.
9. People with shovels cleared the snow from the frozen pond.
10. The goals were scored by Mateson and Kruger.

Practice C **Write sentences with active and passive verbs.**

Choose three of the verbs below. Use each one in two sentences. Use the verb once in the active voice and once in the passive voice.

EXAMPLE: write

Charles Dickens wrote Great Expectations.

Great Expectations was written by Charles Dickens.

eat

applaud

scrub

photograph

fix

write

throw

give

I. Irregular Verbs   On your paper write the correct form (past tense or past participle) of the verb in parentheses. (Lesson One)

EXAMPLE: We _____ every day last summer.   (swim)

swam

1. We _____ for three hours in the mountains without seeing a house.   (drive)
2. Within a short time, the boat had _____ to leak badly.   (begin)
3. The campers have _____ enough food for a week.   (bring)
4. The fund-raising committee _____ an excellent job last year.   (do)
5. The tomato plants have _____ to a height of three feet.   (grow)
6. They said they had _____ down the box of dishes very carefully.   (set)
7. Have you ever _____ into an unripe peach?   (bite)
8. Out of the corner of my eye, I _____ a long-lost friend.   (see)
9. The captains have _____ their teams.   (choose)
10. That job _____ three hours of hard work.   (take)

533

II. Verb Tenses   On your paper write the form of the verb indicated in parentheses. (Lesson Two)

EXAMPLE: They _____ our house.   (*like*, past)

liked

1. Some people _____ a hard time waking up.   (*have*, present)
2. Last night I _____ four hot dogs.   (*eat*, past)
3. I _____ the window in a few minutes.   (*open*, future)
4. I _____ a person to represent our school at the fair.   (*choose*, present perfect)

5. Todd _____ the window with a football.   (*break*, past perfect)

6. By tomorrow they _____.   (*arrive*, future perfect)

7. Fred _____ *War and Peace* for a book report.   (*read*, present continuous)

8. The dog _____ at a rabbit in the field.   (*bark*, past continuous)

9. Frank _____ on the car all day tomorrow.   (*work*, future continuous)

10. He _____ hard to get ready for the track meet.   (*train*, present perfect continuous)

11. I _____ you set up your booth at the flea market.   (*help*, future)

12. Mr. Ariel _____ his cottage by September first of this year.   (*close*, future perfect)

13. Cynthia and Millicent _____ their piano duet all morning.   (*practice*, past perfect continuous)

14. I _____ my work by the time you get here.   (*finish*, future perfect)

15. Laurie _____ both cashier and bookkeeper in her aunt's store for the past six months.   (*be*, present perfect)

16. The man whom Charlie introduced to me insisted that he and I _____ before.   (*meet*, past perfect)

17. Calvin says that he _____ in training his cat to sit up and "sing" the school song with him.   (*succeed*, present perfect)

18. The students denied that they _____ the reference books out of the school library without telling the librarian.   (*take*, past perfect)

19. We _____ forward to seeing you next Friday.   (*look*, present continuous)

20. If you _____ in this contest last year, please raise your hand.   (*compete*, past)

III. Irregular Verbs and Tenses Choose five of the verbs listed below. For each verb you choose, write three sentences. Use the past tense in the first sentence. Use the present participle in the second sentence. Use the past participle in the third sentence. (Lessons One and Two)

EXAMPLE: ride

Elka rode her horse yesterday.

Ed is riding a unicycle down the street.

Ezra has ridden an elephant at the zoo.

Verbs:

pay	stand
hold	shut
set	bring
lead	get
begin	be

IV. Active Voice and Passive Voice Write the verb or verb phrase from each sentence. Then indicate whether it is in the *active* voice or the *passive* voice. (Lesson Three)

EXAMPLE: My name was called.

was called   passive

1. The man in the bank counted the money.
2. This book was written by Frank Jones.
3. Allison closed the garage door.
4. She wore his ring on a chain.
5. The unusual shell was found by Patti.
6. Debi received a letter yesterday from Bob.
7. The vase had been broken.
8. The state scenery is being painted in the art room.
9. Vince will make a cherry cheesecake for the bake sale.
10. Invitations will be sent to all of the advisers.

Using Verbs Correctly in Your Writing

Every sentence you write has at least one verb. Without verbs, your sentences wouldn't make any sense:

> I you.
>
> Pete the dishes.
>
> Marjorie late.

The verbs you choose to use, however, have many different forms. You learned about many of these forms in this unit. It's not always easy to choose the correct form, or the best word, to express your thoughts. By practicing, though, you can make the job easier.

Here are a few ways to complete the thoughts expressed by the above groups of words. How many different verbs can you think of to use in each sentence?

> I love you.
>
> I have left you.
>
> Pete has broken the dishes.
>
> Pete bought the dishes.
>
> Marjorie will arrive late.
>
> Marjorie was late.

The following exercises will give you practice in writing sentences with verbs.

Practice A   Use continuous forms.

Use a continuous form of a verb in parentheses to complete the following sentences.

1. I (arrive) at the station and am waiting for you.
2. The dog (sleep) all the time lately.
3. All day tomorrow we (hear) the fireworks.
4. Charles (take) the same route to work for ten years.
5. Next Christmas we (open) the presents together.

Practice B   **Write sentences using verbs correctly.**

Follow the directions below for writing sentences.

EXAMPLE: Write several sentences about school. Use these verbs: *sit, study, listen.*

In class, I listen carefully to my teacher. At home, I study at least an hour a day. When I study, I sit in the corner of the couch.

1. Write several sentences about summer. Use these verbs: *was hoping, have played, will try.*
2. Write several sentences about your family. Use these verbs: *are, have, live.*
3. Write several sentences about the future. Use these verbs: *hope, will be, might.*
4. Write several sentences about a meal. Use these verbs: *have prepared, was eating, had spilled.*
5. Write several sentences about yourself. Use these verbs: *am, was, have been.*

Using Modifiers Correctly

Circle Line Tours, New York City, around 1960
Garry Winogrand, courtesy of Fraenkel Gallery and the Estate
of Garry Winogrand

Using Modifiers Correctly

You won't believe the following story, but you will see its point.

There were two students named Adjective and Adverb. One day when they came home from school they noticed that their house was on fire. Adverb said to Adjective, "I'll fight the fire with the garden hose. You run next door and phone the fire department. Tell them to come *real swift.*"

Adjective dashed halfway to the neighbors' house, but then stopped and dashed back. "You're the one who ought to phone the fire department," said Adjective to Adverb. "Tell them to come *really swiftly.*"

By the time they settled the argument, their house had burned down.

Which is correct, "Come real swift," or "Come really swiftly"? In the following unit you will find the answer to this and other questions about how to use modifiers correctly.

L E S S O N   O N E

Choosing Between Adjectives and Adverbs

In the preceding story, the student named Adjective was correct in insisting that the firemen be told to "come really swiftly." *Swiftly* is an adverb modifying the verb *come. Really* is an adverb modifying the adverb *swiftly. Real* and *swift* are adjectives. They can modify nouns and pronouns but not verbs or adverbs.

Is it important to use adjectives and adverbs correctly in your speech and writing? It depends on where you are and what is happening. If your house is burning down, grammar doesn't matter. But if you're sitting at your desk writing a letter or a composition, it does matter.

When you're dealing with adjectives and adverbs, your problems often come in pairs. Among adjective/adverb pairs that are often misused are *easy/easily, real/really, bad/badly,* and *good/well.* If you learn to handle these words correctly, you should have no trouble with other adjective/adverb pairs. The rule is the same for all.

P O I N T S   T O   K N O W

To modify a noun or a pronoun, use an adjective. To modify a verb, an adjective, or an adverb, use an adverb.

This rule is easy to apply. Look at the following examples:

> The first problem on the test was (**easy, easily**).

The modifier modifies the noun *problem*. Since only an adjective can modify a noun, the correct choice is *easy*.

> The runner won the race (**easy, easily**).

The modifier modifies the verb *won*. Since only an adverb can modify a verb, the correct choice is *easily*.

> Louise is a (**real, really**) kind person.

The modifer modifies the adjective *kind*. Since only an adverb can modify an adjective, the correct choice is *really*.

> Sam threw the ball (**real, really**) hard.

The modifier modifes the adverb *hard*. Since only an adverb can modify an adverb, the correct choice is *really*.

The pairs *quick/quickly* and *slow/slowly* do not always follow the rule. The adjective members of these pairs, *quick* and *slow*, are sometimes used as adverbs to modify verbs. However, they are used as adverbs only in very short clauses. For example:

> Come **quick!**   Drive **slow.**

In longer clauses the adverbs *quickly* and *slowly* sound better.

> He turned his head **quickly** when he heard the door open.
> The truck took the sharp turns **slowly.**

Which Word Is Being Modified?

In the examples you have seen so far, it is easy to tell which word the modifier goes with. However, it is less easy to pick out the modified word in sentences with certain verbs. When the modifier follows a verb like *feel, taste, appear, look,* or *sound,* some writers become confused. They are not sure whether the modifier goes with the verb or with the subject.

Here are some examples:

Calvin looked (**nervous, nervously**) as he stood up to speak.

Calvin looked (**nervous, nervously**) at his notes as he stood up to speak.

In the first example, *looked* is a linking verb. It joins the subject *Calvin,* with a word in the predicate that describes the subject. Since *Calvin* is a noun, the modifier must be an adjective.

Calvin looked **nervous** as he stood up to speak.

In the second example the verb *looked* expresses action. The modifier modifies the action verb; it tells how Calvin looked at his notes. Therefore, the correct modifier is the adverb.

Calvin looked **nervously** at his notes as he stood up to speak.

Another verb that can be either a linking or an action verb is *feel.*

Linda felt (**weary, wearily**) after working all day.

Linda felt (**weary, wearily**) in her pocket for the car keys.

In the first example, *felt* is a linking verb. It should be followed by the adjective *weary,* which describes the subject, *Linda.*

In the second example, *felt* is an action verb. It should be modified by the adverb *wearily,* which tells how Linda performed the action of feeling for the car keys.

Bad/*Badly* and *Good*/*Well*

Two pairs that cause more than their fair share of mistakes are *bad/badly* and *good/well.* We use these words often in everyday speech, and they can sound right even when they aren't.

▶ The adjective *bad* should be used following a linking verb.

Alex felt **bad** about his quarrel with Jan.

Here *bad* means "regretful" or "sorry." In the following example, *bad* means "ill" or "uncomfortable."

The stuffy air in the room made Sally feel **bad**.

▶ *Badly* is used to modify a verb or an adjective.

While trying to carve a wooden bowl, Gwendolyn cut herself **badly**.   (*Badly* modifies the verb *cut*.)

The **badly** frightened child was crying for his mother.   (*Badly* modifies the adjective *frightened*.)

▶ The adjective *good* should be used following a linking verb.

The coat looks **good** on you.

Good modifies the subject, *coat*. Here's another way of saying the same thing:

You look **good** in that coat.

Again *good* modifies the subject, which in this sentence is *you*. In both these examples *good* means "nice" or "attractive."

▶ *Well* is used to modify a verb or an adjective.

The coat fits you **well**.   (*Well* modifies the verb *fits*.)

He is a **well**-known businessman.   (*Well* modifies the adjective *known*.)

▶ *Well* can also be used as an adjective meaning "in good health" or "in satisfactory condition." Here are some examples:

I hope you are feeling **well** today.

Dr. Stein's patient is getting **well** fast.

The watchman walked through the cobblestone streets, swinging his lantern and calling, "Ten o'clock and all's **well**."

Practice A Choose the correct modifier.

Number your paper from 1 to 10. Each sentence that follows has an adjective/adverb pair in parentheses. Choose one of the two modifiers, whichever is correct in the sentence. Write the modifier on your paper next to the number of the sentence.

1. The other team was beaten (bad, badly).
2. Their coach (sure, surely) looked discouraged.
3. The food in this restaurant smells (good, well).
4. Doris's cold is making her feel (miserable, miserably).
5. Louis is afraid that he did (bad, badly) on the exam.
6. The patient is (good, well) enough to sit up in bed.
7. His parents are (real, really) proud of him.
8. I feel (bad, badly) about missing your birthday party.
9. She learned the song (easy, easily).
10. This lemonade tastes (bitter, bitterly).

Practice B Choose the correct verb.

Number your paper from 1 to 10. Each sentence that follows has two verbs in parentheses. Choose either the linking verb or the action verb, whichever makes the sentence correct. Write the verb on your paper next to the number of the sentence.

1. Sara (was, spoke) sad about her dog's death.
2. The seaweed salad (tasted, was tasted) cautiously by the guests.
3. A few of them said it (was, had) a delicious flavor.
4. The other guests (seemed, smiled) weakly and said nothing.
5. Clyde (is, drives) careful most of the time.
6. Tina (sounded, sang) good after she overcame her nervousness.
7. You should not (feel, talk) so guilty about what happened.
8. They (became, protested) angrily when the mayor refused to see them.
9. The defendant (looked, stared) calm as the jury announced its verdict.
10. The ladder (felt, shook) unsteady under my feet.

Practice C   **Write sentences with modifiers.**

Write a sentence of your own for each item below.

EXAMPLES: happy

Robin looked happy as she read the letter.

surely

I was surely surprised to see him.

1. really
2. good
3. well
4. bad
5. badly

L E S S O N   T W O

Comparing Adjectives and Adverbs

Suppose you make this statement:

Bobbie, Lou, and I are **tall**.

You are stating that all three of you have a certain quality—tallness. However, the adjective *tall* does not indicate how much of that quality you and your friends have. Nor does it tell how you compare with each other in tallness.

Now suppose you decide to rank your friends and yourself according to tallness. You make a chart, and it looks like this:

tallness

Bobbie   1
Lou   3
I   2

To compare the three people in words, you would use three forms of the adjective *tall*, like this:

Lou is **tall**.

I am **taller** than Lou.

Bobbie is **taller** than I

Bobbie is the **tallest** of all.

▶ An adjective has three forms, which express three degrees of the quality that the adjective refers to. The three degrees are called the *positive,* the *comparative,* and the *superlative.*

Here are some more examples:

Positive	Comparative	Superlative
weak	weaker	weakest
early	earlier	earliest
careful	more careful	most careful
surprising	more surprising	most surprising

There are two ways to form the comparative and superlative degrees. One way is to add *-er* and *-est* to the end of the adjective. The other way is to put the words *more* and *most* in front of the adjective. The method used depends on the length of the adjective.

▶ An adjective of one syllable takes the endings *-er* and *-est.*

neat	neater	neatest
rough	rougher	roughest

▶ An adjective of three or more syllables takes the words *more* and *most.*

beautiful	more beautiful	most beautiful
interesting	more interesting	most interesting

▶ Adjectives of two syllables vary. Some add *-er* and *-est,* some add *more* and *most,* and some can be compared by both methods.

happy	happier	happiest
famous	more famous	most famous
common	commoner	commonest
common	more common	most common

▶ Many adverbs can be compared, too. Those that can also serve as adjectives are compared with *-er* and *-est*.

Positive	Comparative	Superlative
hard	harder	hardest
late	later	latest
slow	slower	slowest

Other adverbs are compared with *more* and *most*.

suddenly	more suddenly	most suddenly
clearly	more clearly	most clearly

▶ Some adjectives and adverbs form their comparative and superlative degrees in special ways. Here is a list of the most common irregular forms.

good	better	best
well	better	best
bad	worse	worst
badly	worse	worst
little	less, lesser	least
many	more	most
much	more	most
far	farther, further	farthest, furthest

▶ You can compare adjectives and adverbs "downward," too. Just add *less* and *least* in front of the modifier.

fair	less fair	least fair
exciting	less exciting	least exciting
cheerfully	less cheerfully	least cheerfully
gently	less gently	least gently

547

Write comparative and superlative forms of adjectives and adverbs.

Number your paper from 1 to 10. Copy each adjective or adverb that follows. After each modifier, write its comparative and superlative forms.

EXAMPLE: soon

soon, sooner, soonest

1. quietly
2. heavy
3. far
4. discouraging
5. recklessly
6. bad
7. complicated
8. eagerly
9. high
10. well

Practice B **Write sentences with modifiers.**

For each modifier that follows, write one sentence in which you use the modifier correctly.

EXAMPLE: more gently

He handled the cat more gently than he did the dog.

1. cheaper
2. least confusing
3. more quickly
4. stronger
5. best
6. more carefully
7. faster
8. most politely
9. less embarrassed
10. more annoying

L E S S O N   T H R E E

Using Modifiers in Sentences

You will seldom have trouble forming the positive, comparative, or superlative degree of an adjective or adverb. However, you may sometimes have trouble deciding which form is correct in a certain sentence. Here are some rules that will help you avoid mistakes.

▶ To compare two people or things, use the comparative degree. To compare three or more, use the superlative degree.

Marylou is **younger** than Sue.   (Two people are being compared, so the comparative form is used.)

Are these oranges **sweeter** than those?   (Two groups or types of oranges are being compared, so the comparative form is used.)

This flashlight is the **best** of the four I tried.   (Four flashlights are being compared, so the superlative form is used.)

Sometimes writers make the mistake of using the superlative when they are comparing only two items. They say, for example:

You should buy shoes to fit your **largest** foot.

Since a human being has only two feet, the statement should read:

You should buy shoes to fit your **larger** foot.

▶ In comparing one member of a group with other members, include the word *other* or *else*.

The following examples show what happens when these important words are left out of a comparison.

Pete works harder than anyone in his class.

Since Pete is a member of his class, *anyone* refers to him as well as to the other students. Thus, the sentence says that Pete works harder than Pete does. To correct the sentence, add the word *else*.

Pete works harder than anyone **else** in his class.

▶ Do not use the word *any* with a superlative modifier.

When you use a superlative modifier, you are comparing three or more people or things. The word *any* refers to just one person or thing. That's why the following sentence does not make sense.

Jim's story was the funniest of any.

To correct the sentence, substitute *all* for *any*.

Jim's story was the funniest of **all**.

549

▶ Avoid double comparisons.

As you know, there are two ways to form the comparative and superlative degrees of a modifier. You can use the endings *-er* and *-est,* or you can add the words *more* and *most.* When you use both methods with the same modifier, the result is a double comparison. For example:

> This is the **most happiest** day of my life.
>
> He's a lot **more better** at hockey than I am.

To correct these sentences, just remove *most* and *more.*

> This is the **happiest** day of my life.
>
> He's a lot **better** at hockey than I am.

▶ Avoid double negatives.

If you use *not* and *never* together in the same clause, the result is a double negative. If you use either *not* or *never* with another negative word in the same clause, the result is the same—a double negative. The other negative words to watch out for are *no, nobody, no one, none, nowhere, nothing, neither, nor, hardly, barely,* and *scarcely.* Here are some examples:

> You must **not never** forget this rule.
>
> We asked for some more ice cream, but there **wasn't none** left.

The second clause in this sentence combines *not* (in its contracted form, *n't*) and *none.* There are two ways to correct the sentence. You can remove *not.* Or you can remove *none* and substitute *any.*

> We asked for some more ice cream, but there was **none** left.
>
> We asked for some more ice cream, but there **wasn't any** left.
>
> Rudi could **not hardly** walk after he sprained his ankle.

To correct this sentence, remove the adverb *not.*

> Rudi could **hardly** walk after he sprained his ankle.

Practice A   Correct errors in modifiers.

If a sentence is correct as it stands, write *C* after its number on your paper. If it contains an error, rewrite it correctly. In some cases there will be more than one way to correct an error.

EXAMPLE: Which of these two movies is best?

Which of these two movies is better?

1. New York City has many tall buildings, but the World Trade Center towers are the tallest of any.
2. We never shop at that store no more.
3. Both of my eyes are weak, but the right one is the worst.
4. We have scarcely begun to understand our problems, let alone solve them.
5. Cliff eats more slowly than anyone I know.
6. This book is the best of any I have read this year.
7. People who know the twins well say that Martha is the most talented of the two.
8. However, Sue is more friendlier.
9. Scott made more points than any other sophomore.
10. Paul will borrow your records without asking, and he won't return them, neither.

Practice B   Write sentences using modifiers correctly.

For each of the following items, write a sentence illustrating its correct use.

EXAMPLE: anything else

We like the cheese omelet better than anything else on the menu.

1. of all
2. the stronger
3. hardly
4. any other
5. the most expensive.

Misplaced Modifiers

The sentences you write are perfectly clear to you. But are they always clear to your reader? If they contain misplaced modifiers, they may be quite confusing. For example, suppose you wrote a sentence like this:

Fred looked at the person running ahead of him **carefully.**

The sentence seems to say that the person ahead of Fred was running carefully. However, the writer probably meant to say that Fred looked carefully. To make this idea clear, the writer should have placed *carefully* next to *looked*.

Fred looked **carefully** at the person running ahead of him.

P O I N T S   T O   K N O W

▶ A modifier should be placed as close as possible to the word it modifies.

The reason for this rule is that a modifier will attach itself to the nearest word that it can modify. When the nearest word is the wrong word, the modifier is said to be misplaced. Often the result is a joke that the writer never meant to make.

Built of oak and cedar in the early 1800's, I took some beautiful pictures of the covered bridge.

The phrase *built of oak and cedar in the early 1800's* attaches itself to the subject, *I*. But of course it is the covered bridge that is wooden and very old, not the writer. The phrase should be moved close to the noun *bridge*:

Built of oak and cedar in the early 1800's, the covered bridge made a beautiful subject for my camera.

The adjective phrase in the example above begins with a past participle, *built*. Here is a misplaced adjective phrase that begins with a present participle.

Glowing with neon lights, people jammed the amusement park.

This sentence says that the people were glowing with neon lights. The following correction puts the lights where they belong.

Glowing with neon lights, the amusement park was jammed with people.

The next sentence contains a misplaced prepositional phrase.

Phyllis watched the pitcher wind up and throw the ball **through her binoculars.**

The prepositional phrase *through her binoculars* should modify *watched,* not *throw.*

Through her binoculars Phyllis watched the pitcher wind up and throw the ball.

The misplaced modifier in the next example is also a prepositional phrase. However, this phrase is more complicated. The preposition, *after,* is followed by a gerund, *running.*

After running seventy yards for the winning touchdown, Hugh's teammates carried him off the field on their shoulders.

As you know, a gerund is the -*ing* form of a verb used as a noun. Since it is a verb form, a gerund expresses action. A person or a thing mentioned in the sentence performs the action. Who or what seems to perform the action of the gerund *running* in this sentence? It sounds as if all of Hugh's teammates ran for the touchdown. However, we know that they couldn't have done that. In the following improved version, Hugh does the running.

After running seventy yards for the winning touchdown, Hugh was carried off the field on his teammates' shoulders.

The next example has a misplaced elliptical clause. You probably remember studying elliptical clauses in Unit Twenty-five. An elliptical clause is one from which one or more words have been omitted. The reader mentally fills in the missing word or words. However, when the elliptical clause is put in the wrong place in the sentence, the reader is likely to fill in the wrong word.

When first released, the critics raved about this movie.

The main thing lacking in this elliptical clause is a subject. The closest word that can serve as a subject is *critics*. Thus, the reader might complete the clause this way:

When they were first released, the critics raved about this movie.

Of course the writer means that the movie was released. The following correction makes the idea clear:

When this movie was first released, the critics raved about it.

Our last example contains a misplaced appositive. Strictly speaking, an appositive is not a modifier. It is a noun or pronoun that is placed next to another noun or pronoun to identify or explain it. Like a misplaced modifier, however, a misplaced appositive can cause trouble in your writing. Usually it will either confuse or amuse your reader.

A gooey mess, I had to eat the fudge with a spoon.

Although the writer may have been a gooey mess, he or she didn't mean to say so. The appositive belongs with the noun *fudge*.

A gooey mess, my fudge had to be eaten with a spoon.

or

The fudge was a gooey mess that I had to eat with a spoon.

Practice A   Place modifiers correctly.

Each item that follows contains a modifier plus two or three groups of words in parentheses. From the groups of words in parentheses, choose the one that combines correctly with the modifier. Together, the modifier and the chosen group of words should make a correct sentence. Write the whole sentence on your paper.

EXAMPLE: While driving east toward the sunrise, (the sky turned pink/we saw the sky turn pink).

While driving east toward the sunrise, we saw the sky turn pink.

1. Bored by the long wait, (a book that had been left on the bench caught my attention/I picked up a book that had been left on the bench).

2. Sitting in the highest row at the circus, (they felt as if they were watching toy elephants/the elephants looked like toys to them).

3. Cold and hungry, (the last mile seemed like ten to the hikers/the hikers thought the last mile seemed like ten).

4. While visiting my aunt, (the announcer on the radio said a storm was coming/I heard the announcer on the radio say a storm was coming).

5. Standing on the curb, (Sheila was splashed with muddy water by a car/a car splashed muddy water on Sheila).

6. As a new subscriber, (the cost of the magazine to you will be only forty cents a copy/the magazine will cost you only forty cents a copy/you will pay only forty cents a copy for the magazine).

7. Having gotten over the shame of being late, (the party began to be fun/we began to have fun at the party).

8. After making the beds, (the roar of the vacuum cleaner frightened the kitten/I frightened the kitten with the roar of the vacuum cleaner/the kitten was frightened by the roar of the vacuum cleaner).

9. Learned by heart, (you will be comforted by this poem in times of trouble/this poem will comfort you in times of trouble).

10. When cleaned and pressed, (you will look much better in the suit/the suit will look much better on you).

555

Practice B Correct misplaced modifiers and appositives.

On your paper rewrite each of the ten following sentences. Correct the misplaced modifiers and appositives. You may change the wording of the sentence if necessary.

EXAMPLE: Leaning out of the window, the street below me was filled with soldiers.

Leaning out the window, I saw that the street below was filled with soldiers.

1. The toothbrush in the green glass with the extra-soft bristles is mine.

2. Having studied hard, Elaine's answers to the questions were all correct.

3. Buried deep in the tool chest, Cass found the wrench.

4. Now serving her second term as a senator, Mrs. Stanhope's record is excellent.

5. By saving money now, Charlie's chances of going to college will be improved.

6. An ambitious person, working long hours does not bother my cousin.

7. When tacked on the bulletin board, the children will learn all about dogs from this colorful poster.

8. Dry and tasteless, Ben threw the peach into the garbage can.

9. Doreen likes to watch her favorite TV newscaster sitting cross-legged on the floor.

10. The student leaning against the lamppost with the tall fur hat is the drum major of the band.

R E V I E W   E X E R C I S E S

I. Choosing Between Adjectives and Adverbs Number your paper from 1 to 10. In each sentence, choose the correct modifier from the two in parentheses. Write the chosen modifier on your paper after the number of the sentence. (Lesson One)

1. I thought the book was (real, really) interesting.
2. Except for a slight cough, Uncle Ed feels quite (good, well).
3. It is natural to feel (bad, badly) when you lose an election.
4. Carrie looked (hopeless, hopelessly) at the scoreboard.
5. The law says you must drive through the tunnel (slow, slowly).
6. I'm afraid I did (poor, poorly) on my English test.
7. Henry was (sure, surely) disappointed when the concert was cancelled.
8. Joanna seems to learn very (quick, quickly).
9. Whenever I baby-sit for Mrs. Collins, the children behave (good, well).
10. Ladd solved the problem (easy, easily).

II. Comparing Adjectives and Adverbs Number your paper from 1 to 10. For each sentence, choose the correct form of the modifier in parentheses. Write the modifier on your paper after the number of the sentence. (Lesson Two)

EXAMPLE: This year my friends play badminton _____ than they did last year.   (well)

better

1. Tara is not exactly unfriendly, but she is _____ than her brother.   (friendly)

2. That is the _____ joke I have ever heard.   (bad)

3. Which spacecraft has traveled the _____ from Earth?   (far)

4. In a relay race, should the _____ runner on the team go first or last?   (fast)

5. According to her class yearbook, Kirsten was voted "_____ to remain calm in a crisis."   (likely)

6. Sam plans his time _____ than he used to.   (carefully)

7. My room is usually the _____ in the house.   (messy)

8. This mouthwash was not very effective; in fact, it was the _____ we have ever tried.   (effective)

9. As the _____ employee, Ken is given all the jobs that the others don't want to do.   (new)

10. If you get there _____ than I do, save me a seat.   (early)

III. Using Modifiers in Sentences Number your paper from 1 to 10. If the italicized expression in a sentence is correct, write *C* after the number of the sentence. If the italicized expression is incorrect, rewrite it correctly on your paper. (Lesson Three)

EXAMPLE: These socks are the most popular of *any type we sell*.

of all the types we sell

1. She married *the youngest* of the two brothers.

2. I bet I walk *more farther* every day than you do.

3. Which is *worst*, being criticized or being ignored?

4. You *haven't hardly* had the chance to sit down all day.

557

5. Milton eats *more than anybody* in his family.
6. Herb will take either the selling job or the job with the phone company, whichever opens up *sooner*.
7. My new shoes are *more comfortable than any* I own.
8. The neighbors *never see no lights* in the house at nights.
9. Betty has *the best handwriting of any student* in her class.
10. *The most highest praise* he ever gives is "pretty good."

IV. Misplaced Modifiers Each sentence below contains one or more modifiers or appositives. If the sentence is correct as it stands, write *C* after its number on your paper. If any modifier or appositive is misplaced, rewrite the sentence correctly on your paper. You may change the wording of the sentence if necessary. (Lesson Four)

EXAMPLE: Lying in our sleeping bags, the stars shone brightly.
Lying in our sleeping bags, we gazed up at the brightly shining stars.

1. She glanced at my book about jogging with a smile.
2. A shy animal, Dr. Lee is in China studying the giant panda.
3. He struck a match and leaned over to light the candles in his broad-brimmed hat.
4. Anxious to say the right thing, my heart was beating hard as the interviewer questioned me.
5. Convinced that her son was still alive, the news came as a terrible shock to the woman.
6. Lifting the cover of the box, the rich smell of chocolate tempted me.
7. If captured by the enemy, your name, rank, and serial number are the only information you should give.
8. While unlocking her door, Valya's phone began to ring.
9. The only dentist in town, you must wait weeks for an appointment with Dr. Doshi.
10. Wearing patched jeans, the boy sped along on his bicycle.

Using Modifiers Correctly in Your Writing

You use modifiers all the time when you speak and write. In fact, it would be difficult to communicate without them. However, as you have seen in this unit, using a modifier incorrectly can result in miscommunication.

Since the basic reason for writing and speaking is to communicate ideas, it's important to know and use the rules of our language correctly. The exercise that follows will give you a chance to practice using modifiers.

Practice   **Write a paragraph using modifiers correctly.**

Write a paragraph of at least ten sentences comparing three people, three places, or three things. The three people might be friends, relatives, or celebrities. The three places might be parks, shopping malls, or movie theaters. The three things might be cameras, computers, or cats. Use adjectives and adverbs wisely, and be sure you have placed all modifiers where they belong.

Punctuation

A view of mountains near Ahmadabad, India, 1965
Henri Cartier-Bresson, Magnum Photos, Inc.

Punctuation

You know how important traffic and road signs are. As you drive along, the signs constantly give you information and advice:

CENTER LANE MUST TURN LEFT

CITY LIMITS

STOP

PASS WITH CARE

Signs and signals are important when you read, too. Of course, the signs in printed material are small, unimpressive marks like commas and periods. But these punctuation marks constantly give you information and advice:

The sentence stops here.   (period)

Is this a question?   (question mark)

"This is a direct quotation."   (quotation marks)

What happens when you write? Then you're the one who gives the signals—*punctuation marks*—for others to follow. You can make your reader's task easier by putting the right signs in the right places.

LESSON ONE

End Punctuation

There are three punctuation marks that can come at the end of a sentence. They are the period (.), the question mark (?), and the exclamation point (!). The mark you choose depends on the type of sentence you are writing.

▶ A sentence that makes a statement or declares something is called a *declarative sentence*. It ends with a period.

> The capital of Kentucky is Frankfort.
>
> Theda is a splendid actress.

▶ A sentence that asks a question is called an *interrogative sentence*. It ends with a question mark.

> Did you like the movie?
>
> Where are your friends?

▶ A sentence that makes a request or gives an order is called an *imperative sentence*. It ends with a period or an exclamation point.

> Please don't leave.
>
> Take off your hat!

▶ A sentence that states something with emphasis or emotion is called an *exclamatory sentence*. It ends with an exclamation point.

> What a miserable day!
>
> Our team won the championship!

Practice   Add end punctuation.

563

The sentences that follow do not have end punctuation. On your paper, copy each sentence and add the correct end punctuation.

EXAMPLE: Please help me set the table

Please help me set the table.

1. Is this all that's left of the pie
2. Tell me about your adventure in Peru
3. Two's company, but three's a crowd
4. The building's on fire
5. Leontyne Price is singing in the opera *Aida* this evening
6. Watch out for that car

7. Sally is trying to figure out her income tax

8. A whale is a mammal, not a fish

9. Isn't that the letter you were supposed to mail

10. What a fine picture you've drawn

L E S S O N   T W O

Abbreviations

An abbreviation is the shortened version of a word or phrase. People use abbreviations in order to save both space and time. Following are some of the rules for abbreviations.

P O I N T S   T O   K N O W

▶ Periods are used after most abbreviations of words.

Co. (Company)

Corp. (Corporation)

Inc. (Incorporated)

Ltd. (Limited)

qt. quart

kg. kilogram

▶ Periods are used with initials and with abbreviated titles of people.

Mr. Alfred Newman   **Gov.** John B. Swainson

Ms. Rita Malone   **Sen.** William Proxmire

T. H. White   **Prof.** H. Evalyn Baron

▶ A period is used with the abbreviations for *senior* and *junior*.

Christopher T. Adams, **Sr.**

Christopher T. Adams, **Jr.**

▶ Periods may be used with the abbreviation of an organization's name. However, the trend today is toward leaving out the periods.

YWCA (Young Women's Christian Association)

SAG (Screen Actors' Guild)

CIA (Central Intelligence Agency)

ABC (American Broadcasting Company)

Exception: Periods are always used in the abbreviation for the United States: U.S.

▶ Periods are usually left out of acronyms. An acronym is a set of initials pronounced as a word.

ZIP code (Zone Improvement Plan)

NATO (North Atlantic Treaty Organization)

▶ Use a period after an abbreviation in an address.

Senate Office **Bldg.** (Building)	Filbert **St.** (Street)
Apt. 17B (Apartment)	Sidney **Blvd.** (Boulevard)
Clove **Rd.** (Road)	Yute **Pkwy.** (Parkway)
Sixth **Ave.** (Avenue)	Juniper **Dr.** (Drive)

▶ In postal ZIP codes, names of states and names of Canadian provinces are indicated by two capital letters without periods.

NY (New York)	**AZ** (Arizona)
ME (Maine)	**ON** (Ontario)

▶ Periods are used with abbreviated expressions of time.

4:00 **a.m.** or **A.M.** (Latin *ante meridiem,* "before noon")

6:15 **p.m.** or **P.M.** (Latin *post meridiem,* "after noon")

16 **B.C.** (before Christ)

A.D. 1984 (Latin *anno Domini,* "year of our Lord")

▶ In informal writing the year is sometimes abbreviated. An apostrophe takes the place of the first two numbers.

the class of **'86**

the summer of **'42**

the stock market crash of **'29**

However, if there is a chance that a reader might be confused by your abbreviation, do not abbreviate the year. For example, when you refer to the stock market crash of '29, you mean 1929. But if your reader might think you are referring to a stock market crash in 1829, you should write out the complete date:

the stock market crash of 1929

Practice A   Write abbreviations correctly.

Copy the following 10 items on your paper. Correct any items that are incorrect.

1. Esther M Potter
2. York Ave
3. Main St
4. Skyview Pkwy
5. Ms Holly Hunter

6. 7:10 p.m.
7. 16 BC
8. Dr. Paul Daniels
9. Z.I.P. code
10. Calvin Webster, Jr

Practice B   Write sentences.

Write ten sentences. In each sentence include at least one abbreviaton.

L E S S O N   T H R E E

Commas in Sentences

Commas can be very helpful to the reader, especially in a long or complicated sentence. However, you should use commas only when they are needed to serve a specific purpose.

P O I N T S   T O   K N O W

▶ Use commas where they are needed to separate words in a series.

The fisherman caught bluefish, grouper, and tilefish.
After supper we talked, sang, and told jokes.
Kevin spoke in a low, rumbling, grouchy voice.

In the sentence about Kevin, the three words that are separated by commas are adjectives. But not all adjectives in a series need commas. Look at the following examples.

The old electric train still ran after ten years.

Here there is no comma between *old* and *electric*. The reason is that *old* and *electric* are not two adjectives of equal rank, both modifying the noun *train*. Instead, *electric* has a special relationship with *train*. The two words are so closely linked that they form a single unit of thought. The adjective *old* modifies the unit *electric train*.

A cute little dog raced up to us.

The adjective *cute* modifies the unit *little dog*; therefore, no comma is needed.

▶ Use commas where they are needed to separate phrases in a series.

We saw a herd of goats, a flock of birds, and a swarm of bees.

Horses with ribbons, elephants in sequins, and camels in blue blankets walked in the parade.

▶ Use commas where they are needed to separate clauses in a series.

Some of the students walk to school, some come on the bus, and some ride bicycles.

Notice that a comma is placed before the conjunction *and* in a series. Leaving out the comma before the conjunction can lead to confusion. Here is an example:

You may choose two vegetables from a list that includes green beans, cauliflower, beets, corn, potatoes, peas and carrots.

That sentence is not clear. Are the peas and carrots served together as one dish? Or do they count as two vegetables? A comma clears up the confusion:

You may choose two vegetables from a list that includes green beans, cauliflower, beets, corn, potatoes, peas, and carrots.

The comma before *and* separates the peas and carrots into two dishes.

▶ Use a comma after an introductory word or phrase.

Yes, I'll be there.
However, I may be late.
Unfortunately, it's time to leave.

▶ Use a comma after an adjective or series of adjectives, after an adjective phrase, or after an appositive that begins a sentence.

Angered, the girl slammed the door.
Slim and graceful, the dancer walked onto the stage.
His smile widening, my brother listened to the coach's words.
Jumping to their feet, the fans cheered wildly.
An excellent swimmer, Steve is learning how to dive.

▶ Use a comma after an adverbial infinitive phrase that begins a sentence.

To build a fire, first get some dry wood.

Most other adverbial phrases do not need to be followed by a comma:

Here and there you will find clues to the mystery.
Before dinner you'd better clean your room.

▶ Use a comma after an adverbial clause that begins a sentence.

After the thunder cracked, the group headed for shelter.
When we saw you, we thought you were ill.
Although it is snowing, we can still go outdoors.

▶ Use a comma to set off a name used in direct address. If the name comes in the middle of the sentence, use two commas.

Talia, where have you been?
I'm sorry, Greg, that you had to wait.
Are you leaving now, Dr. Tyler?

▶ Use a comma before the coordinating conjunction in a compound sentence.

Ice is good for a burn, but butter will not help.
Mr. Prather met us for lunch, and then we went to a movie.

The comma may be left out if the clauses are short:

> We bowed and they applauded.
>
> It's dark and I'm frightened.

▶ Use commas to set off *nonessential* phrases and clauses. Do not use commas to set off *essential* phrases and clauses.

An **essential** phrase or clause identifies the noun or pronoun it refers to. It answers the question *which one?*

> The house where I was born has been torn down.

The clause *where I was born* is essential to the meaning of the noun it modifies, *house*. The clause is essential because it tells the reader which house the speaker is referring to.

A **nonessential** phrase or clause does not identify the noun it refers to. The meaning of the noun is clear without the phrase or clause.

> Warren G. Harding, who was considered a weak President, coined the word "normalcy."

Here the clause adds information about Harding, but it is not essential to the meaning of the sentence. Without the clause the sentence would still make sense:

> Warren G. Harding coined the word "normalcy."

Following are some more examples of nonessential phrases.

> The boat, with its deck freshly painted, waited for us at the dock.
>
> Their dog, the winner of many prizes for obedience, chewed a hole in my rug.

▶ Use commas to set off interrupting words in a sentence.

> This is, I believe, your last chance.
>
> I wonder, however, how long this will last.
>
> Rex decided, finally, to see a dentist.

▶ Use a comma between an expression like *he said* and a direct quotation that follows it.

> He said, "That cat belongs to the neighbors."
>
> I asked, "How are you feeling today?"

▶ Use a comma whenever one is needed to avoid confusion.

I fed the dog, and my mother bathed it.

Anyone who laughed then, was laughing to keep from crying.

Practice A   Add commas.

Rewrite the following sentences on your paper, adding commas where they are needed.

EXAMPLE: Entering the fairgrounds we stared in amazement.

Entering the fairgrounds, we stared in amazement.

1. We went to the fair in the morning in the afternoon and again in the evening.
2. Going from booth to booth we sampled many kinds of food.
3. Some of the rides especially one called the Whip looked too scary to me.
4. Jeremy his family and the ticket-seller said "Try it!"
5. Because the ride went very high I knew I didn't want to risk it.
6. Dangling high in the air one of the customers began to scream.
7. I said to the ticket-seller "No that ride is not for me."
8. I could see my life which had barely begun ending that very day on the Whip.
9. Even Jeremy's father Mr. Ryan couldn't get me to go.
10. Mr. Ryan as a matter of fact began to look worried himself.
11. Finally each of us decided to go on either the Whip the Monster or the Crusher.
12. These names probably invented by former customers were good descriptions of the rides.
13. The screeching roaring Monster was my choice.
14. I thought that ride was going to remove my shoes my socks and even my stomach.
15. However I kept all three and I even went on the ride again.

Practice B   Write sentences with commas.

Write five sentences, following the directions below.

EXAMPLE: Write a compound sentence with a coordinating conjunction.

The movie was disturbing, but it had an important message.

1. Write a sentence that contains a series.
2. Write a sentence with an introductory word.
3. Write a sentence that begins with an adverbial clause.
4. Write a sentence that includes a name used in direct address.
5. Write a sentence that contains an interrupting word or words.

L E S S O N   F O U R

Other Uses of Commas

In Lesson Three you practiced using commas to make the meaning of a sentence clearer. In this lesson you will learn a different kind of use for the comma. The rules that follow tell you to use commas in letters, addresses, and dates. These commas do not affect the meaning of what you write. Using them in these places is just a matter of custom.

P O I N T S   T O   K N O W

▶ Use a comma after the greeting of a friendly letter.

   Dear Erica,

▶ Use a comma after the closing of a friendly or business letter.

Sincerely,   As ever,
Yours truly,   Your friend,

▶ Use a comma to separate the city and the state in an address.

   San Francisco, California 94121
   Minneapolis, Minnesota 55417

Notice that a comma is not used to separate the state and the ZIP code.

▶ When you write a sentence in which you refer to a city and its state or country, set off the state or country with commas.

We'll travel to Milan, Italy, next summer.

▶ When writing a date, use a comma to separate the day from the year. If the year comes in the middle of the sentence, put a comma after it, too.

We met on October 1, 1974, soon after I moved here.

If you are writing only the month and the year, a comma between the two is acceptable but not necessary.

The accident took place in April, 1986.

The accident took place in April 1986.

Practice **Add commas.**

On your paper, copy each of the ten items below. Insert commas where they are needed.

1. Mr. Frederick M. Marston
   50 Gramercy Park Drive
   Bowling Green Kentucky 12345
2. Dear Fred
3. Sincerely yours
4. Vienna Austria has been the home of many great composers.
5. Orville Wright was born on August 19 1871 in Dayton Ohio.
6. Dear Aunt Marian
7. Our ship sailed along the Inland Passage from Puget Sound Washington to Skagway Alaska.
8. 300 East 19th Street
   Beanblossom Indiana 54321
   May 24 1984
9. Is there any other city besides New York New York that is located in a state of the same name?
10. Your friend

Semicolons

Semicolons are used to separate words and phrases from each other. The semicolon is stronger than the comma, but not as strong as the period. The following rules will help you use semicolons correctly.

P O I N T S   T O   K N O W

▶ Use a semicolon between independent clauses in a compound sentence when there is no conjunction.

The salmon are swimming upstream; I see them every day now.

In this sentence the semicolon takes the place of a comma and a coordinating conjunction.

▶ Use a semicolon instead of a comma before a coordinating conjunction when the clauses are long. Also use a semicolon when there are commas within the clauses.

Our house has been damaged by fire, eaten by termites, and shaken by hurricanes; and now it faces a visit from twin boys.

▶ Use a semicolon between two independent clauses when the second clause is introduced by a word like *however, nevertheless, thus, therefore*, or *consequently*.

Jennie was eager to move to New York to begin a career; however, Muriel persuaded her to think it over.

▶ Use semicolons to separate items in a series when one or more of the items contain commas.

Three people who won blue ribbons at the county fair were Jim, who grew a giant squash; Lulu, who baked the best cherry pie; and Sal, who raised a beautiful cow.

Among the state capitals that were named for people are Madison, Wisconsin, named for President James Madison; Juneau, Alaska, named for a man who discovered gold there, Joe Juneau; and Bismarck, North Dakota, named in honor of the German statesman Otto von Bismarck.

▶ Use semicolons in place of commas when commas might cause confusion.

We visited Knoxville; the capital of North Carolina; and Washington, D.C.

Practice A   **Add semicolons.**

On your paper copy each sentence, putting in semicolons where needed. In some places you will be replacing a comma with a semicolon.

EXAMPLE: For six days Tony shopped unsuccessfully for a new coat finally he decided to wear his old one.

For six days Tony shopped unsuccessfully for a new coat; finally, he decided to wear his old one.

1. His father was Spanish, therefore, he learned at an early age to love Spanish food.
2. The members of the quartet are Dolores Ricci, soprano, Janine Godfrey, contralto, Larry Morton, tenor, and Charles Hao, bass.
3. I disliked the movie that you raved so much about that is, I disliked most of it.
4. The author, Mary Hinkein, of Wilmington, Delaware, is primarily a poet however, this book is about space travel and time warps.
5. The mayor handed out these awards: first prize, a vacation in San Juan, Puerto Rico, second prize, a home computer game, third prize, a bicycle.
6. Winter will be here soon it's time to put in the storm windows.
7. I have driven to Wyoming, flown in a plane to London, and ridden a horse across most of Colorado, but I don't know how to ride a bike.
8. The people who run the theater told us that the movie was terrific they were wrong.
9. Olive had a cramp in her left leg during most of the marathon nevertheless, she managed to keep going till she reached the finish line.
10. Vernon's cousin has a part in the school play he is very excited.

Write sentences with semicolons.

Follow the directions below for writing sentences of your own. You may look back at the rules and sample sentences if you need to.

EXAMPLE: Write a compound sentence with two independent clauses and no coordinating conjunction.

I put my eye to the peephole and peered out; there was no one there.

1. Write a compound sentence with two independent clauses and no coordinating conjunction.

2. Write a compound sentence with two independent clauses. Start the second clause with *however, nevertheless*, or *therefore*.

3. Write a sentence that contains a series of proper nouns. The proper nouns should be the names of cities and their states.

L E S S O N   S I X

Quotation Marks

Quotation marks are used to enclose direct quotations. A *direct quotation* repeats the exact words that were spoken by the person being quoted. Here is an example:

"I don't like soap operas," said Richard.

The words inside the quotation marks are the exact words that Richard spoke.

Here are the rules for using quotation marks:

P O I N T S   T O   K N O W

▶   Use quotation marks to enclose a direct quotation.

The principal said, "You are doing much better in English this semester. Your writing has really improved."
I replied, "Thank you. I'm trying hard."

Notice that quotation marks are placed both before and after the exact words of a speaker. Notice, too, that a new paragraph begins every time a different person speaks.

▶ Do not use quotation marks around an indirect quotation. An *indirect quotation* does not repeat the speaker's exact words. It presents the speaker's main idea in slightly different words.

The principal told me that I was doing better this semester.

▶ Use two sets of quotation marks when a quotation is broken into two parts.

"I can see the bus coming," she called. "Hurry up!"

"Well," Jim said, "let's not quarrel about it."

In the first example, the first word of the second part is capitalized because it starts a new sentence. In the second example, the first word of the second part is not capitalized because it does not start a new sentence.

▶ Use quotation marks to enclose exactly quoted words and phrases taken from a speaker's statement. Since the quoted words are not the speaker's complete statement, the quotation does not start with a capital letter.

Robert Frost spoke of home as "the place where, when you have to go there, they have to take you in."

The candidate described himself as "the way-down-under dog" in the race.

▶ Use single quotation marks (' ') to enclose a quotation within a quotation.

Mary said, "Robert Frost also wrote, 'Something there is that doesn't love a wall.' "

Mary's words are enclosed in double quotation marks. The words of Robert Frost that Mary quoted are enclosed in single quotation marks.

▶ Use quotation marks to enclose the definition of a word.

To me, the word *obstinate* means "thickheaded."

▶ Place a period or a comma inside the closing quotation marks.

The announcer said, "It's time for the show."

"This should be good," Roy whispered.

▶ If a question mark or exclamation point is part of the quotation, place it inside the closing quotation marks.

"What a strange creature!" the crowd murmured.

Sybil asked, "Why are you here?"

▶ If the entire sentence is a question or an exclamation, place the question mark or exclamation point outside the quotation marks.

Did you say, "Una has to leave"?

The actor was supposed to say, "Forgive me—I bet the money," but he got mixed up and said, "Forgive me—I met the bunny"!

▶ Place a semicolon or a colon outside the quotation marks.

The captain of the plane announced, "Passengers on the right will have a good view of the Statue of Liberty"; but I was on the left.

The following people will give a dramatic reading of "Casey at the Bat": José, Sylvia, Barbara, Clyde, and Bruce.

▶ Use quotation marks to enclose titles of short works, such as songs, short stories, poems, chapters of books, newspaper and magazine articles, and television programs (but not television series).

"Blue Moon"   (song)

"June Recital"   (short story)

"Ode to Autumn"   (poem)

"The Digestive System"   (chapter of a book)

"The Mysterious Stranger"   (television program)

Practice A   Add quotation marks.

Copy the sentences and add the necessary quotation marks.

EXAMPLE: Wally said, The dance is tomorrow.
Wally said, "The dance is tomorrow."

1. Did you see Edith Has Jury Duty on television last night?
2. I have just finished a story entitled Thomas Edison's Dog.
3. I saw that movie and came out humming the song Hopelessly Devoted to You.

4. The police officer kept repeating, You're under arrest; the suspect kept yelling, I haven't done anything!

5. The teacher asked, Have you ever read the story The Monkey's Paw?

6. I heard the waiter say, Are you the gentleman who asked for soda water?

7. The article in *Newsweek* was called France's Close Election.

8. Look out! I cried.

9. The President said, This is going to be a difficult year; he was right.

10. Rory said, I've always loved that famous line from Patrick Henry's speech: Give me liberty or give me death!

Practice B   **Write sentences with quotation marks.**

Follow the instructions below for writing sentences of your own.

EXAMPLE: Write a sentence that includes the title of a song.

Mike has a record of Judy Garland singing "Over the Rainbow."

1. Write a sentence that includes the title of a short story.

2. Write a sentence with a quotation in which *he said* or *she said* breaks the quotation into two parts.

3. Write a sentence that includes the title of a chapter of a book.

4. Write a sentence that includes a quotation within a quotation.

5. Write a sentence that includes an indirect quotation.

6. Write a sentence in which you quote someone warning another person of danger.

7. Write two sentences in which you quote a conversation between two people.

8. Write a sentence in which you quote someone asking a question.

9. Write a sentence in which you quote one word or a few words taken from a person's statement.

10. Write a sentence that includes a famous quotation.

Apostrophes

A small punctuation mark that does three important jobs is the apostrophe ('). It is used to show possession, to form contractions, and to form the plurals of letters, numbers, and symbols. Study the following rules so you will be able to use apostrophes correctly.

P O I N T S   T O   K N O W

▶ To make most singular nouns possessive, add an apostrophe and an *s* ('*s*).

> the cat**'s** paw
>
> the team**'s** victory

What should you do if a noun already ends in *s* or *z*? Should you add '*s*? Say the word out loud. If adding '*s* makes the word awkward to pronounce, add only an apostrophe. This rule applies to nouns of two or more syllables. However, some two-syllable nouns are correct either way.

> Achilles**'** heel
>
> Miss Jabez**'** coat
>
> Miss Jabez**'s** coat

▶ To form the possessive of a plural noun ending in *s*, add only an apostrophe.

> the ducks**'** food
>
> our cousins**'** house
>
> the Joneses**'** car

Some nouns have an irregular plural form that does not end in *s*. For example, the plural of *woman* is *women*. The plural of *mouse* is *mice*. In these cases, treat the plural noun as if it were singular and add an apostrophe and an *s*.

> women**'s** rights
>
> mice**'s** tracks

▶ To make a compound noun possessive, add an apostrophe and an *s* or an apostrophe alone at the end of the compound.

my father-in-law**'s** office

the Princess of Wales**'** wardrobe

▶ To show that two or more persons or things possess something together, add the sign of possession to the last name mentioned. This rule also applies to names of companies and organizations.

Bill and Ken**'s** canoe

Procter and Gamble**'s** products

However, when two or more persons or things own something separately, add the possessive ending to each noun.

Tim**'s** and Mark**'s** shoes

the Harrises**'** and the Fernandez**'** cars

▶ Remember that possessive pronouns already show ownership and never require an apostrophe.

The bird brought food to **its** mate.

Other possessive pronouns are *hers, his, ours, yours*, and *theirs*.

▶ Use an apostrophe to show where a letter or figure has been omitted. When two or more words are combined in a *contraction*, the second word loses one or more letters. For example:

you + will = you'll   (The *w* and *i* are omitted.)

should + not = shouldn't   (The *o* is omitted.)

▶ In the following phrases, figures have been omitted:

the class of '84

the spring of '73

▶ Use an apostrophe and an *s* to form the plural of a number, sign, letter, or word referred to as a word.

There are four **7's** in his address.

You've used too many *very's* in this paragraph.

Practice A   Choose the correctly spelled word.

Number your paper from 1 to 10. In each sentence below choose the correctly written word in parentheses. Write the word next to the number of the sentence.

1. (Is'nt, Isn't) that your friend Alonzo?
2. My (sister's-in-law, sister-in-law's) job pays well.
3. (Josie and Steven's, Josie's and Steven's) families are great friends.
4. All the (church's, churches') schedules are printed in the Saturday paper.
5. (It's, Its) a long way to Houston from here.
6. I know that (childrens', children's) shoes are expensive.
7. You haven't crossed all of your (ts', t's).
8. The (fox's, foxes') den is empty; they must be out hunting.
9. Is this book (your's, yours)?
10. That (record's, records) sales have been amazing.

Practice B   Form words with apostrophes. Form possessives and contractions.

In each sentence that follows there is an italicized word or phrase. Change each italicized word or phrase so that it contains an apostrophe. Rewrite the whole sentence on your paper. You will have to add or leave out one or more words when rewriting some sentences.

EXAMPLES: The car that belongs to *Dad* is his pride and joy.
Dad's car is his pride and joy.

You *will not* be disappointed.
You won't be disappointed.

1. *We are* going to the track meet this Friday.
2. The songs of *Rodgers and Hammerstein* are among my favorites.
3. The class of *1979* gave the school this drinking fountain.
4. The answers of *those witnesses* were not convincing.
5. I buy the products of *Joseph and Herron*.
6. The tennis racquets of *the men* were stolen.

7. The paintings of *Rembrandt* are priceless.

8. *She is* far from home, and she cannot find her way.

9. The hats of *Miss Estey and Mr. Tomlin* were blown away.

10. *Was not* the temperature above 100 at this time last year?

L E S S O N   E I G H T

Other Punctuation Marks

In this lesson you'll learn the correct uses of four other punctuation marks: the colon (:), the dash (—), the hyphen (-), and parentheses ( ). You will also learn the correct use of italics (underlining).

P O I N T S   T O   K N O W

Colon

▶ Use a colon to introduce a list.

He made the following promises: to be on time, to be better organized, and to laugh more often.

Four film stars here tonight have won Academy Awards: Diane Keaton, Warren Beatty, Sally Field, and Woody Allen.

▶ Use a colon to separate hours and minutes when writing the time.

You can be booked on a flight at 6:43 p.m. or 5:01 a.m.

▶ Use a colon after the greeting in a business letter.

Dear Senator Bush: Dear Ms. Jason:

Dash

▶ The dash is sometimes used instead of a colon to introduce a list. Both of the following sentences are correct.

You'll need a few items for the trip: sturdy shoes, a map, and your lunch.

You'll need a few items for the trip—sturdy shoes, a map, and your lunch.

▶ A dash may also be used to show a sudden break in thought.

The teacher said, "If Tommy Sperling were here—by the way, where *is* Tommy Sperling?"

▶ A pair of dashes may be used in place of a pair of commas to emphasize the word or words enclosed.

We were late, and we ran to the train—which, fortunately, hadn't left yet—as fast as we could.

As the carnival began, hundreds of small children—their faces bright with joy—gathered at the entrance.

Hyphen

▶ When you must break a word at the end of a line, use a hyphen (-) to show that the word is completed on the next line. In the following example, the hyphen shows the reader that *light* is only part of the word.

We sat at the window and watched the lightning make jagged cracks in the sky.

Always break a word between syllables, never within a syllable. This rule means that a word having only one syllable cannot be broken at the end of a line. The hyphen in the following example is incorrect because *blamed* has only one syllable.

I can't understand why everyone in the class blamed me for what happened.

▶ Use a hyphen with compound numbers from twenty-one to ninety-nine and with fractions used as adjectives.

He was the thirty-first principal of our school.

We counted forty-two ducks in the pond.

To change the rules of the club, we must get a two-thirds majority to agree.

Parentheses

▶ Use parentheses to set off explanatory material in a sentence.

Martin Luther King, Jr. (1929-1968) was awarded the Nobel Peace Prize in 1964.

Deer can run up to 40 miles an hour (65 kilometers an hour).

A recent poll shows that the candidate is preferred by 56 percent of women voters (see chart below).

Italics

In Lesson Six of this unit you learned that quotation marks are used to enclose the titles of short works. *Italics* (slanted letters) are used by printers to set off titles of long works such as books, films, plays, and television series. The names of newspapers and magazines are also italicized in most printed publications. (This rule does not apply to the Bible.)

When you are typing or writing by hand, underline words that would be italicized in print.

▶ Italicize titles of long works.

The House of the Seven Gables   (book)

The Maltese Falcon   (movie)

Morning's at Seven   (play)

Good Morning America   (television series)

Rigoletto   (opera)

The *Atlanta Constitution*   (newspaper)

Do not italicize the word *the* before the name of a newspaper or magazine unless *the* is part of the official title.

▶ Italicize foreign words.

The *gendarmes* (policemen) of Paris are a familiar sight to tourists.

▶ For words referred to as words, you may use either italics or quotation marks.

Did I hear the word "lunch"?

Did I hear the word *lunch*?

In England the hood of a car is called the "bonnet."

In England the hood of a car is called the *bonnet*.

▶ Italicize the names of ships, trains, and planes.

Captain Bligh commanded the *Bounty*.

Would you like to ride on the *Orient Express*?

The *Kitty Hawk* was the Wright brothers' first plane.

Practice A   **Add the correct punctuation marks.**

Copy each sentence below on your paper. Add colons, dashes, hyphens, parentheses, and italics (underlining) where they are needed.

EXAMPLE: The Outsiders is a novel by S. E. Hinton.

The Outsiders is a novel by S. E. Hinton.

1. The train is scheduled to leave at 605 a.m.

2. Was your article accepted by the Daily News?

3. The Italian word bella means "beautiful."

4. I'm trying to sell my old bike for twenty five dollars say, would you like to buy it?

5. Hannibal 247-183 B.C. is famous for leading an army of forty thousand men and a number of elephants across the Alps.

6. Your first-aid kit will include the following adhesive tape, iodine, gauze, and insect repellent.

7. Thomas Jefferson lived in this part of Virginia for many years see map, p. 341.

8. You will find many definitions for the word subject in the dictionary.

9. We subscribe to the Reader's Digest and New York magazine.

10. Sportswriters used the following words and phrases to describe the rookie shortstop amazing sharp-eyed, superspeedy, and worth his weight in diamonds.

Practice B   Write sentences.

Follow the directions below to write sentences of your own.

EXAMPLE: Write a sentence about a grocery store. Use a colon.
Our local grocery store had the following items on sale: paper towels, yogurt, and peaches.

1. Write a sentence about a famous person. Use parentheses.
2. Write a sentence about a book you've read. Use italics (underlining).
3. Write a sentence that contains at least one compound number.
4. Write a sentence that includes a word referred to as a word.
5. Write a sentence that refers to a certain time, including the hour and the minute.

R E V I E W   E X E R C I S E S

I. End Punctuation and Abbreviations Copy each sentence on your paper. Add the correct end punctuation to each sentence. Also punctuate each abbreviation correctly. (Lessons One and Two)

EXAMPLE: The man asked us not to move the lamp
The man asked us not to move the lamp.

1. Benita Foster lives at 4321 Bedford St in Holiday, Vermont
2. Have you been to Dr. Kilroy's house
3. How wonderful it is to see you looking so well
4. Her father is the new U S ambassador to Italy
5. Our entire family joined the YMCA
6. Did you understand the question
7. Mr. Joe Bruno will be visiting our community soon
8. The Leaning Tower of Pisa is a favorite tourist site
9. The new child is named Harrington Jones, Jr
10. Will you help me wrap my ankle for the game tonight

II. Commas Rewrite the sentences below on your paper. Add commas where they are needed. (Lessons Three and Four)

1. My uncle a florist always brings us fresh flowers.
2. A golden retriever a collie and a toy poodle were playing together.
3. I have enjoyed every book I've read by that author for she always writes well about animals and their habits.
4. When winter comes I'll be ready with shovels salt and warm clothes.
5. His hobby which is collecting rare birds is beginning to annoy his neighbors.
6. Plymouth Massachusetts was named after Plymouth England the city from which the Pilgrims sailed.
7. Running around the track the horse would keep looking for its jockey.
8. Jeane Kirkpatrick the former U.S. ambassador to the United Nations was appointed by President Reagan.
9. If the prediction of the *Farmer's Almanac* is correct this will be a very severe winter.
10. The American Revolution came to an end when British forces surrendered at Yorktown Virginia on October 19 1781.

III. Semicolons Rewrite each item that follows as one sentence. Each of your sentences should include one or more semicolons. (Lesson Five)

EXAMPLE: Jane wants to be a lifeguard this summer. However, her mother is against the idea.

Jane wants to be a lifeguard this summer; however, her mother is against the idea.

1. My house has a roof made of red shingles. It also has aluminum siding.
2. There are many mysteries in nature. For example, no one knows where elephants go when they die.
3. We searched all day for Dana's contact lens, which was lost during the volleyball game. But we never found it.

4. Our club can't decide on how to spend our extra money. Therefore, we're going to ask the principal for her advice.

5. Thad knows how to play chess like a master. He was taught by his father.

IV. Quotation Marks Copy the following dialogue on your paper, placing quotation marks and other punctuation correctly. Remember to start a new paragraph whenever a different person begins to speak. (Lesson Six)

Have you seen the new singer at the Peppermint Club asked Chris. No answered Trina what's he like? He's great Chris said. He has purple hair and green lips, and he wears a silver and green jogging suit that glows in the dark! What does he sing Trina asked eagerly. His biggest hit is You're a Smash Chris said, but the song I liked best was Beautiful Garbage. It tells a story that he acts out, with the help of the audience. It sounds terrific said Trina. Can we go tonight? Not tonight Chris said. My clothes are still at the cleaner's, having the garbage stains removed.

V. Apostrophes Number your paper from 1 to 10. In each set of choices below, only one is correct. Write the letter of the correct phrase after the appropriate number on your paper. (Lesson Seven)

1. (a) Harry's bike   (b) Harrys bike   (c) Harrys' bike

2. (a) the mens gym   (b) the men's gym   (c) the mens' gym

3. (a) your sister's-in-law reasons   (b) your sister-in-laws reasons   (c) your sister-in-law's reasons

4. (a) Bill and Richard's pet raccoon   (b) Bill's and Richard's pet raccoon   (c) Bill and Richards pet raccoon

5. (a) its mine   (b) it's mine   (c) its' mine

6. (a) wouldnt' know   (b) would'nt know   (c) wouldn't know

7. (a) not enough d's   (b) not enough ds'   (c) not enough ds

8. (a) the class of '81   (b) the class of 81'   (c) the class of 1'81

9. (a) is that yours'?   (b) is that your's?   (c) is that yours?

10. (a) haven't gone   (b) have'nt gone   (c) havent' gone

VI. Other Punctuation Marks Rewrite the sentences on your paper. Add colons, hyphens, dashes, parentheses, and italics (underlining) where they are needed. (Lesson Eight)

EXAMPLE: The correct term for a young swan is cygnet.

The correct term for a young swan is cygnet.

1. The main crops of Czechoslovakia are the following wheat, sugar beets and potatoes.
2. You can take that English class at 915 or 1125.
3. This low-budget film it cost only ninety three thousand dollars to make has won several awards.
4. Mauna Kea, on the island of Hawaii, is an extinct volcano 13,796 feet 4277 meters high.
5. The earth's crust its outer surface contains more aluminum than any other metal.
6. There are twenty six state capitals that I've never visited.
7. Pigs are intelligent; that's why George Orwell real name: Eric Blair showed them ruling the other animals in his book Animal Farm.
8. In China dim sum is a special breakfast consisting of different kinds of dumplings.
9. We lived in Peru for three years Peru, Indiana, that is!
10. My teacher complains that I have used the word hopefully in correctly twenty one times in ten papers!

VII. Punctuation If a sentence is written correctly, write *C* after its number on your paper. If a sentence has one or more mistakes in punctuation, rewrite it correctly on your paper. (Lessons One to Eight)

EXAMPLE: The road up the hill was narrow steep and slippery

The road up the hill was narrow, steep, and slippery.

1. Mr and Mrs Kiesel took a cruise down the Mississippi River on a paddle-wheel boat, the Delta Queen.
2. You didnt blow out all the candles Donald, said Lucy, so you wont get your wish.
3. Jeff's father who is an accountant will help Walter Green fill out his income tax form this spring.

4. Will you please read the following poems: "The Tailspin," by Edward Field; "Superman," by John Updike; and "Junk," by Richard Wilbur.

5. If you would like to try out for a part in the play come to the audition on Monday.

6. Running across the parking lot Clive yelled Hey! What are you doing in my car

7. The Declaration of Independence was adopted by the Continental Congress on July 4, 1776.

8. Each person must bring these items a knapsack a sleeping bag and a pair of hiking boots.

9. Our neighbors want us to deodorize our pet skunk however we don't think it is necessary

10. Please don't use the words should and shouldn't when you are talking to me! said Karen

Using Correct Punctuation in Your Writing

In this unit, you learned about the many signals that you can give your reader through careful use of punctuation marks. As you studied these signals, you may have noticed that they fall into two broad groups. One group includes signals that you give not because they are necessary, but because they are customary. For example, you write *Mr.* with a period just because an "educated writer" is expected to do so.

The second group includes signals that make a difference in the meaning of a word or sentence. For example, the difference between *well* and *we'll* lies in a tiny mark called an apostrophe. And the difference between the following sentences lies in two commas.

Students in our class who wrote ten compositions this semester will get free movie tickets.   (Only those who wrote ten compositions will get tickets.)

Students in our class, who wrote ten compositions this semester, will get free movie tickets.   (All students in our class wrote ten compositions and all will get tickets.)

Now that you know most of the rules of correct punctuation, you will want to apply them to everything you write.

Practice   **Write a paragraph using correct punctuation**.

Write a paragraph with at least ten sentences about something that happened recently. It could be something exciting like receiving an excellent grade on a test or visiting a friend whom you haven't seen for some time. It could be something rather ordinary, like waking up this morning, eating breakfast, and rushing off to school. In your paragraph, try to use at least one example of each of the different kinds of punctuation marks you studied in this unit. Of course, you will use some of the punctuation marks many times more than once.

591

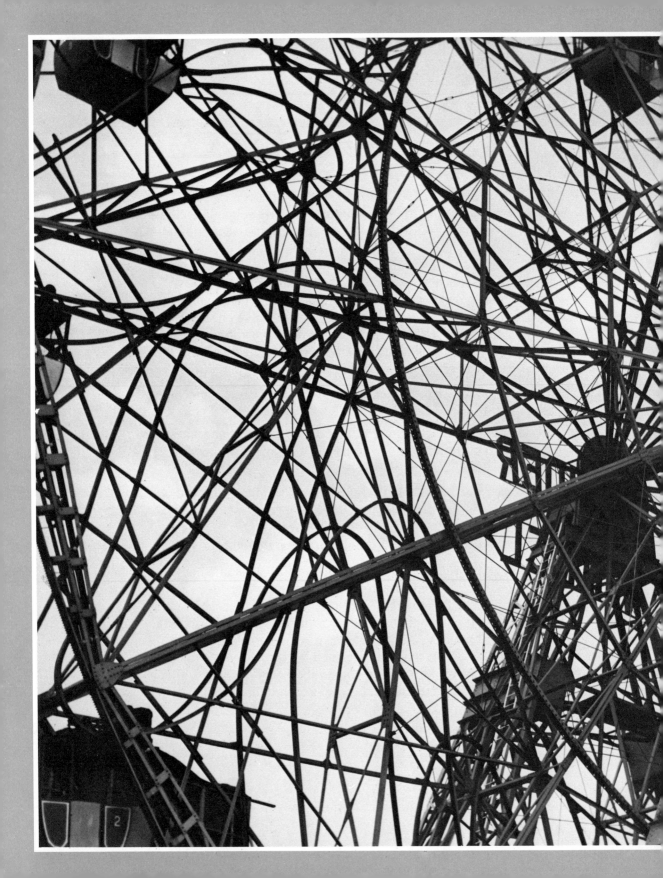

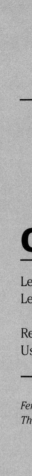

Capitalization

Ferris Wheel at Coney Island, New York City, around 1950
The Bettmann Archive

Capitalization

Suppose someone asked you what the difference was between the following two words.

robin   Robin

"One is a bird and the other is a person," you might answer. But then suppose the person asked you to explain how you came to that conclusion. "Well," you would probably say, "one begins with a capital letter, and the other doesn't."

Capital letters are signals to your reader. They may seem like minor details, but they can make a big difference in a word's meaning. That's why it's important to learn the rules of capitalization. If you know when to use capital letters, you can be sure to give your readers the correct signals. In this unit you will study the rules for correct capitalization.

LESSON ONE

Capitalize First Words

One of the functions of capital letters is to mark the beginning of a sentence or a direct quotation. They tell the reader that what is coming is a new thought.

POINTS TO KNOW

▶ Capitalize the first word of a sentence.

Fencing with swords was first developed as a sport by the Germans.

Have you ever seen anyone fence?

Michael took fencing lessons in college.

▶ Capitalize the first word of a direct quotation.

> Suzette asked, "**W**here are my shoes?"

> "**T**hey're in the oven, getting dry," Bruce replied.

Often a direct quotation is interrupted by explanatory words, such as *she said*, or *he asked*, as in the following example.

> "**I**f you don't come with us this time," he warned, "we may never invite you again."

In this quotation the word *we* is not capitalized because it does not begin a new sentence. You can see this if you take away the interrupting words *he warned*. The quotation now reads:

> "**I**f you don't come with us this time, we may never invite you again."

▶ Capitalize the first word in the greeting and in the closing of a letter.

Dear Tom,	**S**incerely,
Dear Senator Fong:	**Y**ours truly,
My dear friend,	**B**est regards,

Practice A **Correct errors in capitalization.**

Number your paper from 1 to 10. If a phrase or statement is capitalized correctly, write *C* after its number. If the phrase or statement is incorrect, rewrite it correctly.

EXAMPLES: Yours truly,

C

he is here now.

He is here now.

1. dear Aunt Sally,
2. Jane asked, "where will the carnival be held?"
3. sincerely yours,
4. We knew the answer right away.
5. the customer bought a book.

6. Dear Mr. Lowell:

7. is that your father?

8. our friend called to us from across the field.

9. "what a wonderful view!" exclaimed Laura.

10. This is a good time for questions.

Practice B   Correct errors in capitalization.

The following passage contains ten errors in capitalization. Find them, and write each of the incorrect words on your paper. Correct the words by using capital letters where they are needed.

EXAMPLE: my friend and I had never seen this bird.

My

the bird was rare. it hadn't been seen in our part of the country for many years. So when someone reported seeing it in a nearby woods, we birdwatchers got excited.

"Maybe if we camped near where it was sighted," Fran said, "we'd get a chance to see it."

"that's a good idea," I agreed. "let's go."

That same evening we pitched our tents near the spot. by dawn the next day a crowd had gathered.

"there it is," someone shouted, "near the top of that big oak tree!"

All of us looked through our binoculars. then a man behind me said, "why, that's nothing but an ordinary robin!"

Some people laughed, while others groaned in disgust. the noise scared the robin away. as for the rare bird, it never did show up.

L E S S O N   T W O

Capitalize Proper Nouns and Proper Adjectives

As you learned in Unit Nineteen, a proper noun is the name of a particular person, place, or thing. It starts with a capital letter.

common nouns: boy, park, book

proper nouns: Jimmy, Riverside Park, *A Wrinkle in Time*

► Capitalize all proper nouns.

Proper nouns can be divided into groups according to what they name. Study the groups and the examples listed on the following pages.

1. Capitalize geographical terms.

   cities and states: **Miami, New Mexico, Oklahoma**

   countries: **Sweden, Argentina, Nigeria**

   continents: **Africa, North America**

   bodies of water: **Atlantic Ocean, Mississippi River, Lake Michigan**

   streets and roads: **Long Island Expressway, Vincent Lane**

   buildings: the **Washington Monument**, the **Chrysler Building**

   parks: **Yosemite National Park, Central Park**

   bridges: the **Whitestone Bridge**, the **Golden Gate Bridge**

   mountains: **Mount Williamson**, the **Pyrenees**

   regions: the **West**, the **Far East**

Note: The words *north, south, east* and *west* are not capitalized when they refer to compass directions.

   The house is on the south side of town.

   The cowboy rode east to St. Louis.

2. Capitalize the names of people and animals.

   Kimberley Bennett

   Matt brought his dog Spike to the vet.

3. Capitalize the official and professional titles of people when they precede a personal name. Also capitalize the courtesy titles *Mr., Mrs., Ms.,* and *Miss.* (*Note:* This group includes one word that is not a noun but a pronoun: *I.* The personal pronoun *I* is always capitalized.)

   Professor Plum

   Dr. Harold Bekins

   Prime Minister Margaret Thatcher

   Mr. David Jones

When a noun of kinship, such as *mother, father*, or *grandma*, is used in place of a name in direct address, it is capitalized. (Direct address is the act of addressing, or speaking to, a person directly.)

"Thank you for helping me, Grandma."

"Hey, Mom, did you hear the good news?"

"Father, I made this dessert especially for you."

4. Capitalize the names of organizations, companies, institutions, and government bodies.

Democratic Party, State Department

National Football League, Rotary Club

American Telephone and Telegraph

Museum of Broadcasting, Northwestern University

5. Capitalize the names of religious groups, sacred works of literature, and words referring to the deity.

Lutheran Church, the Old Testament, Judaism

the Lord, Buddhism, God, the Bible, Jehovah

6. Capitalize important events of the past and present. Capitalize the names of geological and historical periods. Also, capitalize the names of historical documents.

the Battle of the Little Bighorn

the Industrial Revolution, the Super Bowl

the Devonian period, the Civil War, the Middle Ages

the Declaration of Independence, the Monroe Doctrine

7. Capitalize the names of the days of the week, the months of the year, and holidays.

Tuesday, December, Sunday, Labor Day

August, Halloween

Do not capitalize the names of the seasons.

spring, summer, winter, autumn, fall

8. Capitalize brand names.

Chevrolet, Anacin, Smith-Corona, Kodak

9. Capitalize the names of individual ships, trains, planes, and spacecraft.

ship: the *Queen Elizabeth II*

train: the *Super Chief*

space shuttle: *Columbia*

10. When a proper noun is made up of more than one word, capitalize the first word and all other important words. Words such as *of, and, a, for,* and *the* are not capitalized.

Federal Bureau of Investigation

Volunteer Services for Children

Forbes Wilson and Company

11. Adjectives formed from proper nouns are called *proper adjectives*. Capitalize proper adjectives.

Proper Noun	Proper Adjective
Greece	Greek food
China	Chinese art
France	French language
Alaska	Alaskan pipeline
Congress	Congressional hearing

12. Capitalize the titles of works of literature, works of art, and musical compositions. Capitalize the first word, the last word, and all other important words in titles of works. The term *works* includes books, stories, poems, TV shows, movies, magazines, newspapers, paintings, plays, songs, symphonies, and operas.

You may wonder what is meant by "all other important words." It means all words except articles (*the, a, an*), coordinating conjunctions (*and, but, or*), and prepositions of fewer than four letters (*to, on, for*).

Old Possum's Book of Practical Cats is a collection of poems by T.S. Eliot.

Of Mice and Men was written by John Steinbeck.

"The Catbird Seat" is a funny short story by James Thurber.

The Boston Globe was delivered to our house by mistake.

Have you read "**O**ne **O**rdinary **D**ay, **W**ith **P**eanuts," by Shirley Jackson?

We have tickets to see *The Doctor in Spite of Himself*, a play by Molière.

Titles of school courses are capitalized. However, names of school subjects are not, unless they are proper nouns.

American **L**iterature II, **a**rt, **B**iology 213, **g**eometry, **P**hysical **E**ducation 1B, **I**talian

---

Practice A   Add capital letters.

Rewrite the following sentences on your paper, adding capital letters where they are needed.

EXAMPLE: the fourth of july is my favorite summer holiday.
The Fourth of July is my favorite summer holiday.

1. On their trip to the far east they visited Indonesia.
2. Ernest Hemingway's novel *for whom the bell tolls* takes place in spain.
3. i have an interview with burton industries on friday at their office on first avenue.
4. She went to tufts university, where she majored in european history.
5. When you visited the south, did you swim at myrtle beach?
6. Has dr. williams read the *new england journal of medicine* yet?
7. Who served as secretary of state under president john f. kennedy?
8. The manager of the team, carlos martinez, says every player should read *the boys of summer*, by roger kahn.
9. Mr. Kelly lawson, the principal of our school, spoke about the bill of rights.
10. Did you read about the senate's decision in *time, newsweek,* or *the washington post*?

Practice B   **Write sentences with proper nouns.**

Write sentences that include one specific item for each general category listed below.

EXAMPLE: a person mentioned in history books

The story about George Washington and the cherry tree is not true.

1. a book
2. an athlete or entertainer
3. a song
4. a company or organization
5. a national holiday
6. a famous building or monument
7. a river, lake, or ocean
8. one of the fifty states
9. a season of the year
10. a foreign country

R E V I E W   E X E R C I S E S

I. Capitalization Number your paper from 1 to 10. Give an example of each of the the following items. Be sure to use capital letters correctly. (Lessons One and Two)

EXAMPLE: an adjective formed from a proper noun

American

1. the title of a song
2. the name of your school
3. a brand name
4. a company or store
5. a holiday
6. the name and title of a public official
7. your complete address
8. an ocean, river, or lake

9. a building or monument
10. a day of the week

II. Capitalization Number your paper from 1 to 10. If a phrase or statement is capitalized correctly, write *C* after its number. If a phrase or statement is incorrect, rewrite it correctly. (Lessons One and Two)

1. *the enemy* is a short story by pearl s. buck.
2. "are you going skiing in vermont?" asked Sylvia.
3. fondly, Greg
4. please do not smoke in this area.
5. we had to read the constitution in History class.
6. My parents visited the Louvre Museum when they were in Paris.
7. Suddenly, Dan yelled, "Watch out!"
8. beth's father works for new york telephone.
9. You should go see the movie *Back to the future*.
10. Sandy called and made an appointment with dr. Lawford for tuesday, March 24.

Using Correct Capitalization in Your Writing

You probably don't have much trouble remembering to capitalize the first word of a sentence. Most likely, you perform that skill automatically, without having to think about it. But, from time to time, you may have trouble deciding whether some of the other words in a sentence should be capitalized. To be prepared for these occasions, it's a good idea to get to know the rules for correct capitalization.

Practice   **Write sentences with capital letters.**

Follow the directions below for writing sentences of your own.

1. Write several sentences about a friend. Include at least three words, other than first words of sentences, that require capital letters.
2. Write several sentences about a movie you saw recently. Include at least five words, other than first words of sentences, that require capital letters.
3. Write several sentences about your state. Include at least five words, other than first words of sentences, that require capital letters.

Spelling

An Inuit, Jack Angaiak, seal hunting in the Bering Sea at Tununak, Alaska, 1975. This photo is from the book The Last and First Eskimos, *by Alex Harris.*
Alex Harris, Archive Pictures, Inc.

Spelling

L E S S O N   O N E

Matching Sounds and Letters

As you know, the letters of the alphabet stand for sounds. When you spell a word, you write down the letters that stand for the sounds in the word. Spelling would be easy if you could always use the same letter or combination of letters to stand for the same sound. But, unfortunately, you can't. Often there are several ways of spelling a sound. You have to pick the one that is correct for the word you are writing.

For example, take the long *a* sound. That's the sound you hear when you pronounce the name of the first letter of the alphabet: *A*. The sound can be spelled in several different ways. The most common spellings of long *a* are shown in these words:

station	train	obey
date	weigh	say

You can learn to spell the long *a* sound and all the other sounds in English if you are willing to study and practice. Here are four steps to good spelling that you can take:

▶ Learn the basic spelling rules. There aren't many of them, so this step is not hard. You will find several of the most useful rules in the first three lessons of this unit.

▶ Keep a list of the words you misspell in your writing. Say them and spell them out loud. Practice writing them correctly.

▶ Get into the habit of using your dictionary. Whenever you're unsure of a spelling, look the word up.

▶ Study lists of "spelling demons"—words that almost everybody has trouble with. There is one such list in Lesson Four of this unit.

Spelling Words With *ie* or *ei*

The letters *e* and *i* are often combined to spell certain vowel sounds. But many people have trouble remembering which comes first in a given word. Is it *their* or *thier*? Is it *liesure* or *leisure*?

▶ When the sound is a long *e* (*bee*), use *ie* after any letter except *c*.

grief	thief	relief	fiend
chief	piece	tier	shriek
belief	niece	pierce	field

Exceptions: **ei**ther, n**ei**ther, s**ei**ze, w**ei**rd, l**ei**sure, prot**ei**n, caff**ei**ne, sh**ei**k

▶ When the long *e* sound follows the letter *c*, write *ei*.

rec**ei**ve	dec**ei**ve	c**ei**ling
rec**ei**pt	dec**ei**t	perc**ei**ve

▶ For any other sound except long *e*, write *ei*.

fr**ei**ght	w**ei**ght	rein	their
feign	veil	reign	forfeit
vein	neigh	sleigh	counter**fei**t
weigh	neighbor	eight	height
foreign			

Exceptions: fr**ie**nd, misch**ie**f, s**ie**ve

607

Spelling Words That End in "Seed"

A dozen common words in English end in the sound "seed." All are verbs. Since they are derived from two different Latin verbs, you might expect them to have two different spellings. But that would make things too easy for you—the fact is, the "seed" verbs have three different spellings: *sede, ceed,* and *cede.*

▶ Only one word ends in *sede*:

supersede

The *sede* comes from the Latin verb *sedere*, meaning "to sit." The literal meaning of *supersede* is "to sit above." One person or thing supersedes another in rank, importance, force, or usefulness. Here is a sample sentence containing the word:

The new dress code **supersedes** the one announced last spring.

▶ Only three words end in *ceed*:

suc**ceed**   ex**ceed**   pro**ceed**

These words are derived from the Latin word *cedere*, "to go." Logically, they should be spelled *cede*, but these three words are spelled with a double *e*.

▶ All other "seed" words end in *cede*. These words are also derived from Latin *cedere*.

pre**cede**   (to go ahead of)

re**cede**   (to go back)

con**cede**   (to go with; that is, to agree or acknowledge—usually with reluctance: "He **conceded** that he had been wrong.")

inter**cede**   (to go between in order to bring about an agreement: "Our teacher **interceded** with the principal to get permission for our class trip.")

ac**cede**   (to go to, to consent: "The principal **acceded** to our request.")

se**cede**   (to go apart, to withdraw: "The Confederate States **seceded** from the Union.")

ante**cede**   (to go before)

608

Practice   Choose the correctly spelled word.

In each sentence choose the correctly spelled word in parentheses.

Write the word on your paper after the number of the sentence.

1. The elephants (proseded, proceeded) slowly around the ring.
2. Our cat gets into a great deal of (mischief, mischeif).
3. Have you (received, recieved) your invitation yet?
4. Bill is my best (freind, friend).
5. Jim lost the (receipt, reciept) for the coat he bought last week.
6. Who is the (thief, theif) who stole my lunch?
7. The Rudins have been our (nieghbors, neighbors) for years.
8. The flood waters are beginning to (resede, recede).
9. Can you tell me the (hieght, height) of that mountain in meters?
10. (Neither, Niether) of us can figure out the problem.

L E S S O N   T W O

Spelling the Plurals of Nouns

As you learned in Unit Nineteen, Lesson One, a word that names one person, place, or thing is a singular noun. A word that names two or more persons, places, or things is a plural noun. The following rules will help you spell most plural nouns correctly.

P O I N T S   T O   K N O W

▶   Most nouns form their plural by adding *s*.

trucks	piles	typewriters	records

▶   To form the plural of a noun ending in *s, sh, ch, z,* or *x*, add *es*.

churches	glasses	bushes	foxes

▶   To form the plural of a noun ending in a consonant and *y*, change the *y* to *i* and add *es*.

community	communities
study	studies
sky	skies

▶ To form the plural of a noun ending in a vowel and *y*, add *s*.

key	key**s**
trolley	trolley**s**
tray	tray**s**
monkey	monkey**s**

▶ Some nouns that end in a consonant and *o* add *s* to form the plural.

piano	piano**s**
solo	solo**s**
soprano	soprano**s**

Others add *es*.

lasso	lasso**es**
potato	potato**es**
tomato	tomato**es**
hero	hero**es**
echo	echo**es**

Still others form their plural by adding either *s* or *es*.

torpedo	torpedo**s** or torpedo**es**
volcano	volcano**s** or volcano**es**

▶ To form the plural of a noun ending in a vowel and *o*, add *s*.

cameo	cameo**s**
studio	studio**s**
zoo	zoo**s**
radio	radio**s**

▶ Some nouns ending in *f* or *fe* form their plural by changing the *f* or *fe* to *ve* and adding *s*.

scarf	scar**ves**
wife	wi**ves**
leaf	lea**ves**
shelf	shel**ves**

▶ To make a hyphenated compound noun plural, add *s* or *es* to the principal noun.

sergeant-at-arms	sergeant**s**-at-arms
mother-in-law	mother**s**-in-law
half-truth	half-truth**s**

If there is no noun in the compound, add *s* or *es* at the end.

sit-up	sit-up**s**
merry-go-round	merry-go-round**s**
hand-me-down	hand-me-down**s**

▶ To make a number, letter, or symbol plural, add an apostrophe and an *s*.

7's   y's   &'s

▶ Some nouns that name animals are the same in both the singular and the plural.

sheep	salmon
trout	fish
deer	moose

▶ The plurals of some nouns are formed irregularly.

man	**men**	child	child**ren**
mouse	**mice**	woman	women
foot	**feet**	goose	g**ee**se
tooth	t**ee**th		

Practice A   Choose the correctly spelled plural nouns.

Number your paper from 1 to 10. From the parentheses in each sentence choose the correctly spelled noun. Write it on your paper.

1. Have the (turkeys, turkies) for Thanksgiving arrived yet?
2. Cows have four (foots, feet).
3. The (leafs, leaves) on the maple tree turn bright red in the fall.

4. My dog has several (enemies, enemys) in the neighborhood.
5. Have you had your (tooths, teeth) cleaned this year?
6. His (beliefes, beliefs) have been shattered.
7. The (tomatoes, tomatos) in this salad aren't fresh.
8. How many (9s, 9's) are there in your address?
9. Dad caught six (trout, trouts) last week.
10. I have two (sister-in-laws, sisters-in-law).

Practice B   **Write sentences with plural nouns.**

Use the plural form of each of the nouns below in a sentence of your own.

EXAMPLE: church

The churches in our town are holding a bazaar.

1. stereo
2. child
3. spy
4. waltz
5. key
6. crutch
7. bus
8. shelf
9. get-together
10. salmon

L E S S O N   T H R E E

Spelling Words With Prefixes and Suffixes

Sometimes you add a syllable at the beginning or end of a word to change the word's meaning. For example, suppose you add the syllable *re-* at the beginning of *read*. You get a new word, *reread*, with a new meaning, "to read again." Or suppose you add the syllable *-ful* at the end of the word *joy*. You get *joyful*, meaning, "full of joy."

A **prefix** is a letter or group of letters added at the beginning of a word.

> **un** + cover = **un**cover

A **suffix** is a letter or group of letters added at the end of a word.

> total + **ly** = total**ly**

When a prefix is added to a word, the spelling of that word is not changed.

> mis + spell = misspell
>
> un + available = unavailable
>
> re + enter = reenter
>
> over + take = overtake
>
> il + legible = illegible
>
> over + rate = overrate

When a suffix is added to a word, the spelling of the word does not always change:

> casual + ly = casually
>
> hard + ness = hardness
>
> ring + ing = ringing

But there are times when a suffix causes a change in the spelling of the word it is added to. Here are the rules for spelling words with suffixes.

▶ When adding a suffix beginning with a vowel to a word ending in *e*, you usually drop the *e*.

> have + ing = hav**ing**
>
> like + able = lik**able**
>
> sincere + ity = sincer**ity**

Exception: If the *e* is preceded by *c* or *g*, keep the *e* when adding a suffix beginning with *a*, *o*, or *u*. The *e* is needed to indicate that the *c* or *g* is soft.

> service + able = service**able**
>
> courage + ous = courage**ous**

▶ When adding a suffix to a word ending in a consonant and *y*, change the *y* to *i*.

> marry + age = marriage
>
> floppy + er = floppier
>
> mercy + ful = merciful

Exception: If the suffix begins with *i*, do not change the *y* to *i*:

> carry + ing = carrying

▶ If a one-syllable word ends in one consonant preceded by one vowel, double the consonant when adding a suffix that begins with a vowel.

> drop + ed = dropped
>
> swim + ing = swimming
>
> run + er = runner

This rule also applies to words of more than one syllable if the accent falls on the last syllable.

> refer + al = referral
>
> omit + ed = omitted
>
> regret + able = regrettable

Practice A Choose the correctly spelled word.

Number your paper from 1 to 10. In each sentence choose the correctly spelled word in parentheses. Write it on your paper.

1. The space capsule will (reenter, renter) the earth's atmosphere next Tuesday.
2. The cow walked (droopyly, droopily) to the pasture.
3. Jack (carryed, carried) the ball for sixty-three yards.
4. Did the packages arrive (safely, safly)?
5. His problems are (geting, getting) worse all the time.
6. His calls for help went (unoticed, unnoticed).
7. Ray seemed (really, realy) sorry for his nasty remark to Julia.

8. That swimmer's (timing, timeing) is not very good today.

9. My cousin's (sincereity, sincerity) is touching.

10. The team's (wearyness, weariness) was written on their faces.

Practice B Form words with prefixes and suffixes.

Combine each of the following words with the prefix or suffix indicated. Write the new word on your paper. Then write a sentence containing it.

EXAMPLE: argue + ed

argued

The class officers argued about the plans for the prom.

1. un + necessary
2. sincere + ly
3. permit + ed
4. control + ing
5. lonely + ness

6. il + legal
7. dis + appoint
8. cozy + ness
9. beauty + ful
10. easy + est

L E S S O N   F O U R

Words Often Confused

Some things resemble each other but have different uses. For example, salt and sugar look alike, but they taste very different. If you're making a stew or a cake, you need to know which is which.

Certain words in English resemble each other; they sound the same or almost the same, but they have different spellings and different meanings. When you speak, there's no problem. But when you write, you need to know which is which. Here is a list of pairs or sets of words that confuse many writers.

Words	Definitions
accept	to agree to take
	I accept your offer of help.
except	other than
	I go to the gym every day except Sunday.

Words	Definitions
advice	(noun) an opinion about what should be done
	Ann Landers gives advice to readers of her column.
advise	(verb) to offer an opinion
	What would you advise me to do?
affect	(verb) to act on, influence
	The snow affected our football game; we kept fumbling the ball.
effect	(noun) result
	The effect of the storm can be seen in our backyard.
effect	(verb) to bring about, to accomplish
	The new owner has effected several improvements in the store.
already	before or by a certain time
	Our guests are already here.
all ready	completely ready
	I am all ready to take the road test for my driver's license.
altogether	entirely
	This room is altogether too messy!
all together	all in the same place
	Father called us all together for a family meeting.
brake	a device for stopping a vehicle
	The brake on my bike needs adjusting.
break	(verb) to crack or smash
	Don't break that vase, please!
break	(noun) a rest from a certain duty
	May I take a break from this gardening?

Words	Definitions
clothes	covering for the body
	I need some new clothes very badly.
cloths	(the plural of *cloth*) pieces of fabric
	Please bring me those dust cloths.
fourth	being number four in order
	I was the fourth customer in line.
forth	forward; onward
	Let us go forth to meet the challenges of the future.
its	belonging to it
	Have you given the snake its dinner?
it's	contraction of *it has* or *it is*
	It's been a long time since I last saw you.
	It's a pity we don't meet more often.
lose	to fail to win; to be unable to find
	We're going to lose this game unless we can score a field goal.
	You will lose those coins if you're not careful.
loose	not fastened or confined; not tight
	Who let the parakeets loose from their cage?
	This belt is too loose.
past	(noun) time gone by
	She never talks about the past.
passed	(past tense of *pass*) went by
	A man on horseback passed our stalled car, and he yelled, "Get a horse!"
personal	private
	This letter is personal.
personnel	people employed by a company
	All of the company's personnel were given a bonus.

Words	Definitions
principal	(adjective) most important
	Our principal goal is to raise money for charity.
principal	(noun) director of a school
	Our principal asked us to attend the meeting.
principle	rule of action or conduct; fundamental law or doctrine
	We talk about high moral principles, but we do not always live up to them.
	The principles of democracy include liberty, equality, and justice.
stationary	remaining in one place
	For several minutes Jerry remained stationary while the other dancers swirled around him.
stationery	writing paper and envelopes
	I gave Meg some stationery with her initials printed on it in gold.
than	in comparison with
	Yogurt is better for your health than fudge.
then	next in time or place
	We'll play bingo, and then we'll have popcorn.
there	in that place
	The newspaper is over there, on the table.
their	belonging to them
	Their house was sold quickly.
they're	contraction of *they are*
	They're looking at the map and talking about their vacation.

Words	Definitions
threw	past tense of *throw*
	Harry threw the ball into the bushes.
through	from one end to the other
	Sheila walked slowly through the park.
to	in the direction of
	Is anybody going to the post office?
too	also; more than enough
	I'll be there, too.
	There are too many people here.
two	the number between one and three
	I'll try to save two seats.

Practice A   Choose the correctly spelled groups of words.

Number your paper from 1 to 15. Choose the correctly spelled phrase or clause in each pair. Write the letter of the phrase or clause on your paper.

EXAMPLE:

a. you, Ben, and Kirsten, too

b. you, Ben, and Kirsten, two

a

1. a. break his promise
   b. brake his promise
2. a. her advise
   b. her advice
3. a. It's time to go.
   b. Its time to go.
4. a. new cloths for the wedding
   b. new clothes for the wedding
5. a. loose his keys
   b. lose his keys
6. a. the distant past
   b. the distant passed

619

7. a. The cake is already.

   b. The cake is all ready.

8. a. through the trees

   b. threw the trees

9. a. their new pet

   b. they're new pet

10. a. the house over there

   b. the house over their

11. a. the forth in line

   b. the fourth in line

12. a. pretty blue stationery

   b. pretty blue stationary

13. a. This medicine has no side-affects.

   b. This medicine has no side-effects.

14. a. It is altogether too much trouble.

   b. It is all together too much trouble.

15. a. I will not except the blame.

   b. I will not accept the blame.

Practice B   **Write sentences.**

Write ten sentences of your own. In each sentence use correctly one of the commonly confused words listed in this lesson. Underline the word whose use you are illustrating.

EXAMPLE: *Everyone was <u>accepted</u> into the National Honor Society.*

R E V I E W   E X E R C I S E S

I. Matching Sounds and Letters Each of the following sentences contains one misspelled word. Write each misspelled word correctly on your paper. (Lesson One)

EXAMPLE: Her cheif problem is lack of friends.

chief

1. Have Jim and Esther suceded in selling their house?
2. I believe Mr. Thomas's hairline is beginning to receed.
3. Yolanda is one of my eight neices.
4. The height and wieght of the elephant are being measured.
5. Neither of these boys got a reciept for the clothes he bought.
6. Did you receive a ticket for exseeding the speed limit?
7. We will prosede with our plans for the sleigh ride.
8. My mother spends her leisure time iether reading or practicing the piano.
9. She acceded to my request for another peice of pie.
10. The theif was seized by an off-duty police officer.

II. Spelling the Plurals of Nouns Number your paper from 1 to 10. For each of the following sentences, choose the correctly spelled plural noun from the two in parentheses. Write the noun on your paper. (Lesson Two)

EXAMPLE: Two (foxs, foxes) got into the chicken coop.

foxes

1. Which of these (men, mans) would you like to help you?
2. Franklin caught three (salmon, salmons) in Maine last week.
3. Eddie has to do twenty (push-ups, pushs-up) before he can leave gym class.
4. There are many (zoos, zooes) in the country that don't have cages.
5. How many (e's, es) are there in your last name?
6. Here the (skys, skies) are not cloudy all day.
7. The (trollies, trolleys) have been shut down for repairs.
8. A flock of (geese, gooses) heading south flew past us.
9. Do you really need three (pianos, pianoes) for the concert?
10. I read a story about a man long ago who had several (wives, wifes).

III. Spelling Words With Prefixes and Suffixes Number your paper from 1 to 10. To each word that follows, add the suffix indicated. Write the correctly spelled word with the suffix on your paper. (Lesson Three)

EXAMPLE: train + ing

training

1. shop + er
2. love + able
3. loyal +ly
4. enjoy + ed
5. beauty + ful
6. fame + ous
7. regret + ed
8. happy + est
9. mean + ness
10. change + ing

IV. Words Often Confused Use each of the following words correctly in a sentence of your own. (Lesson Four)

EXAMPLE: except

I'll take all of these books except An American Tragedy.

1. advise
2. fourth
3. altogether
4. principal
5. passed
6. break
7. its
8. personal
9. stationery
10. loose

Using Correct Spelling in Your Writing

Suppose you wrote the following note to a friend.

> I am taking a brake from my auto mechanics class to write you this note. We are planing to visit you this weak end and hope to here all the latest noose. Sea you then!

Your friend would understand what you meant, but he or she would also have a laugh at your expense.

Probably you never misspell easy words like the ones in our humorous example. But if you have trouble with more difficult words, you'll find it worth your while to look them up in a dictionary. That way, your reader will be able to concentrate on your ideas instead of on your spelling.

The exercise that follows will give you practice in writing words with correct spelling.

Practice   **Write a paragraph with correctly spelled words.**

Write a paragraph with at least ten sentences about school. In your paragraph, include the following:

1. at least one word that has *ie* in it;
2. at least one word that has *ei* in it;
3. at least one word that has a *seed* sound in it;
4. at least one word that has a prefix; and
5. at least one word that has a suffix.

When you finish, check to be sure all your words are spelled correctly.

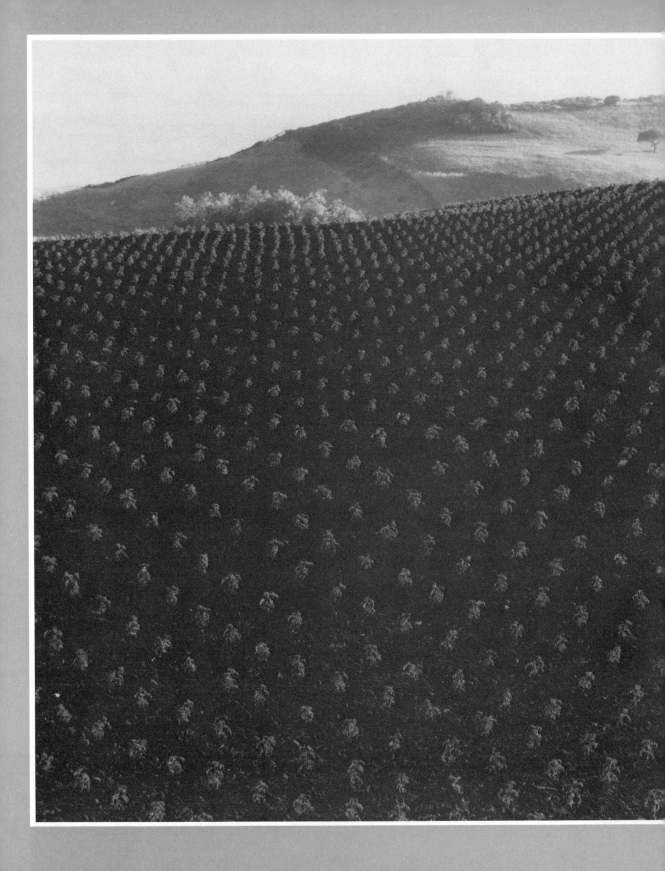

Sentence Patterns

"Tomato Field," 1937
Edward Weston, courtesy of Arizona Board of Regents, Center for Creative Photography, University of Arizona, Tucson

Sentence Patterns

When you speak and write, you arrange the words in your sentences in a certain order so that they make sense. You are able to understand the meaning of the following sentence, for example, because the words in it follow a standard English sentence pattern.

Eduardo passed the science exam.

There are several different ways of rearranging these words, but none of them make sense.

Passed exam science Eduardo the.

Science the passed exam Eduardo.

Exam the Eduardo science passed.

The words in these examples are not arranged in one of the fixed patterns of the English language. Therefore, their meaning is not easily understood.

In this unit you will learn about five standard sentence patterns.

L E S S O N   O N E

The N V Sentence Pattern

The simplest English sentence pattern is called the N V sentence pattern. In it, the *N* stands for the noun or pronoun in the complete subject. The *V* stands for the verb or verb phrase in the complete predicate.

Each sentence in the chart on page 627 follows the N V sentence pattern. Notice that each of the first two sentences includes only a subject and a verb or verb phrase. The last two sentences include modifiers as well: *my, now,* and *well.* All these sentences follow the N V sentence pattern.

Subject	Predicate
N	**V**
Zelda	swims.
Zelda Jones	has been swimming.
My friend	is swimming now.
You	swim well.

Practice A   Use the N V sentence pattern.

Make a chart for the N V sentence pattern. Label one column *Subject.* Label the other column *Predicate*. Below the subject label, write *N.* Below the predicate label, write *V.* Put the simple subjects and verbs from the following sentences in the correct columns.

1. We are listening.
2. They left.
3. Matilda has been waiting.
4. Brett is whistling.
5. Jennifer Jackson smiled.

Practice B   Use the N V sentence pattern.

Make a chart like the one in Practice A for the N V sentence pattern. Write the simple subjects and verbs from the following sentences in the chart. Omit all other words from your chart.

1. Five teenagers are reading in the library.
2. Someone has been staring at me.
3. The lost dog was whimpering.
4. My best friend moved to another city.
5. We will write often.
6. Harry Holmes is studying quietly.
7. Mary worked hard all day.
8. The delighted audience applauded loudly.
9. Honi is fishing today.
10. The plane will land soon.

Practice C   Add simple subjects and verbs.

Copy the chart that follows. Complete the sentences by filling in each blank with either a simple subject, or a verb or verb phrase. Make sure each of the five sentences makes sense.

	Subject	Predicate
	N	**V**
1.	Teresa	_____.
2.	_____	is sleeping.
3.	Flowers	_____.
4.	_____	coughed.
5.	_____	_____.

L E S S O N   T W O

The N V N Sentence Pattern

This sentence pattern has three parts. As in the N V sentence pattern, the first *N* stands for the noun or pronoun in the complete subject, and the *V* stands for the verb or verb phrase in the complete predicate. In this pattern, the second *N* stands for a direct object.

You learned in Unit Twenty-one, Lesson One, that a direct object is a noun or pronoun that answers the question *whom?* or *what?* after a transitive verb. It is one of the four kinds of complements you have studied in this book.

Here are examples of sentences that follow the N V N sentence pattern. Modifiers have been included in the chart. Each modifier is placed in the same column as the word it modifies.

Subject	Predicate	Complement
	Verb	**Direct Object**
N	**V**	**N**
The bird	has recently built	a nest.
My mother	ordered	a lemonade.
Gus and Jim	have fixed	their bikes.

Practice A   Use the N V N sentence pattern.

Make a chart with three columns for the N V N sentence pattern. Label the first column *N*, the second column *V*, and the third column *N*. Write every word from the following sentences in the correct column. Place a modifier in the same column as the word it modifies.

1. Ezra easily caught the fly ball.
2. The loggers hauled the tree trunks.
3. Hal and Eileen have eaten their dinner.
4. We played chess.
5. Many people enjoy stamp collecting.
6. Oliver is reading a science magazine.
7. We will fly our kites later.
8. Grandma is holding her grandchild.
9. Andrea is brushing her dog Happy.
10. Jim planted a large herb garden.

Practice B   Use the N V N sentence pattern.

Make another chart like the one in Practice A for the N V N sentence pattern. Place only the simple subjects, verbs or verb phrases, and noun or pronoun direct objects from the following sentences in your chart. Omit all modifiers.

1. A kind person donated food for the needy.
2. Mary and Tommy will drive their car to the beach.
3. The waves pounded the seaweed-strewn beach.
4. The dog opened the front door with its paw.
5. Fran has visited Bob in Ohio.
6. Bill wants to buy a good used car.
7. Someone in the class is using my ruler.
8. Hurricane Bertha destroyed the old shack.
9. The knight crossed the moat.
10. The welcoming committee provided a nice lunch.

Practice C   Add subjects, verbs, and direct objects.

Copy the chart that follows. Complete the sentences by filling in the blanks with subjects, verbs or verb phrases, and direct objects. Use modifiers as well, to make your sentences as interesting as you can.

Subject	Predicate Verb	Complement Direct Object
N	**V**	**N**
1. My sister	will bring	_____.
2. _____	bought	some spy novels.
3. _____	have returned	_____.
4. I	_____	_____.

L E S S O N   T H R E E

The N V N N Sentence Pattern

The first two parts of this sentence pattern are the same as in the other two patterns you have studied so far: the first *N* stands for the noun or pronoun in the complete subject; the *V* stands for the verb or verb phrase in the complete predicate. However, in this pattern, the second *N* stands for the noun or pronoun indirect object, and the third *N* stands for the noun or pronoun direct object.

In Unit Twenty-one, Lesson Two, you learned that an indirect object answers the question *to or for whom?* or *to or for what?* before a direct object. It is one of the four kinds of complements you have studied in this book.

Following are examples of sentences in which the N V N N pattern is used.

Sarah made her friends dinner.

Tom and Jim bought their parents a VCR.

On the next page are more examples of sentences that follow the N V N N sentence pattern. Modifiers have been placed in the same columns as the words they modify.

Subject	Predicate		
	Verb	Complement	
		Indir. Object	Direct Object
N	V	N	N
Willy	has sent	me	two tickets.
My father	brought	Zeke	his sweater.
Opal	is writing	her friend	a postcard.
I	made	myself	a big lunch.

Practice A   Use the N V N N sentence pattern.

Make four columns on your paper for the N V N N sentence pattern. Label the first column *N*, the second *V*, the third *N*, and the fourth *N*. Write all the words from the following sentences in the correct columns. Place a modifier in the same column as the word it modifies.

1. The young child brought her parents great joy.
2. Pat sent Tommy a shirt.
3. The teacher asked me a question.
4. Lawrence handed Lance a silver trophy.
5. Our grandparents showed us their picture album.
6. I saved you some cake.
7. The gardener gave the lawn a thorough watering.
8. The young girl offered the older woman her seat.
9. Barbara is buying her niece a winter jacket.
10. The doctor gave the patient a complete check-up.

Practice B   Use the N V N N sentence pattern.

Make a chart like the one in Practice A for the N V N N sentence pattern. Place only the simple subject, verb or verb phrase, and noun or pronoun direct and indirect objects from each sentence in your chart. Omit all modifiers.

1. We bought Dorothy a lovely present.
2. Someone has sent you a long note.
3. Jenny will sing her classmates a song.

4. Ernie served us grilled fish.

5. Harry will give his brother his old bike.

Practice C   **Add subjects, verbs, and direct and indirect objects.**

Copy the chart that follows. Complete the sentences by filling in the blanks with words of your own. If you wish, use modifiers to make each sentence as interesting as you can.

Subject	Predicate	Complement	
	Verb	Indir. Object	Direct Object
N	**V**	**N**	**N**
1. _____	sent	Xavier	_____.
2. Ralph	_____	_____	the ball.
3. _____	_____	me	_____.
4. _____	_____	_____	forty dollars.
5. _____	_____	_____	_____.

Practice D   **Identify the N V, N V N, and N V N V sentence patterns.**

Copy each of the following sentences on your paper. After each sentence, write the sentence pattern it follows: N V, N V N, or N V N N.

1. Bettina and Claude have been studying hard.

2. Justin gave his baby sister a hug.

3. I am writing a very funny story.

4. Hannah won the race!

5. My brother told me a joke.

L E S S O N   F O U R

The N LV N Sentence Pattern

In this sentence pattern, the first *N* stands for the noun or pronoun in the complete subject. The *LV* stands for the linking verb. The second *N* stands for the noun or pronoun in the predicate that follows the linking verb. This noun or pronoun is called a *predicate nominative*.

In Unit Nineteen, Lesson Three, you learned that a linking verb "links" or joins the noun or pronoun subject with a word in the predicate that renames or describes the subject.

The most common linking verbs are forms of the verb *be*:

be	been	is	are
was	were	being	am

In Unit Twenty-one, Lesson Three, you learned that a predicate nominative is a noun or pronoun that follows a linking verb and refers to, describes, or explains the subject of the sentence. A predicate nominative is one of the four kinds of complements you have studied in this book.

Here are examples of sentences that follow the N LV N sentence pattern. Modifiers have been placed in the same columns as the words they modify.

Subject	Predicate Verb Linking Verb	Complement Pred. Nominative
N	LV	N
Jimmy Carter	is	a former President.
Kit Robinson	is	my first cousin.
Annie	has been	a loyal friend.
My sisters	are	both lawyers.

Practice A Use the N LV N sentence pattern.

Make a chart for the N LV N sentence pattern. Label the first column *N*, the second *LV*, and the third *N*. Write all the words from the following sentences in the correct columns. Place a modifier in the same column as the word it modifies.

1. Today is Monday.
2. Paul Cunningham is a sailor.
3. Breakfast can be a delicious meal.
4. My parents became American citizens.
5. Charlie Chaplin was a talented actor.

6. Power saws are useful tools.

7. My friends are concert pianists.

8. Janine will be an actress.

9. Alaska is a cold state.

10. Kahlua is a Siamese cat.

Practice B   Add subjects, linking verbs, and predicate nominatives.

Complete the sentences by filling in each blank with either a subject, linking verb, or predicate nominative, plus modifiers to make each sentence interesting.

Subject	Predicate Verb Linking Verb	Complement Pred. Nominative
N	LV	N
1. Sean	is	_____.
2. _____	are	large cities.
3. Summer	_____	_____.
4. _____	was	_____.
5. _____	_____	_____.

Practice C   Write sentences.

Make a chart like the one in Practice B for the N LV N sentence pattern. Write five sentences of your own that follow this sentence pattern. Place each word from your sentences in the correct column.

Practice D   Identify the N V N and N LV N sentence patterns.

Copy each of the following sentences on your paper. After each one, write whether it follows the N V N or the N LV N sentence pattern.

1. Heidi is an artist.

2. Pierre paints portraits.

3. Gorillas are primates.

4. Nurses help sick people.

5. My brother became a lab technician.

The N LV Adj Sentence Pattern

In this sentence pattern, the first two parts are identical to the first two parts of the N LV N sentence pattern: the *N* stands for the noun or pronoun in the complete subject, and the *LV* stands for the linking verb. The new part in this pattern is the Adj. It stands for the adjective in the complete predicate that follows a linking verb.

In Unit Twenty-one, Lesson Three, you learned that an adjective in the predicate that describes the subject is called a *predicate adjective*. It is one of the four kinds of complements you studied in this book.

Here are examples of sentences that follow the N LV Adj sentence pattern. Modifiers have been placed in the same columns as the words they modify.

Subject	Predicate	Complement
	Verb	
	Linking Verb	Pred. Adjective
N	LV	Adj
Danielle	is	very tired.
That hamburger	tasted	terrible.
The bananas	look	ripe.
Your idea	sounds	terrific.

Practice A   **Use the N LV Adj sentence pattern.**

Make a chart with three columns. Label the first column *N*, the second *LV*, and the third *Adj*. Write all the words from the following sentences in the correct columns. Place modifiers in the same columns as the words they modify.

1. This soup tastes bland.
2. George appeared content.
3. Your sister looks quite lovely.
4. The concert was delightful.
5. That comedian is so funny!

635

6. Some school subjects are extremely interesting.

7. Helen feels much better today.

8. That assignment was difficult.

9. The decorations look festive.

10. Otters are cute and furry.

Practice B   **Add subjects, linking verbs, and predicate adjectives.**

Copy the chart that follows. Complete the sentences by filling in each blank with words of your own. Make the sentences as interesting as you can.

Subject	Predicate Verb Linking verb	Complement Pred. Adjective
N	LV	Adj
1. Giraffes	are	_____.
2. _____	looks	happy.
3. _____	seem	_____.
4. You	_____	_____.
5. _____	_____	_____.

Practice C   **Write sentences.**

Make a chart like the one in Practice B for the N LV Adj sentence pattern. Write five sentences of your own that follow this sentence pattern. Fill in the columns with subjects, linking verbs, and predicate adjectives, plus modifiers.

I. Identifying the Five Sentence Patterns The words in each sentence follow one of the five sentence patterns you studied in this unit. Write the sentences on your paper. After each, write the sentence pattern that it follows. Write *N V, N V N, N V N N, N LV N,* or *N LV Adj.* (Lessons One to Five)

1. Dana showed us the trail.
2. It was narrow and winding.
3. We hiked vigorously.
4. Jonah had packed everyone a delicious lunch.
5. George and I ate early.
6. We saw deer.
7. Deer are beautiful animals.
8. We offered them some food.
9. They ran away quickly.
10. Hiking is excellent exercise.

II. Writing the Five Sentence Patterns Write five sentences of your own. Each one should follow the specific sentence pattern given below. (Lessons One to Five)

1. N V
2. N V N
3. N V N N
4. N LV N
5. N LV Adj

Diagraming Sentences

"New York," 1946
Elliott Erwitt, Magnum Photos, Inc.

Diagraming Sentences

Diagrams are often used to help people understand relationships. The "family tree" diagram is an example. Suppose you have a friend who boasts that he is one-sixteenth Sioux Indian. When you look skeptical, he says, "Here, I'll show you." He draws a diagram representing five generations of his father's side of the family. It has five levels of boxes joined by lines. In one of the boxes at the top he writes the name of his great-great-grandmother Dawn Star. In a box at the bottom he writes his own name. The diagram helps you understand the relationship between your friend and his Sioux Indian ancestor.

In a similar way, a sentence diagram helps you understand the relationships between the words in the sentence. It shows how each word functions in the sentence and how all the words work together to express meaning.

In a sentence diagram, each word has a specific position. The words are written on horizontal, vertical, and slanted lines. The lines are solid or dotted, depending on how the words function in the sentence.

Only words that are capitalized in the sentence are capitalized in the diagram. No punctuation, except apostrophes, appears in a sentence diagram.

Following are some examples of sentence diagrams.

George is laughing.

George	is laughing

Someone told me a funny joke.

Someone	told	joke

me

a   funny

Everyone in the audience applauded loudly.

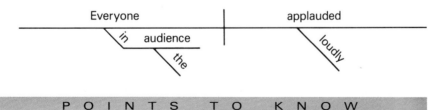

▶ Only words capitalized in the sentence are capitalized in the sentence diagram.

▶ No punctuation, except apostrophes, appears in a sentence diagram.

L E S S O N   O N E

Diagraming Subjects and Verbs

Every sentence contains at least one subject and one verb. The subject and verb are placed on a horizontal line, separated by a vertical line that crosses the horizontal line. The subject is written to the left of the vertical line; the verb or verb phrase is written to the right of the vertical line.

Following are diagrams of sentences that have only subjects and verbs.

Josephine studied.

Josephine	studied

Josephine has been studying.

Josephine	has been studying

641

Diagram subjects and verbs.

Diagram the following sentences.

1. Dogs bark.
2. Kites are flying.
3. Jonathan has been surfing.
4. Someone is whispering.
5. Michael Kent should have come.

L E S S O N   T W O

Diagraming Sentences With Adjectives

An adjective is written on a solid slanted line directly below the noun or pronoun it modifies. (For a review of adjectives, see Unit Nineteen, Lesson Four.) Here is a diagram of a sentence with adjectives.

A light, cool rain fell.

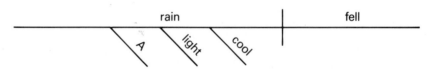

Possessive nouns and possessive pronouns are diagramed as adjectives. The possessive pronouns are *my, your, his, her, its, our,* and *their.* Following are two examples.

Our new kitten is purring.

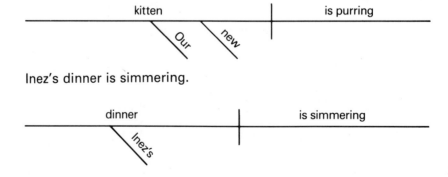

Inez's dinner is simmering.

Practice **Diagram sentences with adjectives.**

Diagram the following sentences.

1. Our old yellow car has stalled.
2. The new bushes are blooming.
3. High, rough waves pounded.
4. Dan's enormous radio is blasting.
5. Cool, wet breezes blew.
6. His small sailboat sank.
7. A delicious fruit pie was baking.
8. The delighted crowd clapped.
9. Tired, hungry people are waiting.
10. A bright, twinkling star is shining.

L E S S O N   T H R E E

Diagraming Sentences With Adverbs

An adverb, like an adjective, is written on a solid slanted line below the word it modifies. (For a review of adverbs, see Unit Nineteen, Lesson Five.)

An adverb can modify a verb, an adjective, or another adverb. Following are sentence diagrams that include these three kinds of adverbs.

When an adverb modifies a verb, draw a slanted line from the horizontal line beneath the verb. Write the adverb on the slanted line.

Beulah does not speak loudly.

When an adverb modifies an adjective, draw a line parallel to the adjective line and beneath it. Connect the two lines and write the adverb on the lower line.

Very strong winds have been blowing.

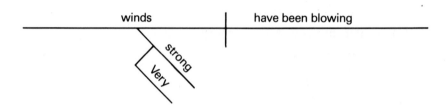

An adverb that modifies another adverb is diagramed the same way as one that modifies an adjective.

Oliver skis quite gracefully.

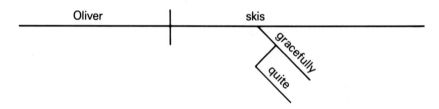

Practice   **Diagram sentences with adverbs.**

Diagram the following sentences.

1. Lifeguards work hard.
2. I slept too late.
3. Extremely noisy children have been playing outside.
4. The violinist practiced daily.
5. The snake slithered slowly.
6. A very shrill siren sounded.
7. This old car moves haltingly.
8. Surprisingly few people have called.
9. We will arrive quite early.
10. Many serious accidents have occurred lately.

Diagraming Sentences With Prepositional Phrases

A prepositional phrase can act as an adjective or an adverb. (For a review of prepositional phrases, see Unit Twenty-three, Lesson One.)

When you diagram a prepositional phrase, you write it below the word it modifies. However, a prepositional phrase includes more than one word, and each word has a specific position in the diagram.

Following are some rules for diagraming prepositional phrases.

P O I N T S   T O   K N O W

▶ Write the preposition on a solid slanted line directly below the word that the phrase modifies.

▶ Write the object of the preposition on a solid horizontal line connected to the end of the slanted line.

▶ Write any modifiers of the object of the preposition on solid slanted lines below the horizontal line.

The prepositional phrase in the following sentence modifies the noun *student.*

The student in the first row is writing slowly.

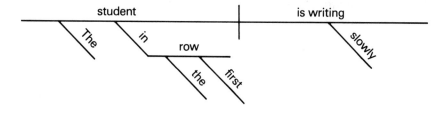

The prepositional phrase in the next sentence modifies the verb *has been sleeping*.

Cory has been sleeping on the blue couch.

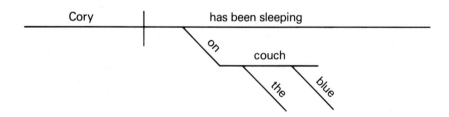

The prepositional phrase in the following sentence modifies the adverb *late*. Both the preposition and the adverb must be placed on slanted lines. Notice that an extra line is used to connect the two slanted lines.

The Sperlings arrived late in the afternoon.

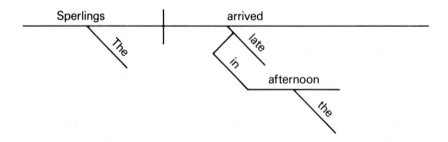

Practice A   Diagram sentences with prepositional phrases.

Copy the diagram skeletons onto your paper. Diagram all the words in each sentence below.

1. A man with a long black coat is dancing.

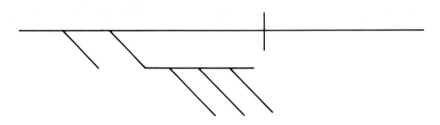

2. The birds are soaring high in the sky.

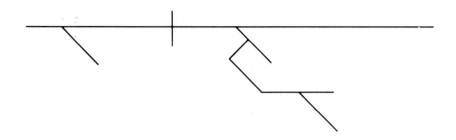

3. The dog on the front porch is eating hungrily.

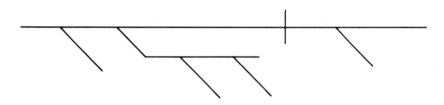

4. The campers have been hiking for the entire weekend.

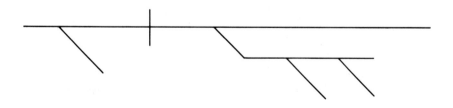

5. My relatives from Austria will stay until Independence Day.

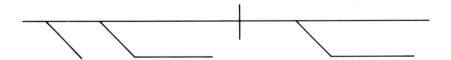

Diagram sentences with prepositional phrases.

Diagram the following sentences.

1. Emily is walking past our house.
2. The person in that car is sleeping.
3. Rhonda will practice early in the afternoon.
4. The movie on the television has ended.
5. Morris will be moving late in the year.

L E S S O N   F I V E

Diagraming Interrogative, Imperative, and Exclamatory Sentences

In interrogative sentences, the subject usually follows the verb or part of the verb. However, in a sentence diagram, the positions of the subject and verb never change. The subject is always written to the left of the vertical line, and the verb is always written to the right.

Here are two interrogative sentences and their diagrams.

Has Ben gone to the zoo?

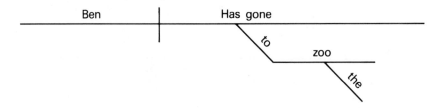

Is that person with the four dogs crying?

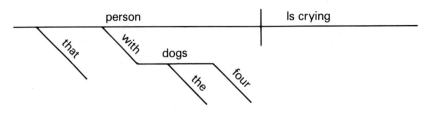

In the first example, the *h* in *has* is capitalized. In the second example, the *i* in *is* is capitalized. That's because they are capitalized in their original sentences. (For a review of interrogative sentences, see Unit Twenty, Lesson Five.)

In many imperative sentences, the subject is not stated; it is understood to be *you.* In these cases, you diagram the subject by writing *you* in parentheses to the left of the vertical line. (For a review of imperative sentences, see Unit Twenty, Lesson Five.)

Stand still.

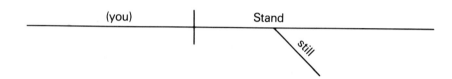

Notice that the verb is capitalized in the preceding diagram. That's because it is capitalized in the original sentence.

Exclamatory sentences are similar to interrogative sentences, except that exclamatory sentences end with exclamation points, not question marks. In some exclamatory sentences, the subject is hard to find. If that's the case, rewrite the exclamatory sentence as a declarative sentence.

Exclamatory sentence:

Does Adrienne sing well!

Declarative sentence:

Adrienne does sing well.

Now it is easy to see that the subject is *Adrienne.* You diagram exclamatory sentences as you would any other sentence.

Does Adrienne sing well!

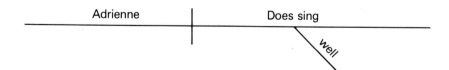

Practice   **Diagram interrogative, imperative, and exclamatory sentences.**

Diagram the following sentences.

1.   Does Tommy draw often?
2.   Will you call later?
3.   Can my mother paint!
4.   Write soon.
5.   Have these patients been waiting for a long time?

L E S S O N   S I X

Diagraming Sentences With Conjunctions

Conjunctions connect words, phrases, and clauses. (For a review of conjunctions, see Unit Nineteen, Lesson Seven.) In a sentence diagram, a conjunction is placed on a dotted line between the words it connects.

The long and boring film finally ended.

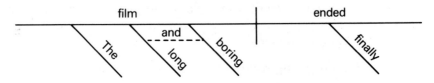

Practice   **Diagram sentences with conjunctions.**

Diagram the following sentences.

1.   The exhausted but happy winner waved.
2.   I type quickly and carelessly.
3.   That dancer moves effortlessly and gracefully.
4.   A young and talented gymnast will perform.
5.   Is that old and beautiful building still standing?

Diagraming Sentences With Compound Subjects and Verbs

A compound subject consists of two or more subjects that share the same verb. The parts of the compound subject are connected by a conjunction. (For a review of compound subjects, see Unit Twenty, Lesson Four.)

Following is a diagram of a sentence that has a compound subject.

Lee, Cary, and Ben are swimming in the pool.

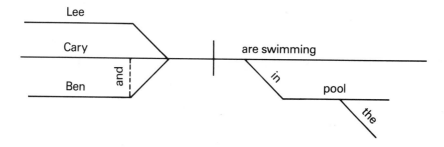

Follow these steps to diagram a sentence with a compound subject:

☐ Write each subject on a separate solid horizontal line. Make all the subject lines the same length and parallel to each other.

☐ Join the subject lines to the horizontal main line.

☐ Move a short way to the right of the point where the subject lines join the main line. This short section of the main line will be the "stem" of the compound subject line. Now draw a vertical line crossing the horizontal main line to divide the compound subject from the verb. Write the verb on the horizontal main line to the right of the vertical line.

☐ Draw a dotted vertical line between the last two parts of the compound subject. Write the conjunction on the dotted line.

☐ Write any adjectives or adverbs on solid slanted lines below the words they modify.

An adjective or a prepositional phrase can modify the entire compound subject or a part of it. When the adjective or prepositional phrase modifies only a part of the compound subject, it is placed under the part it modifies. When it modifies the entire compound subject, it is placed under the stem, to the right of the compound subject.

In the following example, notice the position of the adjectives. The word *our* modifies both parts of the compound subject. Therefore, it is written to the right of the compound subject. The word *four* modifies only the word *nephews,* so it is written directly under that word.

Our niece and four nephews are visiting.

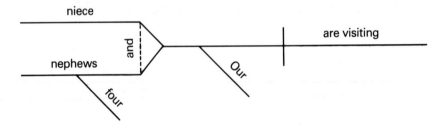

Compound Verbs

A compound verb consists of two or more verbs that share the same subject. The parts of the compound verb are connected by a conjunction. (For a review of compound verbs, see Unit Twenty, Lesson Four.) Following is a diagram of a sentence with a compound verb.

Libby trots slowly, canters, or gallops swiftly around the corral.

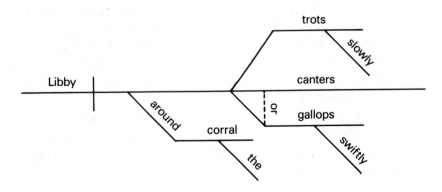

Following are the steps for diagraming a sentence with a compound verb.

- ☐ Write the parts of the compound verb on separate, parallel, solid horizontal lines.

- ☐ Join the lines to the horizontal main line for the subject. Leave a short stem to the left of the compound verb.

- ☐ Draw a vertical line through the horizontal main line, to divide the compound verb from the subject. Write the subject on the horizontal main line, to the left of the vertical line.

- ☐ Draw a dotted vertical line between the last two verbs in the series. Write the conjunction on the dotted line.

- ☐ Write any adjectives or adverbs on solid slanted lines directly below the words they modify.

An adverb or prepositional phrase can modify the entire compound verb or a part of it. An adverb or phrase that modifies the entire compound verb is placed under the stem, to the left of the compound verb. Notice in the following example that the adverb that modifies both parts of the compound verb is placed below the stem. The adverb that modifies only one part of the compound verb is placed directly below that part.

Mavis reads and sometimes dozes during the afternoon.

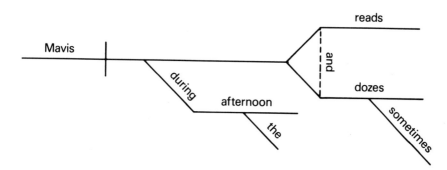

Helping verbs are diagramed according to the way they are used in the sentence. If the same helping verb is used for different parts of the compound verb, the helping verb is placed on the stem of the diagram.

Emma has been swimming, sunning, and surfing.

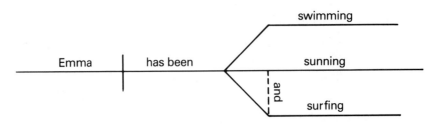

If compound verbs have different helping verbs, each helping verb is written on the line with its verb. Notice that in the following example the adverb *soon* modifies only the verb *will fall*, so it is placed on a slanted line below that verb.

The blossoms are withering and will soon fall.

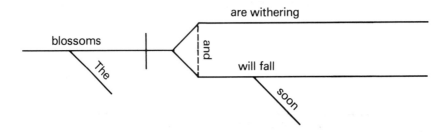

Practice   **Diagram sentences with compound subjects and verbs.**

Diagram the following sentences.

1. Giraffes, lions, and tigers are eating in their cages.
2. We laughed, talked, and joked throughout the afternoon.
3. Our dog and cat fight often.
4. My friend and his brother will help later in the day.
5. I have studied hard and will now relax.

Diagraming Sentences With Direct Objects

A direct object follows a transitive verb and completes the thought begun by the subject and verb. It answers the question *Whom?* or *What?* after the transitive verb. (For a review of transitive verbs, see Unit Nineteen, Lesson Three. For a review of direct objects, see Unit Twenty-one, Lesson One.)

To diagram a direct object, write it on the horizontal main line after the verb. Separate the direct object from the verb with a short, solid vertical line that does not cross the horizontal main line. See the following example.

Mike waved the flag.

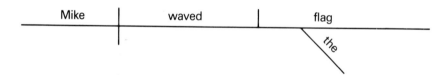

You diagram compound direct objects the same way you diagram other compounds. Each part of the compound is written on a separate horizontal line. The conjunction is written on a vertical dotted line connecting the last two parts of the compound. Notice that in the following sentence diagram the adjectives are placed directly below the words they modify.

Nadia ordered a cheese sandwich and a cold drink.

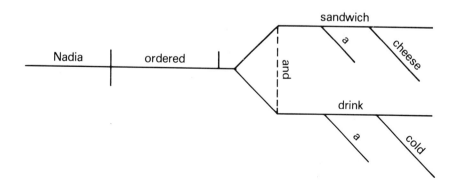

If an adjective modifies more than one part of the compound, it is placed on the stem between the short vertical line and the direct object, as in the following example.

Larry called his friends and relatives.

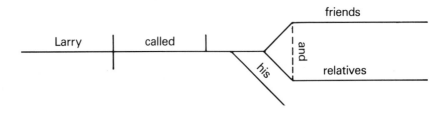

Practice   **Diagram sentences with direct objects.**

Diagram the following sentences.

1. Robert brought his stereo and tapes.
2. Eric Jones easily caught the fly ball.
3. Marlene sang a lovely song.
4. Irving collects rare coins.
5. Tony and Michael watered the rose bushes and the herb garden.
6. Anne and her brother saw a funny movie yesterday.
7. Samantha heard the news.
8. Eddie bought two apples, an orange, and some grapes.
9. Buddy read two poems aloud.
10. Fay bought a shirt, two jackets, and a red sweater at the boutique.

L E S S O N   N I N E

Diagraming Sentences With Indirect Objects

An indirect object is a noun or pronoun that follows a transitive verb and precedes a direct object. It answers the question *To or for whom?* or *To or for what?* before the direct object. (For a review of indirect objects, see Unit Twenty-one, Lesson Two.)

To diagram an indirect object, write it on a short horizontal line below the verb. Connect the indirect object to the verb with a slanted line. Below the indirect object write any adjectives or prepositional phrases that modify it.

Gerald handed his sister her yellow jacket.

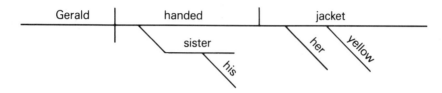

To diagram a compound indirect object, write the parts of the compound on parallel horizontal lines below the verb. Write the conjunction that connects the last two parts of the compound on a vertical dotted line. See the following example.

Peter wrote his mother and Sadie long letters.

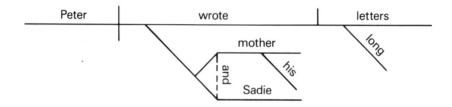

Practice   Diagram sentences with indirect objects.

Diagram the following sentences.

1. Maurice gave Judith a beautiful scarf.
2. My grandmother told my mother and me a funny story.
3. Cary offered his sister and brother a ride.
4. Mel brought Amy and Stuart some records.
5. Pat built her neighbors a bookcase.
6. Perry showed his history teacher an interesting book.
7. Sing us a song.
8. Douglas and his sister taught my friend and me some Spanish.

9. I sent you some flowers.

10. Inez gave Enid a funny look.

L E S S O N   T E N

Diagraming Sentences With Predicate Nominatives

A predicate nominative is a noun or pronoun that follows a linking verb and renames or identifies the subject of the sentence. (For a review of predicate nominatives, see Unit Twenty-one, Lesson Three.)

To diagram a predicate nominative, write it on the horizontal main line to the right of the subject and verb. Separate the predicate nominative from the verb with a short, solid, slanted line. Write any words that modify the predicate nominative on solid slanted lines below it. Here is an example.

Morton is an excellent drummer.

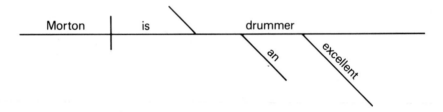

A compound predicate nominative is diagramed the same way a compound direct object is, except that a slanted line rather than a vertical line separates the compound and the verb. Write the parts of a compound predicate nominative on parallel horizontal lines, one above the other, after the slanted line. Write the conjunction on a vertical dotted line that connects the last two parts of the compound. Here is a diagram of a sentence with a compound predicate nominative.

Morton is an excellent drummer and a talented singer.

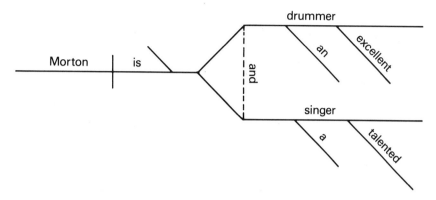

Practice   **Diagram sentences with predicate nominatives.**

Diagram the following sentences.

1. I am a writer.
2. The Mississippi is a long river.
3. Alberta is a Canadian province.
4. France is a European country.
5. Hiram was a master welder.
6. Saturday and Sunday are my favorite days.
7. Soccer is an exciting spectator sport.
8. My father is a volunteer firefighter.
9. Georgia and Alabama are Southern states.
10. Jean's mother is a librarian and an English teacher.

L E S S O N   E L E V E N

Diagraming Sentences With Predicate Adjectives

A predicate adjective follows a linking verb and modifies the subject of the sentence. (For a review of predicate adjectives, see Unit Twenty-one, Lesson Three.)

In a sentence diagram, a predicate adjective is written in the same place as a predicate nominative. A predicate adjective follows the verb on the horizontal main line and is separated from the verb by a short slanted line. Any adverbs or prepositional phrases that modify the predicate adjective are written directly below it.

This new stereo was fairly inexpensive.

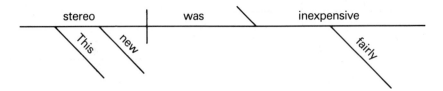

Compound predicate adjectives are diagramed the same way that compound predicate nominatives are. The parts of the compound are written on parallel horizontal lines, one above the other. The conjunction is written on a vertical dotted line that connects the last two parts of the compound. Here is a diagram of a sentence with a compound predicate adjective.

Our new dog is homely but extremely smart.

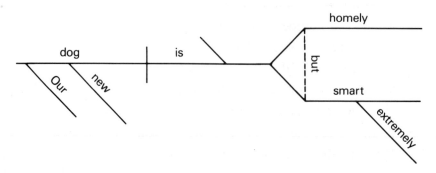

Practice   **Diagram sentences with predicate adjectives.**

Diagram the following sentences.

1. Robert seems quite discouraged.
2. This film is thrilling.
3. Their new home is small but comfortable.
4. Rudy looks very thin and terribly pale.
5. My new shoes are black and light brown.

Diagraming Compound Sentences

A compound sentence is two or more simple sentences that have been combined to form one sentence. (For a review of compound sentences, see Unit Twenty-two, Lesson Four.)

To diagram a compound sentence, you diagram each of the simple sentences separately, one below the other. Then join the verbs with a vertical dotted line. Write the conjunction on this dotted line. Write any modifiers directly below the words they modify. Here is an example.

Randy wrote a children's book, and Ted drew colorful illustrations.

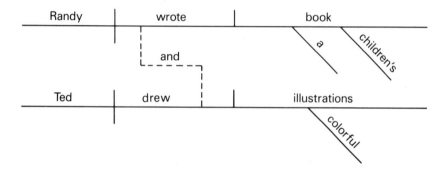

Practice   Diagram compound sentences.

Diagram the following sentences.

1. Leon might go to college, or he might attend a vocational school.
2. Mary read three books, and she wrote three book reports.
3. Raquel is a talented actress, and she is a fine athlete.
4. Abe wrote his mother a letter, and he called his brother in Utah.
5. John seems exhausted, but he will not sleep.
6. The ocean is quite rough, but it is extremely beautiful.
7. Are you studying today, or will you visit your cousins?
8. Nathaniel might drive to Canada, or he might fly to Australia.
9. Most people are leaving now, but we will wait.
10. I live near the school, and you live near the library.

INDEX

PHOTO CREDITS

American Broadcasting Company: 284
Ansel Adams, Ansel Adams Publishing Rights Trust: 82–83
Archive Pictures, Inc.: 168–169 (Mary Ellen Mark); 394–395 (Bill Burke); 604–605 (Alex Harris)
Peter Arnold, Inc.: 26 (Ginger Chih); 286–287 (David Scharf); 327 (Sybil Shelton)
Benyas–Kaufman: 234
The Bettmann Archive: 592–593
Black Star: 173 (Martin A. Levick)
Center for Creative Photography: 204–205, 624–625 (Edward Weston)
Culver Pictures, Inc.: 50–51; 136–137; 228–229; 514–515 (Dorothea Lange)
Jerome Ducrot: 221
Florida Department of Tourism: 63
Fox Studios: 175
Fraenkel Gallery: 538–539 (Garry Winogrand)
William A. Garnett: 242–243
George Eastman House: 434–435 (Samuel J. Castner)
Arlene Gottfried: 281
Ken Heyman: 412–413
Richard Hutchings: 209
International Talent Management, Inc.: 135
Sidney Janis Gallery, NY: 118–119 (Duane Michals)
Steve Joses: 212
Keystone Press Agency: 215
Dick Lewen: 150–151
Library of Congress: 100–101; 374–375
Magnum Photos, Inc.: 306–307 (Burt Glinn); 560–561 (Henri Cartier–Bresson); 638–639 (Elliott Erwitt)
MGM: 128
Museum of Modern Art: 460–461 (Ken Josephson)
Monkmeyer Press Photo Service: 40 (Mimi Forsyth); 46 (David S. Strickler); 66 (Fritz Henle); 73 (Mimi Forsyth); 105 (H. Saunders); 108 (Irene Bayer); 110 (Mimi Forsyth); 123 (Leonard Lee Rue); 143, 148, 153, 202 (Mimi Forsyth); 299 (David Strickler); 304 (M. Rogers); 308 (Mimi Forsyth); 315 (Sybil Shelton)
Dan Nelken: 117
The New York Times: 488–489 (George Tames)
Nova Scotia Film Bureau: 321
Photo Researchers, Inc.: 18–19 (Robert Doisneau); 85 (Leonard Lee Rue); 126 (Guy Gillette); 126 (Mary Eleanor Browning); 162, 165 (Robert Houser)
David Plowden: 68–69
Rainbow Adventure Film: 120
Arnold J. Saxe: 30
Scholastic/Kodak Photo Awards: 77 (Garry Luce)
Scholastic Photo Library: 80; 239; 289
Ed Sievers: 258
Springer/Bettmann Film Archive: 244
Stock, Boston: 187 (Mike Mazzaschi)
Erika Stone: 89, 97
Taurus Photos: 21 (Joan Menschenfreund); 158 (Don Rutledge); 197 (Ellis Herwig); 262 (Frank Siteman); 318 (Shirley Zeiberg)
George Tice: 93
United States Postal Service: 59
Universal City Studios: 180
UPI/Bettmann: 224 (Masaharu Hatano); 184–185; 276–277
Victoria and Albert Museum: 264–265 (Francis Frith)
Warner Brothers: 53
Daniel Wolf, Inc.: 34–35 (Milton Rogovin); 330–331 (Helen Levitt)
Woodfin Camp & Associates: 37 (David Burnett); 139 (Timothy Eagan); 191 (Wendy Watriss/Frederick Baldwin); 251 (David Burnett); 269 (Jim Anderson); 273 (Ira Berger)
World Telegram: 231 (A.L. Aumuller)